Mychailo Wynnyckyj

Ukraine's Maidan, Russia's

A Chronicle and Analysis of the Revolution of Dignity
With a foreword by Serhii Plokhy

UKRAINIAN VOICES

Collected by Andreas Umland

The book series "Ukrainian Voices" publishes English- and German-language mono-graphs, edited volumes, document collections, and anthologies of articles authored and composed by Ukrainian politicians, intellectuals, activists, officials, researchers, entrepreneurs, artists, and diplomats. The series' aim is to introduce Western and other audiences to Ukrainian explorations and interpretations of historic and current domestic as well as international affairs. The purpose of these books is to make non-Ukrainian readers familiar with how some prominent Ukrainians approach, research, and assess their country's development and position in the world. The series was founded in 2019, and the volumes are collected by *Andreas Umland*, Dr. phil. (FU Berlin), Ph. D. (Cambridge), Senior Research Fellow at the Institute for Euro-Atlantic Cooperation in Kyiv.

1   *Mychailo Wynnyckyj*
     Ukraine's Maidan, Russia's War
     A Chronicle and Analysis of the Revolution of Dignity
     With a foreword by Serhii Plokhy
     Paperback edition: ISBN 978-3-8382-1327-9
     Hardcover edition: ISBN 978-3-8382-1300-2

Mychailo Wynnyckyj

UKRAINE'S MAIDAN, RUSSIA'S WAR

A Chronicle and Analysis of the
Revolution of Dignity

With a foreword by Serhii Plokhy

Bibliografische Information der Deutschen Nationalbibliothek

Die Deutsche Nationalbibliothek verzeichnet diese Publikation in der Deutschen Nationalbibliografie; detaillierte bibliografische Daten sind im Internet über http://dnb.d-nb.de abrufbar.

Bibliographic information published by the Deutsche Nationalbibliothek

Die Deutsche Nationalbibliothek lists this publication in the Deutsche Nationalbibliografie; detailed bibliographic data are available in the Internet at http://dnb.d-nb.de.

Cover picture: Street riot during the Ukrainian revolution. © copyright 2014 by Andrii Gorb. Reprinted with kind permission.

Paperback edition: ISBN 978-3-8382-1327-9
Hardcover edition: ISBN 978-3-8382-1300-2
© *ibidem*-Verlag, Stuttgart 2019
Alle Rechte vorbehalten

Printed in the EU

Contents

Endorsements by Scholars

"Many of the major trends of international politics in the twenty-first century are best seen from Ukraine. Understanding the Ukrainian revolution of 2013–2014, and the Russian invasion that followed, are absolutely essential to any informed discussion of the state of the world. This book, rich in chronology, evidence, scholarly analysis, and human insight, is a major step towards such an understanding. It should be widely read by those interested in Eastern Europe, the European Union, digital war, and the possibilities for new forms of politics."

Timothy D. Snyder, Richard C. Levin Professor of History, Yale University

"Wynnyckyj's excellent book is a major contribution to the debate about the tumultuous events of 2013–14. It is even two books in one. The first provides the insights and detailed chronology of a well-grounded eyewitness that have been sorely missing in most accounts to date. The second adds an analytical perspective. Wynnyckyj argues that the Maidan was neither geopolitical, conspiratorial, or material; but ideational and a 'great', nation-building revolution, most like the American War of Independence, and an exemplar of heterarchical identities and mobilisations of broader relevance to all students of social change."

Andrew Wilson, Professor of Ukrainian Studies, UCL School of Slavonic and Eastern European Studies

"Mychailo Wynnyckyj's magnificent account of Ukraine's 2014 Revolution of Dignity easily surpasses every other book on the subject and sets a standard of excellence that will be hard to beat. Wynnyckyj brings to his analysis a unique combination of viewpoints. As a Ukrainian Canadian who has made Kyiv his home, he offers the perspective of native Ukrainians. As a participant in both Ukrainian uprisings, those of 2004 and of 2014, he offers an insider's view. And as a superb scholar well-versed in Western social science, he can place the events he witnessed and made into a theoretical context that explains just why Ukraine's 2014 upheaval was of world-historical importance. Get rid of all your other books on the Ukrainian Revolution, read Wynnyckyj, and get ready to be enlightened."

Alexander J. Motyl, Professor of Political Science, Rutgers University,
Newark

"Back in early 2014, hundreds of people regularly read, examined, and shared Mychailo Wynnyckyj's blogpost 'Thoughts from Kyiv'. For the concerned contemporaries, it was a priceless source of information – a first-hand on the ground account of a truly historical drama, which opened with an inspirational and tragic EuroMaidan in Kyiv, proceeded with the Russian occupation of the Crimea, and culminated in the eastern bloodlands of Ukraine's Donbas. By writing the Revolution of Dignity, the author allows today's reader to relive the tumultuous, heart-breaking, and emotional story of Ukraine's Maidan and Russia's war. Friends of Ukraine shall find here the reason for being optimistic. Ukraine's foes shall learn about her indestructible spirit."

Vlad Mykhnenko, Associate Professor of Sustainable Urban Development,
University of Oxford

"During the Maidan demonstrations and their aftermath, I eagerly awaited Mychailo Wynnyckyj's blog updates—they offered what engaged intellectuals can do best. He not only communicated the 'feel' of revolution's possibility, and anxiety, but also helped us to appreciate the broader conditions and more general significance of this great transformation in Ukraine. With time to reflect, Wynnyckyj has lost neither of these great qualities, but in this book added another we so desperately need. He has written a text inscribing Ukraine's place in a global history and political philosophy that moves dignity and hope to the center of our time's narrative, even when war and violence surround. This volume, then, is not only for those aware of Ukraine's importance. His agent-centered account also could guide those looking to develop their own knowledge activism suitable for shaping alternative futures in other parts of the world. Ukraine, and Wynnyckyj, inspire."

Michael D. Kennedy, Professor of Sociology and International Affairs,
Brown University

Acknowledgments

Apparently, in November 1917, Lenin wrote that it was "more pleasant and useful to go through the experience of revolution than to write about it."[1] A century later, as I complete this book, I am convinced he was wrong — in more than just this claim, but that is another matter. Experiencing the Maidan protests and Russia's subsequent invasion of Ukraine first hand was both thrilling and inspiring but writing about these experiences on social media (and now in this book) was most pleasant and (I hope) useful as well. A word of thanks to all those who follow me on Facebook and read my occasional "Thoughts from Kyiv". Your kind and critical remarks inspired me to write more.

Once things settled down in Kyiv, I was tempted to return to the daily routine of making a living through teaching and consulting. I am grateful to Lviv Business School (LvBS) of Ukrainian Catholic University (UCU) for recognizing that this was not an acceptable option; that this book needed to be written, and that its author needed a fellowship grant to concentrate on the result.

This book would not have been possible without the loving encouragement of my family. During the height of the protests, my brother Roman (Moko) managed the email list through which "Thoughts from Kyiv" were delivered to a non-Facebook audience, and occasionally offered an "outside-but-engaged" Ukrainian diaspora perspective on events. My sister Oksana, Canada's Honorary Consul in western Ukraine, offered moral support, and an "official" perspective from Lviv. Our mother Iroida did what mothers do best: she worried, she encouraged, she loved (as always), and occasionally, she rebuked me for not having completed this book sooner. She took care of our father Ivan (John) in his illness, and occasionally reminded me of the books that he had always planned to write but was unable to complete in time.

But no one deserves my thanks, love, and appreciation more than my wife Marta. In addition to her patience and encouragement during the write-up phase, she emboldened me to spend time in Kyiv's city-center throughout the protests — by supporting my (sometimes) naïve desires to simply "be there", and by ensuring my safety when my exuberance risked getting me in trouble.

Our children—Bohdan, Anastasia, Roksolyana, and Solomia—deserve thanks. Somehow, they understood during the Kyiv-phase of Maidan that their parents just had to be involved, and when the war became personal and close, they responded with inspirational expressions of resolve and wide-eyed patriotism. They patiently tolerated their father's busy schedule and the time stolen from their lives as this text was being completed. I dedicate this book to them. In it they'll read how we tried to build the foundation for their future—always with love and conviction.

May you cherish peace and prosperity, and always remember the sacrifice of those who made them possible.

List of Figures and Tables

Figures:

Tables:

List of Maps

Foreword:
Making the Revolution Happen

"Nothing has really happened until it has been described," goes by far the best-known quotation lifted from the writings of Virginia Woolf. Mychailo Wynnyckyj has taken up the task of ensuring that the Ukrainian Revolution, known as the Revolution of Dignity or Euro-Maidan, has indeed taken place. An active participant in the Maidan protests of late 2013 and early 2014, he began describing them at first in "real time" through his insightful posts on Facebook and has continued to do so in this book, which combines an eyewitness account of events with the interpretation of a Western-educated social scientist.

Mychailo Wynnyckyj has impeccable credentials as both an activist and a scholarly analyst that go beyond his participation in the first stage of the revolutionary protests and commentary on them. His career as an activist began early. On one occasion, as an undergraduate student from Canada taking part in an exchange with the University of Dnipropetrovsk during the final months of the Soviet Union, he attached the blue-and-yellow Ukrainian national flag to his dormitory window—the first public display of the Ukrainian national symbol in a city that would not fully shed its Soviet legacy on the symbolic level until a quarter century later. As a consequence of the Revolution of Dignity, the city adopted a shorter form of its name, "Dnipro," in 2016 to remove a reference to the Ukrainian communist leader Hryhorii Petrovsky, and the name of the Dnipropetrovsk region was changed to Sicheslav in 2019 to reflect its Cossack past.

This revolutionary in terms of the symbolic meaning of the names change required a lot of time—a point that Wynnyckyj, as an analyst and scholar, raises in his account of the Revolution of Dignity. Apart from undergraduate studies in Canada and a short stint as an exchange student in Ukraine, his academic background includes two degrees from Cambridge University, first an MPhil in the sociology and politics of modern societies and, second, a PhD in economic sociology, as well as teaching at the Kyiv Mohyla University in Ukraine, where Wynnyckyj moved in 2003. A regular contributor to the Kyiv Post and other Ukraine-based media outlets, in this book he offers a unique perspective on the revolutionary events in which he took part.

As an activist and commentator, the author comes to the fore in the first part of the book, which is essentially an eyewitness account of events leading from the Kyiv Maidan of 2013 to its political victory in February 2014. This resulted in the ouster of President Viktor Yanukovych in the wake of the mass killing of protesters, followed by the Russian invasion and annexation of the Crimea and the subsequent destabilization and invasion of the Donbas, which led to the protracted and ongoing war in the region. Wynnyckyj allows us to hear the voices of the revolution as he quotes his own Facebook posts and those of his friends and acquaintances. The posts are embedded in the author's reconstruction of events as they took shape on both sides of the revolutionary divide.

Wynnyckyj never fails to indicate on whose side he was and continues to be — the side of the revolution. He is still engaged in the information war that began in 2013, rejecting the argument that Russian aggression against Ukraine was provoked or caused by NATO encirclement and the portrayal of Ukrainians as mere victims of the geopolitical struggles of others. He stresses the local roots of Ukrainian developments and the agendas of their participants, debunking the notion that most of the protesters were ideological nationalists.

Making sense of the events of the Revolution of Dignity, rather than recounting and commenting on them, is the main task of the second part of the book. The key question raised there is whether the Maidan and its consequences qualify as a revolution. Since the author answers in the affirmative, there follows a new set of questions focused on defining the kind of revolution it was. In both parts of the book, Wynnyckyj focuses attention on the local agents of revolutionary change, discussing the broader significance of their actions and analyzing them with the assistance of key Western texts on the essence and variety of revolutions.

Like many books written in the previous century about the phenomenon of revolution, especially in Ukraine, this book begins with a quotation from Vladimir Lenin. But unlike books that became prominent during the rise of the Soviet Union and the Cold War, whose authors attempted to develop the ideas of the father of the Russian revolution or draw on them to legitimize their own views, this one rejects Lenin's authority and seeks to chart a new course. If for Lenin the revolution was first and foremost about class struggle and changes in political structure, for Wynnyckyj it is about new ideas brought to life by revolutionary change. His main authority in that regard is not Theda Skocpol, with her focus of the transformation of societal and class structures, but Hannah Arendt, with her emphasis on the importance of ideas that lead to revolution and are further shaped by it.

Wynnyckyj embraces Arendt's definition of revolution as a violent act in which the participants are driven by the pathos of novelty. He is no supporter of violent methods of revolutionary struggle, considering them tragic and highly undesirable agents of change. This is apparent from his account of events on the Maidan and his highly emotional description of his children's classmates, some of whose parents laid down their lives in the ensuing war. But he welcomes other markers of revolution identified by Arendt as he recognizes them in the Ukrainian events, especially the desire to "constitute an altogether different form of government, to bring about the formation of a new body politic, where the liberation from oppression aims at least at the constitution of freedom." Wynnyckyj asserts that the revolution is in the process of realizing those goals — the events on the Maidan were only the beginning.

The author regards the Revolution of Dignity as three revolutions in one: national, bourgeois in terms of changes to the economic and social order, and conceptual or personalistic. Unlike Volodymyr Vynnychenko, a leader of the Ukrainian Revolution of 1917 who wrote of his own experience as a rebirth of the nation, Wynnyckyj, an activist of a "leaderless" revolution, is ambiguous in defining the momentous upheaval on the Maidan, referring to it as a (re)birth. As he sees it, the revolution resulted from a protracted and regionally based process of Ukrainian nation-building. The new Ukrainian nation as he describes it is multiethnic and multilingual, not unlike the class of the Kyiv school that his children attend. The national solidarity produced by the events on the Maidan makes the Ukrainian Revolution comparable to the American Revolution and helps explain why the upheaval of 2014 was not followed by a reign of terror, which another theorist, Crane Brinton, identified as a marker of true revolution.

If there is an aspect of Wynnyckyj's analysis that draws on Skocpol's thinking and puts one in mind of Lenin, it is his definition of the Ukrainian Revolution as "bourgeois." He notes the major role of the Ukrainian entrepreneurial class, which rebelled against the "neo-feudal" post-Soviet model of political rule embodied in the increasingly authoritarian regime of Viktor Yanukovych. In that regard, Wynnyckyj sees Ukrainians not only following in the footsteps of the great revolutions of the past but also making a new contribution. He argues that the revolution promises to deliver a type of economic and social liberalism that never gained a foothold in Europe because of the dominance of socialist ideas. Once again, he draws a parallel with the American Revolution, which, like the Ukrainian one, took place on the geographic periphery of the Western world and produced novel ideas that went on to change its center.

The third aspect of the revolution inspired by the Maidan, in Wynnyckyj's opinion, has little or nothing in common with the major historical revolutions. It is associated with the particular Ukrainian understanding of the term "dignity" (hidnist'), which, unlike the English or French notion of "dignity," is not rooted in the idea of equalizing individuals of diverse social rank but in a person's comprehension of "their civic worth and civic responsibility." For Wynnyckyj, this is a sign of the arrival on the European scene of "personalism." which he defines as "a worldview that emphasizes the centrality of the socially embedded person." By placing personalism rather than individualism at the center of its discourse, the Ukrainian Revolution, argues Wynnyckyj, has not only distanced itself from Enlightenment-era revolutions with their "individualistic" values but also introduced new values to the world it is striving to change.

Wynnyckyj argues that the Revolution of Dignity opens the door to a new set of ideas that will change the world and should therefore be treated on par with the American, French, and Russian revolutions.

He contrasts the ideas and values promoted by the Revolution of Dignity with those declared officially by the European Union. If the EU seeks to deemphasize the significance of nations and national sovereignty, the Revolution of Dignity embraces them; it counters the EU orientation toward social-democratic models of economic order with a program of economic liberalism, and European "individualism" with its own "personalistic" understanding of dignity.

There are various ways to interpret the features of the Ukrainian Revolution as identified and discussed in this book. A conventional response in the Orientalist tradition would be that Ukraine is simply lagging behind and trying to catch up with Western and Central Europe, whose national and bourgeois revolutions were completed long ago. From this viewpoint, the "postmodern" aspiration to outdo the old European revolutions merely puts a brave face on Ukraine's "premodern" identity, which prevents it from shaking off its traditional collectivism and embracing the individualism that made Europe so successful.

The importance of this book lies in its rejection of such conventional thinking and its search for different ways of explaining the "non-European" features of the pro-European revolution in Ukraine. Wynnyckyj's emphasis on the novelty of its ideas corresponds to the "pathos of novelty" that Hannah Arendt identified as an indicator of true revolution — a revolution in the making, at least, as the Revolution of Dignity has yet to deliver on its promises. But then, if one trusts Virginia Woolf, nothing happens until it is described; hence writing about the revolution is akin to making it, and this book is part of that multifaceted process.

Serhii Plokhy
Harvard University
Cambridge, Mass.

xix

Preface

Our family's apartment is located two subway stops from Kyiv's Independence Square (*Maidan Nezalezhnosti*) — the epicenter of Ukraine's revolution. For me, as for most of the 43 million residents of Europe's largest country (in terms of land mass), the three-month period between 21 November 2013 and 22 February 2014 represented a roller coaster ride of euphoria and trauma. Individually, we experienced the essence of what it means to be human — dignity, self-sacrifice, pride, fear, sorrow, joy, communion. Collectively, we experienced a *people* becoming a *nation*.

Then came the Russian invasion of Crimea, and the war in the Donbas. Although geographically removed (Kyiv is approximately 700 km from Donetsk), the violence touched our family directly: children of so-called "internally displaced people" became classmates of our kids (over 1.4 million IDPs were registered by Ukrainian authorities in 2015), and several of my friends and students volunteered to fight. Many returned from the war with limbs severed and/or psyches wounded irreparably.

Throughout the three months of the Maidan protests I posted regularly to Facebook, and to an email distribution list (several of my "Thoughts from Kyiv" were subsequently published),[1] trying to provide the English-speaking world with on-the-ground analysis of the situation in this seemingly forgotten European nation. On the night of February 18, during what seemed the darkest period of the previous three months, I wrote the following as a "status" post:

> Feeling very sad and incredibly angry. My city burns tonight. The capital of the country that I love (my adopted home and the land of my ancestors), today lost any sense of innocence that may have been left here. Tonight, the center of Kyiv has become a war zone.

> This place of peace, of multiple languages and religions, of intellectual vibrancy, of tolerance and mutual understanding, today is drenched in the blood of protesters whose only demand was to be led by a just and non-corrupt government.

1

As I write these words, the church tent on the Maidan where I have prayed for peace countless times during the past 2 months, burns — set on fire by riot police. Don't look for logic behind such an act — there is no logic that can explain the work of thugs taking orders from an uber-thug desperately holding on to power.

So far, we know of 10 confirmed deaths today (in addition to the 5 who died in January's clashes on Hrushevskoho St.) and hundreds injured. Tonight, we cry. We mourn those who innocently believed freedom could be won peacefully.

Tomorrow we'll regroup. There will be no more false beliefs. There will be no more negotiations. There is nothing to talk about. Tomorrow we'll take back our city and the day after we'll take back our country. There is no way that a few thousand riot police can hold back millions. God help them if they try...

To all my friends throughout the world: I ask for your prayers for those who lost their lives today, and for those whose lives will be lost in the coming days. Pray for those who are sped away in ambulances outside our windows. May their wounds heal quickly. Pray for the heroes who are desperately trying to stop the inevitable advance on Maidan to-night. They face thugs in police uniforms, armed with live rounds. Many will not return home tomorrow.

My world turned black and white today — there is no grey. Academic impartiality be damned. Evil must be stopped.

At the time I was expressing the emotions of many who had attempted to conjoin activism with commentary. We were experiencing history first-hand, and the status of bystander was simply not appealing. The text came quickly and easily. Tears flowed as I typed.

The next morning, I ventured into the center of Kyiv and spent several hours on the burnt-out Maidan. I tried to support the protest-ers as much as I could, but I understood that my role was to chronicle their brave actions, and to relay their monumental task to the world. When the Kyiv phase of Maidan ended, and the Russian invasion of Ukraine began, I continued in this role, travelling to the Donbas sev-eral times — although never actually summoning the courage to get closer than 15km to the front line. Two years after the climax of the protests in Kyiv I wrote the following:

February 19 is a very emotional day for me.

Two years ago on this day, less than 3 meters from where I stood, a man was shot by a "Berkut" officer. We were on the burnt-out Maidan in Kyiv—unaware that within a few days all this would be over, and the next violent chapter in Ukraine's modern history would begin.

One year ago, our family sat glued to the television screen. We watched thousands of men from Ukraine's Army and Volunteer Battalions retreat from the northern Donbas city of Debaltseve. Within the paradigm of war, where every millimeter of territory gained or lost counts, this looked like a defeat. We now know that Putin's victory was short-lived. Notwithstanding repeated attempts to move his forces further into the country, the line drawn by Ukraine's troops after their withdrawal from Debaltseve has become the effective new border with Russia's proxy "republics" in the Donbas. And the line has remained unchanged for a year.

Today was another day of emotions. I attended a commemorative ceremony at our children's school in the Podil region of Kyiv. Two years ago, Oleksandr (Sashko) Plekhanov, a young architecture student who had graduated from our school just 4 years before, was shot dead by a sniper in the center of Kyiv. He was/is/always will be one of the Heaven's Hundred. A stone plaque with his image was erected last year in the vestibule of the school, and photographs from his childhood in various classes and in the school yard hang near the entrance. Today the school remembered its former student with flowers, a solemn candle, and a brief student-led ritual.

The ceremony was organized by our son's teacher. Grade 7. His class is typical of any class in Kyiv. There's Sofia, whose grandmother still lives in Slovyansk (Donetsk oblast), who retold stories that "babushka" tells her of how Ukrainian soldiers liberated their town after two months of sheer hell of the "DPR". There's Vanya, who joined the class last year after his parents fled the city of Donetsk; he misses his old apartment in the city-center, but now he suspects his building is just rubble. And those are just the kids from refugee families.

Then we have Vlada whose father was a lawyer, and one of the co-organizers and then a field commander of the Azov battalion. He saw action near Donetsk airport in the village of Pisky, then in Shyrokino near Mariupol. Vlada is an orphan.

Nadia's father is an explosives expert. She doesn't want to talk about where he's stationed, except that he received training in Yavoriv (Lviv oblast). Nadia's father clears mines in the ATO.

Olya's father was a medic on the Maidan. He volunteered for service in the Army immediately after Yanukovych's flight. His unit liberated Popasna and Lysichansk (Luhansk oblast). He was taken prisoner by Russian regulars in August 2014 during the battle of Ilovaysk, spent several weeks in a Donetsk basement, and was then released in a prisoner exchange in October. He returned to the front in 2015 as a volunteer medic.

Our son's class is no different from the others in our school. Our middle daughter (Grade 3) has 3 classmates whose fathers are currently at the front. My wife met two others during a recent parents' meeting — both were decommissioned last year; both have missing limbs.

Today's commemorative ceremony — nominally in remembrance of the Heaven's Hundred, but in fact honoring all of Ukraine's freedom fighters — took place in the open area at the entrance of our school (the vestibule). It was moving. The kids sang the Ukrainian anthem. They placed flowers to Plekhanov's monument. They hummed the Maidan funeral chant "*Plyve Kacha*" ["The duckling swims"]. The texts they recited boiled down to one simple message: No matter what, we will overcome! Life is hard, and death is always just around the corner, but our cause is just, and our heroes never die. Words on paper can't convey the emotions. The kids meant it!

As a social scientist I can't avoid noting a fascinating moment of identity construction that I witnessed today. The vestibule of our school is home to two gold busts of Heroes of the Soviet Union. Both were students of the school; both died during World War 2. Between the two busts, the plaque on the wall lists the names of 31 individuals under the heading "Teachers and students of this school who were killed in battle for the freedom and independence of their Soviet motherland." This plaque was the backdrop for our son's class during today's remembrance ceremony. For some reason the blue and yellow flag next to this plaque, and the flowers and candle beneath the monument to Plekhanov, and the kids' blue and yellow drawings of Heaven's Hundred symbolism — none of it clashed with the hammer and sickle on the plaque behind them. In fact, somehow, the seemingly contradictory historical representations seemed to complement each other. The names on the Soviet plaque reflect the ethnic make-up of Podil district in Kyiv: Mandryk, Kimmelblatt, Banvelman, Pavlovsky, Vynokurov, Bilan, Livshitz, Chaikovsky... No different today really: families speak Ukrainian, Russian, Hebrew at home, while they learn English, French and German at school. The language in the school yard is a mixture (Surzhyk) that is becoming increasingly Ukrainian with every passing year.

Today, the symbolism on the walls (whether of Soviet or of Maidan origin), was all Ukrainian — without contradiction. Most importantly, the faces of the kids — these were all Ukrainian. The trident, the flag, the language, the songs — these are now elements of their identity that each has personally suffered for. As adults they will not give them up lightly.

The faces of the kids I saw today (even those whose eyes filled with tears as they spoke of their fathers) looked forward, not backward. They honored their ancestors (whatever their ethnicity or historical uniform) for having defended their homeland. And for these kids Russia is now their lifelong enemy. I guess we should thank Mr. Putin for that. But I prefer to thank the fathers of our children's' classmates. Heroes — each of them. Plekhanov's legacy lives on...

This nation is indestructible!

This book is about the indestructible Ukrainian nation. It is about a people transformed through revolution, and about the broader civilizational consequences of these events. Experiencing Maidan firsthand provided me with what social scientists call "thick data", and it would be wrong to duck the opportunity to use this data to engage in scholarly theoretical debates that pervade my field of study. I do so on several occasions in the text. On the other hand, I am very conscious of the fact that my account of Ukraine's Revolution of Dignity lacks "academic distance" — I simply cannot detach myself from my own experiences of both protest and war, nor can I claim neutrality with respect to those whose limbs, eyes, organs, and lives were lost defending their (my) country against invaders. My academic contribution is therefore, of necessity, biased.

But this book is not intended to be a purely academic text. First and foremost, I seek to relay the highly personalized, yet social; objectively dangerous, yet engendering feelings of complete safety; emotionally charged, yet intellectually stimulating events that I lived through during the Maidan protests and during subsequent months of war with Russia. I seek to demonstrate both the excitement of a successful popular uprising (passionate elation), and the experience of feeling threatened by violence (intense fear) resulting from war. However, in addition to personal reflections, this book also seeks to contribute to social science thinking about revolutions, human progress (modernity and post-modernity), and about the ideational vs. material roots of social change. I seek to dispel the numerous stereotypes about Ukraine that have been purposefully or inadvertently (I make no judgments as to motives) perpetrated by both journalists and academics. These include the myth according to which the Kremlin's military aggression in Crimea and the Donbas was somehow justified by the threat to Russia posed by NATO's eastward expansion a decade earlier.[2] A word of warning: if you believe the change of political regime in Kyiv that resulted from the Maidan protests in 2013-14 to have been a "fascist coup", or that Russia did not engage in an unprovoked invasion of the sovereign territory of Ukraine in February 2014, or that the Kremlin did not foster continuous war in the Donbas thereafter, you will not enjoy this book.

From this brief preface the reader will have concluded that the author is highly opinionated. Such an appraisal is accurate, but I assume a degree of empathy on the part of the reader. I will make every effort to back-up my opinions with facts and take full personal responsibility for any errors or misconceptions that may have creeped into the text because of my biases.

Chapter 1:
Introduction

In late 2013 and early 2014, over multiple weeks in sub-zero temperatures, hundreds of thousands of protesters in Kyiv (and in other cities across Ukraine), displayed amazing levels of civic activism, restraint, self-organization, and spontaneous cooperation while demonstrating their individual and collective displeasure with their rulers. Their protest achieved its primary goal (the ouster of President Viktor Yanukovych), but victory came at enormous cost: three months of continuous blockade of the central area of Ukraine's capital, and a climax during which over 100 civilians were gunned down by riot police and snipers. Over subsequent months, during Russia's invasion and subsequent war with Ukraine, tens of thousands more were injured or killed, and almost 2 million displaced from the country's eastern Donbas region (approximately 1.6 million moved to other areas of Ukraine; the rest to Russia). The Crimean Peninsula—an autonomous region within the sovereign territory of Ukraine—was annexed by the Russian Federation in an illegal act that substantively undermined political stability on the European continent. The Russian armed forces then flexed their muscles in Syria (with disastrous consequences for the people of Aleppo), and repeatedly threatened the airspace of several NATO countries. By the fifth anniversary of the start of the "Maidan" protests in Kyiv, evidence of significant covert intervention by Kremlin-backed hackers in the 2016 US Presidential election process had become public, and Russia's use of an illegal nerve agent on UK soil had caused significant diplomatic tension with the West. Amid all the accusations and denials, the term "post-truth" came to epitomize the problems associated with analyzing global "hybrid" war.

Maidan and the Russian invasion changed our world profoundly. This author's first-hand experience of the Ukrainian revolution,[1] which included both protests in the capital and other centers, and war in the eastern Donbas region, is presented in the first half of this book, where I offer a participant observer's perspective on events. As noted in the Preface, for me Maidan was an emotional place—a place of euphoria, sadness, fear, anger, solidarity, and pride. It was a place where I experienced Humanity; where all was possible because there was "we". It was also the place where I saw Death for the first time, and it was the place where I witnessed what has been cogently called "the Birth of a Nation."[2] Then, after 3 months of protest in freezing temperatures, just as we thought victory was ours, war broke out. In 2014 Russia inserted troops into Ukraine, sparking a military conflict that continues to this day. Ukrainians throughout the world banded together in resistance: volunteering, giving, displaying patriotic defiance. And simultaneously, we worked hard to change the country internally—many by taking up formal roles in government; others by becoming engaged in civil society; others still by working to change everyday practices to reflect the activism and values that engendered Maidan.

Revolutions are (by definition) complex. They usually involve violence, inevitably lead to circulation of a state's political elite, and sometimes (in the case of "great" revolutions) result in more fundamental social change than would be expected from momentary political upheaval. An analytical frame for understanding Ukraine's Revolution of Dignity (a series of events that I contend constituted just such a "great" revolution) is expounded in the second half of the book. I am proud to have been part of these events and privileged to offer my interpretation of these processes from the perspective of a participant social scientist.

Experiencing Maidan and the war

History books often present revolutions as abrupt events. In fact, revolutionary socio-political change, though rapid, takes time. The process involves elite circulation, restructuring of economic activities, reorientation of social relations, transformation of institutionalized ideas, norms and practices. For our family, the Ukrainian revolution began in late 2013, and in the years that followed, we experienced a rollercoaster ride of emotions and lifechanging experiences. In the beginning we commiserated with the students who had been savagely beaten by police in the early hours of 30 November 2013 (several had attended my lectures at Kyiv-Mohyla Academy just a few days before); we joined the awestruck million of our fellow citizens who filled the streets of Kyiv on December 1 (and again on December 8, and many Sundays thereafter) to show their displeasure at the brutality of the authorities. During those very early (and heady) days, in our hearts we knew the Yanukovych regime's days were numbered, but that confident belief did not always make the journey any easier.

Temperatures dropped, and the snow fell. "Euromaidan" transformed into "Maidan" with the "euro" prefix becoming increasingly irrelevant to the protesters — although remaining a convenient label for western journalists. We prepared for a drawn-out struggle. By mid-December we had pushed back an attempt by the regime to disperse our protest camp by force. As the slogan on Maidan proclaimed, each of us was just "one drop in an ocean", but together we were unstoppable. We celebrated the New Year with several hundred thousand countrymen on Kyiv's central square, and many million more glued to television screens, singing Ukraine's national anthem in an act of defiance — emotional, peaceful, righteous protest.

Then came the farcical assault on democratic norms when on 16 January 2014, a legislative majority in Ukraine's Parliament (made up of Yanukovych-controlled MP's) violated all procedural norms, and pushed through what we (Maidan activists and demonstrators) viewed as dictatorial laws: they banned public protest, the wearing of helmets and masks during demonstrations, road processions of more than five cars (essentially outlawing the AutoMaidan — see Chapter 3), and they legalized trials in absentia. The protesters' reaction was swift. Three days later, the country that had prided itself on being the only post-Soviet state that had avoided political violence during the two decades that followed the collapse of the USSR, lost its innocence: tyres burned, Molotov cocktails flew, tear gas and bullets (first rubber, and then real) went into play. Then came the first deaths in the city-center, followed quickly by kidnappings and beatings on the outskirts of the capital.

Hopes for a peaceful solution were raised when US and European politicians became involved as brokers in negotiations between the Yanukovych regime and opposition politicians, but all that was dashed on 18-20 February 2014. First riot police and paid thugs attacked peaceful demonstrators near the Parliament buildings; then they attempted to clear Independence Square by force, and finally snipers were deployed onto the rooftops of buildings in the city-center. With pinpoint accuracy their high-powered rifles targeted the necks, heads and hearts of protesters armed with wooden shields and (in a few cases) shotguns or pneumatic pistols.

On 22 February we thought the worst was over. The regime crumbled. We celebrated victory, and simultaneously mourned the deaths of the Heaven's Hundred — Ukraine's now-mythical heroes who sacrificed their lives during the climax of the Kyiv phase of the Maidan protests. Meanwhile, Yanukovych fled: first from Kyiv to Kharkiv and then to Donetsk, only to be extracted to Russia via Crimea on a vessel of the Russian Black Sea Fleet.[3] Little did we know (or expect) that even before the President's ouster, the Kremlin had already launched preparations for the seizure of Ukrainian territory, and organization of its aggressive response to the victory of Maidan.

The second half of the story of 2014 continued into 2015 and beyond. The massacre on Maidan was followed by the Russian military being called to action in Crimea: first to support a self-proclaimed Crimean "government" (established by a minority of elected local leaders — see Chapter 5), and later, to clear the peninsula of Ukrainian troops. On 18 March 2014, the Russian Federation proclaimed Crimea to be a constituent part of its territory (i.e. officially announced its annexation), thereby violating a fundamental principle of the international order — the inviolability of inter-state borders. Western economic sanctions against the Russian Federation, and political isolation of the Kremlin followed.

As it happened, the Crimean affair turned out to be just the start of the Kremlin's anti-Maidan reaction. Within weeks, Russian Special Forces were again active in Ukraine fostering armed conflict in Donetsk, Luhansk, Slovyansk, Mariupol, Horlivka, Kramatorsk, and other towns in the Donbas region. There, during the spring of 2014, protesters egged on by Russian intelligence officers,[4] proclaimed the "Donetsk" and "Luhansk People's Republics" to be independent of Kyiv. Russian troops and heavy artillery poured into the region — a fact that was documented by multiple social media sources, and later confirmed by NATO. In July 2014, Ukrainian forces advancing against the separatists were repeatedly shelled from Russian territory.[5]

As if to dispel any doubts as to direct Russian involvement, on 17 July 2014 Malaysian Airlines flight MH17, travelling from Amsterdam to Kuala Lumpur, and overflying Donetsk oblast at an altitude of over 10 km (over 33 000 feet), was shot down by a Russian manufactured high-tech BUK surface-to-air missile killing all 298 passengers and crew on board.[6] Five weeks later, as Ukrainian troops advanced on the crash site in a pincer movement aimed at cutting off separatist fighters and Russian Special Forces lodged in the city of Donetsk from supply channels crossing the Russian-Ukrainian border, Russian Army regulars crossed into Ukraine northwest of Rostov-on-Don to engage the Ukrainian army advancing in a north-easterly direction from Mariupol.[7] The two sides met near the town of Ilovaysk with the professional Russian army inflicting massive casualties on its poorly trained and underequipped Ukrainian volunteer adversaries.[8]

Scrambling to avoid further humiliation and territory loss, Ukrainian President Poroshenko travelled to Minsk Belarus to meet with his Russian counterpart in the presence of German Chancellor Angela Merkel and French President Francois Hollande. The meeting resulted in an agreement that came to be known as Minsk-1 (signed on 5 September 2014) which nominally instituted a ceasefire. But combat on the frontlines died down just slightly and for a very short time. By January 2015 hostilities had again intensified: the southern city of Mariupol was shelled by Russian multiple-launch "Grad" rockets; formerly liberated areas of the Donbas (including Donetsk airport) were again occupied by Russian-backed "separatist" irregulars. Artillery barrages and renewed troop movements near the town of Debaltseve foreshadowed another direct military engagement between Ukrainian forces and Russian regulars.[9]

In an attempt to halt a full-scale Russian invasion, a second round of high-level EU-brokered talks was held in Minsk in February 2015, leading to yet another "peace" accord — this time signed personally by the Russian, Ukrainian and French Presidents, and by the German Chancellor. Although few in Ukraine judged Minsk-2 to be any more permanent than Minsk-1, the avoidance of full-scale invasion allowed Ukraine to strengthen its defenses, mobilize, equip and organize its armed forces, and to access training and equipment from several NATO countries.[10] Most importantly, a relative pause in hostilities allowed the country's leadership to shift attention to long-delayed domestic problems. Reform of the police, state procurement, higher education, and energy sectors followed. Judicial reform stalled — a fact that resulted in a number of Yanukovych-era officials avoiding prosecution (most fled to Russia after having been granted bail, or after having received warning of their impending arrest).[11] But on the positive side, relative "peace" brought much needed economic reform, and a reorientation of Ukraine's exports from east to west. Economic growth was finally restored in 2017 after three years of catastrophic decline.

The Minsk-2 peace agreement may have reduced the intensity of war, but it did not lead to real peace. On the contrary: throughout 2015 news broadcasts reported 1-3 Ukrainian soldiers killed per day in artillery barrages across the line of contact in the Donbas; an additional 3-5 were reported injured daily. By mid-2016, after 6 months of low intensity conflict (15-25 artillery incidents per day), fighting again intensified (daily artillery incidents numbering up to 100); Russia massed troops and equipment along the Ukrainian border, poured massive reinforcements (armor, tanks, artillery, personnel) into the Donbas. Renewed invasion was somehow avoided. Nominal "peace" along the contact line (now fortified by a network of trenches) continued to be maintained throughout 2017-2018, but with both sides experiencing casualties from regular artillery and small arms skirmishes. At time of writing, the official death toll during 4 years of war between Russia and Ukraine (from April 2014 onward) had topped 10 thousand. Continued shelling along the contact line left no doubt that the death-toll would continue to rise over subsequent months.

In 2014-15 Putin's plan, apparently, was to split Ukraine in two by establishing "*Novorossiya*" on the territory of its 8 eastern and southern oblasts (regions). However, despite enormous resources poured into propaganda (in the region and worldwide), the Kremlin's portrayal of the Kyiv-based revolutionaries as representing a "fascist junta" convinced far too few to matter. A majority of Ukraine's ethnic Russians and Russian-speaking Ukrainians did not identify with Russia, nor with the "Russian World" (*Russkiy mir*) civilizational project offered by the Kremlin. Instead, throughout Ukraine's southeast, ordinary citizens and regional elites mobilized an astonishingly effective line of defense against Moscow's subversive activities. Tens of thousands of volunteers from across the country (a majority of whom were Russian-speakers) mobilized spontaneously and volunteered to fight against what were widely perceived as the forces of a foreign invader. In the end, Ukraine's territorial loss due to Crimea's annexation and the ongoing war in the Donbas amounted to a mere 7%.

Agency on the frontier of Europe

This book is not about the roots of Russian aggression in Ukraine. Nor is it about the geopolitics of the region. Although these topics are touched upon, this book is primarily about the domestic transformation of Ukrainian society through what has come to be known as the Revolution of Dignity. I adopt an agent-centered analytical approach: in contrast to those who would interpret the Maidan protests, and the subsequent Russian-Ukrainian war as manifestations of a geopolitical conflict between Russia and the West (EU, NATO, G7, etc.),[12] I argue that understanding events in Ukraine during and after the Maidan protests requires appreciation of the role of *local* agents. For them, Maidan and war in the Donbas represented ideational struggles related to Ukraine *per se*. Although, their revolution catalyzed broader civilizational change that has had, and I contend will continue to have, global consequences, for the protesters, volunteers, and activists — and indeed for the population as a whole — the regional and/or global significance of Ukraine's political struggles, and the fundamental importance of their country in the broader European context were at best a secondary concern.

On the other hand, as sociologist Michael Kimmel has pointed out, "an analysis of revolution, however morally compelling, must rest on more than the ideational objectives of the participants."[13] This advice is taken seriously in the chapters that follow. Understanding Ukraine's Revolution of Dignity requires a process perspective that admits both domestic agency, and multi-dimensionality. The values, interests, and actions of the protagonists are important to constructing an accurate narrative of the course of events of Ukraine's revolution, but this effort behooves both local and international contextualization. In other words: elites matter, geopolitics matters, grassroots agents matter, but what matters most are the historically situated ideas that unite and/or divide all of the above. During periods of relative stability, these ideas define the institutions of a given social system or (at a macro level) civilization. They infuse legitimacy into everyday social practices, defining the proper forms of social interaction, the acceptability of political and economic structures, the validity of decision-making procedures, etc. But when the prevailing ideas underpinning order in a society come into question, political and social upheaval commonly ensues. When new ideas regarding the proper form of organization of society are both the catalyst and ultimate product of a cataclysmic event, social scientists refer to such an occurrence as a "great" revolution.[14]

In the mid-18th century, at the start of the historical process that has come to be known as the civilizational shift to modernity,[15] few would have predicted that the epicenter of this "great" revolutionary transition would be the backwater colonies that later became the United States. Arguably, it was the civilizational marginality of the American revolutionaries that facilitated their substantive contribution to the development of social institutions, philosophical senses, and identity constructs that shaped the evolution of what has come to be known as the "West". Frontier status was an advantage. I contend that in the early 21st century, the epicenter of an analogous civilizational discontinuity (both geo-political and ideational) was located not in the center of Europe, nor in North America, but on the periphery of western civilization: in a frontier country on the eastern fringes of the EU where one would hardly expect changes of such magnitude to occur.

European historiography is remarkably western-oriented. The region east of the border of the former USSR is studied as a place of long military campaigns (e.g. Napoleon, Hitler), and heinous crimes against humanity (e.g. Holocaust, Holodomor), but not one where events of civilizational significance for the rest of Europe are meant to occur. Thus, according to the narrative espoused by many European and North American observers of global politics, Ukraine's Maidan represented a kind of modern equivalent of the assassination of Crown Prince Ferdinand of Austria prior to the start of the First World War. In the context of the emergence of very real dangers to the West posed by a resurgent and/or unstable Russia, Kyiv (the focal point of the Ukrainian revolution) was a kind of modern Sarajevo — significant for its catalytical effect on subsequent events, but marginal as a determinant of global outcomes.

This perspective misses the mark. As in the American case almost 250 years before, the protagonists of Ukraine's revolution generated ideational (and especially discursive) novelty that could only have been created and articulated on the margin of European civilization. This novelty, I argue, referenced the next stage of development of modernity as a civilizational project (see Chapter 10), but also contradicted several of the foundational principles of the EU (e.g. reduction of the importance of "nation" as a political identity marker; hegemonic institution of *social* market policies). At the height of the protests, and especially during the most challenging periods of the war with Russia, many Ukrainians believed themselves to be defending (or even advancing) "European civilization." French playwright and philosopher, Bernard-Henry Levy, speaking from the Maidan stage on 9 February 2014 said as much: "…the real Europe is here…and Kyiv is the continent's capital…"[16] Belief in the broader significance of the social phenomenon Levy witnessed was shared by those who heard him on Kyiv's Independence Square that day. Sadly, in later months the idealistic message became overshadowed by the geopolitical (territorial, separatist) narrative inherent to the military conflict that followed.

The Ukrainian revolutionaries' radical break with the "Russian world" was perceived as a "correction" of the flow of history,[17] and a *return* to Europe. Ukraine's political and economic disassociation from its former metropole in Moscow was framed as a "civilizational choice", and it elicited a violent reaction from the Kremlin. Throughout the Russian-Ukrainian war that followed the victory of the Maidan protests, in everyday discourse, Ukrainians persistently claimed to be defending "European civilization" from the "Mordor" of Putin's Russia.[18] One author described the conflict between Kyiv and Moscow a as a war between the "world of roads" and the "world of borders."[19] From this perspective, the fundamental difference between the nominally "European" and "Russian" civilizational spaces involved perceptions of the means to collective wellbeing: through openness, communication and trade, or through building fortresses to protect from dangerous intruders.

Ironically, given the refugee crisis that gripped Europe in 2015-16, characterizing "European civilization" as unquestionably open to the outside world may have been dubious, but as was seen on multiple occasions during the Revolution of Dignity, it was the ideational meaning of symbols, rather than their actual institutional manifestations that engendered mobilizational power. In other words, for Ukrainians, "Europe" was a symbol, rather than a central demand.[20] European institutions (i.e. the procedural instantiations of values in EU structures) and European civilization — the totality of culture (including values) and way of life of the continent — were two very different things. The former was distant. The latter was here and now, and worth fighting for — particularly when the alternative was the Russian World (*Russkiy mir*), as it was officially labelled by President Putin.

Regardless of the objective validity of Ukrainians' image of this "European home" there is little doubt that the conflict between Russia and Ukraine was (and remains) a conflict of values and ideas. Indeed, Ukraine's Revolution of Dignity represented a demonstrative shift in values (cosmology, ideological beliefs) the significance of which stretched far beyond Ukraine and surpassed the realities of actually-existing Europe.

Was the Maidan a revolution?

In the social science literature on revolutions, two classic works stand out: Hanna Arendt's *On Revolution* and Theda Skocpol's *States and Social Revolutions*. The first presents an idealist conception of social change, according to which the proliferation of new ideas regarding the proper form of organization of society is identified as both the catalyst and ultimate result of political upheaval. According to Arendt, powerful ideas such as political freedom, economic liberty, fraternal (national) community, and representative government acted as drivers for the progenitors of the American and French revolutions,[21] and gained global currency as founding principles for state governance in the modern world in their wake. By contrast, Skocpol emphasizes the largely material (structural) causes and consequences of political revolutions, focusing on the political-economic (class) relations that such social upheavals reconstitute.[22]

I am convinced: to understand Ukraine's Revolution of Dignity, one need read less Skocpol and more Arendt. The Kyiv-based phase of Maidan was driven by idealism (verbalized in terms such as dignity and national liberation; symbolized in countless emotionally stimulating ways, some of which will be described in subsequent chapters); Putin's military aggression in Crimea and the Donbas was driven by idealism (gathering the "Russian" lands, consolidating and protecting the "Russian World", etc.). Material interests were secondary as progenitors of protest—notwithstanding both Ukrainians' dire material conditions under Yanukovych, and the desperate economic state their country spiraled into after his ouster. Had material interests been the prime motivator of President Putin's actions in Ukraine in the aftermath of the Maidan protests, the industrial infrastructure of Donbas would not have been destroyed as part of the "separatist uprising" there, the Crimean economy would not have been allowed to decline precipitously, and the Kremlin would never have thumbed its nose at the world in the face of the West's debilitating economic sanctions.

As Arendt pointed out, revolutions are characterized by violence, but their protagonists are driven by a pathos of novelty, a broad-based feeling of building a new society that is to replace the old—even at the expense of their own wellbeing:

> Only where this pathos of novelty is present and where novelty is connected with the idea of freedom are we entitled to speak of revolution. This means of course that revolutions are more than successful insur-

rections and that we are not justified in calling every coup d'état a revolution or even in detecting one in each civil war... (O)nly where change occurs in the sense of a new beginning, where violence is used to constitute an altogether different form of government, to bring about the formation of a new body politic, where the liberation from oppression aims at least at the constitution of freedom can we speak of revolution.[23]

In this book I argue that the *"formation of a new body politic"* aimed at the *"constitution of freedom"* in multiple dimensions, captures precisely the aims of Ukraine's Revolution of Dignity.

However, fulfilling this pathos of novelty was (is) not a matter a single act or event. Revolutions take time, and any truly revolutionary process inevitably encounters opposition. In the Ukrainian case, this counter-revolutionary opposition was not only supported by Russia, but was in fact directed by officials and agents receiving orders from the Kremlin (as has become clear from intercepted emails and documentary evidence).[24] In the aftermath of Yanukovych's ouster, the Russian government's motives for invading Ukraine were widely debated,[25] but consensus quickly emerged that one of the primary drivers of the Kremlin's aggressive policies was its need to *contain* (and discredit) the Maidan revolution—a social phenomenon antithetical to the "managed democracy" (in fact—authoritarianism) underpinning the Putin regime. Russia's goal seems not to have been the restoration of Yanukovych as President, but rather a restoration of the vassal status of Kyiv vis-à-vis Moscow—an essential prerequisite of Russia's reinstatement as a "great power" on the global stage.[26]

Ironically, the fact that Russia invaded Ukraine in the aftermath of Yanukovych's ouster in 2014, may have been a blessing for the Maidan revolutionaries. If one follows Crane Brinton's classic *The Anatomy of Revolution* (a comparative study of the "stages" revolutionary social transformations have tended to follow in history), after the overthrow of Yanukovych's "Ancien Regime" in February 2014, and the election of President Poroshenko (a clear "Moderate") in May 2014, the natural lifecycle of Ukraine's Revolution of Dignity should have entailed an "Ascension of extremists" (i.e. overthrow of Poroshenko) followed by a "Reign of Terror" (i.e. dictatorship).

Throughout 2015 many in Ukraine predicted a "Third Maidan" (referencing 2004 and 2014 as the first two)[27] possibly involving violence against the country's numerous "oligarchs" and others who had been more or less prominent in politics during the previous post-Soviet decades.[28] Had Ukraine's revolution not become (in the words of Crane Brinton) "predominantly a territorial and nationalistic revolution," thereby approximating the American case rather than the English, French or Russian revolutions that the classic author described as having all had "a social or class rather than territorial or nationalistic basis",[29] one could have expected some form of Reign of Terror to have emerged in Ukraine.

As it happened, patriotism seems to have trumped the Ukrainian population's desire for vengeance against members of the 'ancien regime'. Crowd-funded grass-roots organizations purchased, packed and delivered aid to the troops; volunteer battalions (most of which were later integrated into a reconstituted Ukrainian Army and National Guard), vocally, visibly, and materially supporting the seemingly sacred cause of defending the country's sovereignty and territorial integrity. Under such circumstances, little social energy was left for a "Reign of Terror." When evidence emerged in 2018 of a planned coup attempt by MP Nadia Savchenko—a Ukrainian Army officer who has been captured and jailed in Russia in 2015, then released and awarded the "Hero of Ukraine" medal in 2016—Ukrainians' reaction was sooner ridicule and outrage than support.[30] Clearly, even the country's most active citizens—many of whom voiced regular and vocal disappointment as to the pace of reforms under Poroshenko—had little appetite for repression and/or despotism.

The intensity of the patriotism exhibited by Ukraine's population in the wake of Russia's aggression surprised many and was widely misinterpreted in the West as reflecting a turn by Ukrainians towards "radical nationalism." Although national liberation was a central component of the discourse of the protesters on Maidan, and later of the volunteer battalions fighting in the country's east, the Revolution of Dignity was about much more. Amidst the tents, barricades facing police lines, speeches from the stage, songs and poetry heard in unlikely places, and never-ending negotiations between the opposition party leaders and the regime, people's value systems changed; the terminology used in their conversations transformed; the symbols they used to express themselves began to morph. The Maidan was a collective social actor that spoke in multiple voices — none of which was really in synch with any group within Ukraine's established political elite. To simplify this phenomenon to a classic "protest movement"[31], or to a coup d'état driven by "right-wing nationalism"[32] would be to reduce Maidan to an absurdity that it certainly was not.

Unlike the "revolutionary coup d'état"[33] of 2004, when the country experienced a rotation of elites supported by popular protest, but minimal actual social or political change thereafter, in the aftermath of the Maidan protests of 2013-14, Ukraine's economy and society transformed dramatically: sectoral and regional political economies shifted, foreign trade partnerships were transformed, the banking sector cleansed. New faces, drawn from the country's "bourgeois creative class" (see Chapter 9) entered government service. Many became civil servants on a quasi-voluntary basis, and so were unable to last long in their positions on the limited salaries offered by the state, but nevertheless their short-term effect was to create an "internal Maidan"[34] in many ministries, in the General Prosecutor's office, in the General Staff of the Armed Forces, and in the Presidential Administration. The reform program that they instituted gained massive financial support from international donors and laid the foundation for a new Ukraine — one that may well evolve (ironically) into a very unEuropean bourgeois (rather than "social") market economy.

According to Hannah Arendt, "pathos of novelty" is a hallmark of "great revolutions." The Ukrainian case is no exception. Nominally barricaded from the outside world during the Kyiv protests, the Maidan became a space for intellectual exchange; for the formation of new ideas, their discussion, acceptance/rejection, and popularization. During the freezing winter months beginning in December 2013, and lasting well into March 2014, it was a place where new paradigms were constructed, molded, and engendered in discourse, symbols, and other communicative artefacts. After Yanukovych's ouster, the topic of discussions shifted to defense, activism, volunteering, and the institutionalization of reform ideas. At time of writing, this process was far from over. Ukraine's social transformation continues, and (as argued in Chapter 10) its essence seems to exemplify the shift from sensate to idealist values described by the sociologist Pitirim Sorokin as constituting a fundamental dynamic that embodies humanity's transition from modernity to some form of *post*-modern.

If what constitutes a "great" revolution is demarcated in its effect on human development, and more specifically, on the elaboration of new senses, new paradigms, new conceptual archetypes of human behavior and organization then, I argue, Ukraine's Revolution of Dignity (including both the protest phase and the ensuing war) are to be treated on par with those of 1776-89 in the United States, 1789-1814 in France, and 1917-33 in Russia. These comparisons will be elucidated in more detail subsequently.

Outline of the book

This book is somewhat eclectic. Although recounting events that surprised the world and led to a redefinition of Europe's political landscape may be the purpose of the "Maidan Diary" presented in chapters 2-4, and of the "Eulogy to Novorossiya" (i.e. Russia's failed counter-revolution) expounded in chapters 5-6, my overall intent in this book is not simply to chronicle the most significant events of the Ukrainian revolution. In Part II (chapters 7-11) I present an analysis, according to which the Maidan is embedded in a broader social science theoretical perspective. I suggest that the significance of what came to be known as the "Revolution of Dignity" was (is) not limited to Ukraine, but in fact reflected an ongoing fundamental civilizational shift with consequences far beyond eastern Europe. Understanding the significance of this transformation requires examination of the events of Maidan and the Russian-Ukrainian war in multiple dimensions.

Firstly, I argue that Ukraine's Revolution Dignity represented a profound rejection of the previously taken-for-granted assumption underpinning (ironically) the EU project, according to which "modernization" should of necessity be accompanied by a decline in the importance of "nation" as a locus of solidarity. In Chapter 8, in the context of appreciating Maidan as a "trajectory correcting" event for

Ukraine that actually strengthens (rather than contradicts) historical European civilizational development trends, the centrality of symbolic allegiances is examined. Solidarity was crucial to the success of Ukraine's revolution. It was manifest in a previously unseen "de-statized" pride in belonging to an idealized nation that I suggest has confusingly been labelled "political nationalism" when in fact its true essence approaches "apolitical patriotism" — a form of territorial identity that transcends ethno-linguistic differences but is simultaneously ambivalent to the institutions of the state.

Secondly, I submit that in reacting to the neo-feudal oligarchic regime which had developed in Ukraine on the ashes of a collapsed Soviet system, Maidan spawned the (re)birth of entrepreneurial/bourgeois self-reliance as a formative paradigm of political programming — a form of liberalism that had never previously gained traction on the European continent (unlike in North America) due to the traditional influence of socialist ideas. As witnessed by the ideological preferences of many of the Maidan activists who volunteered for government service following the collapse of the Yanukovych regime (see Chapter 9), economic (neo)liberalism may yet have a future in Europe — although in a modified form that is likely to find expression in new (possibly distinctly Ukrainian) forms of socio-economic organization.

Thirdly, I argue that the naming of Ukraine's revolution was no accident. The symbolism and discourse generated by the protesters represented a novel reformulation of latent conceptual contradictions inherent in European modernity — one of which is the fundamental concept of human *dignity*. Specifically, the Enlightenment tradition in western Europe led to the *individual* becoming enshrined in both law and ethics, and *material* criteria of his/her wellbeing becoming the basis for judging the performance of social, political and economic institutions. The Maidan protests represented a social phenomenon that did not fit the paradigm. Long-term collective solidarity, material sacrifice, leaderless agency, and popular sovereignty reflect *personalism* rather than individualism — a fundamental shift from sensate to *ideational* values with a heavy emphasis on the transcendent-social aspect

of the human condition that has yet to find incarnation in lasting political or legal institutions. Nevertheless, it was these values that the
Maidan protesters identified as being "European", and for which they
sacrificed.

Part I – A chronicle

Understanding the complex social movement which engendered and
fed the Maidan protests for over three months during the winter of
2013-2014 is no easy task. The catalyst for protest was the Yanukovych
government's abrupt policy shift with respect to the Ukraine-EU Association Agreement. Few at the time believed these demonstrations
would result in a change of government. None foreshadowed Russia's
reactionary invasions of Crimea and the Donbas.

Regional ethno-linguistic differences had been central to
Ukraine's political discourse during the previous two decades, and
certainly presented challenges to state-building, but the threat of mass
social unrest was considered miniscule. For all of Ukraine's problems,
its population was generally considered passive and tolerant; the geopolitical context was stable. On the other hand, some limited signs of
discontent with the status quo were prevalent prior to November
2013: the late 2010 "Tax Maidan" protests (numbering several thousand), the July 2012 student hunger strikes in Kyiv against the passage
of a new "Law on languages" (peaking at several hundred protesters),
the mass demonstrations (over 10 thousand) prompted by a gang-rape
by police officers which led to the burning of the police headquarters
in the village of Vradiyivka (Mykolayiv oblast in southern Ukraine) in
July 2013. In retrospect, some basis for popular revolt may have been
present in Ukrainian society, though not detected until later.[35] Among
the seeds of revolution one may identify university students who had
grown up idolizing the student protests of 1990—an event that was
taught in Ukrainian schools as having precipitated the country's independence. And many more remembered having lived through the Orange Revolution of 2004 as children and craved a chance to experience
similar heroics now that they had entered university themselves. Understanding these antecedents, and the character of the first phase of
the protests, will be the task of Chapter 2.

Policy change with respect to European integration sparked the initial protest, but after the late-night attack by riot police on peaceful student demonstrators on 30 November 2013, the fundamentals of the movement changed. Kyiv's previously passive, self-absorbed, apolitical residents took to the streets *en masse*. Journalists filming the demonstrations were beaten by police. Within days, the protests became entrenched. The city-center transformed into a fortified protest camp surrounded by barricades manned by young and middle-aged representatives of Ukraine's working class and unemployed, who received regular financial, material, and moral support from Kyiv's professional classes. This motley and heterogeneous encampment (unsuccessfully attacked by the regime on December 11) subsequently became the focal point for a vibrant community of activists, radicals, entrepreneurs, white collar professionals, and liberal romantics who mixed naturally with dispossessed vagrants.[36] As discussed in Chapter 3, students were largely sidelined during the second phase of the Maidan protests, and the same occurred with established political opposition figures. Kyiv's business community, public sector workers, pensioners, and white-collar administrators all seem to have spontaneously organized. A single charismatic leader was conspicuously absent. Although it seemed like "civil society" was appearing before our eyes, a more accurate characterization of the mood of the protesters would be "affective idealism" — repeated outbursts of pent up collective emotion (both positive and negative), patriotism, and a romanticized desire to change their government.

In mid-January, the peaceful nature of Maidan changed suddenly. As discussed in Chapter 4, during the third phase of protest, the demonstrations rapidly spiraled into violence. After Ukraine's Parliament passed a series of laws that limited the right to assembly, Molotov cocktails, tear gas, rubber bullets and water canon (in subzero temperatures) went into play. The regime's response to the demonstrators became uncompromising: several Maidan activists were abducted and left to die in the snow in fields and forests outside of Kyiv after having been savagely beaten; video footage of Mykhailo Havryliuk, the protester with a Cossack hairstyle who had been captured by police, stripped naked and paraded in the snow in freezing temperatures to the delight of several officers dressed in riot gear, went viral. While the Maidan in Kyiv radicalized, protest camps in several other cities sprang up (predictably in the west, but notably also in the eastern and southern regions), and local elites were pressured to take sides. In an atmosphere of seeming collapse of all state institutions (e.g. police officers in Lviv simply refused to report for duty), EU leaders brokered a peace agreement between the nominal opposition leaders and the regime, but the *de facto* leaderless Maidan demonstrators rejected the deal. With snipers on the rooftops of government buildings in Kyiv with orders to shoot, it seemed Ukraine was destined to descend into chaos.

On 22 February 2014, Ukraine awoke to the shocking news that Yanukovych had fled the capital. Parliament quickly convened and passed a resolution entitled "On self-withdrawal of the President of Ukraine from performing his constitutional duties and on setting early elections of the President of Ukraine." Given that Ukraine's Constitution does not allow for "self-withdrawal" by the President, a legitimacy crisis ensued, and was not effectively resolved until 25 May with the election of a new President.[37] The power vacuum needed to be filled quickly due to the immanent counter-revolutionary threat emanating from Russia first in Crimea, and then in the Donbas. Shielded by an impressive global propaganda campaign, "little green men" — the euphemism that came to be used to identify Russian Special Forces personnel active on Ukrainian territory — facilitated an effective coup d'état in the Autonomous Republic of Crimea and supervised an illegitimate and falsified "referendum" that purportedly demonstrated the overwhelming desire of the Crimean population to join Russia. The peninsula was annexed to the Russian Federation, but the attempt to stage a similar "separatist uprising" in Ukraine's eastern and southern oblasts (in the regions Putin later referred to as "*Novorossiya*" or "New Russia") failed. With the post-revolutionary government in Kyiv facing hybrid war both on its borders and in the court of international public opinion, the Ukrainian state effectively collapsed, but its people responded with grass-roots activism (forming volunteer battalions, supplying materiel to troops engaged in combat, neutralizing possible subversives) at a level that surprised even the keenest observers of Ukrainian society. The highly tense 3-month period spanning the final days of February until the end of May is reviewed in Chapter 5.

President Poroshenko was elected on 25 May 2014 with an unprecedented plurality: no Ukrainian presidential candidate had ever been able to win a majority in all of Ukraine's regions. In many ways this was symbolic of the completion of the national-awakening aspect of the Maidan revolution, and indeed the groundswell of patriotism that characterized Poroshenko's first year in office was also reflected in the composition of the new Parliament—elected on 26 October 2014. However, the Kremlin-sponsored insurgency in the Donbas continued. For months, tens of thousands of Russian troops massed along Ukraine's eastern border, and men and materiel were poured into the Donbas. Despite the downing of MH-17, and the deaths of almost 300 civilians; despite the flagrant invasion of Ukrainian territory by Russian regulars near Ilovaysk in August 2014, and cross-border artillery shelling of Ukrainian troops before that; despite the bombing of civilian areas in Mariupol, and despite multiple violations by the Russian side of cease-fire agreements signed in Minsk, western support for Ukraine was largely limited to the imposition of economic sanctions against Russia, and diplomatically worded declarations of concern. In Chapter 6 the main battles of the Russian-Ukrainian war are chronicled, and the "moderate reforms" that the two post-Yanukovych Ukrainian governments (led by Prime Ministers Yatseniuk and Hroysman) are reviewed. Under extraordinarily difficult economic circumstances, and under constant threat of further invasion by the largest army in Europe, Ukraine managed to implement a number of fundamental reforms—though the pace of their implementation was decidedly slower than had been expected (demanded) by Maidan activists. In the Donbas, the military conflict gradually stabilized, but four years into the war with Russia, Ukrainians could see no end to fighting along the length of the front, and no prospects for returning sovereignty over Crimea.

Part II – Understanding the revolution and its aftermath

The social (cultural and structural) transformations spawned by events in Kyiv in 2013-14 were multi-facetted, deep, and at times obscured by more pressing superficial political events. The purpose of Part II is to contribute to unraveling the complexity of Ukraine's Revolution of Dignity: a transformation that I argue was simultaneously national, bourgeois and post-modern in character. In these three dimensions Maidan reflected a moment of historical completion (correction), a moment of political birth (transition), and an idealist naissance of novel senses. In Chapters 8-10, each of these dimensions of Ukraine's Revolution of Dignity and Russia's violent counter-revolutionary reaction will be dealt with in turn. [38]

However, before developing our own analytical frame, we begin (in Chapter 7) with a critical examination of more established approaches to analyzing the Maidan protests and their aftermath. Sadly, the most popular (and wrong) descriptions of the "Ukraine Crisis" — a label that relegates Ukrainians to the status of objects of great power politics — are Russo-centric.[39] According to these accounts, the Maidan protesters were nothing more than puppets in a geopolitical game, and Putin's invasion of Ukraine was a (legitimate) reaction to a supposedly aggressive West. Such analyses are not only offensive to Ukrainians (i.e. deny their agency), they are largely inaccurate in their interpretations of facts: the 2014 protests in Kyiv posed no objective threat to Moscow — except in the mind of Vladimir Putin and those in the Kremlin who sought to restore Russia's imperial hegemony in the region. The Maidan represented a multi-facetted *domestic* revolution: national, socio-economic, and ideational. As a *revolution* (rather than just a protest) Ukraine's Revolution of Dignity followed a defined lifecycle that *began* (rather than ended) with Yanukovych's ouster. The protagonists of the violence (and their more moderate supporters) were not acting on anyone's orders: theirs was an (idealistic) leaderless agency aimed at achieving revolutionary change within their own country. Tragically, their desire for domestic change engendered international consequences — local war and a broader recalibration of the balance of power on the European continent. It is this *multi-faceted revolutionary process* that will be the subject of examination in subsequent chapters.

The most obvious lens through which to interpret the Maidan protests and the subsequent war with Russia is that of nation-building. Accordingly, the multiple expressions of grassroots patriotism witnessed during the 2013-14 protests, and subsequently in Ukrainians' response to Russia's invasion, may be understood as phenomena comparable to the 1848 "Spring of Nations" in Eastern Europe—reactions to post-Soviet neo-colonialism. However, the national dimension of Ukraine's revolution is controversial: both Maidan protesters and volunteer battalion fighters often adopted symbolism used by the WWII Ukrainian Insurgent Army and Organization of Ukrainian Nationalists—organizations that were vilified in Soviet historiography for having apparently collaborated with Nazi Germany. In Chapter 8, we examine the national dimension of the Ukrainian revolution, questioning the accuracy of the portrayal of the protesters and volunteer defenders of Ukraine's territory as "radical nationalists". A new Ukrainian nation (defined territorially rather than ethno-linguistically) seems to have been (re)born during the Maidan protests, and hardened in ensuing months by Russian aggression. I argue that this (re)birth represented the completion of a multi-year process of nation-building that finally established a distinct polity—a necessary precondition for the further development of durable social institutions.

In Chapter 9 we turn to the socio-economic aspect of Maidan. This second dimension of Ukraine's revolution belies prevalent social science views, according to which revolutions are instigated by or for the benefit of the working class. In fact, I argue, Maidan constituted a protest of Ukraine's nascent "bourgeois creative class" against post-Soviet "neo-feudalism". The drivers of the protests, and the main protagonists of reform after the ouster of Yanukovych, were representatives of a new socio-economic group that had appeared in Ukraine well before the events of 2013-14 but had been hardly noticed by observers. This author's research (conducted at the turn of the millennium) showed Ukraine's socio-economic structure as having bifurcated during the early post-Soviet period: on the one hand the state had become captured by "oligarchs" who used their access to political leverage to monopolize significant portions of the country's industrial and agricultural sectors, establishing corrupt hierarchical structures engineered to strip assets and funnel wealth to offshore havens; on the other hand, Ukraine's domestic economy had evolved with services growing to contribute over 60% of GDP. Entrepreneurial companies embedded in this services sector spawned a new socio-economic "class" of urban professionals, concentrated in Ukraine's large cities, and engaged in education, IT services, entertainment, finance, consulting, etc. It was this "bourgeois creative class" that rebelled against the neo-feudal structures and practices of the Yanukovych regime: they organized the AutoMaidan, and they financed the volunteer movement when the country's territorial integrity came under threat. In the aftermath of regime change, they entered government demanding "liberal" reforms: minimization of the state, replacement of the previous system of clan decision-making with meritocracy, fundamental changes to the country's judicial, police, education, health care and tax systems.

The political program of Maidan's main protagonists (Ukraine's "bourgeois creative class") was not simply a reflection of socio-economic interests. Indeed, I argue that the third dimension of Ukraine's revolution was conceptual (ideational). The Maidan was a declaration of dignity: a reflection of a shift of values from a state-centered Soviet-era heritage and paradigm to a nominally "post-modern" worldview. Superficially, one can declare that such a worldview cannot tolerate a regime that tortures and maims its own citizens. This is of course true, but more fundamentally, the "habitus" of Ukraine's bourgeois "creative class" accessed deeper philosophical notions: Maidan became a producer of phenomenological senses that represented novelties not only for Ukraine. They were new for Europe as well. I submit that in this respect Ukraine's revolution represents a possible step forward for what has come to be known as "western" civilization. This aspect of the contribution made by the Maidan to broader philosophical (ontological) discourse is the focus of Chapter 10.

In Chapter 11 we sum up the argument of the book, namely that the Maidan was a triple revolution (patriotic, bourgeois, and phenomenological), and offer some thoughts as to the priority areas of the country's development given these dimensions. We also elucidate the long-term threat to Europe presented by Russia, for whom Ukraine is a battlefield in a broader civilizational war. The events of Ukraine's Revolution of Dignity laid bare the previously latent "Russia problem" for which the West has yet to find a solution — one that of necessity must be multifaceted: political, military, economic, intellectual and moral. Ukraine is likely to be the epicenter of both the search for solutions and their implementation.

The underlying thread that ties all the chapters of this book together is the claim that Revolution of Dignity was a catalyst, or at least a punctuation mark, in a process of transformation that affected a broader geography than just that of Ukraine. This claim is somewhat presumptuous. Nevertheless, we might recall that in history, events of global significance often began with seemingly peripheral incidents: the assassination of Austrian Crown Prince Franz Ferdinand in the backwater city of Sarajevo in 1914 is one example; the Boston Tea Party protest leading to the establishment of the United States is another. In late 2013, few would have predicted that a sudden government about-face on what amounted to a free trade deal between Ukraine and the EU would start a mass uprising, nor by any means a revolution. Certainly (despite arguments to the contrary),[40] this agreement was not the cause of the subsequent war between Russia and Ukraine, nor of the Kremlin's later aggression in other places (e.g. the bombing of Aleppo in Syria, covert intervention in the 2016 US election, use of chemical weapons agents in the UK in 2017, etc.). But in retrospect the analogy to other seemingly peripheral historical pivot points is obvious: the Yanukovych regime's refusal to sign the Ukraine-EU Association Agreement as planned in November 2013 seems to have catalyzed a series of events that not only changed Ukraine, but profoundly affected the structure of relations between the West and Russia with broad institutional consequences. Indeed, what came to be known at the "Ukraine Crisis" gave birth to disagreement between the US and Europe (and within Europe) as to the future of NATO and spawned global debate as to the effectiveness of the UN.

Multiple aspects of the 21st century's new realities were brought forward by the Revolution of Dignity with consequences far beyond the East European regional or even global geopolitical contexts. The process was accompanied by violence, and five years after the start of Moscow's war in Ukraine, the violent "clash of civilizations" (though not in the sense intended by Huntington) between Russia and the West seems far from over. More violence seems likely, in a wider geography, until a new civilizational order is established on the ruins of the old.

Part One — A Chronicle

Chapter 2:
Antecedents of Revolution

Throughout its post-Soviet history — prior to late 2013 — Ukraine's society had been, for the most part, civically inactive: seemingly resigned to authoritarianism (except during the Orange protests of 2004); regionally divided with ethno-linguistic cleavages apparently accentuated by differing interpretations of history and geopolitical preference; incapable of consolidated political action because of pervasive divisions within its political elite. According to the commonly accepted narrative, Ukraine is a divided country split along ethno-linguistic lines. Apparently (so said the Ukraine experts prior to Maidan),[1] residents of the predominantly Russian-speaking eastern and southern regions of the country preferred closer integration with Russia, whereas the predominantly Ukrainian-speaking west was pro-EU. Given these conditions, the speed and scale at which the (Euro)Maidan protests organized throughout Ukraine in November-December 2013 was astounding. Their duration, and then the unity of Ukrainians' reaction to Russian interference in their affairs, dumfounded many.

Accounting for how Ukraine's Revolution of Dignity began (describing its precursors and antecedents) will be the task of this chapter. In hindsight, the (Euro)Maidan should not have been as bewildering as it was for many observers of Ukraine. Shock is often a result of stereotype, simplification, and acceptance of half-truths that inevitably evolve into fallacies. We begin our story with the most fundamental of stereotypes surrounding Ukraine: that it is a cleft polity, regionally split, and historically passive. We then examine the "student factor" of the early demonstrations — its roots in previous Ukrainian protests. Finally, some personal reflections on the author's experiences of the early days of the Maidan are outlined. Certainly, in retrospect, some of what Ukraine lived through in late 2013 was predictable. Unfortunately, few anticipated eventual descent into violence, but fewer still foresaw (or recognized) the vastly improved country that emerged because of revolution.

Ukraine's regional cleavages

Unsurprisingly, a country the size of Ukraine (over 43 million inhabitants; landmass of over 600,000 sq. km.) exhibits regional diversity. Throughout the 2000's, during numerous elections, candidates and parties that promised increased integration with Russia persistently polled higher in the east and south where the majority of the population speaks Russian in their everyday interactions. Accordingly, if given the choice, Russian-speakers were said to prefer eastward rather than westward political association/integration. However, as became obvious during the crucial months of 2014 when Ukrainians in the south and east chose loyalty to the Ukrainian state over the "Russian World" (*Russkiy mir*), manifestly rejecting Putin's "New Russia" (*Novorossiya*) project, the equation of language preference with political identity proved a fallacy.

When asked to name their ethnicity during the 2001 census, a clear majority (77.6%) of Ukraine's population identified themselves as ethnic Ukrainians; 17.3% identified as ethnic Russians, and only 4.9% as representing other ethnicities. When asked as to their "native" language, 85.2% of ethnic Ukrainians (nationally) named the Ukrainian language, and 95.9% of ethnic Russians named Russian. Aggregating these numbers: 67.5% of the country's population claimed to consider Ukrainian to be their native language, while 29.6% were Russophone — including both Russian-speaking ethnic Ukrainians, and the vast majority of ethnic Russians.

Data collected through surveys painted a more equivocal picture. Throughout the 1990's and the early 2000's, the Kyiv International Institute of Sociology (KIIS) conducted multiple surveys of representative samples of Ukraine's population, using questionnaires that queried multiple topics. Each interview began with a question as to the respondent's language preference for the survey,[2] and then an additional question on ethnicity. In all KIIS surveys, almost one third of respondents consistently registered as ethnic Ukrainians who preferred to speak Russian in their everyday interactions (ethnic Russians preferred to speak Russian in over 95% of cases). Furthermore, Russian-speaking Ukrainians tended to be concentrated in the eastern and southern regions where there were also higher concentrations of ethnic Russians and other minorities (e.g. Greeks, Armenians, Crimean Tatars, etc.) — as shown in Table 1 below.

Ethno-linguistic identity	Region[3]				
	West	West-Central	East-Central	South	East
Ukrainian-speaking ethnic Ukrainian	92.1%	72.8%	41.2%	17.1%	12.3%
Russian-speaking ethnic Ukrainian	1.9%	16.5%	44.3%	42.8%	49.4%
Russian-speaking ethnic Russian	1.7%	6.0%	9.2%	26.4%	30.2%
Other (incl. Ukrainian-speaking ethnic Russians)	4.3%	4.8%	5.4%	13.6%	8.1%

Table 1:   Ukraine's ethno-linguistic identity by region[4]

Given that language is a primary determinant of identity, these data led many (including, it would seem, the Kremlin) to assume that the predominantly Russian-speaking residents of Ukraine's southern and eastern regions identified more with Russia than with Ukraine. This proved a mistake: when the question of joining Russia finally became concrete, the regions' choices proved different. The Russian-speaking Ukrainian patriot who hailed from Dnipropetrovsk, Kharkiv, Mykolayiv and/or Kherson, became the bulwark of Ukraine's defense against Russian invasion (see Chapter 8). It would seem that the pro-Ukrainian choice of the former Soviet republic's southern and eastern regions — in evidence during the 1 December 1991 referendum to confirm the Ukrainian Parliament's Declaration of Independence from the USSR — in fact reflected the regions' real identity choice. In subsequent years it had been downplayed.

    In fairness to observers of Ukraine who misconceived differences in political preference for identity cleavage, the unanimity of the

Ukrainian polity demonstrated during the independence referendum in 1991 (a vote that transcended ethnic background, region, and linguistic preference, when voters registered overwhelming support in all regions—91% nationally—including majority votes in the Crimean peninsula and the port of Sevastopol) did not translate into unity with respect to domestic political issues thereafter. In 1994, within three years of the USSR's collapse, regional ethno-linguistic cleavages became the dominant feature of Ukraine's electoral geography when the largely Russian-speaking Leonid Kuchma (the former director of the "Pivdenmash" rocket factory in the east-central city of Dnipro, who had served briefly as Prime Minister in 1993) squared off with the Ukrainian-speaking incumbent Leonid Kravchuk in a pre-term Presidential election. Kuchma won by securing the votes of the eastern, southern and east-central regions (see Map 1). Ethnic Russians and Russian-speaking ethnic Ukrainians dominated the pro-Kuchma vote, and it was assumed (wrongly) that President Kuchma would adopt pro-Russian foreign, economic and cultural policies once in office.

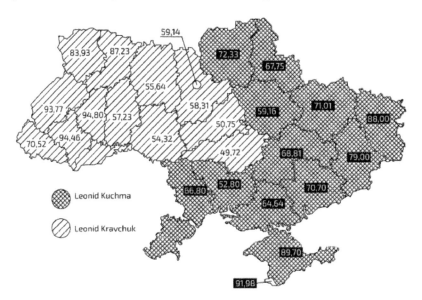

Map 1:   1994 presidential election results by region

In fact, Kuchma adopted a "dual-vector" foreign policy while down-playing the language issue. The country's Constitution, adopted in 1996, proclaimed Ukrainian as the sole state language, but also guaranteed "the free development, use and protection of Russian, and other languages of national minorities" (Article 10). During the 1990's and early 2000's, a policy of "soft-Ukrainianization" in schools was instituted — often justified as an affirmative action mechanism aimed at reversing decades of Soviet-era russification. Textbooks and teaching materials were published in Ukrainian, and prestigious universities began requiring Ukrainian literacy for entry. The use of Ukrainian by urban residents gradually increased — partly due to the requirement that all administrative paperwork be filed in the state language; partly as a byproduct of very gradual and non-coercive nation-building policies aimed at increasing the prestige of Ukrainian as a language of urban interaction.[5]

The influence of such policies was particularly weighty in the traditionally agrarian regions of left-bank (i.e. east of the Dnipro river) regions of central Ukraine. Although the language of conversation in the central part of the country remained primarily Russian or *surzhyk* (a mixture of Ukrainian and Russian),[6] by the mid-2000's, bilingualism in everyday interaction (i.e. one person speaking Ukrainian and the other Russian, and neither feeling the need to switch) became common social practice in Kyiv, and in smaller urban centers in the region (e.g. Sumy, Cherkasy, Kremenchug, Poltava).[7] This gradual shift in linguistic patterns seems to have been reflected in Ukraine's electoral map, and may have played a role in the electoral success of the Ukrainian speaking candidate Viktor Yushchenko, over his Russian-speaking opponent, Viktor Yanukovych in 2004.

Orange Revolution

The Presidential election of 2004 was overtly not about language.[8] The campaign eventually boiled over into what became known as the Orange Revolution (named after the color of Yushchenko's campaign) after confirmed reports of widespread electoral fraud resulted in mass protest in Kyiv that captured global headlines for several weeks in late 2004. At the time, the protests seemed to represent an awakening of civil society, but also a dangerous geographical split of the country's electorate.

Viktor Yushchenko (the "west-central" region candidate) was largely viewed as a pro-EU reformer and campaigned on a record of having served as both a successful Prime Minister under Kuchma (2000-2001), and prior to that as the Chair of the National Bank (1993-1999) responsible for the successful introduction of the Hryvnia (Ukraine's post-Soviet currency). His opponent was Viktor Yanukovych, the former governor of Donetsk oblast (1997-2002), and in-post Prime Minister (2002-2005) — an individual who had been twice jailed for violent crimes during the 1980's, and whose links to Donbas-based oligarch Rinat Akhmetov were poorly concealed. The two Viktors clashed in two rounds of voting, with Yushchenko gaining a slight lead in the first round (39.9% vs. 39.29%), and then officially losing to Yanukovych in the second round on 21 November 2004. However, the results announced by the Central Election Commission were immediately contested by Yushchenko's legal team in Ukraine's Supreme Court. Hundreds of thousands of his supporters (displaying their candidate's campaign color — Orange) took to the streets of Kyiv, demonstrating their outrage at having their votes "robbed" through mass falsification during ballot counting.[9]

Throughout the election campaign, Yanukovych's Russian advisors ("political technologists" led by Muscovite Marat Gel'man)[10] had positioned their candidate as the leader of the Russian-speaking industrialized, working-class east, and portrayed Yushchenko as the son of a Ukrainian-speaking "fascist"[11] whose western electoral base sought to exploit the economic benefits produced by the east. Maps were published covertly by the Yanukovych camp, and distributed as supposedly originating from Yushchenko, displaying "three Ukraines" — first-class (west and center), second-class (south), and third-class (east). When mass protests erupted in Kyiv, with thousands of demonstrators chanting "Yushchenko!", the Yanukovych team responded with a show of popular support in the Donbas: on 28 November 2004 a Congress of Deputies from the Eastern and Southern Regions was organized in the Luhansk oblast town of Severodonetsk. Although separatist slogans were muted, candidate Yanukovych famously (in Russian) rhetorically asked when the western "goats would stop interfering in our work" ("*Kogda eti kozly perestanut meshat' nam rabotat'?*"). Kharkiv governor Yevgeniy Kushnariov then roused the crowd by proclaiming that his city would always have its own government ("*U nas vsegda budet' Kharkovskaya vlast'!*" — "We will always have Kharkiv rule!"). Regional passions were clearly stirred by the campaign, and the language issue (coupled with differing interpretations of controversial historical events — particularly focused on WWII) was conveniently exaggerated as a means of mobilizing support.

However, given the contrast between the top two candidates in 2004 — with Yanukovych enjoying the status of heir-apparent despite his criminal past, and Yushchenko having been poisoned during the campaign, and then having the results of the run-off vote falsified to his detriment — simplifying that year's Presidential election to a contest between regions with varying language preferences is clearly too broad-brush. Nevertheless, Russian President Vladimir Putin seems to have interpreted the Orange protests primarily in these terms: as a western inspired coup d'état aimed at depriving Russia of control over territory largely inhabited by its *sootechestveniki* (compatriots).[12] Had the Kremlin (and western observers) been more astute, they would have realized that calls for greater regional autonomy in these regions reflected the aspirations of local elites who, in turn, politicized language and identity issues (including memory politics) to their advantage. Regional ethno-linguistic difference was not a grass-roots issue, but rather an elite-manufactured straw man that served the short-term agendas of those who propagated it.

After the events of late 2004 had run their course, Ukraine's regional elites returned to their power games within a Kyiv-centered paradigm, never overtly calling for a break-up of the country (except in Crimea where openly pro-Russian parties were more vocal — although never polling more than single digit support). Had the twin issues of language and identity reflected fundamental regional cleavages — not mere window dressing — calls for separatism voiced during the Severodonetsk conference in 2004, may have had some chance of success. As it happened, competition between regional elites for power in Kyiv resulted in never-ending debates over language and memory — not vice versa. Instead of establishing a basis for separatism, Ukraine's ethno-linguistic differences proved epiphenomena of regional elite contestation within a unified context of political nation. This reversed causality seems to have been missed by many observers of Ukraine.

To be fair to those who misinterpreted the significance of language to Ukraine's regional political reality in 2004, throughout their respective political careers Yushchenko (largely) spoke Ukrainian, and Yanukovych (largely) spoke Russian. Furthermore, the bases of their support could not have been more clearly polarized: during the "third round" of voting, held on 29 December 2004 and witnessed by thousands of international election observers,[13] Yanukovych was able to garner over 90% support in Donetsk and Luhansk, whereas Yushchenko polled 90% and more in four western oblasts (Lviv, Ternopil, Ivano-Frankivsk, and Volyn). Significantly however, the line that had traditionally separated Ukrainian-speakers in the western and west-central regions from Russian-speakers in the east, south, and east-central regions shifted, with east-central voters in Sumy, Chernihiv, Poltava and Kirovohrad oblasts (regions that had voted for Kuchma a decade earlier) preferring Yushchenko to the Donbas-born Yanukovych.

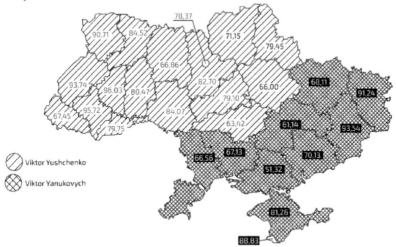

Map 2:   26 December 2004 presidential election "3rd round" results by region

The Yushchenko Presidency (2005-2010) is widely considered to have been a failure for Ukraine. A key component of the settlement that the future President was persuaded to accept in December 2004 as part of the political solution to the crisis (i.e. the price of a Parliamentary decision authorizing a repeat run-off vote), was a change in Ukraine's Constitution. Specifically, the powers of the Presidency were reduced in favor of a revitalized executive chaired by a Prime Minister responsible to Parliament. As a result, the subsequent five years of Yushchenko's presidency transformed into successive periods of "co-habitation"[14] with the President first engaging in open conflict with his former ally and Prime Minister Yulia Tymoshenko, and then (due to his administration's mismanagement of coalition talks following successive Parliamentary elections) being forced to share power with his former rival Viktor Yanukovych when the latter's Party of Regions gained a plurality in Parliament. By 2008, when the remnants of Ukraine's formerly "Orange" forces were able to regain a majority, and Tymoshenko was again confirmed as Prime Minister, the animosity between her and Yushchenko made effective governance impossible. Throughout this time, the political cleavage between the east and south (monolithically supportive of Yanukovych and his Party of Regions), and the now disunited western and central regions (some supporting Yushchenko's "Our Ukraine" and some Tymoshenko's "Batkivshchyna" Party) remained the dominant feature of Ukraine's political landscape.

The January 2010 Presidential run-off, contested by former Prime Ministers Yanukovych and Tymoshenko largely confirmed the cleavage line electorally dividing the country: Tymoshenko won overwhelming support in the west, polling over 85% in Lviv, Ivano-Frankivsk and Ternopil and significant majorities in the central regions (50-70%), but in her native Dnipropetrovsk, and in neighboring Zaporizhzhia support dropped to below 30%. In contrast, Yanukovych won near unanimity in his native Donetsk (90%), and in neighboring Luhansk oblast (89%), with support in the other southern and eastern oblasts ranging between 60% and 75% (78% in Crimea).

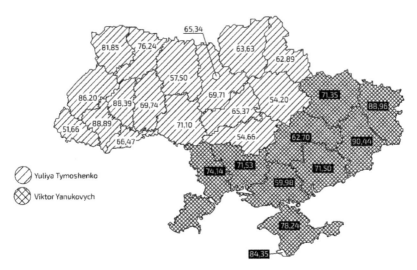

Map 3:   2010 presidential election results by region

Although still interpreted as contest between rival ethno-linguistic regions, the 2010 Presidential race foreshadowed a much more worrisome tendency in Ukrainian politics. Throughout the previous two decades, regional elites (particularly from Dnipropetrovsk, Kharkiv and Odesa) had competed for command over resource allocation by vying for control of key positions in Kyiv. A consequence of this competition was a semblance of low-level equilibrium in Ukraine's economy, and a balance of power in the center that had been maintained skillfully by Kuchma, and less skillfully but still effectively by Yushchenko. However, a key facet of this elite jockeying was a fundamental consensus: once in Kyiv, regional elites became 'nationalized'; they assimilated into the political culture of the capital and adopted the rules of the game of national politics. The exception to this rule were the regional elites of Donetsk who had flirted with national government in the past, but with the ascension of Yanukovych to the Presidency, were now poised to assert their own identity and governance practices on the country as a whole.

The Yanukovych presidency

Having won the Presidency in February 2010 in an election declared free and fair by international observers, Yanukovych proceeded to consolidate his gains by filling key executive posts throughout the country exclusively with officials from his home region. It was in January of 2011 that I first heard the following joke:

> You know, even the homeless in Donetsk are afraid. Black cars have been seen cruising the city streets. They stop and grab whomever they can get their hands on! The next day you're shipped off to some Ukrainian region to head up the oblast administration, militia, tax inspectorate, or some other government office!

As the Ukrainian saying goes "in every joke, there is only a bit of joke." President Yanukovych relied heavily on the loyalty of individuals who came from his region and who were socialized in the same milieu. Loyalty to the authoritarian ruler seemed to have been assumed if one hailed from Donetsk oblast (and better still, from Yenakiyevo or Horlivka—two towns northeast of Donetsk, where Yanukovych was born and raised). Not surprisingly, the regime experienced a shortage of human resources very soon after coming to power. Financial flows were concentrated in the hands of a few trusted allies who topped the hierarchy responsible for extracting billions through graft and extortion. After the Yanukovych presidency ended, its total cost (over 4 years) to the Ukrainian economy was estimated at up to 100 billion USD.[15]

Viktor Yanukovych did not stumble into authoritarian kleptocracy accidentally. Before moving to Kyiv in 2002 as the heir-apparent of former President Kuchma, he transformed the position of Donetsk oblast governor into that of "coordinator" of the activities of several Donetsk-based financial-industrial groups. These included *MetInvest* (ferrous metals), and DTEK (energy generation, Russian abbr. for: Donbass Fuel-Energy Company), both controlled by Ukraine's richest "oligarch" Rinat Akhmetov through his System Capital Management holding company, the business empire of the Kluyev brothers, including *UkrPidshypnyk*—a privatized Soviet-era industrial concern, ActivSolar—Ukraine's largest investor in solar energy, Vistek—manufacturer of welding electrodes, and that of the Landyk family (most notably the "Nord" refrigeration plant). During the 1990's, with the support of local government (including Yanukovych), and not without participation from organized crime groups,[16] these companies became effective monopolies in their respective sectors. Their assets included ferrous metal production, energy generation and distribution, industrial manufacturing, and banking, as well as control over nominally state-owned coal mines of the Donbas region. Their "strategic" status as large employers enabled them to secure subsidies and tax breaks from the central government. These were promptly skimmed off by "clan" members. Kickbacks from state contracts were laundered on a grand scale. According to insiders, the corporate culture of the Donetsk "clan" was strictly hierarchical, and Yanukovych himself was not unwilling to resort to physical force to make his will understood.

Having grown out of these Donetsk regional roots, and finally reached the top of the all-Ukrainian political hierarchy in January 2010, President Yanukovych sought to institute a very clear chain of command—even changing the political rules to suit his needs when necessary. Early in 2010, members of Yanukovych's legal team introduced the so-called "administrative reform" which centralized the executive branch, and greatly increased the President's powers with respect to appointments and dismissals.[17] Then in October 2010, the Constitutional Court ruled that the amendments to Ukraine's Basic Law that had been adopted in 2004 during the Orange Revolution, had been passed with procedural irregularities, and therefore were invalid. Although procedures certainly were violated (the 2004 amendments were passed quickly to avoid violence on the streets of Kyiv), the second part of the Constitutional Court's decision raised many eyebrows: in addition to ruling the amendments invalid, the court ordered the immediate re-enactment of the original 1996 text of the Constitution. In this way, Yanukovych was made effective head of Ukraine's executive branch—a fact that amounted to a coup d'état since his electoral mandate did not presume such powers.[18] But given the lack of unity in the opposition ranks at the time, few questioned the court's decision.

Constitution-changing was not the only area in which Yanu-kovych spawned controversy. On 21 April 2010 in Kharkiv, Ukraine's newly elected President signed an agreement with the Russian Feder-ation according to which its lease of the port of Sevastopol (scheduled to expire in 2017) was extended to 2042. The lease extension for the base of the Russian Black Sea Fleet would be compensated with pay-ment of 100 million US dollars per year, and a one-year 30% discount on the price of imported natural gas. When Parliament convened to ratify the agreement, many MP's saw it as a sell-out to Russia, but de-spite a violent brawl,[19] the ratification vote passed with the support of Yanukovych's Party of Regions, the Communist Party, the Lytvyn Bloc, and several former-Orange defectors who had switched sides af-ter the 2010 elections.

By early 2011, Yanukovych's consolidation of power entered the next logical phase: repression of opposition figures. In May of that year, former Prime Minister (and rival Presidential candidate) Yulia Tymoshenko was charged with abuse of power, and after a very pub-lic trial, sentenced in August 2011 to a seven-year term. The charges were politically motivated, and the judge was obviously biased, but public demonstrations in support of Tymoshenko were small. The for-mer Prime Minister was unpopular among many for her perceived mismanagement of the economy in the wake of the 2008 financial cri-sis, and for epitomizing the perceived failures of the "Orange" elites during the Yushchenko presidency. Nevertheless, her trial was widely condemned in western diplomatic circles as testament to Ukraine's authoritarian development trajectory.[20] By throwing Tymoshenko and several officials from her government team into jail, Yanukovych sent a public message to the country (and to the world) as to who was now "boss" in Ukraine.

However, being boss did not entail commanding respect from the population. The President's lack of popularity was particularly no-ticeable in Kyiv during rush-hour periods when traffic on the northern approaches to the capital was blocked for up to 40 minutes at a time twice daily to allow the President's motorcade to travel between his residence in Mezhyhiriya (16km from the city limits) and the city center. Kyiv drivers trapped in the gridlock would continuously sound their horns in protest, producing a noise that could be heard many miles away. When asked by the press how he justified creating a daily inconvenience for Kyiv's residents, Yanukovych mused that it would likely be more convenient for all if he were to travel by helicopter. In January 2011 a luxurious Augusta 139 was leased for him at a cost to the Ukrainian taxpayer of 1 million USD per year.[21]

Despite being extremely unpopular in Kyiv, throughout the first years of his Presidency, electoral support for Yanukovych's Party of Regions in the Donbas, in Kharkiv in the east, and in Ukraine's southern regions remained high.[22] As shown on Map 4, the Party of Regions won a resounding victory during the October 2012 Parliamentary elections in the Donbas (Donetsk and Luhansk regions) and in the Crimea, and a plurality throughout the south-east. Despite running with its leader in jail, Tymoshenko's "Batkivshchyna" (Fatherland) Party finished first throughout the center and western regions, except in Lviv oblast where they were outpolled by the right-wing Svoboda Party, and in Zakarpattya where local elites threw their support behind Yanukovych. The major electoral story, however, was the persistent split in Ukraine's electoral map: the line between majority Party of Regions (Yanukovych) support and majority "Batkivshchyna" (Tymoshenko/Yatseniuk) support ran exactly through the same geographic regions as the division between Yushchenko and Yanukovych in 2004, and largely reflected the linguistic preference cleavages reported in surveys.

Map 4:   2012 parliamentary election results by region

The persistence of Ukraine's cleft electoral geography hides the underlying story behind the 2012 election, namely the entry into Parliament of a majority of "newbie" MP's: 233 of the 450 deputies elected in 2012 had no previous parliamentary experience.[23] They represented a broad spectrum of political views. On the one hand, the right-wing "Svoboda" (Freedom) Party, for the first time, gained enough votes to organize an independent faction consisting of 36 deputies — primarily from Ukraine's western regions. A new centrist opposition party UDAR (Ukrainian Democratic Alliance for Reforms) led by former boxer Vitaliy Klitschko polled a respectable 13.96% nationally which translated into 42 seats. With its nominal leader Tymoshenko in jail, Batkivshchyna now came to be led by former "Front of Change" leader Arseniy Yatseniuk and fielded 99 MP's. Together, the three opposition parties gathered 177 MP's (117 of which were "newbies") while the Party of Regions and Communists together made up a majority of 240 MP's (an additional 27 nominally independent deputies generally voted with the pro-Presidential majority until early 2014).

The 2012 Parliamentary elections seemed to have convinced Yanukovych that his regime was permanent, and unthreatened. With the opposition forces split between three parties, his regime became increasingly blatant in instituting a kleptocracy that enriched the inner circle around the President (what came to be known as "The Family"). The scale of theft was made fully public only in 2014 after Yanukovych's flight to Russia, but even while in office he enjoyed flaunting his personal wealth.[24] Investigative journalists reported the President's misdeeds regularly, but with little effect except to increase the outrage of those who already opposed the regime. With multiple opposition party leaders jockeying for the status of Yanukovych's main rival in the 2015 Presidential election, interpersonal rivalry resulted in problems with organizing public protests against the regime's excesses. From the outside, Ukrainian society looked passive and serene.

Gradually increasing discontent

Memories die hard. Even a decade after the 2004 Orange protests, deep disappointment in their results translated into widespread suspicion of anyone organizing or engaging in public demonstrations of discontent. Ukrainians felt used by Yushchenko and his immediate inner circle who were said to have profited personally from the efforts and sacrifices of their supporters but had done little to improve their lives in return. Organizing street protests in such conditions proved difficult. In the wake of the 2008 financial crisis, levels of discontent with the status quo in the country rose dramatically, but protest sentiment channeled into the 2009-2010 Presidential campaign. People gathered for mass rallies to protest Ukraine's poor economic performance under Prime Minister Tymoshenko, and the main beneficiary of this discontent turned out to be Yanukovych.

The new President's team encountered their first extra-Parliamentary protests in late November 2010 during the "Tax Maidan" when small business owners pitched tents on Kyiv's Independence Square to demonstrate their dissatisfaction with the Tax Code newly introduced by the government of Prime Minister Azarov. The proposed legislation would have increased fiscal pressure on small businesses significantly. Most controversially, the government proposed cancelling the simplified tax regime for "private entrepreneurs" (small business owners with up to 10 employees) who had paid a set sum monthly since the system was introduced in 1998. To diffuse the crisis Yanukovych and Azarov staged a "good-cop vs. bad-cop" show with the President publicly chastising the PM for his plan to squeeze small business and "extracting" a promise from him to rescind the flat tax cancellation plan. In the end, the promise was kept only partially: the set-rate tax was replaced with a low fixed percentage (5%) on revenue, while social security remittances were increased dramatically. Yet, the regime's promise to concede to the demands of the "Tax Maidan" diffused the situation at the time. After the demonstration dispersed, its organizers faced prosecution on trumped up charges of causing damage to public property.[25]

In mid-2012, Ukrainians' discontent with the Yanukovych administration rose sharply[26] when controversial changes to Ukraine's "Law on Languages" that effectively reversed the soft Ukrainianization policy of the previous two decades were passed by Parliament. A hunger strike was organized in Kyiv's city center with protesters and prominent Ukrainian musicians appealing to the President to veto the amendments,[27] but this time Yanukovych refused. Popular discontent was channeled away from the streets to the polling station (Parliamentary elections were held in October 2012) where the President's Party of Regions benefitted from a well-organized political machine, concentrated electoral support in the heavily industrialized eastern regions, and a pervasively divided opposition. The language issue dissipated in the aftermath of the election. Indeed, the new language law giving individual oblasts, cities, and towns the right to proclaim a "regional" language to be used on par with Ukrainian (effectively instituting Russian as a second state language in these regions) was welcomed in the eastern and southern regions. It was hated in the west and center, but not enough to spark protest. At the time it was understood that if protests were to be effective, they would have to originate in Yanukovych's electoral stronghold in the east and/or south of the country, and their catalyst (if they were to occur at all) would not be language or taxation, but something more fundamental.

In March 2012, several thousand outraged citizens staged a protest in Mykolayiv (southern Ukraine) in front of the local prosecutor's office in the wake of the gang rape and burning to death of 18-year old Oksana Makar. The demonstrations were sparked by the fact that two of the three youths suspected of perpetrating the crime had been sons of local government officials and had been immediately released from custody after their arrest. Within a week, rallies in support of the Mykolayiv protesters were organized in other southern and eastern Ukrainian cities—Kharkiv, Odesa, Donetsk, but dissipated after Yanukovych called cameras into the Presidential Administration to publicly berate Prosecutor General Pshonka for having allowed things to get out of hand. The President then dispatched Interior Minister Zakharchenko to Mykolayiv "to deal with the situation." From the perspective of Kyiv, the problem was resolved.

However, by the summer of 2013, police violence and perceived lawlessness (particularly on the part of local government officials and their children—known by the derogatory term for dandies "*mazhory*") again tested the loyalty of Yanukovych supporters in the south. Here, local authorities (often consisting of imports from Donetsk region) were consistently seen as blatantly disregarding legal and social norms in their interactions with ordinary citizens.[28] When in July 2013 the residents of the southern Ukrainian village of Vradiyivka (Mykolayiv oblast) learned that a local 29-year old woman, Iryna Krashkova, had been gang-raped by three police officers, and that the police commander had covered for his subordinates, the village residents surrounded the police station, and threatened to burn it to the ground with the officers inside. Although the immediate culprits in this case were jailed, the events of Vradiyivka served as a cogent reminder that the patience of Ukrainians when faced with blatant injustice was not without limits.

Regardless of region, irrespective of linguistic preference, Ukrainians' discontent with the Yanukovych regime peeked in 2013. According to a national poll published by the Democratic Initiatives Foundation in June 2013, 25% of Ukrainians claimed to be ready to engage in mass protest against the government if such were organized in their city or town.[29] Another poll published concurrently registered high levels of distrust in the Azarov government (71%); 69% said they lacked trust in the President.[30] In his southern and eastern heartland Yanukovych did not fare significantly better than in the country as a whole, registering approval ratings of 33-35% in the south and 47-49% in the east.[31] In the western and central regions these ratings were in the single digits.

The catalyst

On Thursday 21 November 2013, a surprising announcement appeared on the website of the Cabinet of Ministers of Ukraine. Apparently, in secret session that day, the government of Prime Minister Azarov had voted to cease all preparations for signing the planned EU-Ukraine Association Agreement. The signing ceremony had been scheduled for November 28 when President Yanukovych was to travel to Vilnius for the EU-Ukraine Summit, and although the state visit was still on, according to the announcement, Ukraine's association with the EU (including the Deep and Comprehensive Free Trade Agreement—DCFTA) was on hold.

The government's sudden about-face was shocking given the intensity of diplomatic activity during previous months. In June 2013, the EU had dispatched a mission to Kyiv headed by former Presidents Cox of Ireland and Kwasniewski of Poland who were to observe the adoption by Ukraine of prerequisite legislation (the so-called "Fule list" of laws—named after Stefan Fule, the European Commissioner for Enlargement and European Neighborhood Policy). The mandate of the EU mission was extended several times with legislative changes gradually taking a back seat to political considerations. Yulia Tymoshenko, President Yanukovych's electoral rival three years earlier (in 2010), had been tried and sentenced in 2012 on seemingly trumped up charges of abuse of power. Apparently, the EU emissaries—presumably reflecting the preferences of Europe's political leaders—insisted that Tymoshenko be released prior to the November 2013 Ukraine-EU Summit in Vilnius. Ostensibly, according to Kwasniewski, Yanukovych had promised to consider releasing the former Prime Minister to Germany—officially to receive medical treatment.

Given the public affirmations by Yanukovych and multiple Party of Regions leaders as to the "unchanging nature of Ukraine's European choice,"[32] on the day of the announcement, many in Kyiv (including this author) were skeptical that the government's policy reversal was in fact genuine. After-all, according to Ukraine's Constitution, foreign affairs were the exclusive domain of the President. Why was the decision announced on the Cabinet of Minister's website, rather than on that of the Presidential Administration? Why was the government decision taken at a time when President Yanukovych was on a state visit to Austria?[33] Why was the announcement made public on the day of the ninth anniversary of the start of the Orange protests in 2004? The symbolism of the date was not lost on those who had consistently opposed Yanukovych, and for whom his persona represented all that had gone wrong in Ukraine during the previous decade.

Public reaction to the government's announcement was swift. That evening at 7:54 pm journalist Mustafa Nayem posted the following text (in Russian) on his Facebook page: "Seriously now. Who is ready tonight before midnight, to come out onto Maidan? "Likes" don't count. Only comments to this post with the words "I'm ready". When we get more than a thousand, we'll start organizing." Just over an hour after that first post, Mustafa addressed his Facebook friends with the following text: "We meet at 22:30 under the Independence monument. Dress warmly, bring umbrellas, tea, coffee, good spirits, and friends. Shares (of this post) are most welcome!"[34] That night, 3-5 thousand residents of Ukraine's capital, including Vitaliy Klitschko, Yuriy Lutsenko, Lesya Orobets, Andriy Parubiy and several others who would later become central figures in Ukraine's Revolution of Dignity, gathered on Kyiv's central square. They came not as representatives of any political party, but rather as private citizens expressing their political positions. Popular support for Ukraine's established politicians had fallen consistently during the three years following Yanukovych's presidential election victory in 2010, and so the pro-EU demonstrations were deliberately disassociated from any political party.[35] The next evening, the "Euromaidan" meme was born, and a small protest camp was established on Independence Square ("Maidan Nezalezhnosti").

The Euromaidan protests were not limited to the capital. The day after the first rally in Kyiv, I participated in a demonstration of about 5000 people—primarily students—in the western Ukrainian city of Lviv.[36] According to news reports, similar protests gathered that evening in other western regional centers. These early demonstrations garnered support from local elites—particularly those who were officially not aligned to any major party. For example, the students' initiative that I witnessed in Lviv on 22 November was publicly supported by Ivan Vakarchuk, the former Rector of Lviv State University and a former Minister of Education (2007-2010), by Bishop Borys Gudziak, the President of Ukrainian Catholic University, and by the city's mayor Andriy Sadovyy. Although as in Kyiv, the Lviv student initiative was a grassroots campaign organized primarily through social media, the students received swift and vocal support from local authorities. Similar official support for pro-EU student demonstrations was in evidence in the western Ukrainian cities of Ivano-Frankivsk and Ternopil. But official acquiescence was not forthcoming from Kyiv's city administration, and as one moved eastward, official support for the demonstrators diminished dramatically. For example (and some would say, evidencing the country's endemic regional political cleavages), on the same day as the mayor of Lviv announced his support for the city's pro-EU student activists, all public gatherings in the eastern city of Kharkiv were banned by the mayor—ostensibly due to a risk of flu epidemic. Local elites in the eastern regions were firmly pro-regime—a fact that would result in devastating consequences as events unfolded in 2014.

Student Maidan(s)

Ukrainians have a history of perseverance under tyranny (see the description of the Cossack historical "mythomoteur" in Chapter 8), but as would become clear as the protest movement of 2013-14 gained momentum, once the spark of rebellion is ignited, little can be done to stop the blaze. In fact, despite often being criticized for its passivity,[37]

Ukrainian society experienced several incidents of mass protest during its late- and post-Soviet history. The leaders of most Kyiv-based protests were students, and the focal point of their demonstrations was the capital's central square. This was the symbolic heart of Ukraine. From here the Orange protests had led to the falsified results of the 2004 Presidential elections being overturned. Before that, it was here that the "Revolution on Granite"—a protest (named after the square's stone) in October 1990 by several hundred students, primarily from Lviv and Kyiv—had gathered for a two-week hunger strike that resulted in the resignation of the Prime Minister of the Ukrainian SSR, and in the republican government's acceptance of the protesters' main demand: that young Ukrainian men drafted into the Soviet army be stationed within the territory of the Ukrainian republic The student victory of 1990 became legendary. At the time, the open space in Kyiv's city-center was known as October Revolution Square, but after 1991 it became Independence Square—"Maidan Nezalezhnosti", or simply "Maidan".

The symbolism of Maidan—particularly for Ukrainian student activists—is obvious, and inspirational. In 2001, when the "Gongadze-gate" tape scandal (recordings purportedly made in President Kuchma's office seemed to implicate the in-post President of having ordered the murder of opposition journalist Georgiy Gongadze)[38] developed into the "Ukraine-without-Kuchma" movement, university students were the primary organizers of the demonstrations in Kyiv's city-center. That year Yuriy Lutsenko (a prominent figure in the 2004 and 2013-14 protests) first gained celebrity for organizing a short-lived tent city several hundred meters from Maidan on Khreshchatyk St.[39] He drew inspiration and direct advice from Markiyan Ivashchyshyn (the primary Lviv-based organizer of the 1990 student protests) and from Volodymyr Chemerys (a Perestroika-era Kyiv-based student radical). In fact, according to retrospective accounts, the student "revolutionaries" of the 2000's drew their pedigree from the "Revolution on Granite", and most saw themselves as direct descendants of earlier Soviet-era dissidents.[40]

In 2004, university students again formed the core of the mass demonstrations of what came to be known as the Orange Revolution, forming the radical "Pora!" ("It is time!") organization which acted as a kind of vanguard of the protests. They too pitched tents — first in front of Kyiv-Mohyla Academy, and then on Maidan and Khreshchatyk St. — blocking the center of Ukraine's capital. However, the Orange protests were not limited to students: this time the movement numbered hundreds of thousands.[41] Nevertheless, one cannot be faulted for seeing the 2004 protests as a kind of "dress rehearsal" for the Revolution of Dignity of 2013-14.[42] The Orange protests centered on Independence Square. A stage was erected across from the "stela", and tents set-up along Khreshchatyk (Kyiv's main thoroughfare) from Maidan to City Hall — a tactic that repeated the protest pattern of 1990 and 2001, and was to be replicated 10 years later almost precisely. In 2004, politicians speaking from the Maidan stage communicated in both Russian and Ukrainian in an effort to disavow the "nationalist" (or "fascist") label their opponents tried to hang on them, and signs identifying protesters from the eastern and southern regions were displayed prominently. In both 2004 and 2013-14 Yanukovych's criminal past was highlighted by the protesters in slogans like "we want to live according to the law, not according to "*ponyatiya*" (literally: notions, concepts; here a term that referred to the unwritten rules of the criminal world).

On the other hand, a key difference can be identified between the initial "Euromaidan" demonstrations, and the Orange Revolution of 2004: centralized coordination was absent (and in fact shunned) in 2013. In 2004 the demonstrations were well coordinated by the Yushchenko campaign team, and this element of centralized planning, and top-down organization by a defined (political party) management team obviously distinguished the Orange Revolution both from the protests on Maidan a decade later, and from previous student-centered demonstrations. When the first demonstrators responded to calls transmitted through social media on 22-23 November 2013, their intent was clear: only Ukrainian and EU flags! No party flags or other political party symbolism was to be displayed on the Euromaidan! These protests were to be spontaneous expressions of civil society, led and organized by students and youth without interference or guid-

ance from their elders. After-all, the leaders of previous student protests had become political and civic leaders, and several had achieved
legendary celebrity status (e.g. leaders of the Revolution on Granite:
Oles Doniy, Markiyan Ivashchyshyn, Mykhaylo Svystovych,
Vyacheslav Kyrylenko). Seeing these leaders from the past as their
role-models, the student organizers of the Euromaidan, though
clearly outraged with the government's sudden change of policy towards the EU, sought analogous renown for themselves. They had little interest in seeing the momentum of their movement overshadowed
by established political party machines—particularly since many
blamed the leaders of these same parties for having wasted the social
energy of the Orange protests of 2004 on in-fighting.

Prelude to violence

The students' initial romanticism lasted only for a few days. Although
the numbers gathered through social media and word-of-mouth were
impressive, by Sunday 24 November 2013, the organizational machines of Ukraine's opposition parties kicked in. A large stage was set
up on European Square—300 meters from Maidan Nezalezhnosti (Independence Square) where the students and civil society activists had
established their makeshift camp under the Stella of Independence—
and instructions were sent out to the regional offices of Ukraine's
three opposition parties to gather their members for a mass rally in
Kyiv. The number of people in attendance that day surprised even the
most optimistic of organizers: estimated at over 100 thousand.[43]

The mood on Kyiv's city-center on 24 November was festive. At
the opposition party rally on European Square, popular singers and
bands played both recent hymns and music inspired by the 2004 Orange protests. On Independence Square students and civic activists
set up a kind of open microphone on the steps of the stela from which
anyone could speak their mind. Whereas the political rally on European Square benefitted from a professional sound system, stage and
expert party-political messaging, the gathering on Maidan was less
commercialized, but no less appealing in its atmosphere. My wife and
I attended both demonstrations with our four small children. We felt

safe: a kind of festive carnival with Ukrainian and EU flags everywhere.

However, in a testament to the fact that this was not 2004 when every move of the protestors on the streets was preplanned and controlled, at around 3pm, Oleksandr Turchynov (later to become acting President, but at the time seen as simply a close confidant of the jailed Yulia Tymoshenko) spontaneously called on the crowd on European Square to march towards the Cabinet of Ministers building and then on to the Presidential Administration. Based on the reaction of the demonstration's "speaker" (Yevhen Nishchuk — the MC of the Orange Revolution stage, and later to become the "Voice of Maidan") this call to action was not part of the script. Immediately after Turchynov, Petro Poroshenko was invited to speak. At the time, Poroshenko was a non-aligned MP, former Minister of Foreign Affairs and Economics, and owner of Roshen chocolates and Channel 5 TV. Because of his charisma as a public speaker, part of the crowd remained on the Square to listen. Simultaneously, a large group carrying "Batkivshchyna," UDAR, and "Svoboda" party flags began to move towards the government buildings where they were met by riot police with pepper spray. The skirmishes were minor and localized, but nevertheless, they occurred. Unlike President Kuchma in 2004, this time the Yanukovych regime was indicating clearly that demonstrations of "people power" would not remain bloodless.

Ukraine's opposition leaders were caught off guard by the government's announcement of a policy-about-face on the issue of Europe. Even more, they were caught off guard by the spontaneous protest action organized by pro-EU students and civil society activists who sought to avoid all possible association with the formalized opposition parties. To their credit however, the opposition leaders showed no animosity to the non-political Maidan. In the words of Oleksandr Turchynov:

> We extended an offer to the people on the Maidan to unite our efforts in preparation for the Sunday demonstration... But the journalists and civic activists, Mustafa Nayem, Ihor Lutsenko, Vika Siumar, Ruslana, they said this would be PR for the opposition. They said cooperation with political parties was not in their interests: people were gathering

on their own initiative, and so on Sunday they would try to organize their own event, a kind of alternative to ours. Of course, from our point of view—the opposition's—this was not the best of options—sort of dualism. But we didn't argue and continued to prepare for our demo on November 24th. By that time on the Maidan, under the stela, youth and civil society activists had mounted something like a stage, installed a sound system...[44]

That evening, several of my former students from Kyiv-Mohyla Academy filmed video messages from their lecturers in support of the growing Euromaidan protest movement. I was criticized during subsequent days for foreshadowing possible violence. I said: "Today we did one of two things: we either helped President Yanukovych make a decision, and tomorrow he will in fact announce his intention to sign the EU Association Agreement, blaming the bad Azarov government for stirring up a mess, or today we started the long and drawn out process of revolution, which unfortunately, I'm afraid to say, will not end without blood..."[45]

It did not take long for the prediction to be realized. On Monday 25 November the dangerously spontaneous public gatherings came close to getting out of hand. That evening, according to eye witnesses (I was not on European Square at the time), Tetiana Chornovol, a vocal opposition journalist who unsuccessfully ran for Parliament in the 2012 election, discovered a white van parked near the demonstrators. Inside, were several SBU (Ukrainian Secret Service) agents with electronic eavesdropping equipment. The surrounding crowd (estimated at about 5 thousand) became enraged and started beating the van with rocks—Chornovol herself apparently smashed the sunroof.[46] Riot police were called in to rescue the secret service agents, and according to the opposition parties, were able to successfully retrieve them from the van with the help of Yatseniuk ("Batkivshchyna" leader) and Tiahnybok (leader of Svoboda). According to a source within the riot police squad sent to the scene, the two party leaders were actually orchestrating the whole operation—playing for the cameras and provoking the crowd against the police officers. The Euromaidan side denied any such notion.

Whichever side of the story one believes, it is clear that the mood of these early street demonstrations was electric, and that the patience of the protesters was not without limits. If in 2004, within the first two days the tent city on Kyiv's main square had established a clear chain of command, food supply, and security hierarchy (including, according to some accounts, a communications link with the secret service and police),[47] this time only food and blankets were plentiful in the protesters' tents.

After the contained violence of 24-25 November, the students on Independence Square retreated to the relative safety of the central monument, the "stela". When I visited their demonstration on the morning of November 26, I saw no more than 100 people milling around on the square listening to poetry, drinking tea and trying to keep warm. Although the square was still accessible, the demonstrators were practically surrounded by a ring of police dressed in riot gear—standing at approx. 5-meter intervals.

That day around 10am, the students of the prestigious Kyiv-Mohyla Academy announced a 4-day boycott of classes,[48] and marched across town to join their counterparts at Kyiv's much larger Shevchenko National University. Together they then gathered in large numbers under the Stella on Maidan. Officially both universities were still holding classes, but students were not attending. Serhiy Kvit, the President of Kyiv-Mohyla Academy (later to be appointed Minister of Education after Yanukovych's ouster), issued a statement asking professors not to penalize students for their political activism aimed at encouraging Ukraine's President to sign a pact with the EU.[49] The flywheel of mass protests seemed to be gaining momentum.

Yanukovych's decision

During the week immediately following the November 21 government announcement, many in Ukraine honestly believed President Yanukovych could be convinced by "people power" to sign the DCFTA and Association Agreement with the EU at the Eastern Partnership Summit in Vilnius on 29 November. Personally, when I first heard the Cabinet of Ministers' announcement, I was convinced that it was actually a well-planned ruse put together by Yanukovych's closest advisors. According to my theory, the President's inner circle had anticipated street protests in the wake of a sudden policy shift on the issue of Europe, and had understood that if the cards were played right, their boss could emerge from this seemingly chaotic situation as the popular hero—the man who understood the will of the people, and therefore deserved to be re-elected as the whole nation's President in 2015. Although November 2013 seemed somewhat early to begin campaigning for a vote to be held 14 months later, given the importance of the upcoming race, and the obvious appeal Yanukovych would win in the western and central regions if the EU agreement were signed (the loyalty of his home electorate in the eastern regions was believed to be secure under any circumstances), the theory did not seem farfetched.

But in the end, I was wrong. I had given Yanukovych and his advisors too much credit. On November 26, the day before departing for Vilnius, Ukraine's TV channels aired an extensive discussion between the President and four journalists during which Yanukovych attempted to portray his usual "father-figure" image, and angrily condemned the EU for its laughable offer of aid in the event of a deal. Apparently, to soften the anticipated shock to Ukraine's economy caused by opening trade with the EU, Europe's leaders had proposed a stabilization fund amounting to 610 million euro to be made available to Ukraine in conjunction with an IMF stand-by loan agreement. In Yanukovych's words, this amount of money was like offering "a little bit of candy in a nice wrapper"—an insult to a "serious country".[50] During the televised program the President repeated the phrase "defending our own interests" several times with respect to his motives for signing or not signing any agreement with the EU—clearly pointing to quantifiable economic benefits to the nation as the price for his signature. He discussed gas price negotiations with Putin, Ukraine's trade volumes with Russia and the EU, comparative macroeconomic indicators, import tariffs, aircraft assembly opportunities, unemployment levels, pensions, salaries, and prices.[51] The materialism of this discourse sounded hollow to the protesters gathering in sub-zero temperatures in the center of Kyiv and other cities to demand a deal in Vilnius. Values such as social justice, freedom of movement, expression, and association, and rules-based government (not surprisingly) were not mentioned by the Ukrainian President.

Unlike Yanukovych, the protestors on Ukraine's multiple Euromaidans understood the Agreement not as an economic deal, but rather as a proclamation of common values, and a declaration of Ukraine's European identity. For them, the question of how much money Ukraine's eurointegration would cost was irrelevant. To some extent this non-materialist (romantic) paradigm reflected the youthful exuberance of the students who had gathered on the country's urban squares; many of them were motivated by a desire to live through their own version of a kind of "Orange Revolution" or "Revolution on Granite". Many others—particularly those who had traveled to the EU for studies—were attracted by the communitarian, post-materialist social model of Europe. The contrast between this model of society, and the paradigm of the authoritarian kleptocrat from the industrial heartland of Donbas could not have been more striking.

In the end, Yanukovych's materialist paradigm turned out to be irreconcilable both with the idealist worldview of the Euromaidan protesters, and with the frames of reference of the EU leaders he met in Vilnius. For a deal to have happened, one side needed to give way for the sake of the greater good. For example, the EU leaders could have agreed to sign an Association Agreement without a Free Trade Agreement. Another option may have been to increase the EU's economic aid offer to Ukraine (essentially "buying" Yanukovych's signature in the way Putin did with his 15 billion USD loan commitment— announced on 17 December 2013), and then to use the financial "stick" as a means of ensuring the Ukrainian government kept its promises after the summit. But neither option was deemed sufficiently attractive to EU leaders not accustomed to haggling over the price of joining the European family, nor was Ukraine deemed worth the effort at the time.

In Vilnius, EU leaders faced a difficult decision. They could support the Ukrainian people's desire to join Europe's community of values (visibly and uniquely demonstrated on the streets of the country's cities). But in this case, they risked allowing Yanukovych (a leader that few of them found personally amenable, and an individual many viewed as the embodiment of the antithesis of European values) to return from Vilnius as a hero with a strong chance of re-election in 2015. On the other hand, if the Ukrainian people's aspirations for a European future were denied in Vilnius, the EU risked social unrest on its borders. Although few at the time predicted violence, even a cursory understanding of Ukraine's history indicated that the country of the "Orange Revolution," and countless student protests would not tolerate dictatorship for long. A change of regime through non-electoral means could well cause Ukraine to succumb to its supposed regional ethno-linguistic cleavages—with unpredictable consequences.

The draft of the final communique from the Ukraine-EU Summit in Vilnius included a reference to a signed Association Agreement until the final moment before its publication. On the evening before their trip to the Lithuanian capital, European Commissioners Fule (Enlargement) and Ashworth (Foreign Affairs) both stated that the Agreement remained on the agenda of the meeting. Using diplomatic language, they were saying that the decision to sign or not to sign was up to Yanukovych.[52] But the Ukrainian President did not sign the EU Association Agreement in Vilnius. He returned to Kyiv on 29 November travelling directly from the airport to his Mezhyhiriya residence on the outskirts of the capital. On the Euromaidan in the city center the bad news was greeted with sadness, but not despair. According to Ukraine's opposition politicians, Yanukovych's refusal to sign signaled the start of the 2015 presidential election campaign. By this time Ukraine had become a place of protest, and an eventual descent into violence was not out of the question, but most believed blood would be spilled during the 2015 election campaign. The fact that force was to be used on Maidan the following night was not expected by anyone except perhaps those closest to the regime.

Chapter 3:
Maidan Becomes "Sich"

During the weekend of 30 November – 1 December 2013, events in Kyiv evolved at a dizzying pace. During days prior, the declared aim of the Euromaidan movement had been to pressure President Yanukovych to sign the Association Agreement with the EU. By Friday evening, after the Vilnius Summit had come and gone, most of the demonstrators on Kyiv's Independence Square resigned to the bitter realization that this goal would not be achieved, and so they (like their predecessors who had pitched tents on Maidan in 2010 to protest the government's amendments to the Tax Code, and others who had proclaimed hunger strikes in opposition to changes to the Law "On languages" in 2012) prepared to disperse peacefully and quietly. The students resolved to camp under the Stella for one final weekend. By Sunday evening, if the regime had done nothing, Maidan would have been clear, and Ukrainians throughout the country would have gone about their business — many disappointed, but most passively acquiescent to their own powerlessness.

But, Yanukovych and/or his closest advisors decided to force the issue. At approximately 4am Kyiv time on Saturday 30 November, "Berkut" riot police viciously attacked the few demonstrators who remained camped beneath the Stella monument on Maidan. Video footage distributed via Internet clearly show that the police were not acting with the intent to disperse; their orders were to clear and occupy the central area of Independence Square where the protesters had set up their center of operations. The several hundred young people (mostly university students) who had remained on Maidan overnight did not resist; many were actually sleeping on makeshift mattresses when the attack began. They were savagely beaten anyway. The operation lasted no more than 15 minutes. During the immediate aftermath of the raid, many of the shocked young people were pursued by riot police through side streets, and a small group took refuge in St. Michael's monastery (approximately 750 meters away uphill). The symbolism of this act was not lost on Kyiv residents: the last time this monastery had served as a place of refuge was during the Mongol raids of 1240 AD.

The night that changed Ukraine forever

The evening before, at around 10:30 pm on 29 November, my wife and I strolled through Independence Square to lend our support to the students there. Many were from Kyiv-Mohyla Academy where I teach, and they appreciated moral support from their professor. As we milled around, we noticed multiple groups of young men dressed in track suits with hoods pulled over their heads. Several tried to storm the students' makeshift stage but were pushed back. No fists ever flew, although the provocative behavior of these "guests" was obvious, and I remember expressing my amazement at the students' restraint.

To keep warm, and to diffuse any growing animosity in the face of the provocateurs, the student leaders on the Stella monument began yelling *"Khto ne skache, toy Moskal'"* — a chant that hails from the repertoire of Ukraine's football "Ultras" and roughly translates as "Who does not jump is a Ruskie!" The term *Moskal'* in the context of a football chant is demeaning, but not insulting — like calling an American a "Yank" or a German a "Kraut".[1] The reaction that I witnessed on Maidan was fitting: regardless of linguistic preference or ethnicity, people laughed, and jumped. Music played from the Stella and many danced to keep warm. As we left the square I remember thinking that the scene reminded me of a student rave, but in near freezing temperatures.

On our way to the subway station (the entrance is directly on Independence Square) we met a distant acquaintance — Serhiy Rudyk, a member of Kyiv's city council who had recently joined the Svoboda party. He was strolling through the student demonstration together with Iryna Farion, another Svoboda party activist, and at the time, sitting MP.[2] Both were demonstrably edgy. Whether they knew or suspected that the square would be cleared by police late that night remains unknown.

When we returned to our apartment and tuned our TV to the Friday evening talk show ShusterLive,[3] we noticed the same edginess in the behavior of the program's guests. At around midnight, several leaders of Ukraine's political opposition (Iryna Herashchenko, Serhiy Sobolev, Andriy Ilyenko, Anatoliy Hrytsenko) hurriedly left the studio claiming that they had received messages on their phones of an impending attack on the student demonstrators on Maidan.[4] However, in a live feed from the center of Kyiv, journalist Heorhiy Tykhiy reported no clashes between the protesting students and the hundreds of "Berkut" officers who had surrounded them. Instead, he described a confrontation between the riot police and Arseniy Yatseniuk: apparently the opposition party leader had been asked to facilitate the delivery of a new sound system to the students camped beneath the Stella monument, and had been blocked by police.[5] The atmosphere in the studio was tense—particularly because the broadcast had been interrupted (approximately between 21:00 and 22:00) "for technical reasons." Savik Shuster, the program's host, was visibly shaken, and ended the show after midnight omitting his traditional invitation to tune in the following week. Though no specifics were voiced, the fact that rumors of impending violence were circulating within the political elite that night is beyond doubt.

We now know that at the time of the show's closing, tactical preparations had begun for the forceful clearing of Maidan. According to the testimony of acting Kyiv mayor Oleksandr Popov,[6] on the morning of 29 November, he received a call from National Security and Defense Council Secretary Andriy Kluyev, with instructions to commence the erection of the traditional Christmas tree (a construction that would ironically come to be known as the *yolka*)[7] on Maidan that day. With Independence Square full of protesters, logically this instruction subsumed an operation to clear them, and for this purpose Kluyev ordered Popov to coordinate his actions with Volodymyr Sivkovych, Deputy Secretary of the National Security and Defense Council. That night, according to Popov, he and Sivkovych sat in the office of Kyiv-city police commander Valeriy Koryak and watched on closed circuit TV while 1318 "Berkut" and Interior Ministry officers cleared the remaining 150-200 unarmed students from the square.[8]

Figure 1:   Direction of "Berkut" advances on the Stella monument on Maidan

The police attacked the students from Instytutska St. and from Horodetskoho St., and simultaneously from across Kyiv's central avenue, Khreshchatyk. The formation left few possibilities for flight. The result was a blood bath with 35 young people hospitalized, 68 reporting injuries, 34 arrested, and the rest scattered throughout the city-center, including several who sought refuge in St. Michael's monastery.[9] Interestingly, the "Berkut" officers who pursued the fleeing students there did not break through the monastery gates, but rather staked out in a bus in front of the entrance until chased away by angry Kyiv residents several hours later. The following morning Interior Ministry troops established a security perimeter around the Stella and in front of the Conservatory building. The human fence was manned by police in full riot gear standing no more than one meter apart. Behind them, workers erected the metal frame of what was supposed to be the country's main Christmas tree—the *yolka* carcass which later was to become the main symbol of the Maidan protests. Blood stains from the previous night were washed away.

As news of the beatings spread, thousands gathered on Mykha-livska Square in front of the entrance to St. Michael's monastery. When my wife and son joined the gathering that Saturday afternoon, they witnessed a touching scene. An injured student, with his head bandaged, was met by his middle-aged mother. They moved to a quiet spot near the monastery wall. The mother had brought her son a clean jacket to replace his bloodied coat, and fresh bandages for his head. She kissed him, hugged him, and sent him off — back to the protests. At the time, none of us would have believed that such a scene would become commonplace just a few months later, but with mothers blessing their sons not for protest, but for war…

Uprising

After the early Saturday morning attack on the students of Maidan, a paradigm shift occurred: the protest movement ceased to be about Europe. People on Ukraine's streets were no longer calling for the government to sign the EU Association Agreement — or if they were, this had become a peripheral demand. That weekend, people took to the streets because they had lost all faith in their political leadership.[10] Their government had dared to savagely beat defenseless students in the dead of night! Moderate protesters demanded the resignation of Interior Minister Zakharchenko, and the prosecution of those responsible for the beatings; radicals called for a complete change of government. The word "revolution" — first heard chanted at the 1 December demonstration — suddenly sounded increasingly believable. That day the primary demand of the subsequent months of protest was born: Yanukovych must go![11]

On Saturday 30 November 2013 I posted the following text to my Facebook page under the title *Ukraine's Revolution – Day 1*:

> Last night Ukraine changed forever. This is no longer a post-Soviet state that is trying to muddle through economic and political difficulty. This is no longer a country of peaceful demonstrations that periodically supplies the world media with striking images of hundreds of thousands of smiling protestors with Orange or Euromaidan symbolism. This is now a war zone. And the war is between the Ukrainian government and its people. Soon it could degenerate into outright civil

war (God knows I hope it doesn't but ignoring the realities will not make them go away...).

During the past 24 hours I have realized how stupid (inept? idiotic?) the current leadership of Ukraine is in fact. Previously (like some EU leaders—I suspect) I had given Yanukovych the benefit of some doubt. Assuming some ability to think strategically, I had believed that Ukraine's current President was trying to repeat the electoral story of (President) Kuchma in the 1990's: elected initially thanks to popularity in Ukraine's Russian speaking east, then re-elected five years later by a respectable margin with support from all regions (the fact that Kuchma's second term was a disaster is not relevant to his very real electoral victories). Had Yanukovych signed the EU Association Agreement in Vilnius yesterday, his chances of re-election in 2015 would have been quite good: he would have maintained some support in the east while gaining significant support in the west. After last night's violence, his chances of legitimately winning an election are now nil.

But at this point it is clear that Yanukovych has no intention of even trying to win a fair vote in 2015. Ukraine is today ruled by a would-be dictator who is attempting to consolidate control over his stream of booty by using force against social groups that he considers marginal. He is wrong. The students who gathered on EuroMaidan in Kyiv do not represent a marginal group. The young people on Independence Square that I spoke with yesterday, and the people currently gathering in front of Mykhaylivsky church are intelligent, erudite, and deeply patriotic. They represent the epitome of middle-class European values: they want to live "normal" lives; they want careers (not wealth); they want to work in stable environments; they want to travel freely; they want to raise their children (or future children) in relative safety; they want to be proud of their country. Put simply, they want the personal dignity that life in a European country should offer. And the further west one travels from Kyiv, the more widespread these wants are.

Former Interior Minister Yuriy Lutsenko (one of the leaders of both the Orange Revolution protests in 2004, and organizer of the "Ukraine without Kuchma" demonstrations in 2001, who was jailed in 2011 and amnestied by Yanukovych last year) has not tired of repeating: "the use of force by the state must be countered only by peaceful protest". This is excellent advice, and I sincerely hope that it will be followed. But we need to realize that a thug understands only a thug's language.

International sanctions may help to isolate Yanukovych, but in the end, it will probably take more radical (ugly?) action to displace him. A general strike may be an answer.

More street protests are sure to come—and more blood… God help us!

The above may have sounded like a call to arms, but on 30 November 2013 I did not intend it as such. I spent a few hours on Mykhaylivska Square that Saturday. Not surprisingly, the mood in the city-center had changed since Friday night: no music, no dancing, fewer EU flags, and more radical calls to action (including violence) heard during discussions on the street. I met one of my former students (Hennadiy Zubko)[12] who had been elected to Parliament in 2012 and asked whether calling a general strike was part of the opposition's plans. The answer came: "All in good time. First we block access to government buildings; then we shut down the country." At the time I mused: the flywheel of uprising needs time to get rolling.

On November 30 it was still an open question whether the anger of the protesters had gained enough mass support to eventually prompt regime change. That night, as I was coming home on the metro from the city-center, I noticed that only 4-5 others on the crowded subway car were wearing blue and yellow symbolism on their jackets; when a lady started handing out leaflets calling for people to join the next day's demonstrations, reactions were subdued, and in some cases indifferent. Too many in Kyiv's working class, the previous week's Vilnius summit had been a very distant issue that did not touch upon their daily lives; given the sudden change of focus, they had not yet reset themselves to the new protest reality. Yanukovych was certainly unpopular among Kyiv residents, and although the brutal beating of students on Independence Square mobilized many, critical mass had not yet been achieved. Persistent escalation by the regime, coupled with its intransigence, eventually brought Kyiv residents into the streets in numbers that had never been witnessed in Ukrainian history. But in the early days (i.e. the weekend of 30 November – 1 December) such a turn of events was far from assured.

March of millions

When my wife and I exited Khreshchatyk subway station to join the organized demonstration on the morning of Sunday 1 December, we entered a stream of people that seemed endless. The protest march had started from Shevchenko Park (near Kyiv National University) and had moved slowly towards Independence Square (a distance of about 2 km) gradually gathering momentum. By the time we arrived, the lead protesters had just reached Maidan, and we witnessed several hundred Interior Ministry troops simply abandon their posts surrounding the *yolka* carcass. Clearly, they understood the futility of any attempt to obstruct the tidal wave of people approaching them. Sonya Koshkina, a well-known political journalist, and regular participant in the previous Euromaidan demonstrations, recalls that day in her book *Maidan: An Untold Story*:

> In contrast to November 24th, when people came to the demo like to a party, a kind of safe Sunday stroll, now the people who gathered were very angry. Very! No one talked about politics: politics was moved to the back burner. They had beaten students, practically children, and the authorities continued to pretend nothing much had happened. That, Ukrainians did not forgive. Half a million people – even those who had never participated in any kind of protest actions out of principle – came out onto the streets of Kyiv, to say "We won't forget, we won't forgive!" ...

> Having arrived at Maidan, the people removed the metal barriers, and in a few minutes occupied the entire square. The human sea filled the massive open space, but still there was not enough room for everyone. People filled Khreshchatyk St, further on onto European Square, climbed up the bank near October Palace. Columns continued to approach from the side of Besarabka (the market at the far end of Khreshchatyk St. – approx. 1 km away), and there was no end in sight. In the middle of Maidan, closer to the Conservatory, stood this ugly frame – the skeleton of the *yolka*. Some brave soul clambered up it and attached an EU flag to the very top. His example was followed by other plucky guys, and the *yolka* came to be decorated with homemade banners and signs.[13]

My own recollection matches the above. When the bulk of the crowd reached Maidan, the square turned out to be too small to fit us (estimates of participant numbers range from 300 to 600 thousand). People began to hoist themselves on the roofs of the wooden cabins that had been set up to house Christmas market sellers. The multitude was breathtaking, and strangely, I remember feeling exceptionally safe. I said as much to my wife, in Ukrainian, and our conversation was overheard by others in the crowd, who laughed and commented in Russian "Of course it's safe, this is Kyiv!"

As we stood watching the *yolka* become transformed into the symbol of protest that it would become during subsequent months, a truck with a makeshift "stage" and large speakers on its roof was driven through a hastily organized corridor in the crowd. The sound system was not nearly powerful enough for all to hear, but from our vantage point less than 20 meters from the truck we heard Lyubomir Husar, the Ukrainian Catholic Patriarch tell the crowd "Do not be afraid!" — a message that resonated with us and with those around us. We heard former Polish Prime Ministers Yaroslaw Kaczynski and Jerzy Buzek offer their country's and the EU's support for the Euromaidan cause — both clearly misunderstood that the cause of "Europe" had lost salience after the Friday night attack on students. We heard each of Ukraine's opposition leaders condemn the Yanukovych regime, and call for a change of government. Svoboda leader, Oleh Tiahnybok, roused the crowd with chants of "*Re-vo-lyu-tsiya!*" (Re-vo-lu-tion!) while Vitaliy Klitschko angrily waved off a protester brandishing a mock gable with a Yanukovych doll hanging from the noose. This would not be the last time the two nominal leaders publicly disagreed during upcoming months.

As the crowds gathered in the capital, smaller demonstrations congregated across Ukraine: almost a thousand in Poltava, another thousand in Dnipropetrovsk, 200 in Odesa, 300 in Donetsk, 20 thousand in Lviv.[14] But the scale of the demonstration in Kyiv surprised everyone — including the opposition party bosses. Much was improvised.

The building of the Kyiv City Administration was occupied in a spontaneous act led by opposition journalist Tetiana Chornovol and

Svoboda Party activists. This was not planned by the demonstration organizers,[15] nor did they expect to have to manage a crowd of such magnitude. After just over an hour of speeches Yatseniuk, Klitschko, and Tiahnybok, together with Turchynov, Lutsenko, Parubiy, and others, retreated to the newly occupied Trade Unions building (a large edifice on the edge of Maidan boasting a huge television screen on its wall) to plan their next moves. The Trade Unions building was later to become the headquarters of the Maidan protests, housing a press center, kitchen facilities, a first aid clinic, and sleeping quarters for a radical right-wing group of protesters—those who would eventually call themselves *Pravyi sektor* (Right Sector). But all of this was to happen at some point in the future. That day, no one foresaw such grandiose developments: the opposition leaders entered the building, found an unlocked room and began laying out the contours of their protest camp on a napkin.[16] Areas of responsibility (e.g. logistics, stage, encampments, security, first aid, media relations) were divvied up with Oleksandr Turchynov appointed protest HQ commander.

Meanwhile outside, the crowd did not disperse. The erected frame of the *yolka* was adorned with flags and banners but this trophy was clearly not enough to calm the aroused multitudes. In the words of one activist the general feeling was that the Ukrainian state had ceased to exist.[17] Power and authority had evaporated. All was possible, and the mob ruled. Radicals (some were likely paid agents, but others genuinely craved to make a difference) soon called for occupation of central government buildings. Attention shifted away from Maidan to the Presidential Administration building up the hill on Bankova St.

More blood

The atmosphere in Kyiv's city-center on 1 December 2013 was anarchic (or on the verge thereof). Mobile phone service was sporadic, and no alternative communication links had yet been established between the various pockets of demonstrators milling around near government buildings and the newly formed headquarters in the Trade Unions Building. Streets throughout the city-center were filled with angry and radicalized people, eager to act, but without clear instructions.

The few police officers who were visible, were all deployed in cordons around the entrances to government buildings. Under such circumstances, if violence erupted, the authorities could hardly have been blamed for declaring a state of emergency.

While the opposition leaders addressed the staggeringly large crowd on Maidan, just up the hill on Bankova St., a group of youths numbering up to 200, each wearing balaclava masks and red arm bands for identification, began throwing fireworks at the line of Internal Affairs Ministry troops (primarily consisting of young conscripts) deployed to block access to the Presidential Administration building. Later analysis of video footage revealed that after the main scenes of violence had been effected, several of these supposedly radicalized "protesters" (those who had been particularly vocal) were allowed to pass through the police lines and found refuge with the "Berkut" officers standing behind the initial line of young recruits. But during the afternoon of December 1st, the video footage broadcast by the major global media outlets showed a "far-right radical" street fight with one youth swinging a huge chain towards the police line, and fireworks and explosions injuring young officers. At the time, the protest leaders' hopes of gaining the sympathy of western public opinion seemed dashed.

Soon after the initial attacks on the police line, one of the balaclava-clad youths drove a huge tractor with a backhoe onto Bankova St. screaming his intention to run the grader into the Interior Ministry troops.[18] The fact that anyone was able to drive a tractor unimpeded through the government quarter right up to the Presidential Administration building — at a time when this part of the city-center was under police lockdown — leaves little doubt that the supposedly "radical protesters" who instigated the attacks that day enjoyed (at least tacit) cooperation either from the Yanukovych regime directly, or from powerful minders of the regime who (perhaps) hailed from outside of Ukraine. One theory suggests the radicals' attack on riot police guarding the Presidential Administration building was meant to generate a pretext for proclaiming martial law in Ukraine's capital. According to another theory the provocateurs were led by Russian operatives: Russian state television broadcast footage of the violence on Bankova St.

filmed from the top floor of the Presidential Administration building (i.e. their journalists had access to the building, and the Sunday violence in this part of the city was anticipated by the Russians). A key foundation in the Kremlin's subsequent narrative concerning Ukraine, according to which Kyiv was painted as the hot-bed of "fascist" radicalism was thus placed in the minds of western journalists, and it would not be dislodged for some time.

We now know that the masked youths leading the attack on Bankova St. were not exuberant protesters spontaneously venting their anger. Their assault on police lines was planned and commanded by Dmytro Korchynsky (his face is clearly recognizable on video footage), a leader of the supposedly far-right nationalist "Bratstvo" group. Korchynsky mysteriously fled Ukraine to Russia after being accused of having provoked the incidents.[19] He seems to have manipulated the young radicals under his command: several subsequently became Right Sector fighters, dispatched as volunteers to the Donbas.[20] Whatever the motives of the protagonists, the fact that a street fight with police occurred at all indicates that the opposition leaders, who repeatedly called for peaceful protest, did not fully control the situation in the areas around Kyiv's administrative buildings, and that it is likely that the regime (or someone behind the scenes) did indeed try to capitalize on the situation.

That evening, as news of the backhoe and fireworks spread, journalists from both local and international media outlets began to gather on Bankova St. together with several hundred demonstrators eager to at least witness the action if not to participate themselves. As darkness fell, the police line in front of the Presidential Administration building suddenly came apart, and Berkut officers ran forward. Apparently, these trained crowd dispersers had been kept waiting for action all day. Their attack was vicious and fierce. Anyone with a camera was pounded with a night stick, and a press badge apparently was understood as a request to be beaten. Video footage of defenseless protesters and journalists lying on the ground with hands covering their heads being repeatedly pounded by riot police filled the internet. In the end, official reports counted 165 individuals injured during the evening violence — 52 of them journalists. Those brutalized included a Euronews cameraman, and a correspondent from Polish television—both had bludgeoned heads.[21]

The staged violence on Bankova St. on December 1st seems to have had two concurrent objectives. For the outside world, it was supposed to demonstrate that the Euromaidan protesters (this term was still in widespread use) were far from benign supporters of EU association, but instead represented a far-right violent element of society that needed to be neutralized. The domestic observer on the other hand, was supposed to be frightened. Apparently, the order to introduce martial law was ready for signature as the violence transpired, and several oblast legislatures in the southern and eastern regions of the country were apparently planning *ad hoc* sessions for the following days to ask the President to introduce a state of emergency.[22] But for reasons unknown, Yanukovych decided to wait.

Barricades go up

During the night of December 1-2, despite the violence on Bankova St., up to 6000 protesters remained camped on Maidan. The next morning, they began constructing barricades: on Khreschatyk, separating Independence Square from European Square, and simultaneously on Instytutska St. under the footbridge connecting the October Palace with the Globus shopping center. The latter was built primarily by protesters who had arrived for the Sunday demonstration from western Ukraine, and therefore came to be known as the "Lviv gate." Smaller barricades soon went up blocking Horodetskoho St. (near the Conservatory), on Independence Square itself, and on the far end of Khreshchatyk near the Kyiv City Administration building. Park benches, trash containers, construction materials, and fencing were piled up in make-shift barriers intended to stop (or at least slow) any potential attack by riot police. Although the actual defensive value of these fortifications was minimal, building barricades kept the protesters busy, and the symbolism of the resultant camp design carried great weight.

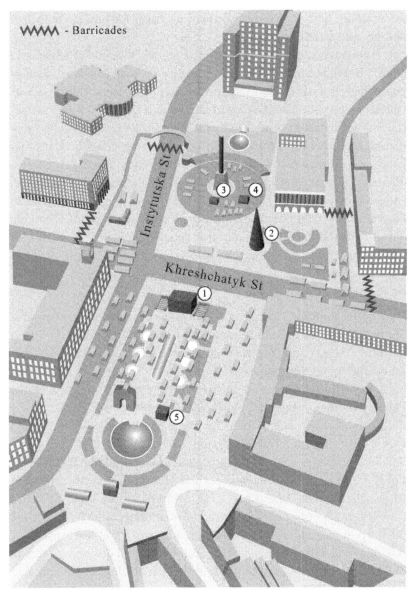

Figure 2:   Maidan with barricades: 1 – Main stage; 2 – Yolka; 3 –
Chapel tent near Stella; 4 – IT tent; 5 – Open University
of Maidan stage

As with the Orange protests a decade earlier, the focal point of the Maidan camp was the stage – its construction began immediately as the crowds began to disperse on December 1. This was to be the spot from which the protest leaders would address the crowds during the evening and weekend demonstrations, and where impromptu speeches could be voiced by ordinary protesters during the day. But, the barricades around Maidan proved a novel innovation (unseen during previous Ukrainian protests), that defined the character of the demonstration in subsequent months. The parallel to the Zaporozh-zhian Sich — the fortified outpost of the free Cossacks that roamed the steppes of southern Ukraine during the 16-18 centuries – was obvious. As with the Sich, a "church" (prayer tent) was set up in the geographic center of the main Maidan (stretching between the stage and the "Globus" shopping center), but in a testament to the fact that the protesters were quite modern, a group of young IT professionals set up an "IT tent" next door. After-all, symbolism and historical nostalgia were important, but so were Wi-Fi and Live Streaming.

Security was established around the perimeter of the barricades from the start, and a strict policy of no alcohol within the limits of the Maidan camp was enforced (although disciplinary issues were reported later — as New Year's approached).[23] Among the tents, people kept busy cooking: huge cauldrons steamed with soups, teas, *plov* (a mixture of rice, meat, and vegetables), and "soldiers' porridge" (corn meal with bits of lard). An impressive logistical operation servicing Maidan was put into place: food, water, medicine, clothing and firewood were delivered in massive quantities regularly. Significant amounts were donated and brought to Maidan by Kyiv residents spontaneously, and voluntarily – particularly during the first half of December. Additional supplies were brought in by the organizational machine headquartered in the Trade Unions building. How much came from grass-roots donations, and how much was organized by the opposition parties is impossible to gauge. However, at no time during the 3 months of protest was there ever a problem with provision of food or basic supplies.

In another nod to historical symbolism, the security forces of the Maidan were organized in "*sotni*" — "hundreds", according to ancient

Cossack traditions and terminology.[24] "*Sotnyky*" (*sotnia* commanders) organized morning marches to key government buildings with several thousand participating every day. For example, on 4 and 5 December protesters set up blockades of police buildings where those accused of organizing the violence three days earlier on Bankova St. were believed to be confined; during the early hours of 4 December a rally of over 100 passenger cars (the original "AutoMaidan") blocked the street in front of the "Berkut" riot police base, honking their horns, and sending the message "if you don't let us sleep at night, we won't let you sleep either." That day, several hundred students who had marched to the Ministry of Education building were successful in forcing the First Deputy Minister to issue a document that officially allowed Kyiv students to participate in public protest (and skip classes) without fear of reprisals. From the protesters' perspective, these were victories; for the regime, each display of civil disobedience provided a pretext for eventually clamping down.

After the attack on students on November 30, and then the violence in front of the Presidential Administration building the following Sunday, few Maidan protesters doubted that force would eventually be used by the regime to clear the city-center. Indeed, on Tuesday December 3, Prime Minister Azarov made his intentions clear in a speech in Parliament. Although he began by promising to investigate the causes of the previous weekend's violence, he went on to say: "We have enough power to clear all blockades of government buildings." This was a poorly veiled reference to the "Berkut" riot police that in recent days had been the regime's primary weapon against the demonstrators, and to the "Tiger" brigade (special interior ministry troops) that had just been relocated from Crimea to the vicinity of the capital. Although the entrance to the "Tiger" base in the town of Vasylkiv had been blocked by demonstrators, there was little doubt that this elite squad could break out of their perimeter in minutes if ordered to do so.[25]

Few at the time knew that prior to the November 21 announcement of the Ukrainian government's decision not to sign the EU Association Agreement, on 10 November 2013 Yanukovych had flown secretly to Moscow to meet with Vladimir Putin.[26] Just prior to that meeting, the President had given a speech declaring his intention to sign the Agreement. He later reconsidered, after Russia imposed new customs procedures for incoming freight causing massive truck queues on the Ukrainian side of the border. The secret meeting with Putin immediately resolved this situation, but what additional deals or plans may have been agreed by the two Presidents remains unknown. Whatever they decided, Yanukovych was apparently not sufficiently alarmed by the scale of the demonstrations in Kyiv to cancel his state visit to China (planned for 3-6 December), but sufficiently irked to order (on 2 December) the partial evacuation of large amounts of cash that he had stashed at his Mezhyhirya residence.[27]

Political games

On 4 December, in a halfhearted effort to diffuse the tense situation on the streets, Ukraine's political elite staged a show of attempting to resolve the crisis through Parliamentary means. On this day, Ukraine's opposition parties tabled a confidence motion. If a majority in Parliament voted in favor, the Azarov government would be forced to resign. But, after a series of carefully planned and scripted statements by the leaders of Ukraine's five parliamentary factions, and a lengthy and emotional speech by the Prime Minister, the motion received only 186 of the required 226 votes.

At first it seemed that the motion would carry. News reports had claimed that Party of Regions deputies were defecting to the opposition in large numbers. Furthermore, Communist Party leader Petro Symonenko (the Party of Regions' coalition partner) began his speech with scathing criticism of the Azarov government, seemingly foreshadowing his faction's support for the no confidence motion. But after 3 minutes, Symonenko suddenly turned his attention to the three opposition factions, criticizing their leaders for wording the tabled non-confidence motion incorrectly: the draft motion identified the government's sudden about-face on EU integration as the reason for Parliament's dismissal of the executive, and this was unacceptable to the Communists. After-all Ukraine's Communists had opposed the pro-EU policy of the government for years, so its sudden reversal could not be a reason for the government's dismissal. Symonenko held up a printed copy of an alternative bill, signed by all 33 Communist Party Parliamentarians, which identified different reasons for firing Azarov, and asked the opposition to support his version.

"Batkivshchyna" faction leader Arseniy Yatseniuk immediately announced that the opposition would support the Communists' motion. Whatever the stated reason, if Azarov could be gotten rid of, the opposition parties would swallow their distaste for the Communists and would support their bill. However, speaker Rybak following strict procedure, called a vote on the original motion. Without the Communists' support the motion failed, at which point Rybak congratulated Azarov, and explained to those watching the proceedings that the Communists' bill had not been previously registered on the Parliamentary docket, and according to the Rada's procedure, it could not be introduced for a vote without first being printed and distributed to all deputies. Prime Minister Azarov's government thereby gained immunity (according to Rada rules, a confidence motion can only be called once per session) until February unless fired by the President.[28]

The "optics" of this situation seemed to suit both sides: The Communists could argue to their supporters that though they had not actually voted for the resignation of the unpopular Azarov government, they had proposed a solution to the stand-off, but were denied by circumstances. Meanwhile, the opposition could legitimately blame both the Communists and Party of Regions (both equally unpopular in opposition constituencies) for their failure and claim that they had tried all options to have Azarov fired. "Optics" secured, the opposition politely blocked the Parliamentary rostrum, and Speaker Rybak quickly closed the proceedings.

Meanwhile, with the Azarov government intact, President Yanukovych departed for a state visit to China where he spent his first day viewing the famous terracotta army in the city of Xian. The irony of the situation was not missed by Ukraine's opposition press (broadcasting on Channels 5 and 24, TVi, and the internet): while thousands gathered on the streets of Kyiv, the President spent the day viewing museum artefacts. The following day's news reports were kinder: Yanukovych would be returning to Ukraine with over 8 billion USD in investment deals signed with the Chinese. However, the most important message of the trip was implied: the protesters were safe from further violence because the man giving the orders was far away, and busy with other matters.

These matters were economic. Unlike the protesters on the Maidan, Ukraine's governing officials were ensuring the welfare of the country's businesses and employees! This was the materialist message that the "Anti-Maidan" demonstrators who first gathered on December 4 on the square and park adjacent to the Parliament, proclaimed. On that day, the Party of Regions bussed in about 2,000 "protesters" who declared their support for the economic policies of the government. Their event was short-lived, but a small group established a camp in Mariyinskiy park that was to serve as the counter-balance to the Maidan on Independence Square during subsequent months. The "Anti-Maidan" participants were regularly shown on news broadcasts highly inebriated, and openly admitted having received 300 UAH (approx. 35 USD) per day for their presence in Kyiv. Testimony of those brave enough to enter the Anti-Maidan camp also suggest that these "protesters" saw themselves as working for pay rather than volunteering for a cause.[29]

What the regime seemed to miss was that unlike the Anti-Maidan, the Maidan protesters were not paid to gather in Kyiv's city-center, and their demands were not economic. For Maidan activists, investment figures and economic agreements with China (or anyone else for that matter) were completely irrelevant. They wanted those responsible for independent Ukraine's first ever incidents of state-sponsored violence to be punished, and more immediately, they wanted the regime to stop persecuting (through selective justice) those who dared to stand-up for their rights and beliefs. Long-term: they wanted personal dignity and rules-based government; they wanted freedom to travel to Europe; they wanted to be proud of their country (which may explain why the national anthem was sung on the Maidan on an hourly basis). But clearly, the regime was not listening — a fact that merely increased the protesters' anger.

Resolve hardens

On Friday 6 December, a court order was delivered to demonstrators occupying Kyiv's city hall: they were instructed to clear the administrative building by the following Monday. The court ruling also referenced the Trade Unions building where the opposition had established its headquarters, and the October Palace concert hall, the premises of which several hundred demonstrators had been using as lodging.

Simultaneously, Prosecutor General Pshonka broadcast a short statement in which he warned that occupying government buildings was a criminal offence, and that those responsible would be punished to the full extent of the law. Meanwhile, several individuals who had been beaten by police on December 1st on Bankova St. were brought before the courts.[30] Maidan activists organized free legal aid for them, but few believed in the impartiality of Ukraine's judiciary.

During his return journey from China, President Yanukovych stopped in Sochi to meet with his Russian counterpart, there to inspect the state of preparations for the upcoming Winter Olympics. According to unofficial reports, while in Sochi, Yanukovych signed a strategic document formally agreeing Ukraine's entry into the Eurasian Economic Union, and eventually into Customs Union with Russia. For those on Maidan who were interested in foreign affairs, this news represented the end of all hope for a potential compromise with the regime. For others, the last straw were the editorial instructions issued to journalists that Friday evening to de-emphasize the protest actions in weekend news reports (several reporters quit their networks that day). For others still, the arrival of more paid Anti-Maidan protesters to the camp near Parliament meant it was time to make a stand.[31] Whatever the motive, the Maidan protesters dug in, and Ukraine's population mobilized.

When on Sunday 8 December, at approximately 1pm, my family and I arrived at Kyiv's Independence Square for the now traditional *viche* demonstration, we were part of a crowd that was unprecedented in Ukraine's history. There were more people in the city center that day than the previous week, and more than we ever saw during the

Orange protests. Estimates of numbers ranged from 500 thousand to 1 million—in reality no one could really tell.[32]

The *viche* (ancient Slavic word for "community gathering") began with an ecumenical service led by clergy from the Ukrainian Orthodox (Kyiv Patriarchate) and Ukrainian Catholic churches who were joined by a Baptist preacher, a Muslim mufti, and Jewish rabbi. Clerics from the Ukrainian Orthodox Church (Moscow Patriarchate) were notably absent. After the service was over, the first speaker was invited to the stage: Professor Myroslav Popovych—Director of the Institute of Philosophy of the National Academy of Sciences. His appearance was meant to signify the support that the protesters enjoyed from Ukraine's intellectual elites. His address was followed by several representatives of the Ukrainian diaspora and foreign dignitaries (the protesters had international support). Then the three opposition leaders spoke, but the speeches were disappointing: they called for early elections, demanded that Yanukovych make public the deal he struck with Putin in Sochi, required that criminal charges be laid against those who ordered the use of force against peaceful demonstrators, demanded the release of those Maidan activists who had been unjustly charged and persecuted, and summoned the Azarov government to resign. It all sounded intellectually and morally sound. And highly unrealistic. Yanukovych was Ukraine's legitimately elected President, and short of a voluntary resignation, that was a fact to live with; after the fiasco in Parliament several days earlier, according to the Constitution, the Azarov government had gained immunity for the duration of this Parliamentary session (i.e. until February 2014). Ukraine's court system was widely believed to be dependent on the will of the Presidential Administration, so the likelihood of prosecutions against demonstrators being dropped was next to nil, and the probability of charges being laid against those who ordered police violence against them even lower. The bottom line was: Maidan must stand. But beyond continued protest, there was no plan.

When the speeches were over, most of the massive crowd dispersed, but some stayed to vent their anger. They had come to be part of revolutionary change, but the message from the stage was "wait." The unwitting victim of the pent-up emotions became a statue—that of Lenin. No one knows who orchestrated the demolition of the Lenin monument, and whether it was truly spontaneous or planned. Svoboda activists claimed responsibility, but the fact that police stood by and watched the destruction is suspect. Video footage of the destruction of Lenin was broadcast extensively by TV channels loyal to the regime with ample Russian-language commentary as to the "neo-fascist" nature of the Euromaidan, and its "hooligans". On the other hand, during subsequent months, Lenin statues were toppled throughout central and eastern Ukraine (they had been removed during the 1990's in the western region), so perhaps the vandalism in Kyiv during the evening of 8 December represented a real desire by (at least some) protesters to demonstrate a symbolic break with the past. One suspects there was a bit of both: pent-up rage coupled with well-placed provocation. That symbiosis seemed to characterize the dynamic of much of the early protest action.

On 10 December, in an apparent reaction to the "hooliganism" of the weekend, and in a grand show of apparent "statesmanship" aimed at demonstrating his desire to diffuse growing popular unrest, Ukraine's serving President met with his three predecessors in the presidential TV studio to discuss current events. The meeting was broadcast simultaneously on 4 networks, and prepared messages were delivered by each participant. The President promised to pressure prosecutors to release the "hooligans" arrested for "organizing" the street riots in front of the Presidential Administration on December 1st (without a guarantee of amnesty); the former Presidents suggested further concessions that Yanukovych might consider (e.g. prosecuting the Interior Minister, firing the Prime Minister, etc.). All agreed that some form of "national round table" negotiations between the opposition and the regime should be enjoined.

Meanwhile, increasing numbers of riot police and Interior Ministry Special Forces ("Berkut", "Tiger", "Jaguar" etc.) were brought into the capital from the regions each day. And each day, more and more people arrived on Maidan from the regions with the intention of staying. On 9 December Kyiv received its first significant snowfall of the winter—about 10cm.

Maidan survives!

On Tuesday 10 December, Ukraine's social media filled with reports of touchingly humane interactions between police and demonstrators. Apparently, many of the young men on the police side were cold, hungry, and lonely. Young ladies from the Maidan brought them hot tea, and sandwiches; in several spots, protestors moved their burning barrels closer to the police line, so that the men in uniform could feel a little warmth in the freezing temperatures. However, these moments of humanity did not last long. Throughout the day Interior Ministry Special Forces were seen deploying to strategic spots in the government quarter, and the demonstrators' outer barricades (put up during the previous weekend but unmanned during weekdays) were quietly disassembled. Rumors were ripe of an impending attack on Maidan. At one point in the evening, Klitschko even called for women and children to leave the city center. The influx of Interior Ministry troops was accompanied by an apparent "bomb scare" that resulted in the closing of 3 subway stations in the city center for several hours. Few believed the bomb threat to be genuine. Most saw it as a regime tactic aimed at minimizing the influx of people to Maidan.

Meanwhile, the opposition leaders were visited by dignitaries from both the EU and the US—a move that was officially censured by both the Russian Duma, and personally by Russian Prime Minister Medvedev, as an "intervention in the internal affairs" of Ukraine. Grandstanding, pressure tactics, and posturing seemed to be everyone's preferred strategy. Few expected the regime to break the peace so soon, and certainly not at a time when the EU Foreign Affairs Commissioner *and* the US Assistant Secretary of State were both in Kyiv. They had come to try to convince Yanukovych to diffuse the situation. Both were disappointed.

During the very early hours of the morning of 11/12/13, in temperatures that dropped to -14 C, several thousand riot police and Interior Ministry troops were ordered to clear the Maidan barricades. They began by dismantling those furthest from Independence Square—on Khreshchatyk St., near the occupied Kyiv City Administration building. Two other columns moved forward in a pincer formation from the direction of Mykhaylivska and Kostyolna Streets, and simultaneously down Instytutska St. through the "Lviv Gate" barricade. The tactical plan was to clear Maidan from three sides.[33] The Kyiv Administration building, and the stage were the ultimate targets.

At about 2am, on the approach from Mykhaylivska St., the "Berkut" troops were met by the opposition leaders—including world boxing champion Vitaliy Klitschko and his brother Volodymyr (another boxing champion). Together with Arseniy Yatseniuk and other opposition politicians, they tried to negotiate with the police commanders.[34] Several thousand protesters were present on Maidan at the time, but it was unlikely that their numbers would suffice to stop the onslaught of police if the order to clear were given. Delay tactics were key: the word had gone out through social media and by telephone that Maidan was under attack. Notwithstanding the night hour, Kyiv residents were assembling at Maidan in their thousands. They came by car, by taxi (cab drivers offered free rides), on foot through the snow in the dead of night. By 5 am the crowd had swelled to over 25 thousand, from a mere 5,000 at midnight.

Mystic stories of that evening abound. Apparently, a monk in Mykhaylivsky monastery, realizing the impending danger to the demonstrators, began ringing the bells on the bell tower in alarm. As the bells started to ring, the "Berkut" riot police broke through the barricade on Instytutska St. They were faced with a chain of protesters several men deep who had locked arms. The priests on the protesters side raised their crosses, and orders were disseminated not to throw projectiles towards the police. The air was filled with the sound of church bells. The two sides pushed up against each other but did not fight. The shoving continued until sunrise when the "Berkut" suddenly withdrew. They were no less than 40 meters from the stage, and were fully armed with riot gear, tear gas and rubber bullets. They did not fire.

On the other end of Khreshchatyk St., as night turned to day, interior ministry troops attempted to storm Kyiv city hall. Three buses pulled up to the front doors of the building, but the troops were blocked from exiting their vehicles: protesters poured water from fire hoses through second floor windows onto the busses in -10-degree (Celsius) weather. When two more busses with police reinforcements attempted to pull up to the building, protesters blocked their path and forced a retreat.

At 10 am, several hundred interior ministry troops maintained a cordon around the Trade Unions building. The scene was surreal. On one side of the police line some thirty thousand people filled the square in front of the stage, from where the singer Ruslana continued to call for peaceful protest: "Every person on Maidan is responsible for Ukraine's image in the world! Let them hear us—We are here!" On the other side of the police line, bumper-to-bumper busses blocked Kyiv's main thoroughfare, providing cover for an almost empty street where city workers slowly removed one of the protesters' make-shift barricades. Meanwhile, 300 meters to the west, the tense face-off between crowds and riot police continued in front of the city hall building.

At 10:07 the three busses with interior ministry troops in front of the Kyiv Administration building succumbed to pressure from the crowd shouting "go home!" and retreated. At approximately the same time, at the other end of Khreshchatyk Street, the troops forming a police cordon separating Maidan from the Trade Unions building boarded their busses. At 10:43 they drove away.

The foreign factor

International reaction to the attempted clearing of Maidan was quick. European Commission Vice President for Foreign Affairs Catherine Aston issued the following statement:

> I am still in Kyiv. I was among you on the Maidan in the evening and was impressed by the determination of Ukrainians demonstrating for the European perspective of their country. Some hours later I observe with sadness that police used force to remove peaceful people from the center of Kiev [sic]. The authorities did not need to act under the coverage of night to engage with society by using force. Dialogue with political forces and society and the use of arguments is always better than the argument of force.[35]

America's Assistant Secretary of State for Europe and European Affairs Victoria Nuland, who had arrived in Kyiv the night before for talks with Yanukovych, visited Independence Square on December 11 immediately after the attempted clearing. She walked through the protesters together with the US ambassador, somewhat comically demonstrating her country's support by handing out cookies and pastry. She later met with the Ukrainian President. Their ceremonial handshake (broadcast on television) was obviously cold.

In subsequent days the protesters were visited by Germany's foreign minister and by his counterpart from Canada. On 15 December US Senators John McCain (R) and Chris Murphy (D) also visited Maidan to lend their support to the demonstrators. McCain did not mince words:

> What we're trying to do is to bring about a peaceful transition here, that would stop the violence and give the Ukrainian people what they unfortunately have not had, with different revolutions that have taken place—a real society... I'm praising their ability and their desire to demonstrate peacefully for change that I think they deserve.[36]

The Ukrainian diaspora around the world mobilized in support of the Maidan with demonstrations held in Toronto, Ottawa, Montreal, Chicago, New York, Washington, Sydney, Melbourne, Munich, London, Paris, and many other places. "Euromaidan" websites and Facebook pages were established by diaspora activists; money was collected in support of the protests, and political leaders throughout the world were lobbied to pressure the Ukrainian regime to avoid further use of force against Kyiv's demonstrators. Journalists on one of Georgia's television channels dressed in blue and yellow for their broadcast. In Warsaw, Ukrainian flags lined the main street, and the Palace of Culture and Science building was illuminated in blue and yellow in solidarity with the Maidan protests. Polish and German border guards for the first time invited Ukrainian passport holders to cross their respective borders using channels labeled for "EU citizens". This privilege had traditionally been denied to Ukrainians and was seen by many as particularly demeaning. Such gestures were very much appreciated on Maidan and were widely reported by Ukrainian media.

The Anti-Maidan

The foreign pressure seems to have worked. The regime stood down—for a while. During public pronouncements Yanukovych repeated his opposition to the use of force against civilian demonstrators, while in private expressing his conviction that as temperatures dropped, so too would the will of most of those on Maidan to remain camped out in the cold.[37] In the meantime, the regime demonstrated its political strength.

On 12 December the Party of Regions announced that a pro-government rally would be held the following Saturday. Presumably this demonstration was to show the world that the Maidan protesters did not represent the will of *all* Ukrainians. The only problem was that Maidan had occupied Independence Square and the Anti-Maidan rally was to take place on European Square. After the attack on Maidan by police on 11 December, Ukraine's opposition parties had called upon their regional organizations to mobilize, and thousands were pouring into the capital daily. The two squares where the two rival demonstrations were to be held were 300 meters apart, and tens of thousands were expected at each rally. The mood was ominous.

The number of "guests" from Ukraine's regions during the weekend of 14-15 December was unprecedented. Independence Square was filled with Ukrainian-speaking westerners: people who had travelled to Kyiv from Lviv, Ternopil, Ivano-Frankivsk, Vinnytsia, Khmelnytsky and smaller cities in the west of the country to support the Maidan movement. Meanwhile, just outside the barricades, groups of Russian-speaking young men from Donetsk, Dnipropetrovsk, Zaporizhzhia and other eastern cities roamed the streets clearly feeling uncomfortable in the capital because its population obviously supported Maidan (according to a poll conducted 10-14 December by the pro-Yanukovych "Research & Branding Group" 64% of Kyiv residents supported the Maidan protests).[38] Besides language, the main difference between the political tourists from east and west was that the latter came to Kyiv in their own cars, or on busses that their local communities had organized for them. Their eastern counterparts were bussed in by the Party of Regions (under threat of losing their jobs — according to multiple reports) and had received instructions not to leave the pro-Presidential demonstration on European Square without permission.

In the end both crowds remained peaceful, but the Anti-Maidan rally — televised on First National TV (the state-owned broadcaster) — proved nothing but comical. First, Parliamentarian Oleh Tsariov gave a very long and boring speech (20 minutes) at the end of which he tried to ridicule the Euromaidan demonstrators' chant "*Khto ne skache, toy Moskal'*" ("Who does not jump is a Muscovite"). Many in the Anti-Maidan crowd misunderstood and started jumping. Then another Party of Regions MP mounted the stage, and immediately after declaring his support for Yanukovych started to encourage the demonstrators to chant "Putin! Putin!" The crowd followed his lead, but the speaker was quickly whisked off stage, and the chant stopped. Finally, the headline speaker, Prime Minister Azarov was introduced. After explaining (yet again) to the uninterested crowd how Ukraine's economy would have been negatively affected had the Free Trade Agreement with the EU been signed, Azarov went on to proclaim that although many in Ukraine would like to see a visa-free regime with Europe, this was impossible because in order to simplify border-crossing procedures, the EU demanded that Ukraine legalize same-sex marriages (!).[39]

To the Anti-Maidan demonstrators, whether Azarov's statements were true or not really didn't matter. After their rally ended, many quietly migrated to their supposed opponents' camp on Independence Square to enjoy the concert of the popular rock group *Okean Elzy*. There, the supposedly pro-regime political tourists were fed and entertained. That evening, most boarded their Party of Regions chartered busses for the long trip home. Those who had been hired on a longer-term assignment returned to the Anti-Maidan camp in Mariyinsky park near Parliament. This Anti-Maidan camp was to remain a mainstay of the Kyiv protest scene during upcoming months — periodically swelling to several thousand, but usually manned by several hundred obviously paid "protesters" hailing from Ukraine's southern and eastern regions.

Barricading for the long term

When I arrived at Maidan the evening after the failed operation to clear the encampment on 11 December, I witnessed a beehive of activity. A fresh sprinkling of snow had covered the layer that had fallen during the previous days, but the stamping of feet by masses of people had made the stone surface of Kyiv's main square slippery. Hundreds of shovels and ice picks were brought to the city-center together with thousands of heavy-duty refuse bags (the kind used for construction waste). Led by former Microsoft Ukraine Director Dmytro Shymkiv,[40] hundreds of activists chipped away at the hardened snow and loaded it into the refuse bags. Others then carried the 10 kg sacks to designated spots where they were transported to the barricade sites. By late that evening, the snow from Maidan had all been collected, and so the protesters expanded their cleaning activities to include side streets. Volunteered passenger cars were used to transport the collected snow bags to the main square. I remember noting that the cars were not cheap, and most had Kyiv city registration plates.

The work continued all night with arc welders (connected to portable generators) brought in to build metal frames. These were reinforced with metal poles and fencing with snow sacks placed on top. The entire construction then had water poured on it, so that the snow hardened into ice. The resultant barricades were impressive feats of engineering. It was that night that I first heard a joke about the paradox of the typical Ukrainian man: "It takes the average husband three months to put up a shelf in the bathroom, but less than three hours to build a barricade."

During the attempted clearing on December 11th, the makeshift barricades had been dismantled, but within 24-hours, new and stronger fortifications were constructed. Inside the Maidan perimeter, the protesters established lodging quarters (tents were fitted with wood floors), soup kitchens, firewood storage facilities, first aid posts—all the requisite facilities for long term encampment. A call went out for thermal camping mattresses. Within two days some 20 thousand were delivered by a local polypropylene manufacturer. Lodging facilities were organized in Kyiv Expo Plaza (a local exhibition hall located five subway stops from the city-center),[41] and at the

Ukrainian Catholic Cathedral complex on the left bank of the Dnipro river. Thousands of Kyiv residents opened their apartments to demonstrators arriving to the capital from the regions for several days. Regular religious services were held in the church tent (clergy from different confessions established a schedule), and an online broadcast facility (called "*Spilnobachennya*") was established next to the IT tent.

Gradually, Maidan transformed. Two surveys of protesters conducted by the Democratic Initiatives Foundation on 7-8 December and 20 December illustrate its changing face:[42] whereas the first registered over 50% of demonstrators as being from Kyiv, the number of locals in the later sample dropped to 19% with 81% of the protesters hailing from outside the capital (approx. 50% from the western regions). These people needed to be housed, fed, and occupied. During evenings and on weekends the crowds would swell (up to 60% of weekend *viche* participants were locals),[43] but as the Maidan evolved, the role of Kyiv residents switched from manning the camp (and protecting it as on December 10-11), to supporting it.

Increasingly, in addition to keeping busy with daily duties in the camp, Maidan activists saw a need for intellectual stimulation. The opposition parties managed the main stage, producing "official" messages, so a soap-box style venue seemed logical. In a testament to the spontaneity and lack of centralized leadership on the Maidan, the idea of establishing an "open university" was picked up by two groups simultaneously. The first initiative was called "Euromaidan university", and its lectures were held in the Academy of Sciences building on European square (freed of Anti-Maidan demonstrators, but not yet occupied by Maidan). Although this venue had the advantage of warmth, it was somewhat removed from Independence Square, and therefore lecture attendee numbers were disappointing. If the purpose of "intellectualizing" Maidan was to be achieved, the "university" would have to be established inside the camp perimeter. On 11 December 2013 the Open University of Maidan ("VUM")[44] was born when an alternative (smaller) stage was set up near the Lyatsky Gate across from the McDonald's on Independence Square. Professors from Kyiv-Mohyla Academy, Kyiv School of Economics, and Kyiv National University (as well as unaffiliated speakers) were invited to give presentations—with a polite request from the organizers to focus lectures on "not overly academic" topics. After-all, holding the attention of a crowd for 40 minutes in subzero temperatures was a challenge.[45]

One of my lectures at the Open University of Maidan was entitled "Buzz: Word of Mouth Marketing"—a topic that I often touched upon during my executive education seminars at Lviv Business School and at Kyiv-Mohyla Academy. The presentation evolved into a discussion with various protesters (including students, entrepreneurs, pensioners, and others) on how to spread the values of Maidan eastward without spending large amounts of money on advertising. Our brainstorm spawned the Russian phrase *"Poymite nas. Zadolbalo!"* which translated means "Understand us. We're fed up!" (the word *"zadolbalo"* is somewhat stronger in connotation than the English equivalent). I whispered this phrase to Ostap Stasiv—an organizer of the Open University of Maidan, and the next day I received a text message "your banner is ready."[46] The 7-meter long banner that Ostap had printed with the collectively created phrase graced the barricade facing European Square throughout the protest, until the night of 18-19 February 2014 when it was destroyed by attacking Berkut special forces. For many, this banner symbolized the idea of the protest, and the reason for its longevity.[47]

Figure 3:   Banner on barricade facing European Square

Institutionalizing Maidan

Getting the Maidan message out to Ukraine's population would need more than clever slogans on barricades in the center of Kyiv. If Yanukovych was to be dislodged (through protest or through presidential elections scheduled for March 2015 — many believed this was the only legitimate way to effect regime change), Maidan needed to transform from an encampment into a national movement. Some form of institutionalized organization was obviously required to coordinate the activities of the various Maidans that had become established in regional centers throughout the country, and to popularize the protesters' message. However, given the skepticism of the demonstrators towards established political parties (including the opposition), this structure could not be a new political party.

On 22 December, during the now regular Sunday mass demonstration on Independence Square, former Tymoshenko-right-hand Oleksandr Turchynov announced the creation of the Popular Assembly "Maidan," or "NOM" (*Narodne obyednannia "Maidan"*).[48] The fact that the formation of a supposedly non-political organization was announced by a very political figure caused significant controversy, but this was to be the least of the new organization's problems. The NOM was proclaimed from the stage as having two governing bodies: a Maidan Council (*Rada Maidanu*) consisting of 32 individuals plus 7 co-leaders: Serhiy Kvit (President of Kyiv-Mohyla Academy), Yuriy Lutsenko (former Interior Minister under Yushchenko and then political prisoner under Yanukovych), Yulia Tymoshenko (former Prime Minister, and currently in jail), Vitaliy Klitschko (leader of the UDAR Party), Oleh Tiahnybok (leader of the Svoboda Party), Arseniy Yatseniuk (leader of the Batkivshchyna party), and Ruslana Lezhychko (popular singer, and hero of the Euromaidan). However, less than one day after its proclamation, the newly formed NOM leadership began to disintegrate. Civic activists Yegor Sobolev and Iryna Karpa — both names had been announced from the stage as members of the Maidan Council — declared that they had not been informed of their inclusion prior to the public proclamation. Ruslana also wrote on her Facebook page that she was resigning from the post of co-leader because "I am not a politician". The "co-leadership" governing body was therefore disbanded, and the Maidan Council was increased to over 40 people with more "non-political" actors included.

Formally, the Maidan Council was supposed to represent the voice of protestors camped on Kyiv's Independence Square; to coordinate their demands and activities with Ukraine's numerous civil society organizations and opposition parties. Finding common ground between such diverse groups was extremely difficult, and although the Maidan Council was eventually to play a role in attempts to find a peaceful compromise at the climax of the protests in February 2014 (see Chapter 4), the organization failed in its stated purpose because of a lack of leadership. The Maidan increasingly rejected any form of institutionalized hierarchy, and so the Maidan Council operated instead as a horizontal discussion forum. Maidan was a focal point for solidarity; for expressing values in a kind of short-hand that was understood by others who believed the same. It was not an organization in the classic sense.

In contrast, the somewhat anarchic and spontaneous "Auto-Maidan" achieved significant success both as a lasting configuration, and as a milieu from which potential new leaders emerged. Its protagonists—Dmytro Bulatov, Serhiy Koba, Serhiy Poyarkov, Serhiy Khadzhynov, Oleksiy Hrytsenko—were idolized as heroes during the early protest phase. Each of these young men hailed from Kyiv's nascent middle class. They owned moderately expensive cars and used social media effectively to organize others like them. Symbolically, they positioned themselves as the "cavalry of Maidan": whereas the protest camp had blocked the city center, the AutoMaidan resolved to harass key members of the Yanukovych regime by bringing the Maidan protests to their homes. In late December they picketed the estate of Prosecutor General Pshonka, the homes of Interior Minister Zakharchenko and Prime Minister Azarov.

On 29 December, after yet another Sunday *viche* during which the three opposition party leaders disappointed the gathered multitudes with general speeches, and appeals to "continue to stand", the AutoMaidan activists organized a "visit" to Yanukovych's private residence 16km outside the Kyiv city limits. On that day, the line of cars travelling to Mezhyhirya numbered over 2000. The column was stopped several hundred meters from the entrance to the President's compound, but the protesters' presence clearly infuriated Yanukovych. During the first two weeks of January, over 1500 car owners whose license plate numbers had been recorded by the authorities as they travelled to Mezhyhirya as part of the AutoMaidan "visit", were stripped of their driver's licenses by regime-controlled courts. An additional 129 vehicles (including the private car of Inna Tsarkova, an employee of the Canadian embassy in Kyiv) were torched by unknown vandals.[49]

The protest geography had expanded, and the regime's patience was not without limits. Although the Maidan camp seemed safe for the duration of the Christmas holiday period, systematic repression of the protest movement was clearly being planned and executed. The early months of the coming New Year would turn out to be decisive.

Chapter 4:
Descent into Violence

By late December 2013, the stand-off between Yanukovych and the Maidan protesters lulled into a surreally festive permanence. On New Year's Eve, the legendary Ukrainian rock group *Okean Elzy* put on a reunion concert with its original band members, and former Eurovision song contest winner Ruslana—a regular on the stage throughout December—organized a show with the 200 000 strong crowd waiving flashlights while singing the national anthem. During the second week of January (Ukrainians generally celebrate Christmas on January 7), traditional "*Vertep*" plays were acted out on the Maidan stage with opposition politicians playing key roles, and evil characters played by actors dressed in Berkut uniforms.

The festive atmosphere hid a grim reality. The Party of Regions and Communists held their majority in Parliament making Yanukovych untouchable; the Azarov government (including Interior Minister Zakharchenko, who most believed to have been responsible for December's violence—including both the student beatings and the attempted clearing of Maidan on 11 December) was immune to dismissal. The previous year's "visits" by the AutoMaidan to the homes of top-level regime officials (including Mezhyhirya), had extended the protests' geography, and clearly angered Yanukovych. Whereas the demonstrators and activists were safe within the barricades of Independence Square, they were under significant threat as soon as they left the Maidan camp.

Kidnappings and beatings

On December 25, opposition journalist and Maidan activist Tetiana Chornovol was attacked and brutally beaten while driving home from Kyiv to Boryspil.[1] Her car was forced off the road, and she was left to die in the snow. Passers-by noticed a parked car on the road side with an open door. Tetiana was in the ditch nearby covered in blood, suffering from a concussion, a broken nose, several broken facial bones,

99

and multiple hematomas. She had been travelling home after spending several nights on Maidan. Her younger son was to take part in a New Year's concert at his nursery the following day.

Chornovol had achieved renown during the years preceding Maidan for her investigative reports of the luxurious residences of Ukraine's high-level functionaries. In 2012 she gained unauthorized access to Yanukovych's lavish residence, built on the territory of a former nature reserve and monastery. Her description and photos from Mezhyhirya were broadcast by the opposition-supporting TVi network[2] — much to the chagrin of the President who apparently took great pride in his regal home and protected the security of the grounds vehemently. Prior to her beating, Chornovol (together with Ihor Lutsenko — another victim of kidnapping) published an investigative report uncovering another of the President's regal mansions in Crimea.[3]

The reaction to the Chornovol beating was swift: the Auto-Maidan paid a visit to the home of Prosecutor General Pshonka on December 28, with activists pasting photos of Tetiana's mutilated face on his fence. The regular Sunday *viche* on December 29 proclaimed "Solidarity against Terror!", and it was on that day that thousands joined the AutoMaidan in picketing Yanukovych's residence in Mezhyhirya. During the first week of January, additional visits to the dachas of Viktor Medvedchuk (widely believed to be Putin's informal representative in Ukraine) in Zakarpattya oblast, and to the home of Interior Minister Vitaliy Zakharchenko were organized.

During subsequent days, other Maidan activists disappeared or were beaten after having left the safety of the barricades. On 3 January, Svoboda MP Andriy Iliyenko and his lawyer Sydir Kizin were attacked outside Shevchenkivskiy district police station in Kyiv. Iliyenko's jaw was broken and he was diagnosed with a concussion.[4] On 21 January, after having been taken to hospital for treatment of injuries suffered during escalating violence (see below), Ihor Lutsenko and Yuriy Verbytsky were kidnapped and beaten in an unknown forest location. Lutsenko survived the ordeal, but Verbytsky was killed.[5] One of the leaders of the AutoMaidan, Dmytro Bulatov, was reported missing by his comrades on 23 January. He turned up a week later in a village near Kyiv having been tortured. Half his ear was cut off.[6]

On 10 January, protesters surrounded a district court on the outskirts of Kyiv where a sham trial of three members of the right-wing "Patriot of Ukraine" organization on charges of "terrorism" was being held. The young men were accused of plotting to blow up the statue of Lenin in the town of Boryspil and were given 6-year sentences. After the court verdict was announced, protesters blocked the prisoner transport van, which led to their being dispersed by riot police with tear gas. Several were injured, but the incident did not end at the court house. The bus with the "Berkut" officers who had just dispersed the protesting crowd was chased by AutoMaidan activists and forced to the side of the road on Prospekt Peremohy (one of the main thoroughfares of Kyiv). Up to 100 cars blocked the bus's further advance to the "Berkut" base, demanding that the officers disembark without their headgear, so that they could be identified. The stand-off lasted for several hours until Yuriy Lutsenko—a former Interior Minister who had been imprisoned then pardoned by Yanukovych—arrived. His attempt to negotiate with the "Berkut" ended with Lutsenko being beaten himself. He and twelve others were later hospitalized with concussions and broken bones. In the end, the "Berkut" exited the bus—most showed their faces very reluctantly. They were not to forgive this humiliation.

On the night of 15-16 January, I went to Maidan for a night vigil. Social and traditional media were buzzing, apparently foreshadowing a possible night attack on the camp, and volunteers were asked to assemble inside the barricades. But the night proved peaceful. I walked the Maidan perimeter with friends, prayed at the church tent, chatted with Anatoliy Hrytsenko and Petro Poroshenko (the billionaire businessman milled around the demonstrators with no personal security detail), sang the national anthem several times, and then drank coffee with Gennadiy Kurochka (future head of PR in the Poroshenko Administration), and with Valeriy Chaly (future Ukrainian ambassador to the US). The conversations were nothing less than fascinating, and the overall experience—inspiring. Little did we know that this would be the last peaceful night in Kyiv for many weeks.

"Dictatorial" laws

The threat of a physical attack by the regime on Maidan turned out to be a false alarm, but on 16 January Yanukovych attacked much more shrewdly. That day, Parliament was to return to plenary session to pass the 2014 budget (the protests had made a vote on the budget in December impossible). According to the docket, only the budget was to be put to a vote that day, but Speaker Rybak clearly knew something else was planned: he quietly asked the opposition to barricade him in his office.[7] According to Parliamentary rules, a session could not be opened without the presence of the Speaker or one of his deputies. Opposition MPs barricaded the office of First Deputy Speaker Kaletnik (Communist Party) as well, but he climbed out the window and via a fire escape entered a side door to the session hall. From there, he opened the session, and announced that because the rostrum and electronic voting system had been blocked by the opposition, MP's would vote that day with their hands. He then put the budget bill to a vote, and then followed with an *additional* 11 bills. Printouts of the latter had not distributed to MPs, and most had no idea what they were supporting. Nevertheless, Volodymyr Oliynyk, a vocal Party of Regions MP who had been confirmed by the ruling majority as the official vote counter (in the absence of a functioning electronic voting system) announced within 5 seconds of each vote that 235 MPs had voted in favor.[8]

The package of legislation (11 bills) established the legal framework for a regime crackdown. It permitted trials in absentia, required all SIM card purchases for mobile phones to be effected only after government registration of passport details of the buyer, permitted the abrogation of internet access by the state, and instituted a blanket amnesty to all "Berkut" officers and interior ministry officials who may have committed offenses against Maidan activists. In addition, its provisions *outlawed* the following:

- Participation in public unrest (broadly defined) – punishable by 10-15-year prison term;

- Travelling in groups of 5 cars or more without previous permission from traffic police—punishable by driver's license suspension for up to 2 years, and vehicle confiscation;
- Participation in a peaceful demonstration dressed in a helmet or uniform—10 days confinement;
- Inciting civil disobedience—punishable with 2-year prison term;
- Erecting tents, stages, sound systems in public spaces without official permission—15 days confinement;
- Collecting information about the whereabouts or spending habits of a judge—punishable with 2-year prison term
- Blocking entry into a private residence—punishable with 6-year prison term; blocking entry into a government building—5 years imprisonment;

The legislative package was signed by Yanukovych immediately and was promulgated on Friday 17 January 2014. The same day, the President fired Serhiy Lyovochkin, the dovish head of his administration,[9] and replaced him with Andriy Kluyev—the now former Secretary of the National Security and Defense Council—widely believed to have been responsible for ordering the beating of students on November 30, and a supporter of a crack-down on the protests. According to reports from the Maidan first aid service, all doctors who worked in the hospital located closest to the city-center (Oleksandrivska) were called in for special duties over the weekend. Maidan protesters braced for the worst.

Fires of Hrushevskoho

On Sunday 19 January hundreds of thousands gathered on Maidan again. That morning, a group of intellectuals[10] published an open letter to the three opposition leaders, calling for unity against the country's descent into dictatorship, and entreating them choose a single leader of the resistance. But during the *viche* Klitschko, Yatseniuk, and Tiahnybok disappointed the roused multitudes yet again. Their speeches were emotional and vapid. The crowd awaited the announcement of a single leader. In response, Batkivshchyna parliamentary leader Arseniy Yatseniuk responded: "You want a leader? I'll tell you who is the leader! The "narod" (the people) is the leader!" This proved to be a fatal error.

The leaders of AutoMaidan (Bulatov, Poyarkov, Hrytsenko) ascended the stage, and again called for "a single leader", but none was forthcoming. Then Serhiy Koba — an AutoMaidan activist whose yellow tuned sports car had become one of the symbols of the movement — grabbed the microphone and proclaimed his plans to demonstrate in front of the Parliament until MPs rescinded the "dictatorial laws" that they had passed 3 days earlier. He presented an ultimatum to the opposition leaders: either they choose a leader within half an hour, or he would lead the protest to Parliament himself.[11]

When later questioned about Koba's ultimatum, Bulatov, Poyarkov, and Hrytsenko all professed to having had no prior knowledge of his intentions. Whether Koba understood the provocative nature of his statement remains unknown, but the effect was immediate: large numbers of protesters began moving away from the stage on Independence Square towards European Square (where the AutoMaidan cars were parked) with the intention of blockading the Parliament building. From my vantage point in front of the stage, I noticed several groups of masked young people dressed in protective gear of the kind used by motorcyclists, march away in organized fashion in the direction of European Square. I remember wondering whether someone had not pre-planned some sort of provocation, but given the spontaneity of Maidan, and diversity of the people gathered there, one could never be sure.

Whatever the level of intentionality among the various groups of protesters, it was clear that the three opposition party leaders had lost control of the situation. For reasons unknown Lutsenko, Hrytsenko, Parubiy, Poroshenko, Ruslana and other "moral authorities" were not on the stage that day. A new name gradually emerged from among the protests: Dmytro Yarosh — the leader of the *Pravyy sektor* (Right Sector) nationalist organization.[12] It was their fighters who first attacked the line of Interior Ministry troops that had cordoned off Hrushevskoho St., thus blocking access from European Square to the Parliament building. They threw the first Molotov cocktails, and set ablaze the police bus parked in front of the gate to Dynamo stadium.

These rock throwing youths were the first to provide the global press with stunning images of Kyiv's city center descending into chaos.

To their credit, the opposition leaders made a valiant effort to diffuse the situation. Klitschko ran from Independence Square to European Square immediately after Koba's ultimatum and stepped between the frontline protesters and riot police. But the aroused youths were not interested in listening to his calls for continued peaceful protest, nor did they hear the leader's warning that violence on the part of Maidan would legitimize a forceful reaction by the regime. The frontline protesters' response to Klitschko's physical obstruction of their path to the police was to spray the former boxing champion's face with a fire extinguisher. About an hour later the three political opposition leaders again spoke from the stage on Maidan calling for peace — to no avail. Klitschko finished his speech by saying that he was on his way to personally speak with Yanukovych — to call on him to end the "war against his own people".[13]

Several hours later, Klitschko returned from his "chat" with Yanukovych to announce that a round table meeting would be held the following day aimed at finding a peaceful resolution to the situation. The meeting was to be chaired by Andriy Kliuyev (the newly appointed head of the Presidential Administration). Later Ukraine's opposition party leaders would refuse to take part in the negotiations unless they were personally attended by Yanukovych. The two sides would finally meet on 22 January — much to the displeasure of the protesters on Maidan, who by that time flatly refused to accept any negotiated settlement with the regime. However, the precedent of a meeting between the opposition leaders and Yanukovych would prove significant a month later, when real peace talks would be engaged.

On 19 January riot police at the base of Hrushevskoho St. faced approximately 10 thousand protesters. Tyres were lit for the first time, and their smoke became symbolic of the Maidan's radicalization. Four police buses were burned that evening. Just after 6pm, the riot police deployed a water cannon – despite temperatures that had dropped to -9 degrees Celsius (Ukrainian law forbids the use of water cannon in sub-zero temperatures). The water doused the fires, but icicles quickly formed on the vehicles' remains, and on the cobblestones of the street. The resultant scene of fire and ice was earie. Many saw the symbolism as significant: according to the Julian calendar 19 January is the feast of the Epiphany—the day when Ukrainian Orthodox and Catholic eastern rite church-goers celebrate the baptism of Christ by submerging themselves into freezing water.

I visited both the Maidan camp that day, and the newly established "war zone" near the Dynamo Stadium gates. The atmosphere resembled that of Mykhaylivska square on 30 November 2013—the morning after the beatings of the Euromaidan students. Songs and carols from the stage were replaced by somber speeches and documentary films. The people standing on European Square nearby were generally middle aged, primarily male, with very grave faces. I would describe their mood as "determined." I dared approach to about 100 meters of the battle line. Rubber bullets were being fired occasionally from the police side, and Molotov cocktails periodically tossed by protesters. Rocks and fireworks also flew occasionally, but most of the projectiles were not reaching their targets. Nevertheless, lots of smoke from burning tyres; smoke bombs and fireworks exploded regularly—all of this to the regular beat of drumming on an oil barrel. Amazingly, cafes and restaurants, as well as the fashion boutiques that lined Khreshchatyk St. and European Square (for the most part) remained open. Not a single window was smashed. No looting was reported. Masked youths dressed in motorcycle armor carrying sticks and Molotov cocktails moved freely among more peaceful demonstrators who went about the daily business of tending to their tents on Maidan and trying to keep warm. Strangely, I felt safe.

By 22 January both sides were reporting casualties. The riot police reported several officers injured. Few believed them. A makeshift first aid point was established to treat wounded protesters on European Square. At approximately 6:30 am, the first death was reported there: Serhiy Nigoyan, a 20-year old ethnic Armenian, who days earlier had been filmed emotionally quoting Ukraine's national poet Taras Shevchenko's epic phrase *"Boritesia—poborete! Vam Boh pomahaye!"* ("Fight on—you will overcome! God aids you!") died of gunshot wounds. At approximately 9 am, Mykhailo Zhysnevsky, a Belarusian who had joined the Maidan protests in December, was shot dead near the Dynamo stadium gate.[14] At 1:30 pm Roman Senyk from Ivano-Frankivsk was shot by police; he died of his wounds in hospital on 25 January. Later investigations concluded that all three were shot with bullets issued only to Ukraine's police forces.[15] Of the first three to fall in what would eventually be called the Heaven's Hundred, two were not ethnic Ukrainians (Zhysnevsky was not even a citizen of Ukraine) — a fact that belied the portrayal of Maidan as an uprising of nationalist extremists.

As news of the first deaths on Hrushevskoho spread, so too did reports of interior ministry and regular army troops being mobilized throughout the country. By the third week of January, all of Ukraine's riot police ("Berkut", "Tiger", "Jaguar" etc.) had been brought to Kyiv, and were already either directly involved in the fighting near European Square, or were on alert awaiting instructions to clear the Maidan camp.[16] Given the size of the protests however, the deployed units required reinforcement, and so additional troops from various non-special purpose units throughout the country were ordered to travel to the capital (e.g. traffic police, local law enforcement, etc.). Their convoys were blocked on the approaches to Kyiv by protesters.

Maidan spreads

By 24 January Maidan had "gone local." While the intensity of violence on Hrushevskoho St. gradually decreased (the protesters built a cobblestone and brick wall between themselves and the police line blocking the street towards Parliament), oblast administration buildings throughout the western and central regions of the country were overrun and occupied by local supporters of the Kyiv protests. Regional governors (Presidential appointees) were forced to write letters of resignation. Central government authority was paralyzed throughout much of the country, including in the central-eastern cities of Poltava, Sumy and Chernihiv. Apparently, this very visible loss of control over the country finally made Yanukovych amenable to compromise.[17]

On 25 January, during negotiations with the opposition, President Yanukovych proposed the post of Prime Minister to Arseniy Yatseniuk, and Deputy PM to Vitaliy Klitschko. Both refused. The suggestion that a government of unity be established was probably a ruse, but many saw it as a sign that pressure on the President was having some effect. Yanukovych also promised to repeal or soften the provisions of the 16 January "Dictatorial Laws" which were seen to

have been the root cause of the violence on Hrushevskoho St. during
the previous days. However, the President's offer was conditional
upon demonstrators freeing all occupied government buildings — a requirement that the opposition leaders could not have fulfilled even if
they had wanted to. They no longer controlled Maidan.

Also on 25 January, several hundred Interior Ministry troops
were discovered hiding in Ukrainian House — the large building facing European Square, from which the newly constructed barricades
on Hrushevskoho St. were clearly visible and easily accessible. The
building was quickly surrounded by several hundred demonstrators,
and it was all the opposition leaders could do to negotiate the late-
night peaceful evacuation of the government forces from inside.[18]
During subsequent weeks the Open University of Maidan moved to
Ukrainian House, as did the sleeping quarters of several hundred protesters. The territory of the protests was thus expanded to include all
of European Square and Khreshchatyk Park (see map below):

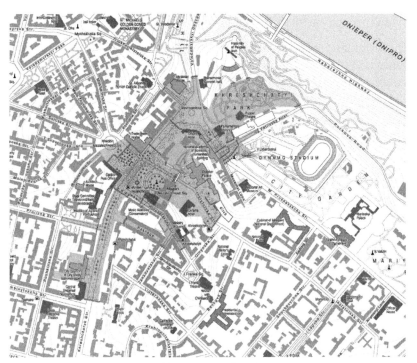

Figure 4:   Maidan controlled areas of Kyiv on 27 January 2014

According to evidence that emerged later in 2014, on 21 and 24 January of that year, Ukraine's Ministry of Internal Affairs officially accepted two special air cargo shipments of crowd-control ordinance (primarily stun- and smoke-grenades totaling over 13 thousand units) from Russia.[19] Presumably these were to be used during any planned clearing of Maidan, and in employing counter-measures against violent protesters. At the time, all we knew on Maidan was that the riot police officers waiting for orders in the government quarter were itching for a fight. When on one occasion during a brief engagement on Hrushevskoho St., they captured several protesters, the "Jaguar" unit's men stripped one of their captives and filmed him being paraded *naked in the snow* to the delight of the officers. The video of "Cossack Havryliuk" was later uploaded to the Internet, and the victim became a national hero.

Regime cracks

During the final days of January 2014, Yanukovych seems to have planned for a state of emergency (or even martial law) — i.e. deploying the military to clear Maidan by force. Whether a disgruntled and demoralized Ukrainian army would have executed the President's order if given will remain forever unknown. Military commanders must have understood that obeyance would have meant mass civilian casualties in the center of Kyiv. According to the testimony of Oleksandr Turchynov, during a secret meeting with Ukraine's President on January 27, he explained to Yanukovych that any forceful resolution of the crisis would lead to rivers of blood.[20] Similar warnings were apparently voiced by Akhmetov — the richest of Ukraine's oligarchs — who sought to avoid the use of force against Maidan. Yanukovych seems to have listened. During the morning of 28 January, Parliament was called to extraordinary session, and Prime Minister Azarov submitted his resignation. Former First Deputy Prime Minister Arbuzov was appointed acting Prime Minister, but more significantly, 9 of the 11 draconian laws passed on 16 January were rescinded.

Few on Maidan rejoiced after the announcement of Azarov's resignation. Many (like me) were cautious that this might be some sort of trap: before noon we pointed out that the resignation still needed to be accepted by Yanukovych; then the Presidential decree dismissing the Prime Minister was published, and the 16 January laws were abrogated, but people were still asking "what's the catch?" After all, Interior Ministry troops continued to be mobilized across the country (that day the Cabinet of Ministers under acting PM Arbuzov passed a resolution increasing the "Berkut" complement from 5000 to 30,000 men);[21] strange concrete barriers were set up overnight around key government buildings in the city-center, and then suddenly disbanded around noon; rumors spread regarding the contents of special telegrams sent by the Presidential Administration to Army officers in the regions; oblast governors, who had previously remained relatively tranquil when faced with mass demonstrations in front of their administrative offices, suddenly became more vocal in their demands for order; police attacks on AutoMaidan leaders continued with several now in jail; ominously, 28 January was the day that Ministry of the Interior Directive №1011 which legalized the use of lethal rounds in firearms by Berkut special forces came into force. The demonstrators on Maidan had many reasons not to trust the regime, and many still believed a declaration of martial law was in the works. Furthermore, they did not fully trust Klitschko, Yatseniuk and Tiahnybok, and so held little stock in their negotiations with Yanukovych.

When I visited the barricades on Hrushevskoho St. after the announcement of Azarov's resignation, I found the mood there twitchy and apprehensive. Tension was particularly high on the "front line" where police barricades were in plain view. Standing next to a burning barrel (day-time temperatures rose only to about -15 C), listening to conversations between helmet-clad young men, it seemed to me that a single "spark" — in whatever form — would be enough to rekindle violence. During the previous days, blood had been shed in Ukraine's central and eastern regions: a demonstration in central Cherkasy had been attacked by *titushky* (thugs hired by the regime — the name *titushky* became colloquial after an incident with Vadym Titushko, a hired thug who attacked two opposition journalists in May 2013; since then, thugs hired by the regime to beat up demonstrators or activists were all labelled *titushky*) and then by "Berkut"; protests in front of the Zaporizhzhia oblast administration building had also been violently dispersed; in Donetsk, the local "ultras" organization (supporters of Donetsk Shakhtar football club) came out to support the several hundred pro-Maidan demonstrators gathered in this eastern bastion of the Party of Regions;[22] their photos and home addresses were immediately published on the internet with the label "fascist" and many experienced reprisals.[23] On the front lines, the young men discussed each of these events: the regime was resorting to violence throughout the country while promising amnesty to the Maidan in Kyiv. Few believed Yanukovych's proclaimed desire for peace to be genuine.

Apparently, edginess was also in evidence in Parliament. The extraordinary session called on 28 January to accept Azarov's resignation was extended for an additional day to enable the adoption of a "Law on Amnesty". Four versions of the bill were tabled with the two main ones authored, respectively, by the leaders of the opposition, and by Yuriy Miroshnichenko, the President's official representative in Parliament. Both bills provided reprieve from prosecution for acts of violence perpetrated during mass protests, but the presidential bill required that all occupied government buildings and public spaces be freed of demonstrators before its provisions were to go into effect. Yanukovych's proposal was an obvious trap for the opposition: Yatseniuk, Klitschko and Tiahnybok did not command the protesters, and so could not guarantee their withdrawal from occupied positions in exchange for amnesty. The opposition politicians' support for such a provisional bill would have been seen as a sell out by the demonstrators.

On the other side, many of the businessmen-politicians in the Party of Regions craved a peaceful resolution to the crisis that would enable a return to some level of normality. Many were unhappy with having been sidelined from the decision-making process on 16 January (most had not read the texts of the "Dictatorial Laws" before their adoption). A split within the ranks of the ruling majority was on offer. In an unprecedented act—likely reflecting his lack of confidence in supposedly loyal MP's—on 29 January, Yanukovych *personally* attended a meeting of the Party of Regions faction in Parliament. The Details of the closed-door discussions were sketchy, but according to rumor, many pro-regime MP's were inclined to support the opposition's amnesty bill, and only personal threats from Yanukovych convinced them to fall into line.[24] Although the ruling Party of Regions had often been considered monolithic, apparently in late January, the Parliamentary faction (187 MPs) had begun to crack.

Seven identifiable groups were represented within the parliamentary faction of the Party of Regions, with four representing the core of the Party. Specifically:

1. The Akhmetov group which was represented in the Presidential Administration by Irina Akimova (on Jan 17 she was appointed the President's representative in the Cabinet of Ministers), and in the government by Deputy PM Oleksander Vilkul, Health Minister Raisa Bohatyriova, Economics Minister Prasolov, and Sports Minister Safiulin. This group included the largest number of the Party of Regions MP's, and was guided in its political preferences by what its members called 'economic pragmatism';

2. The Firtash group, nominally led in Parliament by Serhiy Tihipko, but in fact forming the base of support for Serhiy Lyovochkin, the recently fired Head of Yanukovych's Presidential Administration. According to insider reports, this group was "dovish" in its stance towards the Maidan;

3. The Kliuyev group, led in Parliament by Serhiy Kliuyev, whose brother Andriy served as Secretary of the National Security Council until mid-January, and then replaced Liovochkin as Head of the Presidential Administration; Andriy Portnov (legal counsel of the Presidential Administration) was also considered a member. Insiders suggested that this group represented the "hawks" with respect to Maidan;

4. The Yanukovych group—personally loyal to the President. First Deputy PM Arbuzov (appointed Acting Prime Minister after Azarov's resignation), Justice Minister Olena Lukash, Interior Minister Zakharchenko, and Revenue Minister Klymenko were all considered part of the Yanukovych "family".

The three additional (less influential) groups within the Party of Regions included a) the Ivaniushchenko group—led by the organized crime boss "Yura Yenakiyevsky" (believed to be the main financier of the regime's *titushky* thugs, and of the Anti-Maidan), b) the Russian lobby represented in Parliament by deputies Kolisnichenko (one of the authors of the Jan 16 "Dictatorial laws") and Nestor Shufrych, and in the executive by Education Minister Dmytro Tabachnyk, and Defense Minister Lebedev, and c) the Luhansk group led by Parliamentary faction leader Oleksandr Yefremov, and represented in government by Social Services Minister Nataliya Korolevska.

Prior to the crisis, these groups had balanced their interests by divvying up spheres of economic influence. This balance was delicate, and its fulcrum was the Prime Minister's office: Azarov had suited all sides as a relatively neutral figure. With Azarov gone, the conflicting business and political interests of each group became conspicuous, and a split developed over the twin issues of EU Association and the government's strategy of dealing with Maidan. On the one hand, Firtash and Lyovochkin apparently favored closer ties to the EU, while Kliuyev, Yefremov, and the Russian lobby opposed. Akhmetov and Ivaniushchenko maintained their neutrality with respect to foreign affairs, but supported the regime's efforts to quell the Maidan—until the violence of Hrushevskoho St. when Akhmetov allied with the "doves" and Ivaniushchenko went to the "hawks".[25] On 29 January, Yanukovych made a last-ditch effort to reconcile the rift, but the "Law on Amnesty" simply froze the status quo (cleavage within the Party of Regions and stand-off between the regime and Maidan) rather than resolving the situation, and so suited no one.

Calm before the storm

Immediately after the passage of the "Law on Amnesty" Yanukovych went on sick leave—something no Ukrainian President had ever done before. The President was still formally in control but had now withdrawn himself from decision-making duties. Apparently, the near mutiny of his faction in Parliament had made Yanukovych realize that the lifespan of his perpetual political "balancing act" had come to an end. Difficult decisions would have to be made — something Ukraine's President disliked doing.

At the end of January 2014 Yanukovych suddenly found himself without the political support that he had always taken for granted. He was still surrounded by a loyal inner circle (including Acting Prime Minister Arbuzov, Revenues Minister Klymenko, Interior Minister Zakharchenko, and others), but the financial and political resources that his loyalist group controlled were insufficient to maintain power without cooperating with others. The uncertainty left many questions open: which side within the Party of Regions would Yanukovych choose to ally with? Would he choose the "hawks" (Kliuyev and Ivaniushchenko) and Russia, or Lyovochkin's and Akhmetov's "doves" and Europe? Both groups included individuals from Donetsk with whom Yanukovych had long-standing ties, so the President's decision would not be based on regional preferences — a fact that likely made it even more difficult for him to make a choice.

According to one theory, forcing Yanukovych to make a choice was part of the Kremlin's plan to finally gain control over Ukraine. Previously, the Ukrainian President had tried to mimic the "dual-vector" policy first employed by Leonid Kuchma during the early 2000's, when political rapprochement with the West was balanced with economic openness to Russia. However, Yanukovych's practice of "sitting on two chairs simultaneously" pleased neither side.[26] By the end of 2013, the regime had stripped the coffers of the Ukrainian state bare, and therefore needed to beg its neighbors for financial assistance. Whereas EU leaders found the prospect of buying Ukraine's association distasteful, Putin offered an aid package of 15 billion USD on 17 December 2013 with an immediate pay-out of $3 billion. A likely requirement of this loan was the forceful clearance of Maidan.

A document published by Kyiv Post deputy editor Katya Gorchinskaya in March 2014 (supposedly leaked from a "trusted source" within the Kremlin)[27] suggests that the Russians felt betrayed by Yanukovych when he rescinded the 16 January "Dictatorial Laws." Apparently, the financial aid package that the Ukrainian President had agreed to with Putin involved a promise to crackdown on Maidan *prior* to the start of the Winter Olympics in Sochi (i.e. 7 February 2014).

Both sides understood that a legal basis for such a crackdown was required, and that the adoption of draconian laws aimed at abrogating civil liberties would likely elicit a reaction from the protesters (given likely Russian infiltration into the protester ranks, a reaction could have been provoked if necessary),[28] thus creating a pretext for martial law. Yanukovych seems to have been initially prepared to quash the protests in exchange for large amounts of money from Russia, oblivious to the trap Putin had set for him: had the Ukrainian President ordered a crackdown on Maidan, he would have become a pariah in the West, and completely dependent on the Kremlin. This may well have been explained to him by Akhmetov, or someone else within his immediate circle of loyalists, and certainly was clarified by the multiple western emissaries visiting Yanukovych in late January.[29]

On 28-29 January Yanukovych blinked. The forceful removal of the demonstrators was postponed in favor of a peaceful alternative: clearance of occupied buildings and streets in exchange for blanket amnesty. The likelihood that this resolution could be implemented during subsequent weeks was slim, but Yanukovych seemed willing to try. However, the Ukrainian President may have misunderstood his Russian counterpart's intentions: Putin was not merely interested in the dissolution of Maidan; he wanted the protests to be cleared *by force*.[30] Anything less was treachery that would prompt the Russian President to take more direct and personal control over the course of events. Yanukovych could not be allowed to maintain his balancing act between Russia and the West. He had to become a puppet of the Kremlin, and Ukraine had to come under Russia's control.

On 6-7 February Yanukovych travelled to Sochi for the opening of the Winter Olympics. Initially, the private meeting with Putin that he had hoped for was postponed. Later the two met, but apparently the reception was cold. We now know that by the time of the opening of the Games, the Kremlin had already put plans into place for a Russian military intervention in Ukraine. Likely, the invasion was to be legitimized by a request for military assistance from Yanukovych that would be justified by mass uncontrolled street violence. This violence needed to be kindled and/or staged, and if the Ukrainian regime was unable to do so after encouragement from the Kremlin, Russian covert agents would provoke bloodshed directly.

Madness

On Sunday 16 February, at sunrise, the first passenger car drove through an opening in the barricades on Hrushevskoho St. The opposition leaders had managed to convince the young men manning the defensive positions separating European Square from the government quarter to stand down. That day, the Kyiv City Administration building was also cleared of camped protesters, as were the previously occupied oblast administration buildings in Ternopil, Ivano-Frankivsk, Lviv and Poltava.[31] Because October Palace and the Trade Unions buildings in Kyiv were technically not "administrative" structures, during negotiations between the opposition and representatives of the Presidential Administration, it had been decided to allow the demonstrators to remain in these two buildings, so long as occupied government offices were cleared. As the traditional Sunday *viche* began, it seemed as though the three-month stand-off was gradually winding down. Almost a month after the start of deadly riots on Hrushevskoho St. some semblance of peace had returned to the city-center.[32]

Common ground between the protesters and the opposition leaders would never have been found if not for the Maidan Council — the reformulated "NOM" (see Chapter 3). Initially, this forum gathered to coordinate the activities of the various autonomous groups operating on or around Maidan (including the "*sotnia's*", the Auto-Maidan, the opposition parties, NGO's etc.). Throughout January, the Maidan Council met frequently, providing an interface between the opposition party leaders who were engaged in negotiations with the regime, and the various groups of protesters in the city-center. During a meeting of the Maidan Council on 14 February, Vasyl Gatsko, the leader of Democratic Alliance (a non-Parliamentary political party that had consolidated significant support during the protests) pointed out that although the "Law on Amnesty" had provided an opportunity for the protesters to avoid further bloodshed, its adoption had also diminished the energy of Maidan significantly. To reinvigorate the enthusiasm of the protesters he proposed a peaceful march on Parliament to demand early elections and a return to the 2004 version of Ukraine's Constitution (the amendments adopted during the Orange Revolutions had been cancelled by Ukraine's Constitutional Court in 2010, giving Yanukovych wide reaching executive power). Gatsko emphasized that the march should be peaceful, and the initiative was broadly supported by the Maidan Council.[33] On Sunday 16 February the intention to march was announced from the Maidan stage.

On the morning of 18 February, an estimated 20 thousand demonstrators gathered on the various approaches to Parliament in organized columns. Each was flanked by Maidan Self-Defense force "fighters" carrying wooden shields and wearing makeshift helmets. The largest group approached up the hill from Maidan through the concrete barricades on Instytutska St. Another group gathered near Arsenalna subway station and planned to approach Parliament through Mariyinsky park (blocked by the Anti-Maidan). The third group gathered at the base of Hrushevskoho St. on European Square. In each case the protesters were blocked by "Kamaz" dump trucks and busses parked bumper-to-bumper across the streets, and by lines of Interior Ministry and "Berkut" troops supported by *titushky* (thugs hired by the regime). Those among the protesters who were more astute also noticed multiple snipers deployed on the rooftops of nearby buildings.

According to the protesters' accounts, the Maidan's columns approached the police blockades, and positioned for a stand-off. Apparently, the first shots were fired by the "Berkut" (official reports claim the opposite), but in the end it really doesn't matter: rocks were thrown by demonstrators at police, who responded with tear gas and stun grenades. Someone lit fires under the dump trucks; the Party of Regions office on Lypska St. near Parliament was set on fire; live rounds were fired at the crowds.[34] The "Berkut" attacked fiercely, beating retreating protesters along Instytutska and Hrushevskoho streets, while the hired *titushky* thugs from the Anti-Maidan hunted down injured Maidan supporters in Mariyinsky park. In the chaos that ensued, many hundreds were injured.

Makeshift first aid centers were hurriedly established near Maidan, but these were quickly overwhelmed. Ambulances were not allowed to enter the government quarter. Two spots within the city-center gained infamy that day: Instytutska St. in front of the National Bank building, and Mariyinsky park. In the first case, protesters retreating from the violence near Parliament were trapped, unable to pass through the narrow opening in the concrete barricade. They were beaten repeatedly by "Berkut" and left to suffer for several hours on the cold pavement. Medical assistance was provided only after their arrest—several hundred were transported in paddy wagons to overcrowded police stations where they were charged with assaulting police officers. In the case of Mariyinsky park, the situation was even worse: wounded protesters were beaten with wooden bats and iron prongs while lying prostrate on the frozen ground. Several hundred were treated with concussions and broken limbs. The first deaths were registered here that day—among them Oleksandr Plekhanov, a 3rd year architecture student, and a graduate of our children's school in Kyiv.

At 4pm the Ministry of the Interior and the State Security Service (SBU) issued a joint statement: by 6pm all individuals occupying the city-center were to clear their positions. Even before the allotted time was up, "Berkut" and other special forces units occupied October Palace on the hill above Maidan and attacked the "Lviv Gate" barricade on Instytutska St. under the bridge. Simultaneously, police units descended Hrushevskoho St., cleared Ukrainian House, and approached the barricade between European Square and Maidan. At approximately 8pm, this barricade was rammed with an armored personnel carrier, and by 10 pm the Trade Unions building was set ablaze. A last line of defense through the middle of Independence Square was set up by the protesters in the form of burning tyres and debris. Throughout the night, whatever could be burned was thrown on this makeshift barricade. The resultant black smoke seemed to halt (delay) the regime's advance.

By morning, the Ministry of Health confirmed 25 dead and over 800 injured during the previous night's clashes. Real figures were likely significantly higher. Trains and road transport into the capital were stopped. For the first time since its opening in the 1950's, the Kyiv metro was shut down. Airports remained open, but this seemed temporary. Officially, the Security Service of Ukraine announced the commencement of an "anti-terrorist operation."

Somehow, through the blockade, several busses with reinforcements from central and western Ukraine arrived at Maidan at sunrise. The reinforcements brought weapons. They would be needed eventually, but for the moment the protesters rejoiced in their small victory: Maidan had survived the night.

I spent a few hours on Maidan on 19 February. Like many Kyiv residents, I trekked to the city-center on foot. My intent was to offer support (food, medicine, clothing), and in this I was not alone: thousands walked to Maidan that day carrying provisions. On arrival, I witnessed a surreal scene. Fires continued to burn on the perimeter of the protests. A makeshift hospital (complete with operating room) had been established inside St. Michael's church, and the grounds of the monastery were filled with wounded. Many were in shock. Stocks of food, water, clothing and fuel were piled high, and volunteers were collecting names and telephone numbers of those reported missing by friends or family. As I descended the hill from the monastery towards Maidan, I saw a wounded man being hurriedly carried in the opposite direction on a stretcher.

19 February 2014 was the day that I first witnessed a real act of war. At approx. 5:30 pm, during a brief interlude in the fighting, I spotted one of the frontline demonstrators venturing into the ash and debris of no-man's land — a strip 10-20 meters wide separating the protesters from the line of government forces. He was searching for debris that could be added to his barricade fire; he did not approach the police line; he was not at all aggressive. Suddenly, a "Berkut" officer emerged from behind the Stella with a pump-action shot gun. He fired, and the young man fell. Seconds later, three protesters had jumped over the barricades to retrieve their wounded colleague. They evacuated him to a first aid point nearby. He was lucky. Many others weren't.

By this time Maidan had been cut in half. Government forces had occupied the still burning Trade Unions building, October Palace and the hill beneath it, and the Stella monument. The monument to the founders of Kyiv (on Maidan, adjacent to Instytutska St.) was stuck in no-man's land. The church tent, the IT tent, and all the other temporary structures that had stood on Independence Square for almost three months were burned that night. By morning, the "barricade" (if one could call it that) separating several thousand armed interior ministry and "Berkut" troops from the protesters was no more than a meter high. If the order to storm the stage had been given, Maidan would have been cleared within minutes.

But the order was not given, and hundreds of lives were spared. Why the stage was not attacked that night remains a mystery. The opposition leaders attest that the morale of the government forces declined significantly as the night wore on.[35] Others suggest the burning wall of fire established by the demonstrators reduced the attackers' visibility. Others still attribute Maidan's survival to tactical error: the regime's pincer movement failed. Government forces were supposed to attack the stage both from the side of Instytutska and European Square, and from Khreshchatyk, but the latter approaches were blocked by Maidan Self-Defense forces. The most probable theory involves commanders awaiting an order that never came. Clearing Maidan would have resulted in massive bloodshed and death. Without a direct order from the President, no commander was prepared to take responsibility for such action. And Yanukovych didn't have the stomach to give the order himself.

Negotiated pause

During the 24-hour period spanning 18-19 February, 36 Ukrainians lost their lives (including 11 police officers). 85 protesters were treated for gunshot wounds; over a thousand were hospitalized — primarily with head wounds caused by nightsticks.

But the casualty figures of the day do not reproduce the emotional trauma suffered by the population. The last time Ukraine's capital had seen such violence on its streets was WWII. As the day wore on shock changed to sadness and anger. Reaction in the western and central regions (whose populations generally supported Maidan), was swift and equally violent: over 10 thousand protesters stormed the offices of the SBU and Ministry of the Interior in Ivano-Frankivsk; in Lutsk (Volyn' region) and Zhytomyr, the oblast administration buildings were occupied without resistance from local police; in Lviv, an angry crowd estimated at 15 thousand occupied the local SBU office, and several police stations; in Rivne, another 10 thousand demonstrators sequentially occupied the oblast administration building, the city and oblast prosecutors' offices, police headquarters, SBU and tax inspectorates; in Ternopil protesters set fire to the oblast administration building; in Sumy the Party of Regions office was ransacked; in Poltava street fights caused injuries on both sides when protesters attempted to take control of the oblast administration building guarded by local police; in Khmelnytsky, an attempt to storm the local SBU office ended with two people shot and the building set alight. Throughout the western and some central regions of the country, the regime was clearly losing control.

Throughout the afternoon of the 18th and the morning of the 19th, the opposition leaders had been in touch with Viktor Yanukovych. The President was intransigent: the violence in the government quarter was the opposition's fault, and the only possible resolution to the crisis was the Maidan's capitulation. To allow this to occur, Yanukovych had given the order to pause the advance of government forces, but no further negotiations were engaged. According to Yatseniuk, the President's ultimatum was valid until 6pm on the 19th, at which time the operation to clear the remaining protesters from Maidan was to recommence.[36]

However, when the opposition leaders met with Yanukovych during the afternoon of the 19th (immediately prior to the deadline), his mood had changed dramatically. The agenda for negotiations suddenly included changing the Constitution, possible early elections, reformatting the executive, and a blanket amnesty to demonstrators. Most importantly, the President declared there would be no clearance of Maidan that evening and gave orders to his staff to begin drafting a memorandum aimed at peacefully resolving the crisis. Concurrently, as video evidence from Yanukovych's residence was to show later, an order was given to evacuate valuables from Mezhyhirya.

What caused the President's change of heart during the afternoon of the 19th remains unknown.

During the subsequent two days a peace deal was negotiated by representatives of the Presidential Administration and the three opposition parties. The dialog was mediated by high-ranking representatives of the EU and a special envoy of the Russian President. In the end, as described below, the deal proved too little too late—a fact that painfully demonstrated EU officials' lack of understanding of facts on the ground in Kyiv. The Russians, on the other hand, seemed to know exactly what was going on, and took full advantage. Evidence gained after Yanukovych's ouster shows seven high-ranking FSB (Russian security service) officers landing in Ukraine's capital on 20 February; after touring Maidan incognito, and meeting with their SBU colleagues (many of whom were later to gain refuge in Russia), they departed to Moscow on the 21st, and landed at Simferopol airport in Crimea on 27 February 2014—the first day of the Russian Special Forces operation aimed at occupying the peninsula.[37]

Snipers

Yanukovych's good-natured disposition on the afternoon of 19 February was irrelevant from the protesters' perspective. The crisis was far from over. Despite the police checkpoints that had been established on all approaches to Kyiv, reinforcements from the regions got through.[38] They were angry and vengeful, and for the first time, they brought firearms to Maidan: pneumatic weapons, pistols, and hunting rifles.

At approximately 9am on 20 February, the situation in Kyiv changed dramatically. After having been beaten back to a small strip of territory around the stage, the forces of Maidan counter-attacked against the line of riot police. They fired live ammunition, and the riot police retreated in panic. The protesters efforts were primarily concentrated on the upward slope of Instytutska St. between October Palace and Hotel "Ukrayina", but the police line dividing Independence Square from European Square was also targeted. From European Square, government forces retreated to their original line on Hrushevskoho St. where they hid behind concrete barriers. Ukrainian

House was recaptured. The retreat from Instytutska St. was less well organized. "Berkut" riot police and hired *titushky* thugs ran from the city-center all the way to Pecherska Lavra (approximately 3km away). While the protesters on Maidan set about rebuilding the barricades around their original perimeter, several youths decided to chase the retreating government forces. They were met with sniper fire.

The following eyewitness report was written on 20 February 2014 by Liubomyr Markevych, a Canadian resident in Kyiv who made his way to the city-center at around 10am that day:

> By the time we got to the Maidan... we came across a war zone. Black smoke was already pouring out of one corner of the Conservatory of Music and tyres were burning all along the perimeter of the barricades. Meanwhile a Maidan activist stood on stage and directed the deployment of various 'sotni' regiments to various sectors of the Maidan perimeter to reinforce the Maidan from anticipated counterattacks. More ominously he directed everyone's attention to snipers being spotted on the hill in front of the Zhovtneviy (October) Palace. We were all stunned and it appeared that many around us were equally shocked as well. What was going on and why were they firing? No one seemed to know, but it all became irrelevant as stretcher after stretcher carrying the dead and wounded began to be carried out from the front lines.

> We quickly realized this was war. Live rounds were now being fired and people were being killed. Before retreating we made our way to the Conservatory to ask the activists there why the building was set on fire. We were told the Berkut had lobbed grenades or molotovs into the building where Maidan activists had set up a Red Cross station. It seemed the activists were managing to contain the fire from the inside and indeed it would soon be put out. The next scene however was a jaw dropper. There in the entrance to the Conservatory was a group of about 20 activists armed with semi-automatic weapons getting ready for whatever their orders happened to be. We left.

> Over the next few hours the media was full of reports of armed Berkut units being formed near the Building of Officers and Cabinet of Ministers, ostensibly for an all out assault on the Maidan. Snipers in the meantime continued to do their work and casualties were mounting continuously. Fearing the police would abduct the bodies from city hospitals and secretly cremate them destroying evidence of

death by sniper fire, the Maidan leadership ordered that the bodies be laid out in several spots near the Maidan perimeter and maintained with dignity. Instant shrines began growing around the bodies which lay covered with flags and blankets,–but with faces exposed for all to see. Various media were seen filming the scene and people began congregating to pay their respects. It was surreal.

A few hours later we returned to the Maidan. TV media had announced that some 50 police and one sniper had been taken prisoner near the Maidan area. We saw one Berkut led past the stage and into a tent for questioning. An uglier scene took place near the post office where we saw a provocateur beaten to the ground and then led away. He had Russian identity documents on him.

Many months after the conclusion of the Maidan protests, it was still unclear who shot first, and who was responsible for the mass killings of February 20. That morning, 46 people lost their lives. Four of them were police officers shot by firearms carried onto Maidan by protesters. 16 were shot with bullets from Kalashnikov rifles issued to the "Berkut" special forces and fired as they retreated in the face of the Maidan counteroffensive. One protester died of a pistol wound shot from close range (probably friendly fire).[39] The remaining 25 protesters died of penetrating wounds; in only one case was the bullet found inside the victim's body, and it was a 7,62 x 54 mm piercing round fired exclusively by professional snipers.

During the morning of February 20, Andriy Shevchenko, an MP from the Batkivshchyna party who had maintained a connection with the commander of the "Berkut" unit that had been transferred to Kyiv from Dnipropetrovsk, received an urgent call. Live rounds were being fired at the government forces from the direction of the Conservatory building. Evidently the shooter was a professional because targets were hit in the legs and arms only. Shevchenko alerted Andriy Parubiy (Commander of Maidan Self-Defense), who dispatched several of his men to investigate, but by then the shooter had apparently disappeared, having achieved his goal of catalyzing subsequent events.[40]

The "Berkut" retreated from their positions up the hill, firing their automatic weapons towards the advancing Maidan protesters.[41] They were followed by young activists—some armed with pistols and hunting rifles—carrying wooden shields. The battle between the government and Maidan forces was bloody, but not yet a massacre. The source and caliber of rounds fired at the advancing protesters changed once the "Berkut" troops had retreated up the hill on Instytutska St. Video footage and subsequent ballistics investigations from the scene show shots being fired from the top floors of Hotel "Ukrayina" (the Maidan first aid service had established a triage center in the lobby there), from the rooftop of the Arkada bank building behind the upper entrance to Khreshchatyk subway, from the 7 Instytutska St. residential building just behind the concrete barricade to which government forces had retreated, and possibly from the roof of the Cabinet of Ministers building. The snipers used piercing rounds and targeted heads, necks, and chests. The victims had no chance.

In the aftermath of the protests, several investigators attempted to piece together multiple fragments of video footage filmed by journalists and eyewitnesses at the scene of the massacre.[42] Officials from the post-Yanukovych Ukrainian government accused Russia of deploying the snipers, but at time of writing, no concrete evidence to support these claims had been made public.[43] Kremlin sources have suggested the snipers came from Georgia, the Baltic countries and/or Poland. Others have suggested Ukrainian nationalist radicals conducted a "false flag" operation aimed at sewing chaos in Kyiv, to hasten the overthrow of the Yanukovych regime.[44] This latter theory was supported by a leaked recording of a telephone conversation between the Estonian ambassador to Ukraine and EU Commissioner Catherine Ashton, during which the two discussed the possibility of Maidan provocateurs being behind the mass murder.[45] However, it should be noted that the bugged telephone conversation was first leaked by the Russia Today media outlet, and multiple comparable stories linking the snipers to everyone but the Kremlin have been reported firstly by Russian media. Generating an image of complete chaos on the streets of Kyiv was mostly in Russia's interests (i.e. it provided a pretext for insertion of troops charged with stabilizing the situation), but at time of writing, no direct links between the sniper fire and the Kremlin had yet been made public. The truth may never be known.

Parliament and Parasiuk

During the afternoon of 20 February 2014, after the sniper fire on Instytutska St. had ceased, and the "Berkut" forces had retreated from both Maidan and the government quarter, opposition politicians began calling for MP's to gather in Parliament. Some means of ending the violence needed to be found. The session did not open until around 5pm, and MPs gathered very gradually – apparently several had expressed concern for their own safety in the wake of the day's violence. Initially, only 227 Parliamentarians registered (minimum quorum: 226), but as the evening wore on, several Party of Regions MP's and some nominal independents arrived. By 10pm, 238 out of the total complement of 450 had registered their presence.

The key test came just after 10pm when the speeches ceased, and a draft document was put to a vote. In the end 236 voted in favor of the "Postanova"[46] that ordered the following:

1. All Interior Ministry troops currently in Kyiv were to cease fire and return to barracks;
2. All live ammunition and lethal weapons that had been issued to government forces were to be returned immediately;
3. Blockage of roads and rail lines for the purpose of limiting the movement of people was to cease;
4. All anti-terrorist operations currently undertaken by the SBU and Interior Ministry were to be stopped immediately;
5. Circumstances that had led to deaths and casualties during the protests were to be investigated and the guilty brought to trial forthwith by the Prosecutor General;
6. The Cabinet of Ministers was ordered to provide financial compensation to all victims of the recent violence and their families;
7. Activists arrested for their participation in protests were to be released and all criminal cases against them closed;
8. It was now the exclusive right of Parliament to declare a state of emergency.

Immediately after the vote, the three opposition leaders left Parliament for the Presidential Administration building where the memorandum on the peaceful resolution of the crisis, mediated by three EU officials and a representative of the Russian Federation, was being finalized with Yanukovych's participation. At 7:30 am on 21 February the "Agreement on Settlement of the Crisis" was ready for signing, but the opposition leaders insisted that each should present it to their respective parliamentary factions first, and that the deal should be approved by the Maidan Council. The main points of the Agreement were as follows:[47]

1. Within 48 hours of signature, Parliament was to pass, and the President was to sign, a special law according to which Ukraine's Constitution was to return to its 2004 version (i.e. the text which limited Presidential powers in favor of an executive answerable to Parliament);
2. Within 10 days thereafter, a government of national unity was to be formed with participation from both the opposition and the President's faction;
3. Early presidential elections were to occur by December 2014 at the latest (Yanukovych's full term ended in March 2015, so this was a minimal concession);
4. Occupied government buildings throughout the country were to be cleared, protesters amnestied, illegal weapons turned in, and acts of violence investigated;
5. No state of emergency was to be declared.

These points were negotiated with the assistance of the German and Polish Foreign Ministers and a high-ranking French diplomat, plus an emissary from Russia. When these foreign officials presented the Agreement to the Maidan Council, many members expressed serious concerns as to the legitimacy a deal with the "murderer" Yanukovych. However, the Europeans insisted vehemently that a negotiated deal was the only way to avoid more bloodshed. Polish Foreign Minister Sikorski was caught on video telling one of the Maidan Council members (Prof. Oleksiy Haran from Kyiv-Mohyla Academy) "If you don't sign this deal you will all be dead."[48] Sikorski then sent out the following message on Twitter: "Good compromise for Ukraine. Gives peace a chance. Opens the way to reform and to Europe. Poland and EU support it." Clearly the Polish Foreign Minister misunderstood the social mood on Maidan.

That afternoon (21 February), in accordance with the signed Agreement, the Ukrainian Parliament voted overwhelmingly to re-enact the Constitutional amendments passed in 2004, thus overturning the Constitutional Court decision of 2010 that had consolidated power in the Presidency. Arguably (the bills still needed to be signed by the President to come into force), Ukraine had now become a Parliamentary-Presidential republic again. This meant Yanukovych still retained power over the army, and over foreign affairs (Defense and Foreign Ministers remained Presidential appointees), but the rest of the executive branch had now become accountable to Parliament. A new majority coalition now needed to be created which would then appoint a new Prime Minister and approve all other Ministerial appointments. Immediately after the Constitutional vote, Parliament also passed a new law that granted blanket immunity to all those involved in anti-government activities and violence. A special motion to remove Interior Minister Vitaliy Zakharchenko from office received 332 votes in favor—including 69 from Party of Regions MP's.

But on Maidan, these Parliamentary victories seemed too little and too late. During the evening of 21 February Maidan counted its dead and wounded. When my wife and I went to the city-center, we were joined by thousands of Kyiv residents who came to mourn. Many were crying. All were grim faced. We brought drinking water to the trauma point at Ukrainian House, and then went to Independence Square. A line of uniformed and fully armed police officers from Lviv marched up to the stage, and it was announced that these trained officers had joined the Maidan Self-Defense forces; the cheers were louder than any I had heard ever before. The arrival of armed reinforcements was followed by an announcement of first aid courses being offered to all Self-Defense units. Apparently if more of the Maidan "*sotnias*" had been trained in basic first aid, several deaths could have been avoided during the fighting on the 18-19th. If fighting resumed (so it was said from the stage) first aid skills would be needed.[49] Next, a man from Kharkiv took the microphone and demonstrated a bloody shield on which one of his buddies had died the previous day from a sniper wound. He also showed a grenade to the crowd and promised to go back to Kharkiv after "our victory" and shove it into a bodily orifice of oblast governor Mykhailo Dobkin—a Yanukovych supporter who had proudly worn a "Berkut" T-shirt during a session of the oblast legislature and had called for all protesters on Maidan to be shot.

Not surprisingly, given this atmosphere, when information on the contents of the Agreement signed by the three opposition leaders with Yanukovych was made available, many on Maidan were not pleased. When Yatseniuk, Klitschko, Tiahnybok, Poroshenko and other politicians were invited onto the stage together with priests for the funeral service for the men who lost their lives during the previous days, the crowd (40-50 thousand people) whistled at them. The gathered multitudes were appalled that a peace agreement had been signed with the person they saw as responsible for over 100 dead and several hundred more injured. They were particularly displeased with the prospects of having to wait for Presidential elections until December 2014 (as stipulated in the deal). During Klitschko's attempt to explain to the crowd why he had signed the Agreement with Yanukovych, an open coffin with the body of a dead protester was brought directly to the front of the stage amid screaming "who will answer for this?" and "how could you shake the hand of a murderer?".[50]

Then, Volodymyr Parasiuk, a *sotnia* commander who had personally fought with riot police during previous days, forced his way onto the stage. His short emotional speech, during which he stressed that his unit was armed, ended with an ultimatum to the opposition leaders: either renounce your deal with Yanukovych and force the President's resignation by 10 am the following day, or Parasiuk's *sotnia* would storm the government quarter.[51] Dmytro Yarosh from the Right Sector then mounted the stage to assure the crowd of his fighters' readiness to advance. The threat was real and ominous. Although over a thousand Interior Ministry troops had been withdrawn from the government quarter that day, significant numbers of well-armed SBU troops and representatives of other agencies remained inside the

Presidential Administration and Cabinet of Ministers buildings. If attacked by a crowd from Maidan, they were likely to defend themselves using lethal force.

The evening demonstration lasted until midnight. The crowd in the city-center dispersed gradually: some travelled with the coffins of their fallen comrades to their hometowns and villages to prepare funeral ceremonies; others huddled in tents, apartments, and common areas. Few in Kyiv slept that night. The morning promised to be decisive.

Chapter 5:
Climax & Recoil

What happened in Ukraine after the mass shootings in Kyiv in February 2014 was somewhat predictable. A month before the massacre on Instytutska St., I wrote the following in my "Thoughts from Kyiv" blog:

> According to opinion polls taken in December 2013 (almost a month after the start of the Euromaidan protests), Viktor Yanukovych remains the single most popular politician in Ukraine with a base of support concentrated primarily in the eastern and southern regions of the country that amounts to a national support level of 20%. ... If Yanukovych were to be removed from office by force (e.g. in a revolutionary event), every fifth Ukrainian would likely feel cheated, outraged, and violated. Inevitably, given the concentration of Yanukovych supporters in the east of the country, any radical resolution to the current stand-off would lead to a call for Russian military intervention across the border.

This chapter chronicles the first three months of post-Yanukovych Ukraine: an interlude of short-lived euphoria mixed with mourning for those who had fallen at the climax of the protests in Kyiv; a time of shock in the face of Putin's whirlwind Special Forces operation in Crimea; a period that marked the launch of foreign-inspired violent reaction to the victory of Maidan in the Donbas. During these three months, Ukraine's central government experienced a legitimacy crisis; Russia annexed sovereign Ukrainian territory, and militant separatism flared throughout the southern and eastern regions. Evidence later surfaced of the violence in Donetsk, Odesa, and Kharkiv (and especially in Slovyansk and Kramatorsk) having been orchestrated by the Kremlin as part of a covert operation aimed at splintering off what Putin called "Novorossiya" from Ukraine. However, as events in Crimea and the Donbas unfolded, few in Kyiv (and even less so in the West) understood their artificiality. On the other hand, there was no mistaking their gravity and significance.

Yanukovych runs away

The morning of 22 February 2014 was a strange one. Kyiv awoke with one question: where was Yanukovych? According to news reports, the President had left his Mezhyhirya residence at 22:40 the previous evening.[1] Could it be that Yanukovych had simply skipped town? MP's from the ruling majority seemed to think so: by the end of the day, a total of 70 members of the President's faction had tendered their resignations from the once all-powerful Party of Regions. Speaker Rybak resigned his post, as did his first deputy (Communist Ihor Kaletnik) who immediately fled to Russia.[2] Yanukovych appointees (including the acting mayor of Kyiv, and several regional governors) began resigning *en masse*. Many fled the country. As the regime crumbled, one question remained on the minds of everyone in Ukraine's political class: in the physical absence of President Yanukovych, who was the head of the Ukrainian state?

Nestor Shufrych—a former Minister in Yanukovych's government, and a high-ranking member of the Party of Regions—spoke from the Parliamentary rostrum on February 22. He reminded the session: now that the 2004 Constitutional amendments had been reenacted (a Constitutional majority had voted to do so on the previous day), if the President should resign from his office, his functions were to be carried out by the Speaker of Parliament (not by the Prime Minister, as stipulated in Yanukovych's Constitution). In these circumstances, given Speaker Rybak's resignation, the key issue before Parliament must be the election of a new Speaker. The fact that it was Shufrych who raised this issue, rather than a pro-Maidan MP, was widely seen as confirmation that Yanukovych had indeed skipped the country and/or resigned. However, notwithstanding widespread defections of MP's, Parliament still faced a legal legitimacy problem. The bill which reverted the 2004 version of the Constitution, passed the previous day by an overwhelming majority, had not yet been signed by President Yanukovych.

Yatseniuk rose to the rostrum immediately after Shufrych's speech to explain his view of the situation: Parliament had re-enacted the 2004 Constitution on February 21 with an unprecedented 386 votes in favor—86 more than the required 300 for Constitutional amendments. The vote had been supported by 140 Party of Regions MP's once loyal to Yanukovych.[3] The President had signed an EU-brokered agreement with the opposition corroborating his support for Parliament's decision. Regardless of whether Yanukovych had actually signed Bill 4163, Ukraine had *de facto* reverted to the 2004 version of the Constitution, according to which the Speaker of Parliament should assume duties if the President were incapacitated. The speech was fiery, but in fact, Yatseniuk's argument was based on thin legal ice. According to formal legal procedures, without the President's signature, the Constitutional amendments could not come into force.

On the other hand, with thousands of protesters demanding Yanukovych's arrest in the wake of the massacre of Maidan activists by snipers, and with a majority of oblast- and city-level councils voting to renounce any decrees passed by the President, formal legality took a back seat to substantive legitimacy. If formal procedures had been followed, Yanukovych would have had to have either resigned, or been impeached. According to Article 111 of Ukraine's Constitution, impeachment required a special Parliamentary Investigative Commission to be created to consider any crimes that the President was suspected of committing; then that commission should have submitted its findings to both the Supreme Court and the Constitutional Courts, and only after the rulings of both could Parliament have voted on impeachment. With the institutions of state crumbling, there was no time for such formalities. Besides, on 22 February 2014, Yanukovych was nowhere to be found.

Climax

As it happened, the events of 22 February 2014 turned out to have represented the climax of the protest phase of Ukraine's revolution. But on Maidan, you would never have known. The atmosphere in Kyiv's city-center was one of mourning rather than celebration. The mood was somber. In the rain, the ground on Independence Square was black and sticky—a stark reminder of the previous days' fires. Blood stains were covered with flowers, and memorials set up at each spot where a person had been killed during the fighting. The Stella at the center of the square was turned into a spontaneous shrine covered in flowers; a similar memorial site was set up on the grounds of St. Michael's monastery, and on the burnt-out trucks near the Parliament where fighting had been fierce. On Maidan itself, the coffins of heroes who lost their lives to sniper fire and police grenades were brought to the stage in pairs all day—each was sent off to the music of "*Plyve Kacha*" ("The duckling swims"—the song which was to become the funeral hymn of the protests), in the presence of tens of thousands of demonstrators. "Heroes do not die!" ("*Heroyi ne vmyrayut'!*") was chanted as the bodies were carried past the burnt-out hulk of the Trade Unions building toward waiting vehicles that would take each to their final resting place—to villages and towns throughout Ukraine.

Although few were celebrating, on 22 February, the revolution scored massive political victories. Parliament opened its morning session with an official announcement by deputy speaker Koshulynskiy ("Svoboda") that Speaker Rybak (Party of Regions) and First Deputy Speaker Kaletnik (Communist) had both resigned. Within a few minutes, Koshulynsky announced that two candidates for the post of Speaker had been nominated: Turchynov ("Batkivshchyna") and Poroshenko (Independent). Poroshenko immediately announced that he was taking his name off the ballot, and Oleksandr Turchynov (the original Commandant of the Maidan—chosen on 1 December 2013 when the protesters first took control of the city-center and occupied the Trade Unions building) was elected Speaker.

The legitimacy of Turchynov's election was unquestionable: choosing a Speaker was the sole prerogative of Parliament and needed no external confirmation. However, whether Turchynov's powers extended to those of Acting President was debatable: in the absence of Yanukovych's signature on the Bill reverting Ukraine's Constitution to its 2004 version, could the bill be considered law? According to the 1996/2010 Constitution, if the President should become incapacitated, his powers were to be temporarily transferred to the Prime Minister, but in the wake of Yanukovych's flight, Ukraine's Acting Prime Minister Arbuzov was nowhere to be found either. In an attempt to resolve the issue, immediately after Turchynov's election, "Batkivshchyna" faction leader Arseniy Yatseniuk tabled a Parliamentary

Resolution (*Postanova*) according to which the Rada decreed the Constitutional Bill overturning the 2010 Constitutional Court decision and returning the country's basic law to its 2004 version (adopted the previous day) to be law even in the absence of the President's signature. The resolution was supported by 325 MP's.

The situation required procedural delicacy, and Parliament proceeded cautiously: first MP's voted to confirm Arsen Avakov (Batkivshchyna MP and former mayor of Kharkiv) as Acting Interior Minister. Then Yanukovych-loyalist Viktor Pshonka was removed from the post of Prosecutor General, and former Prime Minister Tymoshenko was freed from jail. All three of these votes were unquestionably legitimate and legal. Parliament had elected a new Speaker and had exercised its power to appoint and remove executive branch officials. Then Speaker Turchynov called a recess — apparently to arrange the details of Tymoshenko's release, and to try to locate Yanukovych.

At approximately 4pm, the President's whereabouts became apparent when his television interview (taped earlier that day in Kharkiv — see below) was broadcast.[4] In that interview, Yanukovych, looking tired and disoriented, stated that in the coming weeks he would be travelling through the eastern and southern regions of the country to "find an answer: what are we going to do with the country?"[5] He claimed that the car he had been travelling in from Kyiv had been shot at;[6] that he would be staying in Ukraine; that extremists in the capital were shooting at Parliamentarians. None of these statements were true.

With Yanukovych's location now established Turchynov tabled a resolution, the legitimacy of which was debatable. According to the text, President Yanukovych was said to have *removed himself* from office and was therefore relieved of his duties. In the words of Yuriy Miroshnichenko — the (now) former President's official representative in Parliament — this document represented a *political* rather than a strictly legal act. According to Parliament's resolution, Yanukovych was not *de jure* removed from office — proposing such a bill would have been clearly unconstitutional. Instead, the President was *relieved of his duties* by a vote of 328 MP's (i.e. a Constitutional majority).

Was this decision constitutional? According to Ukrainian legal procedures, only the Constitutional Court is empowered to rule on this question, and under procedures in force at the time, such a ruling needed to be requested by at least 50 MPs. In late February 2014, gathering the signatures of 50 MPs under such a request to the Court would have been highly unpopular if not dangerous, and effecting a ruling from the Court within three months (i.e. before the early Presidential election scheduled for May 25) would have been a practical impossibility. Thereafter the point was moot.

Fatal mistake

During the 23 February session of Parliament, the former opposition leaders (now newly empowered), emboldened by their rapid success, decided to push the limits of revolutionary expediency. At 12:30 that day, the Rada voted to officially give Presidential powers (temporarily) to Speaker Turchynov. As noted, the constitutionality of this decision was questionable: the legitimately elected President of Ukraine was alive and had not officially resigned, nor been impeached. Even his whereabouts (in Kharkiv) had been established. Nevertheless, the new leaders pressed on, apparently believing that their actions and decisions were required by Maidan.

Votes were called in quick succession. At 12:40 the Rada voted to remove the despised Dmytro Tabachnyk from the post of Minister of Education, and at 12:42 Parliament removed Leonid Kozhara from Foreign Affairs. In both cases, several Party of Regions MP's registered "nay" votes, causing an uproar in the Chamber. In their defense, Nestor Shufrych rose to the rostrum to point out that the Friday accords signed by Yanukovych gave him 48 hours to sign the constitutional amendments that give Parliament full control over the executive. This term expired at 16:00 that day. Couldn't the revolutionaries wait for 4 more hours? This would have given their decisions much more legitimacy. But the new leaders pressed on.

One of the most unfortunate events to have occurred during these first days of post-Yanukovych Ukraine, was the passage on February 23 of a bill that rescinded the Law on Languages, passed in 2012 (co-authored by two notoriously pro-Moscow Party of Regions

MP's—Kivalov and Kolesnichenko), which provided official language status to Russian in those localities (oblasts and/or rayons) where more than 10% of the population requested such status. Given the countless other priorities facing the interim government, the fact that this bill was introduced at all indicates either complete political ineptitude, or ideological extremism on the part of Vyacheslav Kyrylenko—the bill's initiator. Given Kyrylenko's history as one of the co-organizers of the student hunger strikes in 1990 (the "Revolution on Granite"), and his later service as Deputy Prime Minister during the Yushchenko Presidency (and again in the post-Maidan Hroysman government), one would like to think that his misplaced legislative initiative was a mistake, rather than a deliberate provocation. Whatever the case, Kremlin news outlets immediately launched a campaign aimed at frightening the Russian-speaking population of Ukraine's eastern and southern regions with visions of a "nationalist junta" that had come to power in Kyiv.

In the end, Turchynov refused to sign Kyrylenko's bill (his first "veto" as acting President). Three years later, no new Language Law had yet been submitted to Ukraine's Parliament, and so the Kivalov-Kolesnichenko legislation which allowed regions to declare Russian to be an official language for use in their localities remained in force.[7] But the damage to the new post-Yanukovych government's international and domestic image had been done—irreparably.

Kharkiv-Donetsk-Crimea

Late at night on 21-22 February 2014 Yanukovych travelled to Kharkiv where he was to attend the "Congress of People's Deputies of all Levels of Government from the Southern and Eastern Regions, Sevastopol and AR Crimea" the following day. The last time such a meeting had been held was in 2004 in Severodonetsk (in the context of the Orange protests),[8] and there Yanukovych had famously stated that the western "goats" should stop telling him how to live. Other speakers had openly called for the separation of the eastern and southern oblasts from a supposedly "nationalist" west. If similar proclamations were to be made at the Kharkiv gathering this time, it could have signaled

the start of some sort of quasi-legitimate break-up of the country. After-all, by late February 2014, most of the authorities in the west and
center had already overtly sided with the Maidan protesters, and so a
split of Ukraine was not inconceivable with the west and center adopt-
ing a pro-EU/pro-Maidan position, while the east and south proclaiming themselves pro-Russian/pro-Yanukovych.

During the evening of February 21, before their departure from
Mezhyhirya, and just prior to signing his own resignation as Speaker
of Parliament, Volodymyr Rybak discussed the planned Kharkiv
gathering with Yanukovych: Rybak refused to personally attend the
Congress, calling it a Severodonetsk-2.[9] Whether Yanukovych understood the scenario that was to unfold in Kharkiv remains an open
question. According to Rybak and Kharkiv oblast governor Dobkin,
on arrival in Kharkiv from Kyiv, the President showed no signs of
anxiety, and acted as if his power was not threatened. His behavior
was not that of a man fleeing for his life. In fact, he appeared confident
that the deal he had signed with the opposition that day would lead
to the dismantling of the protest camp on Maidan soon. In Dobkin's
words: "He did not create the impression of a person on the run. He
100% expected to return. If he had known that he would not return,
he would have blown up Mezhyhiriya, burned it, destroyed it—it was
that dear to him."[10]

The President's mood changed during the early morning hours
of Saturday February 22 after multiple meetings with Dobkin, and a
phone conversation with his son Oleksander who was in Donetsk. The
Kharkiv governor had tried to convince the President not to appear at
the planned convention (apparently he feared Yanukovych would be
whistled off the stage because the mass killings in Kyiv had led to
enormous popularity losses for the Party of Regions—even in their
electoral heartland).[11] Dobkin's arguments finally got through when
he declared that during the convention, police would not be able to
guarantee the President's safety. With that, Yanukovych seems to
have understood that his crisis was real: he taped a short interview
with a Kharkiv journalist during which he angrily declared his refusal
to sign any of the legislation that the Rada had adopted that Saturday

morning (i.e. reenactment of the 2004 Constitution, amnesty for Maidan activists, freedom for Tymoshenko). He promised to remain in the country, but in fact, immediately after the address was recorded, departed for Donetsk, and later fled to Crimea, and eventually to Russia.

The facts surrounding Yanukovych's flight from Kharkiv to Crimea remain unclear. According to airport logs, the Ukrainian President departed Kharkiv for Donetsk by helicopter at approximately 1 pm on 22 February. Once at Donetsk International Airport, he boarded a private jet, but (amazingly!) was denied permission to depart by local Customs officials. An armed stand-off between the President's bodyguards and Ukrainian border security officers ensued. Yanukovych then de-planed and drove by car to the home of Rinat Akhmetov—his old friend, and Ukraine's richest "oligarch". The following day, the President's cortege of cars headed towards Crimea, avoiding main roads, and apparently leaving the pavement on several occasions.[12] On 25 February Yanukovych finally reached the southern coast of the Crimean Peninsula where he officially decommissioned his state-provided bodyguards, and crossed onto the (leased) territory of the Russian Black Sea Fleet.

On 28 February, the ousted Ukrainian President surfaced at a press conference broadcast from the Russian city of Rostov-on-Don. Viktor Yanukovych looked tired and lacked his normal self-confidence. He had apparently been evacuated on a Russian warship, brought from the port of Novorosiysk to Moscow, and then to Rostov-on-Don where he was staying with "friends". During the press conference, just prior to reading a prepared "apology to the Ukrainian people for allowing events to run out of control", Yanukovych broke the pen that he had been holding in his hands in half. The video image was seen as a demonstration both of his frustration and anger, and of a lack of sincerity of his remorse.

Open questions

Why did Yanukovych concede power? Why did he run away, first to Kharkiv during the early hours of February 22, and then onward to Russia in subsequent days? According to the Kremlin's narrative, President Putin supposedly called his Ukrainian counterpart on the evening of the 21st to tell him that under the circumstances, leaving Kyiv was inadvisable. However, security camera footage from Mezh-yhirya clearly shows Yanukovych supervising the packing of his belongings (including paintings, statues, furniture, and other valuables) three days earlier.[13] The President's departure from Kyiv (or at least the evacuation of valuables from his residence) had been planned before the mass killings in the city-center. Indeed, Yanukovych seems to have started packing immediately after his return from Sochi where he met with Putin on the sidelines of the Olympic Games.

Why did the President flee? Was his departure supposed to be temporary, and what actually occurred was a miscalculation? Is it possible that the purpose of Putin's phone call on the eve of Yanukovych's departure was not to advise him not to leave, but rather to assure him the move was temporary, and that the Ukrainian President's fate was in good hands? Is it possible that Putin (via undercover agents) instigated the chaos in Kyiv on February 18-21, and then planned to have Yanukovych ask for Russia's assistance to counter the coup plotters during the Party of Regions' gathering in Kharkiv?

But Yanukovych did not attend the Kharkiv Congress on 22 February 2014. He failed to use the opportunity to assert himself as the legitimate President of Ukraine; to proclaim Turchynov to be a usurper and the opposition leaders to have staged a coup d'état. Put colloquially, Yanukovych choked. When told by the Kharkiv governor that he could not guarantee the President's safety, Yanukovych decided not to make an appearance at the Congress. Its delegates voted to disavow all decisions taken by the Parliament since the President's departure from Kyiv, and to "take responsibility for protecting the Constitutional order on the territories of eastern and southern Ukraine, until order can be reinstated in the capital."[14] But the resolution did not directly call for separatism, nor for open defiance of the interim Kyiv government. If a separatist Severodonetsk-2 had been planned for that day in Kharkiv, the plan failed.

If Yanukovych had made an appearance at the Kharkiv convention, if he had publicly asserted his legitimacy as President of Ukraine, and the convention deputies had supported a call to arms to counter the "fascist coup" in Kyiv (as Kremlin propaganda referred to Yanu-kovych's ouster), a *de facto* breakup of Ukraine would have been ef-fected. Given the chaos in Kyiv, requests to Moscow to provide polit-ical, economic and military assistance authored by Ukraine's eastern and southern oblast councils (or possibly by Yanukovych himself) would have legitimized Russian invasion. The Turchynov govern-ment would have been denied similar assistance from the West due to its lack of formal legitimacy.[15] Kyiv and the western regions where popular support for Maidan was overwhelming would have found themselves economically and politically isolated, while the eastern and southern regions effectively integrated (formally or informally as client states) with Russia.

Immediately after the Congress' closing ceremony, Governor Dobkin, together with his close friend Hennadiy Kernes — the mayor of Kharkiv — hastily fled to Russia, avoiding confrontation with pro-Maidan demonstrators who had surrounded the conference hall.[16] The border they crossed was by then amassed with Russian troops, artillery and armor, ordered to full alert by Vladimir Putin.[17] Several columns of tanks stood ready to cross into Sumy and Chernihiv ob-lasts from the north, and given the disarray of the Ukrainian army, had the order to invade been given, they would have been in Kyiv within a few hours.[18] But Yanukovych failed to officially request mil-itary support from Moscow during the Kharkiv Congress. Such a re-quest was to be written by the Ukrainian President only after his exile to Russia and was demonstrated on 3 March 2014 with much fanfare by Russian ambassador Churkin during a meeting of the UN Security Council.[19] But by then Yanukovych was no longer seen by Ukrainians as their legitimate Head of State, and so the request carried little weight.

It is unlikely to ever be known with certainty whether Putin's vision of *Novorossiya* (i.e. the territorial breakup of Ukraine) was hatched after Yanukovych's flight from Kyiv, or before, but in retro-spect it seems plausible that it was planned at least in general terms well in advance of the mass killings on Maidan. In September 2013, Putin's special advisor on Ukraine Sergey Glazyev warned that if Kyiv signed the EU Association Agreement, this would amount to "a cessation of Ukrainian sovereignty."[20] At the time this statement was interpreted as a metaphor—the Kremlin's spokesman on Ukraine was trying to persuade Yanukovych not to sign the EU deal and added a little scaremongering to his discourse. But Glazyev may have meant no metaphor at all. In 2015, the Russian Ministry of Defense awarded Special Forces officers involved in the annexation of Crimea (see below) with medals inscribed "For the return of Crimea". These medals bear the dates "20 February – 18 March 2014". The latter date marks the day of Crimea's official annexation by the Russian Federation; the former date is the day snipers first fired on Instytutska St. in Kyiv. On that day, Yanukovych was still in the capital, and no calls for separatism had yet been heard anywhere in Ukraine. Yet a covert plan to dismember Ukraine seems already to have been put into motion.

Crimea

The first pro-Russian demonstrations were held in the Crimean city of Sevastopol on 23 February 2014—the day the Rada voted to strip Yanukovych of his Presidential powers. Sevastopol is a unique city: a military port, home to both the Russian and Ukrainian Black Sea Fleets, with a population consisting primarily of naval personnel and their families. Its primarily ethnic Russian inhabitants generally identified with a Russian historical narrative, according to which Sevastopol was proclaimed the "City of Russian Glory" due to its strategic role in the Crimean War, and in WWII. The Russian media reported 20 thousand participants at this first separatist rally, while local eyewitnesses estimated approximately 3000 with most being wives and family members of Russian Black Sea Fleet personnel stationed there.[21] The protesters chanted "Putin is our President!" and "Ro-si-ya!" ("Russia!") and waved Russian flags. The demonstration "elected" a Russian citizen, Aleksey Chaliy, to the post of "people's mayor", and his first decision was to set up road blocks with armed guards on the roads into the port city. On February 24, the Yanukovych-appointed governor of Sevastopol resigned both his post and his membership in the Party of Regions, stating that "those who appointed me have left."[22]

Although Sevastopol is strategically important (similar to Guantanamo or Gibraltar) it is not the administrative capital of Crimea. That role is played by the land-locked Simferopil, and it was there that most of the events of late February and early March 2014 unfolded. Simferopil is a city of 300 thousand residents. Its center is dominated by a large edifice known as the Crimean Parliament—a proto-legislature which, according to Ukraine's Constitution, enjoyed a higher status than an oblast-level council, but wielded limited real powers. The head of the Crimean executive (*de facto* governor of Crimea, who bore the title Prime Minister) was appointed by the Parliament of the Autonomous Republic, but according to both the Ukrainian and Crimean Constitutions, only candidates submitted by Ukraine's President were to be considered, and no cases of non-approval had ever taken place. Crimea's actual autonomy was therefore limited. Given the closed nature of its political elites, and their often criminal backgrounds, decisions were generally made behind closed doors with a view towards balancing the economic interests of Kyiv and the locals.[23]

On 26 February 2014, the Crimean Parliament was scheduled to gather for a special session. The Prime Minister of Crimea, Anatoliy Mohyliov, a Yanukovych crony who hailed from Makiyivka, Donetsk oblast, was disliked by many, and given the recent change of government in Kyiv, changes in the leadership of the executive branch on the peninsula were likely. Rumors were also circulating of possible separatist initiatives being tabled: only a week before, during a trip to Moscow, the speaker of the Crimean Parliament Vladimir Konstantinov had alluded that any unlawful change of government in Kyiv would be answered with a motion by the Crimean legislature to denounce the 1954 decision of the Supreme Soviet of the USSR, according to which administrative control over the peninsula had been transferred from Russia to Ukraine.[24]

Suspecting an impending act of separatism, over 12 thousand Crimean Tatars, Ukrainians, and pro-Maidan ethnic Russians gathered on the square in front of the Crimean Parliament on 26 February. The pro-Ukraine crowd included "ultra" fans from the Tavria (Simferopil) and Sevastopol football clubs. They faced approximately 5000

activists of the "Russkoye Yedinstvo" ("Russian Unity") party — a political force that had garnered just over 4% of the popular vote during
the last Crimean elections. After a full day of stand-off, and several
incidences of pushing and shoving, and after several hours of closed-
door negotiations between a delegation of Crimean Tatars and
Speaker Konstantinov, at 4pm, the leader of the pro-Russia demonstration, Sergey Aksionov, and the leader of the Crimean Tatar
Medzhlis (assembly), Refat Chubarov, emerged together to ask the
protesters to disperse. For the moment, it seemed, the threat of violence in the Crimean capital had subsided.

But that night, the Kremlin intervened directly. In the words of
acting President Oleksandr Turchynov:

> During the night of 26-27 February, armed men occupied the building
> of the Crimean Verkhovna Rada. I was informed of this early on 27
> February. The signature and the arsenal used left no doubt — this was
> the work of professionals. These were Special Forces of the GRU of the
> General Staff of the RF, armed with automatic rifles, autocannons, gre-
> nade launchers. I understood that if they (the Russians) had taken this
> step, the situation could quickly degenerate into a very real military
> conflict. The very next day, Russian forces without identifying marks
> began their occupation of critical infrastructure, airports, blockades of
> Ukrainian military units. I called a meeting of the NSDC (National Se-
> curity and Defense Council) to work out our priority actions in reac-
> tion to the aggression of the RF. But the situation deteriorated very
> quickly. Concurrently with their attack on Crimea, Russia began to
> transfer army units to our borders. These were storm trooper units,
> ready to cross the line at any time. Concentration of Russian forces be-
> gan along our entire border, and this was not just a scare tactic, this
> was a very real preparation for invasion aimed at overthrowing our
> new government.[25]

On 27 February, with the Parliament building in Simferopil occupied
by heavily armed men, deputies were called by Speaker Konstantinov
for a special session to vote on the appointment of a new Prime Minister. During the previous day, when the Crimean Parliament had
been blocked by demonstrators, only 49 of 100 deputies had attended
the planned session (i.e. insufficient for a quorum); with the building
occupied by armed "little green men", even fewer risked showing up.

Nevertheless, the press service of the Crimean Rada announced that the leader of "Russkoye Yedinstvo" ("Russian Unity") party, Sergey Aksionov, was elected Prime Minister of the Autonomous Republic with 53 votes in favor. Later reports suggested that only 36 deputies actually voted for Aksionov, with the balance of votes registered *in absentia* by Konstantinov using 17 duplicates of his colleagues' voting cards.[26] Aksionov's election was also dubious given the statutory requirement that any candidate for the leadership of the Crimean executive be submitted to the Autonomous Republic's legislature by the President of Ukraine. In Aksionov's case such details were overlooked.[27] As soon as the votes were cast, Aksionov, a businessman reportedly known in the local underworld by the nickname "Goblin"[28] addressed the pro-Russian demonstrators gathered outside the occupied Parliament building: "In this difficult time the Russian Federation, I am sure, will extend a helping hand, and will provide assistance, including financial, so that Crimea will be able to reconstruct its political situation quickly."

"Little green men"

That night, both Belbek military airport (which served Sevastopol), and Simferopil International (the main civilian airport in Crimea) were occupied by heavily armed uniformed men who locals began referring to ironically as "the polite people" (*vezhlivye liudi*) for their tendency to ignore all questions as to their allegiance or origin. During subsequent days, more "unidentified" armed men occupied all local television stations and broadcast centers; cut land telephone lines and jammed mobile phone signals near Ukrainian military bases. Apparently, the actual blockades of these bases were effected by forces of the Russian Black Sea fleet, but the support they received from Special Forces transferred into Crimea from Russia was more than obvious.[29]

Dmytro Tymchuk, the leader of the "Information Resistance" (sprotiv.info) grass-roots intelligence communication agency recalled the start of Putin's Crimean operation:

> After the victory of Maidan, as events in Crimea began, Minister of Defense Lebedev (a Yanukovych appointee) simply disappeared, and

then "surfaced" in Sevastopol; Chief of the General Staff Ilyin also removed himself from office (and also later appeared in Sevastopol). The
entire command of the Ukrainian Navy suddenly "became ill" and
checked into hospitals. The army was demoralized—in the first place
in Crimea, and in the eastern regions where the population generally
did not support Maidan. In this post-revolutionary situation, in a period of *de facto* anarchy in the state, executing a covert operation in Crimea turned out to be a relatively simple matter for the Russians.[30]

On 28 February the Ukrainian Parliament officially appealed to the
United States and United Kingdom—"guarantors" of Ukraine's territorial integrity under the Budapest Memorandum—to intervene to
stop Russia's aggression in Crimea.[31] According to the 1994 agreement, Ukraine had voluntarily given up the nuclear weapons that it
had inherited from the USSR in exchange for security assurances from
the world's nuclear powers.[32] The reaction of the United States government was immediate (yet disappointing): President Obama issued
a statement voicing his "deep concern" over the movement of Russian
troops, and warned that "there will be costs (to Russia) for any military intervention in Ukraine."[33] Meanwhile, the first key infrastructure facilities (transportation and communication) were quietly occupied during the night by Russian Special Forces already in Crimea,
and the first blockades of Ukrainian Armed Forces units were set up
by a mixture of local pro-Russian protesters and heavily armed men
without insignia.[34]

The following day, on March 1, the Federation Council of the
Russian Federation—the upper chamber of the Russian Parliament –
voted unanimously (90:0) to approve President Putin's request for
permission to deploy the Armed Forces of the Russian Federation on
the territory of Ukraine.[35] The *de facto* invasion which had been
launched three days earlier now received a legal basis—though its formal legitimacy was questionable: Putin's request to the Council was
framed as a response to the appeal for assistance from Crimean Prime
Minister Aksionov, but the latter was *de jure* self-proclaimed because
his candidacy had not been approved by Ukraine's President, as required by both Ukrainian and Crimean law. In Kyiv, Turchynov had

signed a decree cancelling Aksionov's appointment,[36] but few in Simferopil or in Moscow took notice because Turchynov's legitimacy as
Acting President was legally questionable as well.

On the ground in Crimea, questions of legal legitimacy of commanders were multiplied by the fervent belief on the part of Ukrainian
troops living in barracks on the peninsula that the troops of the Russian Black Sea Fleet stationed in Sevastopol were their friends and allies. The movement of Russian armor on Crimean roads, coupled with
overflights by battle helicopters, was generally met with confusion.
Ukrainian personnel were instructed by Kyiv to defend their positions, but their officers' loyalties were often questionable at best. For
example, during his first meeting with subordinates in Sevastopol, the
newly appointed Commander of the Naval Forces of Ukraine, Admi-
ral Denys Berezovsky, called on his officers to commit treason, and
himself swore allegiance to "people of Crimea and Sevastopol." On 20
April, after Russia's annexation of the peninsula, Putin appointed Berezovsky (by then an officer of the Russian Navy) Deputy Commander of the Russian Black Sea Fleet.

Throughout the spring of 2014, treason on the part of Ukrainian
military and civilian personnel stationed in Crimea was common. In
Sevastopol and Simferopil, SBU and Interior Ministry troops (especially Berkut units who had been hastily evacuated from Kyiv on 21
February) switched sides almost immediately. Of the 13 468 Ukrainian
military personnel (4637 officers and 8831 soldiers and NCO's) stationed in the Autonomous Republic of Crimea at the end of February
2014, only 3990 remained loyal to their oaths (including 1649 officers)
by the end of April.[37] Most of the Ukrainian military personnel had
families living on the peninsula; they were very much aware of the
discrepancy between their own wages and equipment quality compared to those of their Russian colleagues;[38] they had been brought up
in a narrative of "brotherhood" with Russia (i.e. common Soviet-era
symbols, historical memory, wartime myths, language); they were
skeptical of the new Kyiv administration given the portrayal of the
Maidan protests by Russian and local Crimean television as "fascist",
"nationalist", and opposed to the Russian language. In this context,

Kyiv seemed distant whereas the Russian Black Sea Fleet offered refuge and opportunity to comfortably continue their military careers.

Two incidents of valor and demonstrative loyalty by Ukrainian officers stand out in the midst of the mass defections of Ukrainian troops. The first occurred on 4 March 2014 when Colonel Yuliy Mamchur, Commander of the Ukrainian Air Force base at Belbek, led a column of unarmed officers and personnel of the 204th Tactical Aviation Brigade to face the Russian Special Forces that had surrounded his base. They approached the Russians carrying the Ukrainian flag and the flag of their unit (a red standard bearing Soviet-era symbols—a relic of the Brigade's battles in 1941) challenging the occupiers to shoot. The men sang the Ukrainian national anthem (badly). After a short verbal exchange with the "little green men" that had surrounded the base, Mamchur's officers were allowed to pass, and the Ukrainian flag was again hoisted atop Belbek (it had been replaced by a Russian tri-color hours earlier). The blockade around Belbek airbase lasted until 22 March when Mamchur was finally arrested by the FSB, and later released into mainland Ukraine. In the end, only 38% of his men remained loyal to Ukraine.[39]

The second incident was less militarily significant, though symbolic. On 21 March when command of the prestigious Sevastopol Naval Academy was officially to be transferred from Ukraine to Russia, a small group of cadets stood at attention and loudly sang the Ukrainian national anthem as the Russian tri-color was being raised.[40] Their former colleagues who had recently transferred their allegiance from Ukraine to the Russian Federation stood shocked. When they finished singing, the young Ukrainian cadets sharply completed an about-face and departed the ceremonial square of the Academy. They were later transferred to the Ukrainian Naval College in Odesa, and each was given command of a vessel in the reconstituted Ukraine's Navy after graduation.[41]

In March 2014, the Russian strategy with respect to personnel of the Ukrainian Armed Forces stationed in Crimea, was peaceful though forceful: first they organized blockades of Ukrainian facilities, then offered higher wages to those who chose to switch sides, then announced ultimatums requiring troops who remained loyal to

Ukraine to lay down their weapons, and finally stormed the facilities, organizing the withdrawal of any remaining Ukrainian personnel. Both sides were heavily armed, and so the stand-offs were often highly tense. Despite Ukrainian accusations that the Russians attempted to provoke violence, Moscow's Special Forces effected their mission with extraordinary professionalism: during the entire operation, only one Ukrainian soldier was killed.[42]

"Referendum" and annexation

On 16 March, the new Crimean "authorities", backed by tens of thousands of deployed troops from Russia's Black Sea Fleet and Special Forces, conducted a "referendum". The plebiscite was condemned by the EU, the US, the UK and many other western states as illegal.[43] Nevertheless, on this day, after a "campaign" lasting only 10 days, Crimeans were asked to support one of two versions of their political future:

1. Reunification of Crimea with Russia as a constituent entity of the Russian Federation;
2. Renewal of the 1992 Constitution of Crimea and the status of Crimea as a part of Ukraine.

Continued status as an Autonomous Republic within Ukraine according to the laws in place in 2014 was not on the ballot. The second option (renewal of the 1992 Constitution of Crimea) involved complete autonomy with only foreign affairs delegated to Kyiv. How this would have been implemented in practice if the results of the referendum had shown Crimeans' support for such an option will forever remain unknown. The announced results showed an 81.4% turnout (89.5% in Sevastopol) with 96.77% purportedly supporting union with Russia (95.6% in Sevastopol).

These numbers were exceptionally high and obviously falsified. On the day of "voting" the Crimean "authorities" were caught openly lying. For example, the head of the "referendum commission" Mikhail Malishev stated on 16 March: "By 8pm 1,250,426 people had voted, not counting Sevastopol. If Sevastopol is included, the number is 1,724,563."[44] Accordingly, 474,137 people were said to have voted in Sevastopol. However, according to population registry data from 1

November 2013, Sevastopol's population *totaled* only 385,462 — including underage children who could not vote. Strangely, therefore, 123% of Sevastopol voters were said to have voted in the Crimean "referendum".

A poll conducted by the Kyiv International Institute of Sociology during the period spanning 8-18 February 2014, registered 41% of Crimeans supporting unification of the peninsula with Russia[45] — a number that was higher than any recorded in previous surveys, but still far from the overwhelming support claimed by the "referendum commission." The President of Russia's Council on Civil Society and Human Rights, an analytical group attached to the Kremlin, briefly posted a document on its website which showed just over half of Crimeans supporting unification with Russia with an expected turn-out of 30-50% — likely an accurate estimate given that the leadership of the Crimean Tatars (a minority representing approximately 15% of the total population of the peninsula) had called for a complete boycott of the vote.[46] Credible international observers (e.g. OSCE, UN) were not present in Crimea during the vote, so no independent substantiation of its results were possible.

Nevertheless, despite widespread international condemnation of the "referendum" and of the military action that preceded it, on March 18 Putin officially welcomed Crimea and Sevastopol into the Russian Federation. The President's speech to both houses of the Russian Parliament on the occasion of "Crimea's return" was triumphant and ominous: in addition to presenting a revisionist version of history (Putin described Crimea as the cradle of Ancient Rus; a place of timeless Russian valor), the Russian President proclaimed a manifesto: Russians throughout the former USSR desired and deserved to live within one country; this had been prevented by the United States which broke up the Russian nation after the collapse of communism, and then continued meddling in the neighborhood during the Orange protests, and more recently during the Maidan. Russia would no longer allow mistreatment of its co-ethnics beyond its borders. Most ominously, he referred to Kyiv as the "Mother of Russian cities" and entreated further: "Ancient Rus is our common source and we cannot live without each other."[47] The speech was full of veiled and open threats towards the

West and towards the "neo-Nazis, Russophobes, and anti-Semites" that had supposedly taken power in Kyiv. The audience of Russian Parliamentarians received it enthusiastically (some shed tears of joy).

That day, I was convinced that further invasion of Ukraine by Russian troops was imminent. My fears were confirmed on 2 April 2014 when US Air Force General Philip Breedlove announced that Russia had amassed sufficient forces on Ukraine's eastern border to effect an incursion within 3-5 days.[48] NATO's Supreme Allied Commander in Europe was stating the obvious: Ukraine could not continue the policy of extreme restraint that had been exercised in the face of Russian aggression in Crimea (where land and sea assets were abandoned without a fight), nor were the Ukrainian Armed Forces any match for those of Russia. With tens of thousands of troops massing on Russia's south-western border, NATO commanders were not discounting the possibility of full-scale invasion of mainland Ukraine, and such an act would require more than a mere diplomatic response. No western politician was interested in presiding over the start of World War III, but given Russian belligerence, the prospect of such a turn of events could not be discounted.

Rumbling in the east

As the Crimean crisis unfolded, protests against the new Kyiv government erupted in Yanukovych's electoral heartland. The oblast administration building in Donetsk was first occupied by Anti-Maidan demonstrators on 1 March, and then cleared by the SBU on 6 March. Russian flags were again on display at a protest in the eastern city on 9 March. The demonstrators called for greater autonomy and voiced their displeasure with what they saw as a coup d'état in Kyiv. Overtly separatist demands were muted. Instead, the demonstrators paraded St. George's ribbons (a Russian imperial symbol that was transformed during the 2000's by Kremlin technologists into a memorial symbol of Soviet-Russian victory in WWII), and called for increased linguistic autonomy for their region.

One month later, the protesters returned in more organized fashion: on 6 April the oblast administration buildings in both Donetsk

and Luhansk were occupied. Having denounced the Kyiv government, the demonstrators proclaiming their allegiance to "people's
governors": Pavel Gubarev in Donetsk and Valeriy Bolotov in
Luhansk—both Russian citizens. In Donetsk, the "Donetsk People's
Republic" was proclaimed (the proclamation of the "Luhansk People's Republic" occurred two weeks later), and on the following day
(April 7), the regional SBU headquarters in both oblast centers were
raided. Significant stores of automatic weapons were seized by separatist militants. Given the gradual reduction of Anti-Maidan protest
activity in evidence throughout March, its sudden reemergence immediately after the Crimean "referendum" and Putin's annexation
speech was suspect: the involvement of subversives from the Russian
Federation seemed likely.[49]

The day after the "Donetsk People's Republic" ("Donetskaya
narodnaya respublika"—DNR) was proclaimed, protesters occupied
the Oblast State Administration building in Kharkiv to proclaim the
"Kharkiv People's Republic" ("Kharkovskaya narodnaya respublika"). However, Interior Ministry forces retook the building the following day, and so the separatist project turned out to be short-lived.
The Kharkiv episode demonstrated the three key requirements of for
separatism to succeed in eastern Ukraine: 1) tacit pliancy if not overt
support from local elites, 2) minimal pro-Maidan grassroots activism,
and 3) significant manpower imported from Russia.[50] In Kharkiv,
none of these factors proved present. The city's mayor Hennadiy
Kernes, and former oblast governor Mykhailo Dobkin (both former
Yanukovych loyalists) refused to support calls for overt separatism;
they appeared at Anti-Maidan demonstrations wearing St. George's
ribbons, but their public pronouncements stopped short of calling for
direct Russian intervention in local affairs. The Kharkiv Maidan, led
by the young poet and writer Serhiy Zhadan, gathered regularly in
sizeable numbers near the city's Shevchenko monument before and
after the shootings in Kyiv, and had mobilized sufficient numbers to
surround the conference hall where Yanukovych had planned to
speak on February 22. Finally, although Kharkiv is less than 40km
from the Russian border and only 80km from the Russian city of Bel-

gorod, in early April 2014 the newly appointed Minister of the Interior, Arsen Avakov (a Kharkiv native and former mayoral candidate) beefed up security at the main border crossing. Unsure of the loyalties of local police, he also brought the "Jaguar" unit from Vinnytsia to Kharkiv to clear the Oblast Administration building (ironically, this unit had gained infamy by parading Cossack Hawryluk naked in the snow during the Maidan protests). Thereafter, pro-Moscow demonstrators in Ukraine's second largest city were limited to several hundred (often paid hooligans and "tourists" from the nearby Russian city of Voronezh)[51], and their rallies proceeded peacefully, gradually winding down by mid-May.

The opposite situation developed in the town of Slovyansk. Located approximately 130 km north of Donetsk, on the main road to Kharkiv (175km away), this small city became the epicenter of the pro-Russian militancy that would later transform into the Russian-Ukrainian war in the Donbas. On 12 April 2014, the city's main administrative building, its police station and SBU office were stormed and captured by a group of heavily armed men. These later turned out to be "volunteers" from the Russian Armed Forces under the command of Russian GRU Colonel Igor Girkin (a.k.a. "Igor Strelkov") who had previously taken part in operations in Crimea.[52] During a brief appearance at the occupied police station that day, Slovyansk mayor Nelya Shtepa expressed support for the action,[53] and for the cause of the "Donetsk People's Republic." Thereafter Slovyansk was turned into a fortress that would not be retaken by the Ukrainian Armed Forces until July 2014.

On the same day as local government buildings in Slovyansk were occupied by forces of the "Donetsk People's Republic", in the neighboring town of Kramatorsk, the police station was raided, the Ukrainian flag and trident removed, and the banner of the "DNR" raised. The event was filmed by local journalists whom one of the "militants" asked to keep a safe distance, beyond the *porebrik*. This Russian word means "curb", but it is a term that is used solely in St. Petersburg slang—a fact that gave away the origins of the masked gunman in Kramatorsk and made him famous among pro-Maidan activists when the video footage went viral.

Peaceful demonstrations (even accompanied by calls for separatism) were one thing; occupation of government buildings and infrastructure by heavily armed men was quite another. On 13 April 2014 Acting President Turchynov announced the commencement of an Anti-Terrorist Operation (ATO) to take back control of Donetsk and Luhansk oblasts.[54] As part of his announcement, Turchynov called for volunteers to join Interior Ministry and Army units. According to Ukrainian law, the ATO was to be coordinated and led by the SBU, but in reality this was a military operation from the start: armored vehicles established checkpoints on the main road into Slovyansk, and a Special Forces unit was ordered to retake Kramatorsk airport.[55] On the first day of the ATO, one Ukrainian soldier was killed during fighting at a checkpoint near Slovyansk, and 5 others wounded. Many thousands more would follow during subsequent months and years of fighting in the region.

When the ATO began, Kyiv authorities expected troops to encounter hooligans and swindlers backed by Russian intelligence officers and/or subversives. After-all, the leader of the self-proclaimed "Government of the Donetsk People's Republic", Denis Pushylin, was a former local organizer of the MMM financial pyramid;[56] the self-proclaimed "People's Governor of Luhansk" Valeriy Bolotov was a former driver for Party of Regions heavyweight Oleksandr Yefremov. But to the surprise of many, forces advancing on Slovyansk and Kramatorsk were met with significant resistance from the local population: soldiers attempting to "liberate" separatist-occupied towns and villages were blocked by residents, and on one occasion six Ukrainian armored personnel carriers were captured by "DNR" forces when their crews defected. During these early stages of the ATO, pro-Kyiv (and especially pro-Maidan) sentiments were rare in the Donbas. Throughout April, separatist checkpoints were established on roads throughout Donetsk and Luhansk oblasts. Local government and police buildings were raided and occupied in both oblast centers, as well as in Horlivka, Mariupol, Yenakiyevo, Artemivsk (later renamed Bakhmut), Severodonetsk, and other towns in the regions.

Meanwhile on May 2, Odesa lived through hell. What actually took place that day in Ukraine's southern port city is shrouded in a great deal of confusion, but according to local eyewitnesses, the massacre that resulted in 47 deaths was deliberately instigated by covert Russian operatives acting in alliance with Odesa's corrupt local police.[57] Amateur video footage clearly shows police assisting the pro-Russian armed thugs[58] who later attacked a column of pro-Maidan demonstrators (backed by "ultra" football fans). Outnumbered by the angry pro-Ukrainian mob, the pro-Russian side eventually retreated into the Trade Union Building which was set on fire (by whom remains unclear). Later investigations showed that the walls of the Trade Union Building had been laced with chloroform several days before the tragedy; most of those killed that day died of smoke inhalation. Apparently, the plan was to have the deaths of "peaceful pro-Russian protesters" (many of whom were imports from the nearby Russian-controlled unrecognized region of Transnistria) blamed on the Kyiv government, and to thereby initiate a wave of separatism in this key southern Ukrainian port city. The plan backfired: Odesa chose peace, and its population chose Ukraine.

By early May 2014, the Kremlin's plans to stoke mass protest against the Kyiv government throughout southeastern Ukraine had suffered severe setbacks: the proclamation of the "Kharkiv People's Republic" on April 7 had been stillborn; support for separatism in Donetsk and Luhansk, though evident (particularly in the smaller towns of Slovyansk and Kramatorsk), had turned out to be not as strong as expected; the murder of pro-Russian demonstrators in Odesa on May 2 had not resulted in mass mobilization of locals outraged at the incompetence and/or cruelty of the new Kyiv authorities. Under such conditions, any open invasion of mainland Ukraine by the Russian troops massed on the border would likely have been met with significant local resistance. In addition, since the Crimean annexation on 18 March 2018, the international community had mobilized against the Kremlin, implementing sectoral sanctions and excluding Russia from the G8.[59] Open invasion would be costly.

In mid-April, the US, EU, Russian and Ukrainian foreign ministers met in Geneva, and issued a joint statement that seemed to represent a first step towards diffusing the tense situation in Ukraine's east.[60] But the first real sign of de-escalation came on 7 May during a joint news conference with the President of Switzerland (chair of the OSCE) in Moscow, when Putin first suggested the need for dialog with the new Ukrainian authorities, and publicly asked the leadership of the "Donetsk" and "Luhansk People's Republics" to postpone their planned referendums on independence.[61] This announcement did not immediately end separatist violence in the region (protesters clashed with police at the city administration building of Mariupol on the same day),[62] but Putin's statement was widely received as a sign of de-escalation.

On 11 May 2014, despite Putin's request, the leaders of both the Donetsk and Luhansk "People's Republics" called upon their populations to approve the "declarations of independence" of their "republics." The results were a foregone conclusion. In Luhansk, the self-proclaimed "Central Election Commission" stated that 75% of eligible voters had participated in the plebiscite (1 359 420 ballots cast) with 96% supporting independence. In Donetsk, the self-proclaimed authorities announced that 74.87% of eligible voters had participated, and 89.07% (2,252,867 ballots) had supported the independence of the "Donetsk People's Republic". International observers were not present at either referendum, and no state (including Russia) recognized their results. Indeed, unlike in the Crimean case where a referendum was used as an informational tool to justify illegal annexation, the 11 May "votes" in the two "republics" of the Donbas were widely seen as sham plebiscites. The real electoral turning point for Ukraine (all regions except Crimea and some separatist controlled areas of the Donbas) was to come two weeks later—Ukrainian Presidential elections were scheduled for May 25th.

Governing after Yanukovych

Although Crimea and the simmering conflicts in the Donbas (and in Kharkiv and Odesa) raised significant security concerns both domestically and internationally, mundane economic issues needed to be resolved in Kyiv. After years of mismanagement (and outright theft) by Yanukovych, Ukraine's state coffers were completely depleted: at the end of February 2014, the *national* treasury reported a balance of just over 108 thousand UAH (approx. 12 thousand USD) in its accounts.[63]

Salaries of state employees could not be paid; fuel and materiel for the Armed Forces could not be supplied; health care, education, and pensions could not be financed. Western financial assistance needed to somehow begin flowing, despite the government's legitimacy issues.

Given the extreme financial crisis, and the reluctance of western governments to support the post-Yanukovych government at the scale and speed required, the newly empowered Kyiv leaders sought immediate assistance from those who had money: the country's oligarchs. Controversially, they were offered key regional governor posts.[64] On 2 March 2014, Ihor Kolomoisky, Ukraine's second richest man, who owned (until 2017) the country's largest bank (PrivatBank) and several other large corporations including the popular 1+1 television channel, and Ukraine International Airlines, was appointed Governor of Dnipropetrovsk oblast. Kolomoisky's corrupt relationship to previous successive Ukrainian governments was a poorly guarded secret, and immediately after Yanukovych's ouster his appointment caused an uproar among Maidan activists: how could an oligarch be put into a position of power?[65] Even more controversially, the position of Governor of Donetsk oblast had apparently been offered to Ukraine's richest oligarch, Rinat Akhmetov—a former confidant of the ousted President—but the metals, energy and coal tycoon had refused. Serhiy Taruta—16th in Forbes' ranking of rich Ukrainians, and owner of key metal works in Mariupol—was asked to fill the job. As in Kolomoisky's case, Taruta's appointment was contentious, but given the complete decimation of Ukraine's state finances, and the need for strong, authoritative leadership in the key regions of the east, the decision of the post-Yanukovych leadership to turn to the oligarchs for help was understandable.

Less understandable were the back-room deals struck by the new leaders with key members of the old regime. For example, on 22 April 2014, Presidential candidate Petro Poroshenko, UDAR party leader Vitaliy Klitschko, and two of their confidants, travelled to Vienna to meet with oligarch Dmytro Firtash who had made the Austrian capital home to avoid prosecution. Their encounter was also attended by Yanukovych's former Presidential Administration Head, and

Firtash's business partner Serhiy Lyovochkin. During a 28-hour marathon meeting, the 6 men agreed that Klitschko (whose UDAR party
had apparently been receiving financing from Firtash since 2012)
would not run for President but would receive Poroshenko's support
for his candidacy for mayor of Kyiv. Furthermore, UDAR and Poroshenko would form an alliance during any future Parliamentary
elections.[66] Most importantly, Poroshenko received Firtash's support
(including the campaign machine of the UDAR party) for his Presidential bid. Although the Ukrainian President denied any connection,
years later many Maidan activists were convinced that the leniency of
prosecutors towards Lyovochkin and other seemingly moderate former officials of the Yanukovych regime could be traced to the deal
struck by Poroshenko in Vienna in April 2014.

Back-room deals, and high-level appointments made for great
news and discussion in social media, but in the aftermath of Yanukovych's ouster, the more boring business of government needed to
be done also. Indeed, Maidan had promised that this business would
now be done differently: more openly, eradicating corruption, and
with greater efficiency. Reform became the dominant discourse and
given the lack of capacity for change encountered by the new leaders
within their own ministries (i.e. incompetent in-post civil servants
and/or mass vacancies caused by the departure of government managers who had served under the previous regime), they relied heavily
on volunteers from among Maidan activists. This author personally
became involved in drafting the new Law on Higher Education—
passed in first reading on 8 April[67] and adopted by the Rada in its final
version on 1 July 2014.[68] Other Maidan-initiated reforms included the
"Prozorro" public procurement system,[69] transformation of the Soviet-era Ukrainian militia into a western-style police force,[70] lustration
and creation of anti-corruption institutions. Each of these initiatives
were driven by volunteers who entered the new government from the
Maidan—most had no public sector experience, and many put successful business careers on hold.

Certainly, many of the Maidan-initiated reforms required western assistance. Furthermore, rescuing Ukraine's economy—stripped
bare by Yanukovych and his cronies, but also sapped by the exigencies

of having to fight insurgency in the east — could not be accomplished without external help. Western financial institutions and governments could not legally assist Ukraine until the question of the legitimacy of the new authorities was resolved. Andriy Deshchytsia, Ukraine's extremely able post-Yanukovych top diplomat was titled "acting" Foreign Minister. The same was true for Defense, SBU and Prosecutor General: the Ukrainian Constitution required that candidates for each of these posts be appointed first by the President and then approved by Parliament. Without a legitimately elected President, these executive positions were filled with Parliamentary appointees — a fact that precluded their involvement in international negotiations as equals. Given the disastrous state of the economy, resolving this legitimacy issue was a top priority.

Poroshenko

On 25 May 2014 Petro Poroshenko was elected President of Ukraine, with 55% support nationally, and a majority in all electoral districts except one (Kharkiv oblast — district 178). Residents of Russian occupied Crimea, and of the portions of Donetsk and Luhansk oblasts where violence precluded a safe election did not vote but overall, the election was declared free and fair by both international and domestic observers.[71]

Poroshenko's victory in the first round was unprecedented. No candidate in Ukraine's post-Soviet history had enjoyed such broad-based national support. As the map below demonstrates, in 2014, the regional cleavages that had characterized all previous Ukrainian elections disappeared. Electoral support of this magnitude had not been enjoyed by anyone in Ukraine since the election of Kravchuk in December 1991 — prior to the official dissolution of the USSR.

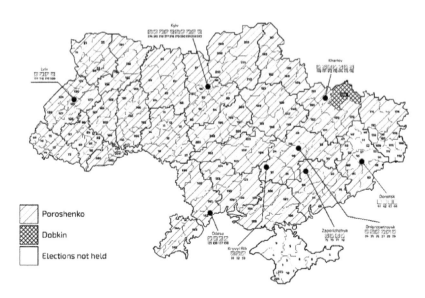

Map 5:   2014 presidential election results by electoral district

During the campaign, Poroshenko avoided criticizing acting President Turchynov openly. However, on the day after the vote, with exit
polls predicting his victory, the President-elect stated that in his opinion, any Anti-Terrorist Operation (ATO) should not last 2-3 months; it
should last for hours; Ukrainian forces should be well paid, well
equipped, and then the effectiveness of the ATO would increase dramatically.[72] These words would prove to haunt Poroshenko in future
months when "ATO" would become a widely criticized euphemism
for what effectively became a full scale war.[73] On the day that Poroshenko beamed optimism as to the prospects of resolving the conflict in the Donbas, the first battle for Donetsk airport was engaged
with over 40 "insurgents" reported killed by Ukrainian forces; later it
was revealed that 34 of the dead were Russian nationals whose bodies
were covertly transported to the Russian Federation for burial.[74]

These initial victories emboldened the new President, and in
those early days, Poroshenko clearly underestimated the likelihood of
direct Russian military intervention in the Donbas. He seemed to be
convinced that a deal with the Kremlin could be reached. During his
first week in office Poroshenko held several secretive meetings with

Russian ambassador Zurabov and Kremlin officials in the Presidential Administration building, and apparently called Putin several times to discuss ways to end the violence in the Donbas. Each time he informed EU and US officials of the results, and although details of the Poroshenko peace plan were not made public, apparently, Ukraine's western partners were encouraged by the efforts of the new President. On June 18, amid news of brutal fighting throughout the region, Poroshenko announced a 14-point peace plan that entailed amnesty for separatists who had not committed violent crimes, safe passage out of Ukraine for foreign fighters, and a promise of increased autonomy for the region. The leadership of the Donetsk and Luhansk "People's Republics" immediately rejected Poroshenko's offer and vowed to continue their insurgency, but on 20 June 2014, Ukrainian forces were ordered to unilaterally cease fire nevertheless.

Chapter 6:
War and Reform

With the election of a new Ukrainian President on 25 May 2014 some measure of stability in Ukraine's domestic politics was achieved. However, peace on the eastern border remained a distant prospect, and the return of sovereignty over Crimea was relegated to some unidentifiable future. Direct and overt invasion by Russia of Ukraine's mainland territory had been foreshadowed many months before, but few really believed the skirmishes and obviously staged protests in the Donbas would degenerate into full-scale war. Indeed, immediately after his election, President Poroshenko promised to put an end to the Anti-Terrorist Operation (ATO) within weeks. After that, the focus of his Presidency was to be domestic reform.

Poroshenko's promise was either overly optimistic or the newly elected President was misinformed because Ukraine's military situation in the spring of 2014 did not indicate a high probability of a quick end to conflict with Russia. Although intelligence from March and April 2014 was not made publicly available until several months later, it is now clear that immediately after Yanukovych's departure from Kyiv, the Kremlin ordered its troops to full combat readiness, and Ukraine's interim leaders were made fully aware of the threat. According to Andriy Parubiy, Acting Secretary of the National Security and Defense Council, over 100,000 Russian troops massed on Ukraine's eastern border throughout the spring of 2014. These forces included at least 370 artillery systems (e.g. "Grad" multiple launch rocket systems), 270 tanks and 140 combat aircraft.[1] According to the transcript of the National Security and Defense Council meeting held on February 28 (i.e. at the height of the Crimean crisis), acting President Turchynov interrupted the discussion of the situation on the peninsula to respond to a phone call from Russian Duma Chairman Naryshkin.[2] Apparently the message from Moscow was direct and unequivocal: the Russian Federation would resort to full-scale war if the "rights of Russians and Russian-speakers in Ukraine *continued* to be threatened." No evidence of such rights actually being threatened was ever provided, but given the troop build-up on the border, Naryshkin's warning was taken seriously. Poroshenko's apparent assumption, three months later, that Putin would not order Russian regular forces into continental Ukraine if his agents' incitement of separatism in the Donbas failed (and especially if it succeeded) was naïve at best.

Admirably however, against the backdrop of impending all-out war with Russia, Ukraine's new leadership embarked on an impressive domestic reform program. The country's dire economic situation left them little choice but to institute fundamental changes to the economy, and many of their reform initiatives were generously supported by western donors. Objectively, more was achieved during the 3-4 years following the Maidan protests than during the previous two decades of Ukraine's independence. But expectations after the Maidan protests were also exceptionally high (both domestically and among Ukraine's international partners), and inevitably many were left disappointed with the pace and results of the reform effort.

This chapter chronicles the main events of the violent military conflict with Russia (ongoing at time of writing—four years after its start) and presents an evaluation of the domestic reforms instituted during this period by Ukraine's post-Yanukovych leadership. The story of the war in Ukraine's Donbas, and the failed attempt to expand hostilities beyond the territorially small but important industrial region is laid out; an account of the valiant efforts of both the fledgling government (particularly on the diplomatic front), and of ordinary Ukrainians to stop Russia's onslaught and maintain the territorial integrity of their country is presented. Finally, the various domestic initiatives aimed at improving the lives of Ukrainians are evaluated.

Mobilization of volunteers

The fighting in the Donbas throughout April-June 2014 escalated on both sides gradually. In the beginning, the separatists enjoined groups of 10-20 armed men to attack and occupy government buildings in the various mining towns in the region: Horlivka, Kramatorsk, Slovyansk, Yenakiyevo, Makiyivka, Druzhkivka, Luhansk, and Donetsk. The industrial city of Mariupol on the Azov Sea was also targeted. The

Ukrainian response was to send in small groups of police, and later (after multiple cases of disloyalty)[3] SBU and Armed Forces personnel, to disperse the armed groups. At their strongest, before the events of August 2014 (see Turning Point below), Ukrainian military units operating in the Donbas rarely numbered more than 80-100 men.

As reinforcements and weaponry became available to the separatist forces (sent clandestinely from Russia), their military engagements became more deadly: on 22 May 2014, 16 Ukrainian soldiers were killed and 12 wounded when a checkpoint near Volnovakha (Donetsk oblast) was shelled with mortars; on 29 May, 14 Ukrainian military personnel were killed, including General Kulchytsky, when a Mi-8 helicopter was shot down by a mobile rocket launcher near Kramatorsk (Donetsk oblast); on 14 June, a Ukrainian Air Force IL-76 transport plane was shot down on approach to Luhansk airport by a shoulder-launched surface-to-air missile killing all 49 troops and crew onboard.[4] By mid-June 2014 it had become clear that what had started as a separatist insurgency fomented by men armed with pistols, rifles and grenades, had evolved into a military operation whose participants had received military training and were equipped with heavy weapons.

On the Ukrainian side, the reaction to the escalation of the Donbas insurgency was to mobilize men and resources. Already in March, Acting President Turchynov issued a decree requiring reservists to report for duty in the Armed Forces.[5] This was followed by a second decree in May, according to which the Ukrainian Armed Forces were ordered to create "territorial defense battalions" in each oblast where volunteers would receive training, and (eventually) be tasked with combat assignments.[6] In the end, 32 volunteer battalions were created in 2014, including "Aidar" (initially created by Maidan Self-Defense activists) which saw action in Luhansk oblast.[7] In addition to the territorial defense units under the command of the Armed Forces, volunteer battalions were formed under the command of the Ministry of the Interior. These were also organized territorially with some of the 22 created units reaching regiment strength, while others remained squadrons. Their primary task was law enforcement, but several—including Dnipro-1 and "Myrotvorets" ("Peacekeeper"—composed of volunteers from Kyiv region) were deployed into small towns in the Donbas for clean-up operations. Three Interior Ministry volunteer units were organized under the auspices of the newly revived (after May 2014) National Guard: the Azov, Donbas and Kulchytsky battalions. Unlike the other units under the command of the Interior Ministry, the National Guard battalions were authorized to directly engage in combat; in 2015 they were supplied with heavy weaponry and armor.

Relations between the command structures of the Armed Forces and those of the Interior Ministry were tense throughout the early years of the ATO. For example: during the battle of Ilovaysk (see below), the leadership of the Donbas battalion publicly accused the General Staff of abandoning their fighters in the Russian encirclement.[8] To some extent, the military brass' skepticism of the Interior Ministry volunteer battalions was understandable: the existence of armed units outside of the structures of the Armed Forces compromised the principle of unified military command. Prospects of the eventual establishment of private armies in Ukraine frightened several observers[9] — not without justification: in 2015, members of the Dnipro-1 battalion, created with extensive financial support from one-time Dnipropetrovsk governor and oligarch Ihor Kolomoisky, participated in the forceful resolution of commercial disputes involving their patron.[10] Furthermore, the Interior Ministry battalions created in 2014 seemed to attract combat-hungry volunteers with radically right-wing political preferences. For example, the leadership of the "Azov" battalion seemed to profess openly racist views;[11] their *Wolfsangel* symbol and balaclava-wearing fighters became the brunt of much criticism.[12] On the other hand, Azov fighters were exceptionally well disciplined and effective in the operation to retake Mariupol in July 2014. Similarly, the Right Sector — led by the understated Dmytro Yarosh — whose members had been among the most active in fighting the "Berkut" riot police during the Maidan protests, and then were among the first to volunteer for military service after Yanukovych's ouster — saw action in some of the hottest battles of the Kremlin-sponsored insurgency. From its inception, the Right Sector attracted young men who were highly skeptical of the formal structures of the Ukrainian state (especially the Interior Ministry); theirs was an anarchic patriotism that co-opted the symbolism of the WWII era OUN-UPA (and so was vilified by Kremlin propaganda),[13] but also attracted individuals for whom the line between defense of the nation and criminality was often blurred.[14]

Right Sector fighters took part in multiple military operations in the Donbas throughout 2014-2015, including the defense of Donetsk airport, the battle for Mount Karachun (near Slovyansk), and the liberation of Avdiyivka (13km from Donetsk). However, rather than co-operating with Armed Forces commanders, their small tactical units coordinated their activities with the SBU, and indeed many Right Sector volunteer fighters eventually gained legal legitimacy by signing up for duty in Ukraine's Secret Service.[15] In July 2014, the informally organized Right Sector officially reconstituted itself as the "Right Sector Ukrainian Volunteer Corps" — a brigade-class military unit with multiple battalions (some organized outside of the Donbas theatre), a command center, medical and training facilities, and a diverse logistical supply system. Impressively, these structures were founded, equipped and maintained without financing from the Ukrainian state. For Right Sector's participants therefore, their loyalty to the state needed to be earned — their cause was the defense of the Ukrainian nation (its territory).

Regardless of one's opinion of the efficacy of constituting what amounted to an independent army outside of the state's structures, the Right Sector phenomenon (together with that of other volunteer battalions) was remarkable, and indicative of a broader trend. Throughout 2014, Ukrainians mobilized. Footwear, uniforms, food, electricity generators, Kevlar vests and helmets — all were sourced through grassroots crowdfunding initiatives.[16] Although arms and ammunition were retrieved from legacy-Soviet stocks, targeting optics for snipers, and night vision equipment were obtained through volunteer networks. Organizations such as "Armiya-SOS" (reconstituted from the "Euromaidan-SOS" volunteer group that had provided logistical support to the protesters), "Wings of Phoenix", and "Come Home Alive" (Povernys' zhyvym) sprang up spontaneously, and on a mass scale.[17] Effectively, they created a logistical support network for Ukraine's Armed Forces (including the volunteer battalions, Right Sector, and more traditional Army units) where none existed prior to the start of hostilities.

As the war in the Donbas wore on, and the logistical systems of the Ukrainian Armed Forces were improved, the need for volunteers diminished.[18] However, in the early months of Russia's aggression, without grassroots mobilization — both of volunteer fighters and of the massive logistical supply effort that supported them — it is doubtful that Ukraine's territorial defense would have been as successful as it was.

Slovyansk

As noted in the previous chapter, immediately after his election, President Poroshenko engaged in multiple attempts at negotiating a resolution of the conflict in the Donbas, engaging the support of Germany and France as interlocutors in talks with Russia. The Geneva Accords, negotiated in April 2015 in a marathon session between US and EU leaders and the foreign minister of Russia called for a cessation of hostilities, amnesty, and OSCE monitoring of the situation in the Donbas, but the deal proved ineffective. Throughout May-June (and thereafter), the Kremlin poured heavy weapons and men (i.e. fighters who were either decommissioned Russian army officers or nationalist paramilitaries)[19] into the Donbas. By mid-June Moscow's equipment supplies to the "separatists" included "Grad" multiple launch rocket systems, armored personnel carriers, and tanks,[20] yet Putin persisted in publicly denying Russia's direct involvement.

With the intensity of clashes increasing (tank duels on the territory of Donetsk airport began in late May 2014 and continued on a daily basis thereafter; clashes with pro-Russian forces near Shchastia in Luhansk oblast resulted in the near complete destruction of the Aidar volunteer battalion; a major battle near the town of Yampil enjoined several hundred soldiers on both sides and led to heavy casualties), the need for de-escalation was increasingly becoming obvious. Throughout the latter part of May and early June, reports from the region increasingly indicated a shift in the population's loyalties: if autonomy was to come at the price of lives and mass destruction, the locals were not prepared for that level of sacrifice. On 20 June, less than one week after the Il-76 incident near Luhansk airport which resulted in the deaths of 49 Ukrainian servicemen, Poroshenko announced that Ukrainian forces would unilaterally cease fire for one week. Concurrently, the Ukrainian President announced his peace plan — only to have it immediately rejected by the "DNR" and "LNR" leadership.

On 1 July 2014, the nominal cease fire announced by Poroshenko 10 days earlier was rescinded. Given that casualty figures had continued to mount, maintaining the semblance of "peace" made little sense. During the first week of July, Ukrainian forces scored decisive victories despite facing heavy artillery and Grad multiple launch rocket barrages on several occasions. Slovyansk — the base of operations for the commander of pro-Russian forces in the Donbas, Russian former GRU Colonel Girkin — was cleared of separatist fighters on July 5. On the same day the towns of Druzhkivka, Kostiantynivka, and Artemivsk (later renamed Bakhmut) returned to government control. Kramatorsk was also recaptured. Controversially, a column of separatist troops was allowed to retreat from the area northwest of Donetsk into the oblast center. They fortified their defenses in the city, expecting Ukrainian forces to eventually besiege it or attempt a storm.

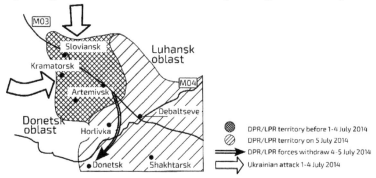

Map 6:   **Ukrainian liberation of Sloviansk and Kramatorsk 1-4 July 2014**

After liberating Slovyansk and Kramatorsk, the Ukrainian Armed Forces' attention switched to dismantling unlawfully established checkpoints along the eastern border of Luhansk oblast and the south-eastern border of Donetsk oblast, and to defending key infrastructure in the oblast centers. The defense of Donetsk airport was eventually to become legendary, but in early July 2014, the epicenter of heavy fighting with tanks, "Grad" multiple launch rockets and heavy artillery was the smaller airport of Luhansk.[21] There Ukrainian paratroopers dug in until the end of August when, because of constant bombardment by artillery and tanks, there was nothing left to defend.

Meanwhile, along the southeastern border of Donetsk oblast, Ukrainian troops advanced quickly until on July 11, near the town of Zelenopillya (due east of Donetsk, 5 km from the Russian border), they were covered by rocket and artillery fire originating from Russian territory. 37 Ukrainian servicemen were killed.[22] During subsequent weeks, shelling by Russian "Grad" and Tornado rocket systems across the border became systematic.[23] Ukrainian troops endured heavy losses. Civilian casualties mounted as well. The advancing Ukrainian forces employed air power on separatist targets, but by early July 2014 the pro-Russian forces had gained access to sophisticated anti-aircraft weaponry, making deployment of airpower by Ukraine risky. After numerous transport and fighter aircraft (helicopters and airplanes) were shot down in early July 2014 over the Donbas, Ukrainian commanders grounded the country's Air Force for the duration of the ATO.

Turning points

On 17 July 2014, the Kremlin's gradual escalation of the conflict in the Donbas hit a climax (one of several that would be forthcoming as the war unraveled). On this day Malaysian Airlines flight MH-17 on route from Amsterdam to Kuala Lumpur and overflying the conflict zone at an altitude of 33,000 feet (just over 10,000 m), was shot down by a hi-tech BUK surface-to-air missile brought to Ukraine from Russia. All 298 persons onboard were killed. Responsibility for the downing of this passenger airliner was never admitted by Moscow, but evidence gathered both by the Dutch-led official investigations into the crash,[24] and by the independent Bellingcat investigative organization[25] proved conclusively that the sophisticated weapon that brought down the Boeing 777 was operated by a Russian crew, and that the system itself originated from the 53rd Anti-Aircraft Missile Brigade based in Kursk.[26] Apparently, the convoy that had transported the BUK missile to the Donbas entered Ukrainian territory on 23-24 June 2014 and was photographed on route on several occasions.

In the immediate aftermath of the MH-17 disaster Valentyn Nalyvaychenko, Acting Head of the SBU, voiced a plausible theory as to what happened that fateful day. Apparently, there are two towns in Donetsk oblast named Pervomaysk (the name translates into Russian as "First of May" — a common Soviet-era designation given to small settlements). According to Nalyvaychenko, the BUK missile system was supposed to have been stationed near the Pervomaysk that is located northwest of Donetsk (near the town of Pisky) but was mistakenly deployed to the Pervomaysk that is south of the town of Snizhne near the border between Donetsk and Luhansk oblasts (adjacent to Torez where the wreckage of MH-17 crashed). If the weapon system had been deployed to the correct Pervomaysk, the BUK missile would have shot down an Aeroflot flight on route from Moscow to Larnaca Cyprus crossing the airspace of the Donbas at a similar altitude and time as MH-17. Nalyvaychenko contended that had that flight been downed (and had the wreckage fallen on government-controlled territory), the Kremlin would have used this event as a pretext for open invasion of mainland Ukraine.[27]

Before the downing of MH-17, the Kremlin had argued with some degree of credibility that the heavy artillery, tanks, and "Grad" rocket systems used by "separatist" forces in their battles against the Ukrainian Army had been captured in battle, or taken from local stockpiles left over from the Soviet era (not imported from Russia), and that the men operating this equipment were local disgruntled residents of the Donbas and/or Russian volunteers operating without direct orders from the Kremlin. Until July 17, evidence of direct participation by Russian forces had been limited — except for shelling across the border (see above). However, the firing of a hi-tech BUK surface-to-air missile was obviously not the work of local insurgent coal miners. Successful operation of a weapon of this type required significant training, and the weapon itself was not readily available in the conflict zone. For western leaders, the downing of MH17 represented the first turning point in the conflict in the Donbas. This war could no longer be considered an internal conflict over differing visions of Ukraine's development: this was a war between two sovereign states in which the aggressor had sought to fight through proxies but was increasingly becoming directly involved (albeit still in a limited way).

On the day MH-17 was shot down, the territory of the Donbas still controlled by the "People's Republics" had shrunk to a fraction of its size just a month earlier. The Ukrainians' strategy after the liberation of Slovyansk and Kramatorsk had involved maintaining control over the north-south road that connected the city of Donetsk and the Azov port of Mariupol, and from there, advancing northeast along the Russian border. The plan was to surround the separatist forces in Donetsk and Luhansk, cutting off their supply lines from Russia by stationing Ukrainian troops between the two oblast centers and the border.

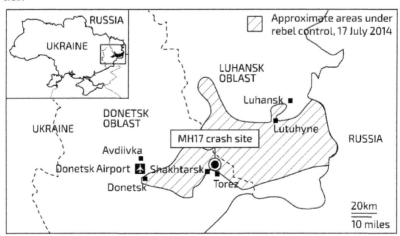

Map 7:   Territory controlled by "People's Republics" on 17 July 2014

By mid-August 2014, looking at the map of the ATO zone one could not be faulted for believing the conflict was on the verge of completion. The city of Luhansk, although not liberated, was completely surrounded by Ukrainian forces, and its outskirts had been entered by volunteer battalion fighters; Donetsk was not yet surrounded, but its main supply line to Russia had been cut; a thin strip of territory stretching eastward from Torez (near the MH17 crash site) through Krasny Luch, Antratsyt and Krasnodon to the Russian border had not yet been retaken by government forces, but this territory included no large cities, and so clearing it of pro-Russian insurgents was deemed a matter of weeks.

The immediate task of the ATO commanders was to surround Donetsk: troops that had pushed eastward along the southeastern Ukrainian border, and had endured shelling from Russia, were now ordered to move north towards the MH-17 crash site; meanwhile forces from Artemivsk (later renamed Bakhmut) were sent south towards Horlivka. Understanding that such a maneuver would result in the complete isolation of the city of Donetsk, Russian military commanders moved to assist their separatist proxies. Ground forces of the Russian army were ordered to cross into Ukrainian territory, and the successes of Ukraine's primarily volunteer forces were quickly reversed.

The exact circumstances and scale of the insertion of Russian Army ground forces into the Donbas conflict remains unclear, but the sequence seems to have occurred as follows:[28] on 23 August Special Forces troops dressed in uniforms without markings set up a checkpoint near Amvrosiyivka, 10 km from the Russian border inside Ukraine; on 24 August a column of 250 Russian vehicles crossed the border into Novoazovsk and took control of the main road leading to the Azov Sea port of Mariupol; on the same day a column of approximately 100 Russian tanks and self-propelled artillery vehicles reportedly crossed the southeastern Ukrainian border, and moved north towards Donetsk through the towns of Starobesheve and Kuteinykove (west of Amvrosiyivka). The presence of Russian tanks and artillery was detected by NATO, which issued a statement estimating 1000 Russian troops had entered Ukrainian territory; Alexander Zakharchenko, the leader of the "Donetsk People's Republic" admitted the number was closer to 3-4 thousand.[29] Whatever the exact number, their presence to the southeast of Donetsk effectively meant the

Ukrainian forces operating in the vicinity of the town of Ilovaysk were surrounded.[30]

On 29 August 2014, after receiving personal assurances from both Russian President Putin and "DNR" leader Zakharchenko that the Russian and separatist forces surrounding the Ukrainian units would allow a corridor for their retreat, the volunteer battalions in the vicinity of Ilovaysk began their withdrawal.[31] As they retreated, their columns were fired upon, and many were taken prisoner. According to official sources, of the over 1800 Ukrainian fighters in Ilovaysk, 368 died that day, over 300 went missing in action (some were later to be confirmed dead), and 310 were taken prisoner.[32] Eyewitness estimates of losses were significantly higher.[33] The Ukrainian Prosecutor General later reported that the Ukrainian forces in Ilovaysk in late August were outnumbered 18:1; the Russian Army had moved tanks into the area, outnumbering the Ukrainian deployment 11:1; artillery—15:1; "Grad" rocket systems—24:1.[34]

The tragedy of Ilovaysk represented a turning point in the ATO from which Kyiv would never really recover. The Ukrainian forces in the battle were highly fragmented with multiple chains of command, and significant difficulty managing inter-unit communications. The volunteer battalions under Interior Ministry command included the Donbas and Azov National Guard battalion, together with the Dnipro-1, Peacekeeper, Shakhtarsk, Kherson and Svitiaz police units.[35] Ukrainian Armed Forces units included: the 17th Tank Brigade, units of the 93rd, 28th and 51st Separate Mechanized Brigades, the 39th, 40th and 42nd Territorial Defense Battalions.[36] According to Ilovaysk participant testimonials, after the Russian regulars surrounded the Ukrainian forces, significant numbers deserted their posts—how many remains unknown.[37]

In ensuing weeks, the demoralized Ukrainian forces regrouped, but lost territory was never recovered. A comparison of two maps of the Donbas prepared just three weeks apart indicates that in mid-August areas formerly controlled by pro-Russian forces had been almost cleared. But most of these were returned to Russian military control by early September, and indeed additional territory (the strip of land connecting the "DNR" to the Azov Sea) was occupied. This line of contact between Ukrainian and Russian forces now constituted the effective border of the separatist enclave with Ukraine and would remain relatively unchanged (at least in Donetsk oblast) until the end of 2014.

Map 8:   Comparison of "DNR/LNR" controlled territory before and after Russian invasion in August 2014.

Diplomacy

While fighting during the summer of 2014 continued in the Donbas, an international "contact group" chaired by Swiss diplomat and OSCE representative Heidi Tagliavini met periodically in Minsk Belarus. The "DNR" and "LNR" were represented at the negotiating table by Aleksandr Zakharchenko and Igor Plotnitsky,[38] whereas Russia delegated its ambassador to Ukraine Mikhail Zurabov. The interests of Ukraine were represented by former President Leonid Kuchma—a fact that raised eyebrows domestically since many remembered the multiple political scandals that plagued Kuchma's second term in office (e.g. the disappearance of journalist Georgiy Gongadze which sparked mass demonstrations in 2001), and his erstwhile support for Yanukovych during the 2004 presidential election which led to the Orange protests. However, despite skepticism as to the choice of representatives, the Minsk Contact Group established a platform for negotiations between the warring parties and for high level meetings.

During the first Contact Group meetings, the direct involvement of Russian troops in Ukraine had not yet been established beyond doubt. After MH-17, and then the battle of Ilovaysk, any doubt that may have existed as to the Kremlin's direct military role in the Donbas dissipated. A hasty meeting between Poroshenko and Putin (mediated by German Chancellor Merkel and French President Hollande) was organized in Minsk in the wake of the battle, and significant resources were mobilized to try bring Russia to heal. The world was shocked by the Kremlin's audacity. During the 24th meeting of the Security Council on Ukraine, Samantha Power, the US ambassador to the UN, dropped any previous diplomatic language:

> Russia has come before this Council to say everything except the truth. It has manipulated. It has obfuscated. It has outright lied. So, we have learned to measure Russia by its actions and not by its words. In the last 48 hours, Russia's actions have spoken volumes.

> On August 26—just this Tuesday—after meeting with Ukrainian President Poroshenko in Minsk, Belarus, President Putin spoke of the need to quote "end bloodshed as soon as possible." End quote. Yet the same day, satellite imagery show(s) Russian combat units–combat units— southeast of Donetsk, in eastern Ukraine. That same day in Luhansk, Ukraine detained regular Russian Army personnel from the 9th brigade…

> The day after those talks, Russia fired Grad rockets from inside Russia at Ukrainian positions in Novoazovsk, and then attacked with two columns of Russian armored vehicles and tanks. Russian armored vehicles and Uragan multiple rocket launchers are positioned on the outskirts of that town as we speak.

> Russia's force along the border is the largest it has been since it began redeploying forces there in late May and includes significant numbers of combat aircraft and helicopters. Russian unmanned aircraft routinely cross into Ukrainian airspace.

> Other Russian deployments into Ukrainian territory include advanced artillery and air defense systems not found in the Ukrainian inventory. These artillery systems have shelled Ukrainian positions outside

Luhansk City in conjunction with the recent separatist counteroffensive.[39]

The US diplomatic position with respect to the Kremlin's aggression in Ukraine was clear. On the other hand, tough talk did not entail action against Russia: NATO troops were not deployed to Ukraine (the alliance was not required to defend a non-member), military aid was not provided (Obama administration officials feared supplying weapons would escalate the conflict), economic sanctions were imposed against targeted officials only (trade with Russia was not stopped completely because this would have hurt the interests of western companies). Stopping further Russian aggression on the ground was up to Ukraine, but with the country's forces routed in Ilovaisk (and further deployments of Russian forces within Ukrainian territory — in addition to Crimea — considered likely), President Poroshenko's bargaining position with Putin was less than enviable.

On September 7, following a very public meeting in Minsk, where Poroshenko was shown on camera reluctantly shaking the hand of a smirking Russian President, the first "Minsk Protocol" was agreed. In what represented a diplomatic victory for the Kremlin, the document was signed by the Ukrainian President and the two leaders of the separatist republics, and merely witnessed by the leaders of France, Germany and Russia (Putin insisted Moscow was not a party to the conflict). The agreement consisted of 12 points, largely reflecting the original Poroshenko peace plan first announced in June:[40] It called upon both sides to:

1. ensure an immediate bilateral ceasefire,
2. ensure the monitoring and verification of the ceasefire by the OSCE,
3. agree decentralization of power in the Donbas, including through the adoption by Ukraine of a special law "On Local Self-Governance in Particular Districts of Donetsk and Luhansk Oblasts,"
4. ensure the permanent monitoring of the Ukrainian-Russian border and verification by the OSCE with the creation of security zones in the border regions of Ukraine and the Russian Federation,

5. secure the immediate release of all hostages and illegally detained persons,
6. agree the amnesty from prosecution and punishment of persons in connection with the events that have taken place in some areas of Donetsk and Luhansk Oblasts,
7. continue inclusive national dialogue,
8. take measures to improve the humanitarian situation in Donbass,
9. ensure early local elections in accordance with the Ukrainian law "On Local Self-Governance in Particular Districts of Donetsk and Luhansk Oblasts",
10. withdraw illegal armed groups and military equipment as well as fighters and mercenaries,
11. adopt a program of economic recovery and reconstruction for the Donbass region,
12. provide personal security for participants in the consultations.

As the Minsk-1 agreement was being finalized, fierce fighting erupted near Mariupol on the Azov Sea. Besides the fact that this city represented one of Ukraine's key industrial centers, it was strategically positioned as the last major urban center between the Russian border and the northern coast of Crimea. If the Russians occupied Mariupol, there would be little to stop them from punching through a land bridge to the newly annexed peninsula. After Ilovaysk, Ukraine was left with no reserves in the area: the entire territory between Mariupol and Odesa was defended by what was left of the 79th Brigade.

In the aftermath of the Minsk meeting however, the Kremlin's appetite for further war in eastern Ukraine seems to have diminished. On 6-7 September 2014 Mariupol was shelled with "Grad" rockets from newly occupied positions to the east (the town of Novoazovsk fell to Russian troops on 27 August), but after several 4-way telephone conversations between Poroshenko, Putin, Merkel and Hollande, the assault was called off. The Ukrainian President visited the city on 8 September 2014 and announced that 1,200 prisoners had been exchanged during the past days, and that prospects for a complete cease fire (as required by the Minsk Agreements) and eventual peace looked favorable.

Donetsk airport and Debaltseve

The President's optimism was belied by the 30-50 ceasefire violations reported daily throughout the autumn of 2014. Although no longer a war of advancing/retreating fronts, intense fighting was reported daily in Donetsk oblast around Donetsk Airport, and in the vicinity of the town of Debaltseve. In Luhansk oblast the primary target of artillery bombardment was the town of Shchastya (ironically this word means "happiness" in Ukrainian and Russian).

Donetsk Airport was primarily a symbolic target: throughout the autumn of 2014, fierce battles were engaged for control of the new terminal—constructed in preparation for the 2012 European Football Championship, and completely decimated 30 months later. Strategically, the airport was marginally significant because of its location on the outskirts of the city of Donetsk, but the fact that it had been continuously held by Ukrainian forces (despite daily attacks) since the first deployment of paratroopers there in late May 2014, gave it emblematic status. The destroyed hulk of the airport's control tower became symbolic of Ukrainian resistance to Russian aggression—comparable to the *yolka* on Maidan. The airport's defenders were called "cyborgs"—reportedly so named by the separatists who claimed the Ukrainians seemed invincible. Throughout November-December 2014 the cyborgs were blasted repeatedly by heavy artillery, mortars, rockets and tank shells. After four months of heavy fighting, their positions finally were overrun by separatist fighters and Russian mercenaries in mid-January 2015. The airport fell on 20 January 2015.

Forcing Ukrainian troops to abandon the airport facilities represented an important symbolic victory for the "DNR". However, their Russian commander-curators set their sights on more strategic targets: the main roads to and from Donetsk. To the south, on the road to the oblast's second largest city Mariupol, stands the town of Volnovakha (liberated by Ukrainian forces in May 2014). On 13 January 2015 the checkpoint on the road outside of the town was hit by a "Grad" attack.

83 rockets were fired from "DNR"-controlled Dokuchayevsk. 12 civilians were killed and dozens more injured. According to a telephone intercept made public by the SBU, the launch was ordered by Shpakov, a Ukrainian citizen who enlisted in the "DNR" armed forces, but whose commander/curator was Col. Sinelnikov of the Russian Army.

To the north of Donetsk, the small town of Debaltseve (pre-war population: 25 thousand) was identified as strategic. It was targeted for three reasons. Firstly, the town hosts a key railway junction, gaining control of which would allow the supply of equipment and ordinance between the cities of Donetsk and Luhansk along the main railway line. Secondly, the road linking Horlivka and Donetsk to the town of Alchevsk and the city of Luhansk passes through Debaltseve. Thirdly (and perhaps most importantly), in a northwesterly direction, the road from Debaltseve heads towards the strategic town of Artemivsk (now renamed Bakhmut—home of Ukraine's largest salt mine, providing over 90% of the country's salt), and then to Slovyansk from where the original "separatist" movement had started in mid-2014, and then on to Kharkiv.

During its mid-2014 advance into Donetsk oblast, the Ukrainian Army liberated Debaltseve from "separatist" forces on 28 July 2014, but the town was held in a "pocket"—surrounded from the east, west and south by the enemy. In January 2015, pro-Russian separatists, and Russian regular army troops massed around this key strategic town and prepared to push forward to retake territory lost to Ukrainian troops earlier. On 17 January 2015, pro-Russian forces began shelling Ukrainian positions in and around the city from all sides. The intense artillery barrage continued for 3 days. When the infantry advance began, Ukrainian forces experienced mass desertions and dereliction of duty,[41] and although Debaltseve itself continued to be held, the town of Vuhlehirsk, 13km to the west, was occupied by "DNR" forces on 27 January. During subsequent days the pro-Russian forces attempted to cut the supply lines of the remaining Ukrainian troops in Debaltseve—to encircle them in the same way as had been done in Ilovaysk.

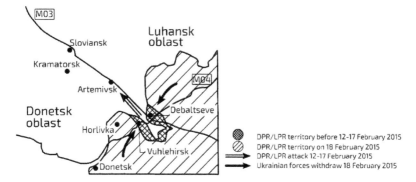

Map 9:   The Debaltseve encirclement

Russian regulars were directly involved in the battle of Debaltseve: Ukrainian soldiers on the ground reported being bombed by Russian aircraft.[42] The town was key to Putin's negotiation strategy in Minsk. According to participants in that 11 February meeting, unlike the German, French and Ukrainian leaders who relied on their advisors and assistants in the negotiations, Putin ran his show alone. According to Poroshenko, the Russian President referred to Debaltseve several times, claiming that the situation there was dire for the Ukrainian forces which had, apparently, been surrounded by their opponents and were preparing to surrender *en masse*.[43] The Russian President believed that a Ukrainian military defeat at Debaltseve was imminent, and that such a defeat would represent the end of Kyiv's ability to project any defensive capacity in the Donbas in the future. This would have strengthened Putin's hand in the Minsk negotiations, allowing him to extract concessions both from Poroshenko and from the Merkel-Hollande tandem that represented the West. As it happened, Ukrainian forces withdrew from Debaltseve under intense fire on 18 February 2015, but a massacre of the kind that occurred 6 months before at Ilovaysk was avoided. Of the approximately 6,000 deployed Ukrainian servicemen, 267 lost their lives in the battle of Debaltseve.

Implementing "peace"

The second Minsk Agreement was signed on 15 February 2015. Its terms differed minimally from of Minsk-1, but this time Putin was forced to admit to being a party to the conflict: at the insistence of Merkel, Hollande and Poroshenko, the Russian President personally signed the deal.

Minsk-2 instituted an OSCE-monitored ceasefire from 15 February 2015 (enforced — in large measure — only after the Ukrainian withdrawal from Debaltseve on 18 February), a withdrawal of heavy weaponry from the line of contact (required pullback distances depended on artillery caliber), and release of prisoners of war (according to the principle of "all for all").[44] These measures raised minimal objections from Ukraine's political class, but the political provisions of Minsk-2 were much more controversial. Specifically, the agreement called for Ukraine to modify its Constitution to enshrine the linguistic, economic and political autonomy of the "Particular Districts of Donetsk and Luhansk Oblasts". These regions were to be given the constitutional right to engage in separate agreements with the Russian Federation (without the consent of Kyiv), and to appoint their own prosecutors and judges. Individuals involved in the "events that took place in the Donbas" (a euphemism for those responsible for separatist violence) were to be granted immunity from prosecution, and the central Ukrainian government would be responsible for the economic restoration of this territory. The agreement also called for the withdrawal of all foreign military personnel from the region and restoration of government control over the Ukrainian-Russian border, but *only after* local elections in the relevant districts had been run.

These provisions were problematic for two reasons. Firstly, if local elections in the contested regions of the Donbas were to occur prior to the restoration of government control over the Ukrainian-Russian border, the likelihood of such a vote being free and fair was minimal: so long as Kremlin operatives crossed the border from Russia freely, both the voting procedure and ballot count would be fully controlled by Moscow. Furthermore, although the agreement required a withdrawal of heavy weapons from the disputed territories, it did not specifically require removal of Russian troops before the elections. Thus, even if these elections were held in accordance with Ukrainian law (as required by the agreement), they would be supervised by the Russian military. Such a provision amounted to a restoration of Ukrainian sovereignty in name only.

Secondly, the Minsk-2 agreement required Ukraine to enact amendments to its Constitution. Previous deals (e.g. the Geneva Accords of April 2014 and the first Minsk agreement in September 2014) had called for Kyiv to adopt a special law granting increased autonomy to the eastern Donbas. Ukraine's Parliament had passed such legislation in September 2014 immediately after Minsk-1 (the bill was signed into law by Poroshenko on 16 October 2014).[45] Its provisions provided significant autonomy for the disputed regions, including the right to create local police forces not subordinate to Kyiv, and to independently appoint judges and prosecutors; locally elected councils and executives could not be dismissed by the central government. After promulgation, the law was valid for a 3-year term and could be renewed on a yearly basis (as occurred in 2017 and 2018). According to Minsk-2, these provisions—amounting to a "special status" within Ukraine with the right to independently engage in foreign relations with Russia, while also requiring Kyiv to pay for the regions' reconstruction—were now to be enshrined in Ukraine's Constitution.

For many (including this author), the requirement of Minsk-2 to enshrine a special status for the disputed regions of the Donbas into the Ukrainian Constitution amounted to a violation of sovereignty. During an August 2015 meeting at the Presidential Administration of the "21 November Initiative Group" (an informal organization of Maidan activists, media and business leaders, and intellectuals created after the ouster of Yanukovych), Poroshenko was reminded of US Founding Father Thomas Paine's statement: "A constitution is not the act of a government, but of a *people* constituting a government."[46] Accordingly, the text of the Ukrainian Constitution could not be the subject of a "peace" deal, nor could the provisions of the Constitution be dictated by Moscow, Berlin or Paris. Poroshenko disagreed with this position vehemently (and emotionally), arguing that increased autonomy for the disputed regions of the Donbas was a small price to pay for peace, and that the constitutional concessions were required to maintain and strengthen the anti-Putin international coalition his administration had assembled.

Unfortunately, some radicals within Ukraine's polity (in this case supporters of the nationalist "Svoboda" party), and many demobilized volunteers disagreed with the President's position: on 31 August 2015, on the day MP's were scheduled to vote on the Constitutional amendments in first reading, demonstrators gathered in front of the Parliament building, and one of them threw a grenade at the police perimeter around the building.[47] Tragically, one National Guard serviceman was killed, and 90 injured.

This event marked the beginning of the end of Poroshenko's political "honeymoon": throughout the next three years, the President's approval rating steadily declined. In the Donbas, the military situation largely remained unchanged with casualties averaging 3-5 per week throughout 2016-2018. Periodic cease fire agreements were announced and promptly violated, and skirmishes across the line of contact (effectively now a frontline) reported regularly. Kremlin aggression continued to sap Ukraine of valuable resources, but because the conflict had become localized, the Russian-Ukrainian war gradually receded from the attention of the global media.[48]

"Frozen" conflict

During the three years of relative "peace" following the Minsk-2 Agreement—with no significant territorial gains by either side, and few major battles along the continuously smoldering frontline— Ukraine rearmed considerably. Within a remarkably short period the Ukrainian Armed Forces improved their fighting capability significantly, and President Poroshenko even boasted in August 2018 that the country's military would soon be one of the strongest in Europe.[49] With over 250,000 active duty personnel at the close of 2018, this claim seemed relatively plausible. A further 180 thousand operational reservists (many with combat experience) could be called up at a moment's notice if threat of war with Russia reemerged.

In the local Donbas theatre, Ukrainians faced an army that (according to US envoy Kurt Volker) had amassed more tanks in the break-away regions than were stationed in all of western Europe.[50] If in 2014 the combined forces of the "DNR" and "LNR" counted 30 tanks that had been captured and/or commandeered from Ukrainian army bases in the Donbas, by mid-2016 the "separatist" forces fielded almost 600. The Kremlin had also increased deployment of armored vehicles tenfold from 124 in 2014, to 1260 two years later. Artillery and multiple launch rocket systems (e.g. "Grad") had increased from 110 units to 1060, and the 50 anti-aircraft weapons (e.g. "BUK" and "Osa") available to the supposed "insurgents" had become 470 two years after the start of the war.[51] Local fighters among those operating this massive force of armaments became increasingly rare as the conflict dragged on: after 2015, Ukrainian troops—though highly motivated to defend their territory—faced better trained and better equipped fighters from Russia.

Training for the Ukrainian forces was provided by several NATO members. The Yavoriv facility in western Ukraine hosted two significant personnel training operations: the US-led Joint Multinational Training Group (overseen by the 7th Army Training Command), and "Operation Unifier" under Canadian leadership. Each enjoined approximately 250 military trainers and support staff. In addition, the US, UK, Canada, Poland and Lithuania established the Multinational Joint Commission on Defense Reform and Security Cooperation with Ukraine in 2015 to coordinate international assistance aimed at reforming the command structures and military culture of the Ukrainian Armed Forces.[52]

The benefits of military cooperation between NATO and Ukraine were mutual. As US Lt. General Ben Hodges pointed out, no NATO country had ever directly engaged the Russian military in combat. Ukrainians on the other hand, had direct experience of Russian electronic warfare capabilities: they had successfully operated while having all their communications jammed by their opponent, and the US needed to understand how.[53] Another former US Army infantry officer who had previously served two tours of duty in Afghanistan, and was dispatched to the Yavoriv training facility, reported:

> Ukrainian soldiers moving and communicating tactically at a level that matched or exceeded most conventional U.S. units... If the Ukrainians continue to train hard and build combat power—and I suspect that their incentive to do so is greater than that of their (mostly Russian)

adversaries — there is a possible outcome here that I have yet seen described in Western media, nor have I heard it in Russian media, either: Ukraine can defeat the separatists. Ukraine can defeat Russia on the battlefield.[54]

Retired British General Grant was less optimistic. He called on Ukrainian military commanders, and the country's political establishment to reduce their complacency:

Ukraine's senior military act as if they believe they are winning because they are fixated on their successes in this very limited tactical war. They and the Defense Ministry are missing the point, because they are not preparing fast enough for a strategic and operational war that would likely be outside the Donbas and would give no time to mobilize large reserve forces... For soldiers to be forced to stay in one defensive position like Minsk demands is always militarily wrong, because it gives the enemy the strategic advantage. Russia is taking advantage of this fact daily... Ukraine's military position in the Donbas is at a critical risk of encirclement, which is a common Russian strategic act. Russian troops practice this tactic regularly during exercises. Trench warfare also breeds an entrenched mentality among soldiers and staff... The Ukrainian Army gets better every day, but overall it is not one of the best in Europe because it has some critical organizational flaws...[55]

Evaluating the scope and levels of success of Ukraine's military reform is beyond the scope of this book, but the final phrase of the above quote — referencing "critical organizational flaws" — encapsulates the broader problems that extended well beyond the military and seemed endemic to multiple aspects of Ukraine's socio-economic and political realities at the start of the Revolution of Dignity. These became the target of concerted reform efforts after the victory of the Maidan protests and will be examined in the next part of this chapter.

The home front – elections

The Maidan had called for a "complete reboot of the political system." The first element of this demand was enacted in March 2014 when Ukrainians elected a new President. In October 2014 they elected a new Parliament. Despite multiple calls to change the electoral law, the latter vote was conducted according to the previously instituted mixed system: half of the Rada (225 seats) was elected according to a proportional representation (party list) system, and half according to a "first past the post" majority system where candidates contested individual constituencies. Because conducting a fair vote in Crimea and in the occupied portions of Donetsk and Luhansk oblasts was impossible, elections were held in 198 of the 225 defined majority constituencies, meaning that the full complement of MPs elected in 2014 numbered 423 instead of the Constitutionally mandated 450.

The result of the 2014 Parliamentary election was encouraging for Ukraine's future for several reasons. Firstly, for the first time in the country's history, the Communist Party—a consistently pro-Russian and far-left (pro-Soviet) political force—failed to gain enough votes to be represented in the legislature. Secondly, the far-right Svoboda and Right Sector parties also failed to pass the 5% barrier in the proportional vote and were therefore represented only by a few MPs who had won majorities in specific constituencies (e.g. Dmytro Yarosh of the Right Sector—constituency №39 in Dnipropetrovsk oblast; Yuriy Levchenko of "Svoboda"—constituency №223 in Kyiv; Andriy Ilyenko—constituency № 215 in Kyiv). Thirdly, the Opposition Bloc, consisting of former Party of Regions MPs, won a mere 29 seats (9.4% of the national popular vote).

Five parties (in addition to the Opposition Bloc) were able to pass the 5% proportional representation barrier in October 2014, and formed the main factions which majority constituency MPs then joined:

1. The Petro Poroshenko bloc (an alliance between Poroshenko's Solidarity Party and Klitschko's UDAR) gained 21.8% of the popular vote which translated into 63 seats in Parliament. This faction was joined by 69 majority constituency MPs and therefore represented the largest bloc within the Rada with 127 seats.

2. People's Front (a newly formed political party whose mem-
    bers broke away from "Batkivshchyna" after Yulia Tymo-
    shenko's return to politics in 2014), led by Arseniy Yatseniuk,
    was surprisingly able to gain the largest proportion of the
    popular vote — 22.1% — giving it 64 seats + 18 from majority
    constituency MPs who joined the faction.

3. "Samopomich" (Self-Reliance), nominally led by Lviv mayor
    Andriy Sadovyy gained almost 11% of the popular vote
    which translated into 32 seats plus one majority MP. This new
    political force gathered Maidan activists (e.g. Yegor Sobolyev
    and Oksana Syroid) and leaders of the "Donbas" volunteer
    battalion, together with non-oligarch sector entrepreneurs
    (e.g. Oleksiy Skrypnyk and Oleksandr Danchenko) under the
    banner "Just Do it!" ("Viz'my i Zroby!") — a slogan that re-
    flected the moto of many Maidan participants. Support for
    this party was not concentrated in any specific region of
    Ukraine, and in fact Samopomich was unable to gain a major-
    ity of the popular vote in any of Ukraine's 198 constituencies
    (see map below), but nevertheless polled respectable support
    throughout the country.

4. Oleh Liashko's Radical Party won 7.4% of the popular vote,
    and entered Parliament with 22 MPs, having won no addi-
    tional majority constituency seats.

5. "Batkivshchyna," led by former Prime Minister and 2-time
    Presidential candidate Yulia Tymoshenko, gained 5.7% of the
    popular vote which meant 17 seats, plus two MPs who joined
    this faction after having won majority constituencies.

Perhaps the most important outcome of the 2014 parliamentary vote
was that Ukraine's traditional east-west electoral divide, although still
somewhat persistent in the east's support for the Opposition Bloc, had
all but disappeared. Previously, in March 2014, Ukrainians had
elected Petro Poroshenko to the Presidency in an unprecedented single round of voting that belied all previous regional cleavages. Now,

the electorate had again proved that its voting preferences were no longer defined by region.

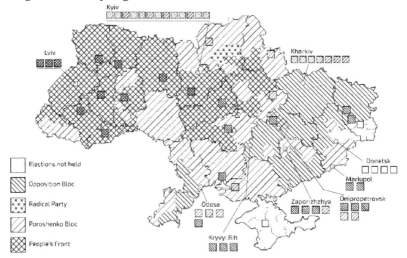

Map 10:   Results of October 2014 parliamentary election popular vote by constituency

Because Arseniy Yatseniuk's People's Front won the popular vote, and because the party had run its campaign under the slogan "Elect Arseniy Yatseniuk as Prime Minister," the leadership of the Poroshenko bloc (and the President personally), agreed to nominate Yatseniuk to the Prime Minister's post—even though his faction had the *second* largest number of seats in Parliament. However, the majority of ministerial seats in the executive branch, and of committee chairs in Parliament, were allotted to Poroshenko Bloc MPs. The candidacy of Oksana Syroid of Samopomich was supported by both factions in her bid for the Deputy Speaker position, whereas the position of First Deputy and Speaker were filled by People's Front and Poroshenko Bloc candidates respectively: Andriy Parubiy and Volodymyr Hroysman.[56]

The five nominally pro-Maidan factions (all elected parties except the Opposition Bloc) signed a grand coalition agreement laying out their agreed legislative plan. The country was in a critical state (facing both military aggression and economic collapse), and so this was deemed no time to jockey for political advantage. Temporarily at least, Ukraine's political class united in a singular understanding that its state and society required reform. Now was the time to institute it.

Revolutionary reform

The reform plan set out by the newly installed Yatseniuk government in early 2015 (publicly supported by Poroshenko) was impressive, and nothing less than revolutionary: based on 6 strategic documents, including the EU-Ukraine Association Agreement Implementation Agenda, the Parliamentary Coalition Agreement, and Ukraine's Memorandum with the IMF, it identified 62 priority measures, and grouped these into 18 key areas. The plan targeted the provision of a wide spectrum of public services as ripe for change: elections, education, energy, taxation, policing, public procurement, health, prosecution service, judiciary, security and defense, local government (decentralization), public service, etc. Monitoring frameworks were established for each reform initiative, and an inter-branch National Reform Council was created to coordinate these broad-based efforts. Chaired by President Poroshenko, the Council included the Prime Minister and relevant ministers, and the Speaker of Parliament and relevant Committee Chairs. Representatives of civil society were also coopted. Dmytro Shymkiv, the former Director of Microsoft Ukraine and a Maidan activist who had been appointed Deputy Head of the Presidential Administration, was chosen as Secretary of the Reform Council; 17 high profile meetings were organized in 2015, and a further 22 in 2016; significant donor funding was engaged; glossy brochures printed, and a website launched to communicate achieved progress, plans, and reform perceptions by sector (based on survey results).[57] The table below summarizes the goals and results of the first two years of execution of Ukraine's post-Yanukovych reform agenda.

Reform Initiative	Objectives	2015	2016
Anti-corruption	- Transparency of incomes, assets of public officials - Merit-based appointments - Effective punishment of (incl. confiscation) for infraction - Watch-dog bodies enable NGO oversight	**Achievements:** - Lustration completed (843 persons registered) - Legislation on integrity checks of public officials adopted; free access to information secured - National Anti-corruption Bureau launched and operating - National Agency for the Prevention of Corruption launched (NAPC) **Failures:** - Delay in launching Special Anti-corruption Prosecutor Office - Software for collection of e-declarations from public servants is flawed	**Achievements:** - Special Anti-corruption Prosecutor Office launched - Over 100 thousand e-declarations showing assets of civil servants and elected officials made publicly accessible **Failures:** - Verification of e-declarations by NAPC delayed - Launch of State Bureau of Investigations delayed - Launch of Special Anti-Corruption Court delayed - No guilty verdicts for suspects charged with corruption-related offenses yet handed down

Decentralization	- Improved effectiveness of local government - Improved service provision for local communities - Transfer of financial resources to local gov't	- Revenues of local governments increased by 42% due to local taxes staying in locality where collected - 794 village and town council voluntarily merged into 159 territorial communities, elections held	**Achievements:** - 1 billion UAH spent on improvements of local infrastructure - New hospital districts formed **Failures:** Further decentralization reforms require Constitutional amendments, and these are hopelessly stalled
Public Administration	- Professional civil service that is responsive to public pressure; capable of both policy development and implementation - Improvement of service provision to citizens - Reduction of staff	- Almost 54,000 central government employees made redundant; efficiency and transparency improved according to WE Forum ranking - New Law on Civil Service passed: competitive selection for all positions; reduction in grades from 15 to 7 - 662 Centers of Administrative Services established providing 51 government services	- Competitive selection of Secretaries of State (permanent deputy Ministers) completed for 9 ministries - Concept of "reform officer" and "reform experts" approved for 10 trial ministries: to be implemented in 2017; EU funding for this initiative is approved - System of electronic document exchange implemented for inter-ministry correspondence by Cabinet of Ministers

Law Enforcement	- Creation of an effective police force that citizens trust - Creation of a renewed and effective prosecutor office	**Achievements:** - Patrol police staffed and operating in 10 cities; training underway in 9; selection underway in 9 **Failures:** - New prosecutors' selection process compromised: pre-Maidan personnel reappointed to key posts at local levels	**Achievements:** - New patrol police operating nationwide; high trust levels **Failures:** - Launch of State Bureau of Investigations delayed - Reform of prosecution service delayed - District police force reform delayed
Health	- Accessibility of quality medicines and vaccines - Improved health care services - Transparent financing that reduces endemic corruption	- Laws allowing procurement of medicine from international organizations without middle-men adopted - reform of the Ministry of Health and decentralization of hospital administration delayed	- Law adopted recognizing the registration of medicines and vaccines in Canada, US, Australia, Japan, or EU as valid in Ukraine. - Autonomation of health care facilities; introduction of pay-per-patient (to replace institutional financing); reform of medical education all delayed due to lack of political will

| **Business Climate** | - Deregulation and decreased numbers of inspections
- Streamlined taxation system
- Harmonization with EU standards | - Number of business activities subject to licensing reduced from 56 to 30; multiple mandatory certificates abolished; moratorium on company inspections introduced
- Payroll taxes reduced from 43% to 30%
- Social Security contribution reduced from 41% to 20%
- Introduction of flat personal income tax – 18%
- Introduction of electronic administration of VAT | - Launch of system of electronic filing of customs documents
- Personal income tax reduced to 17%
- 14,475 Soviet-era standards abolished; over 1000 EU standards adopted
- Ukraine moves from 140th place in World Bank's 2013 Doing Business Ranking to 83rd in 2016 |

Energy	- Liberalization of energy markets - Reduced dependency on Russian natural gas - Increased production of own energy resources	- Gas imports from Russia significantly reduced; replaced by alternative "reverse" supply from EU - Agreement signed with Westinghouse for supply of uranium fuel rods - Energy consumption reduced: electricity by 12%; natural gas by 21% - Share of nuclear power in electricity generation increased from 49% to 56% - State support for coal industry reduced; targeted only for mine drainage and conservation - Introduction of targeted subsidies for vulnerable groups for payment of gas and electricity	- National consumer energy price control body established as independent regulatory agency - Amendments to Law on Renewable Energy introduced to harmonize with EU standards - 2.7 billion UAH in subsidized loans and grants issued to consumers for improvements aimed at energy efficiency - For the first time in history, Ukraine did not buy gas from Russia for a full year
Education	- Modernization of content and learning methods - Equal access to quality primary and secondary education; increased choice - Autonomy for schools and universities	- Implementation of the 2014 Law on Higher Education: introduction of structured PhD programs; academic autonomy for universities; recognition of foreign diplomas; requirement of English proficiency for	**Achievements:** - Over 100 new competence-based Standards of Higher Education developed for the bachelor's level - Concept of "New Ukrainian School" based on competency curriculum developed

			Failures:
		professors' career advancement; transparency of university finances - New Law on Scientific and Scientific-Technical Activity adopted; Ukraine joins Horizon 2020 EU research funding instrument	- Establishment of National Agency for Quality Assurance in Higher Education delayed - Adoption of new Law on Education delayed
Public Procurement	- Transparency of procurement at all levels of government through institution of mandatory electronic auctions - Increased competitiveness of tenders	- ProZorro electronic procurement system developed and piloted – 2300 state customers; almost 6 billion UAH volume - Estimated savings: 500 million UAH	- ProZorro electronic platform is mandatory for all procurement by government at all levels, and large state-owned enterprises - 420 thousand transactions mediated by ProZorro – total volume: over 200 billion UAH - Overall savings estimated at 9 billion UAH - ProZorro receives prestigious "World Procurement Awards" and is recognized at "Open Government Awards"

| Banking | - Financial stability and reliability of banks
- Consumer and investor protection | - Foreign reserves increased from 7.5 billion to 13.3 billion USD; bank refinancing rate decreased from 30% to 22%; inflation stabilized at 12%
- 106 stock market abuse cases prosecuted
- 33 banks deemed insolvent (in addition to 32 in 2014);
- More than 50% of staff of NBU (over 6000 employees) deemed redundant | - Positive assessment of reform progress from IMF: disbursement of 1 billion USD
- Refinancing rate reduced to 14%; inflation – 12%
- 16 more banks deemed insolvent (2014-16 total: 81 banks) Deposit Guarantee Fund disburses funds to consumers with deposits valued under 200 thousand UAH
- PrivatBank (Ukraine's largest bank) nationalized in December, securing liquidity and protecting over 20 million depositors – cost to state: 5.5 billion USD |

Table 2: Reform objectives and major milestones achieved in 2015 and 2016 – based on 2015 and 2016 "Reforms Monitoring Progress" reports of the National Reforms Council

By early 2017 it became clear that although much had been done to change Ukraine during the first three post-Maidan years, the reforms had been poorly communicated to the public: poll results showed widespread skepticism of even the most seemingly successful initiatives (e.g. approval of police reform was at 39%, introduction of "Pro-Zorro" in public procurement at 30%).[58] Although the Poroshenko administration had been prepared for a drop in its popularity resulting from the implementation of several unpopular initiatives (e.g. raising gas and electricity prices to market rates), the ruling elite's appetite for further reform gradually evaporated. Attention increasingly shifted to the upcoming election campaigns: Presidential elections were scheduled for March 2019; a Parliamentary vote for October 2019. In early 2017, Ukrainians were granted visa-free travel rights to the EU, and it would seem that Poroshenko deemed this, together with the signing of the EU Association agreement in 2015, to have been enough to fulfil the Maidan demand for European integration. Although health care reform (which had been lagging behind other reform initiatives during the previous two years) was accelerated thanks to the gutsy system-busting efforts of the Acting Minister of Health, Ukrainian Diaspora-born Ulana Suprun, the creation of a specialized anti-corruption court was delayed, and Parliament's moratorium on the sale of agricultural land extended yet again. Stalled structural reform meant unfulfilled promises to the IMF: the agreed tranche of 1 billion USD scheduled for late 2017 was delayed, and in early 2018, cancellation of the Fund's Stand-by facility by the end of the year could not be ruled out.[59]

Sovereign default was avoided in 2015 after successful negotiations with the IMF resulted in significant financial aid.[60] However, despite some degree of stabilization, Ukraine emerged from two years of political and social turmoil significantly poorer than it had been at the end of the Yanukovych regime. In the 4th quarter of 2015, a slight uptick in GDP statistics (6% quarter-on-quarter growth) was recorded, and 2.3% year-on-year growth was reported for 2016, but given the extreme decline in industrial production of the previous years, coupled with a doubling of consumer prices, and a more than threefold decline in the value of the currency immediately after Yanu-kovych's ouster (from 8:1 UAH:USD to 25:1), minor economic growth was barely noticed. Much needed foreign investment had not materi-alized largely due to the lack of reform of the Procuracy and judiciary (both affecting perceived security of property rights), and due to in-fighting within the political class (mutual accusations of corruption) resulting in overall political instability.

At the end of 2016, Ukraine received its last major dose of eco-nomic shock-therapy. Since the ouster of Yanukovych, 81 commercial banks had been brought under special administration by the National Bank of Ukraine (NBU), and eventually closed. The state guaranteed deposits up to 200,000 UAH (approx. 7,000 USD), but any larger de-posit amounts were generally lost when an institution was declared insolvent. The industry clean-up had been accompanied by significant scandal with several former bank owners suspected of having delib-erately squirrelled away depositors' funds into foreign accounts in off-shore havens prior to NBU intervention. On 28 December 2016, Privat-Bank, Ukraine's largest bank, responsible for the fulfilment of over half of the country's interbank payments—was declared nationalized due to insolvency.[61]

PrivatBank could not be allowed to fail in the same way as other (smaller) institutions. Closing it would have collapsed Ukraine's fi-nancial system. However, despite its massive size, one year after its nationalization, it became clear that this institution had never really been a legitimate bank: over 90% of its loan portfolio consisted of un-secured credit extended to businesses owned or associated with its founders—oligarchs Ihor Kolomoisky and Hennadiy Boholiubov. Ac-cording to documents filed by Ukraine's Ministry of Finance with the High Court of Justice in London, the previous owners of PrivatBank had used over 5 billion USD of their depositors' money to finance highly risky ventures, and to siphon cash out of Ukraine.[62] In Decem-ber 2017, the British court issued a worldwide freeze on assets owned by Kolomoisky and Boholiubov, but the legal wrangling seemed likely to continue for years.

The fact that the PrivatBank case (and the prosecution of other pre-Maidan infractions by oligarchs Firtash[63] and Akhmetov[64]) was brought before western courts rather than being tried domestically, was testament to the slow pace of judicial reform implementation by Ukraine's new elites. In late 2017, a new Supreme Court was finally appointed. Almost a quarter of the nominee finalists had been previously rejected by independent anti-corruption watch-dogs due to their inability to explain the origin of assets accrued while previously serving as lower court judges. They were nevertheless installed in office. Concurrently, inter-agency battles between the National Anti-Corruption Bureau and the Special Anti-Corruption Prosecution Office became public, and in 2018, the IMF openly declared Ukraine's next instalment of bridge financing dependent on implementation of promised anti-corruption initiatives and judicial reforms.[65]

Holding elections that resulted in the removal of high-level Yanukovych regime functionaries was not the same as eradicating corruption. Furthermore, stabilizing the country's economy, reforming the educational, health care and procurement systems, and introducing a new police force (not to mention massively strengthening the army), in the eyes of many, had not yet fulfilled the promise of Maidan to "reboot government." Although elite circulation after the overthrow of Yanukovych was manifest, and significant progress in reforms implementation had been achieved, Ukrainians' generally perceived the transformation of their lives to be too slow. Publicly, the Poroshenko administration declared fighting corruption as its highest priority, but the perception among both Ukrainians and observers abroad throughout the 4 years following the Maidan protests was that the authorities had not done enough to fight the problem. The President was accused by western and local analysts, and by leaders of donor organizations, of systematically stalling anti-corruption initiatives.[66] Some alleged that instead of enabling the overthrow of the oligarchs, Poroshenko had in fact taken charge of their old system of wealth extraction.

In December 2017, the European External Action Service of the European Commission published a progress report evaluating the status and pace of reform implementation as outlined in the Association Agenda (a corollary document to the Ukraine-EU Association Agreement). The report's conclusions were encouraging:

Considerable legislative reforms have taken place in the fight against corruption and new specialized anti-corruption institutions have been set up in Ukraine. Work on implementation of anti-corruption efforts continued over the past year, while further substantial work is still outstanding. Some of the new Ukrainian agencies already participate actively in the fight against corruption, while others remain to be fully operationalized. Ensuring sustainable and tangible changes in the governance system to eliminate corruption opportunities and ensure proper prosecution and punishment for corruption-related crimes remains one of the key challenges Ukraine faces in its reform process hindering the improvement of the business and investment climate.

The year 2017 also witnessed important legislative developments in the spheres of the electricity market, energy efficiency, environment, education and decentralization. Key reforms such as pensions, healthcare and food safety were initiated. Justice sector reform, enabled by the adoption of constitutional amendments back in June 2016, continued with the adoption of a new law on the Constitutional Court and the selection of new judges to the Supreme Court. This allowed the gradual renewal of the judiciary system through mandatory exams for all judges of the newly constituted Supreme Court and now also lower courts. The implementation of the Strategy on Public Administration Reform has advanced, and the reforming of law enforcement bodies continues.

Resolute policy actions taken by the authorities, supported by international partners, have reduced external and internal imbalances and the macro-economic situation continued to stabilize in 2017. As a result, the economy has continued to grow, though at a relatively slow pace. The local currency has remained stable and the international reserves of the central bank have increased steadily. In September 2017, the successful stabilization of Ukraine's economy coupled with the reforms the government has undertaken was marked by its return, after four years, to the international capital markets. Ukraine was able to raise USD 3 billion with a 15-year maturity.[67]

Throughout 2014-2015, the Ukrainian economy experienced dramatic decline. Even excluding the statistical effect of the loss of Crimea (the region contributed approximately 3% to national GDP before the Russian annexation), real GDP declined 6.8% per annum in 2014, and a further 9% in 2015. The drop was accompanied by inflation of 25% in

2014 and over 40% in 2015.⁶⁸ Rising prices were largely the result of a sharp decline in the value of Ukraine's currency which dropped from 8 UAH to 1 USD prior to the Maidan protests to almost 40 UAH to 1 USD in the spring of 2014, settling at a rate of 24-25 UAH to 1 USD by the end of 2015. Not surprisingly, with prices doubling and disposable income declining precipitously, household consumption dropped as well — by almost 70% — and by the end of 2015, Ukrainians' patience with their new government was beginning to run out.

However, in Q4 2016 the economy registered an impressive 4.8% quarter-on-quarter, seasonally adjusted, annualized rate of real GDP growth, and 2.3% growth for the year. Three years after the events that sparked protests on the streets of Kyiv, it seemed the worst of the country's economic decline was over. Growth in 2017-18 was re-strained.⁶⁹ Despite concerted efforts aimed at attracting foreign direct investment, its levels remained muted. On the other hand, exports of both commodity (primarily grains) and non-commodity products (e.g. IT services, machinery components) registered steady gains.

By the end of 2018, Ukraine's post-Yanukovych recession seemed over. The transparent public sector procurement system insti-tuted immediately after the victory of the protests had resulted in the savings of several billion hryvnia for the state budget. Significant loopholes that had previously enabled asset-stripping and tax evasion by oligarchs who exercised effective control over state-owned compa-nies had been plugged (though outright victory in Maidan activists' declared war on high-level corruption was still a distant prospect). Most importantly, the structure of the economy had transformed from one reliant on extractive industry exports (steel, pig iron, fertilizers) that in turn were heavily reliant on energy imports from Russia, to one based on services, high-tech and agricultural exports, and manufac-turing for domestic consumption. By mid-2018, ten consecutive quar-ters of moderate growth had been registered, and growth rates seemed to be accelerating.⁷⁰ Inflation had finally been brought under control,⁷¹ and the country enjoyed a positive balance of trade with IT sector exports almost equaling those of grain. A new Ukrainian econ-omy, transformed by a new neo-bourgeois elite (representatives of the nascent Ukrainian "creative class" — see Chapter 9), seemed to have finally achieved some level of health. But transformation was far from complete. New institutions (both formal and informal) based on the ideas of Maidan had yet to be constructed. The ideational foundations of these proto-institutions, as well as their origins and broader impact on European civilization, will be examined in Part II.

Part Two — Analysis

Introduction to Part II

Two decades after gaining independence, having survived several periods of economic bust (extreme crises occurred in 1993, 1998, 2008,
and in 2014 — each accompanied by major currency devaluations, and
double-digit percentage spikes in consumer prices) followed by exciting spurts of moderately rapid growth;[1] having provided the world
with striking images of peaceful political upheaval during the 2004
Orange protests[2] (only to disappoint both domestic activists and foreign observers in the aftermath); Ukraine again topped the world's
headlines in 2013-14 when millions gathered in Kyiv (and in other urban centers throughout the country) to protest against, and eventually
to overthrow, the Yanukovych government. In the aftermath of regime change in Kyiv came a Russian-sponsored war: a seemingly endless conflict that revitalized old security institutions (NATO), put into
question the efficacy of existing international organizations (e.g. UN,
OSCE), and the functionality of the global order established in the
wake of the collapse of the USSR. By 2016, the confrontation between
Russia and the West seemed to increasingly resemble the Cold War
(although without the ideological component), with numbers of hot
spots of political instability, overt military conflict, and covert operations (including Russian intervention in the 2016 US Presidential election, Kremlin financial backing of European right-wing parties,[3] and
Moscow's use of chemical weapons for assassination in the U.K.), increasing in a seemingly endless progression. Five years after the fateful beatings of students on Kyiv's Independence Square, the outlook
for global security was decidedly pessimistic. Clearly, 2014 was a
pivot point for more than just the history of Ukraine.

What is most extraordinary about Ukraine's Maidan having been
the catalyst of such global transformation is that its events did not
need to happen. Had Prime Minister Azarov's government not issued
a public statement stating that preparations for signing the EU Association Agreement were suspended; had Yanukovych not tried to hag-
gle with EU leaders at the last minute by presenting them with unrea-
sonable financial demands; had Ukraine's President actually signed

the Agreement—the street protests would either never have happened, or they would have dissipated within a few weeks. Most importantly, had there been no violent crack-down on the remaining
protesters on Independence Square during the early morning hours of
30 November 2013, the demonstrators would have simply dispersed.
Certainly, they would not have camped out in the center of Kyiv for
three months in freezing temperatures until Yanukovych's flight to
Russia in February 2014. Very few of the activists (protesters and their
supporters) of Maidan would ever have experienced any intense sense
of patriotism (see Chapter 8), and fewer still would have volunteered
for government service in 2014 (see Chapter 9) had the protests failed.

Conditionality of events continued after Yanukovych's ouster.
Had Russian President Putin not ordered his Special Forces into Crimea in late February 2014, and had they not supervised (at gun-point)
a "referendum" on joining the Russian Federation in March, the peninsula would have remained within the sovereign borders of Ukraine.
Had the Kremlin's aggressive military operation not been expanded
in subsequent months to include the entire southeastern region of
Ukraine, war would not have broken out in the Donbas, hundreds of
thousands of citizens would not have been uprooted, and thousands
of lives (including those aboard Malaysian Airlines Flight MH17)
would not have been lost. On the other hand, had one of Ukraine's
richest "oligarchs" not mobilized his resources in the eastern industrial city of Dnipropetrovsk (later renamed Dnipro), and had the Russian-speaking residents of the Ukrainian southeast not mounted a
concerted grassroots resistance effort against Putin's *Novorossiya* project, Ukraine could well have ceased to exist in 2014. Furthermore, had
the EU, the US, Canada, and other western countries not imposed
sanctions against Russia, and had they not attempted to broker peace
between Kyiv and Moscow, the outcome of the war in Ukraine may
have been different—certainly it would have been even more bloody,
but also it may have remained localized rather than spawning the outbreak of a new global conflict between Russia and the West.

Whereas the purpose of the first part of this book was to present
a chronicle of the Maidan and of the Russian-Ukrainian war that it
sparked, in Part II these events will be contextualized, and a version

of their theoretical generalization will be presented. Our purpose is to unravel the complexities of Ukraine's Revolution of Dignity—a process of social transformation that I contend was simultaneously a national, bourgeois and post-modern revolution, and to identify the character of this three-fold revolution's agency. Furthermore, I seek to position the events of Ukraine's revolution (including both the Maidan protests and subsequent war) within the context of the ongoing shift of global civilization from modern, sensate, materialist, industrial society to some form of post-modern, post-industrial, idealist paradigm of organization. In this context, I argue that viewing the "Ukraine Crisis" strictly through a geopolitical lens (as many analysts do) belittles its significance: Maidan was a punctuation event in the historical process of European civilization's passage from one form to another.

Part II is divided into five chapters. In chapter 7, the theoretical context for depicting Maidan and its aftermath as an ongoing ("great") revolution will be contrasted with the prevailing geopolitical (structuralist, realist) perspectives commonly found in the literature on the "Ukraine Crisis" on the one hand, and with Putin-centered (psychological and conspiratorial) theories on the other. I argue that the narrow geopolitical perspective (most often propounded by "Russia experts") is grounded in a broader materialist paradigm that simply does not apply to analysis of Ukraine's Revolution of Dignity and will increasingly become inappropriate to analysis of social phenomena as western civilization moves beyond sensate modernity to a new condition. Maidan was "ideational" (in the sense proposed by Pitirim Sorokin),[4] as was the motivation for Ukraine's defense when Russia launched its expansionist military operation. I argue therefore, that the real significance of Ukraine's Revolution of Dignity is in its indicative value: as a possible expression of the vector of development for western civilization.

In her classic work *On Revolution* Hannah Arendt described "great revolutions" as being powered by three ideational drivers: historical completion (trajectory correction), political birth (transition), and naissance of novel senses (of regional/global importance).[5] The structure of Chapters 8, 9, and 10 broadly follows this threefold characterization, arguing that Ukraine's Revolution of Dignity was just such a *great* (civilizational) revolution: national, bourgeois, and post-modern.

Thus, analyzing the first dimension (i.e. national awakening, historical completion of Ukraine's nation-building process), in Chapter 8 I argue that the formation of a distinctly Ukrainian, grassroots, leaderless, collective agency represented a key characteristic of the Revolution of Dignity that has been misinterpreted as being reflective of radical nationalism.

The second dimension (political birth), examined in Chapter 9, involved the mobilization of a previously understudied (and largely unnoticed) socio-economic constituency: a non-oligarchic domestic bourgeoisie. It was this urban creative class that generated the financial and organizational resources required by the lengthy protest action, and later for the territorial defense of Ukraine. The most active members of this socio-economic group formed the core network of reformers who implemented much needed changes in key sectors (banking, police, education, public procurement, etc.) during the immediate post-Yanukovych period. Many of these individuals seemed to share a common—broadly termed "liberal"—ideology, and most considered their own lack of previous public sector experience to be an asset.

The fact that many in Ukraine's post-Yanukovych government viewed their entry into politics as temporary and preferred the use of influence (including social networks) over institutionalized power to achieve their goals, reflects what I argue in Chapter 10 was a fundamental novelty of values and practices that developed during Ukraine's Revolution of Dignity. This third dimension of Maidan—its pathos—generated a "horizontality" of relations (a heterarchical political community) that differed fundamentally from the nominally meritocratic hierarchies that have underpinned modern societies. In this dimension, I contend, the Ukrainian revolution generated a new paradigm for social organization that approximates a realization of *personalist* (rather than post-Enlightenment individualist) philosophy, and it was from this novel sense that the name Revolution of *Dignity* originated.

In the final chapter, I offer some thoughts as to the implications of the Ukraine's Revolution of Dignity for the future of Ukraine and the region. Five years after the ouster of Yanukovych, the Maidan agenda remained unfinished: although the issue of national identity seemed to have been resolved in favor of an inclusive, territorial, non-etatist definition of what it means to be Ukrainian, the issue of institutional development — particularly with respect to the creation of a functioning judiciary that would enact the principles of dignity and fairness — remained unresolved. The danger that Ukraine faced in its next phase of revolutionary development was that of a "leftward shift" (to borrow a term from Arendt) in its political discourse. In the run-up to elections in 2019, such a shift from idealism to materialism could give rise to populism, and the propagation of simplistic solutions to economic problems that would inevitably lead to vengeful witch hunts (i.e. some form of terror as predicted by Crane Brinton). With an aggressive neighbor exerting a constant threat to the country, the realization of such a scenario would be disastrous both for Ukraine and for the region. However, the "Russia problem" may in some way have been a blessing in disguise, allowing Ukraine to follow the model of Israel (i.e. vibrant development under permanent existential threat) and/or the early US where revolutionary institution building occurred in the context of a war for independence. Indeed, both examples inspire optimism in Ukraine's future.

For those in the West willing to recognize exemplars of change in unlikely places, Ukraine offers a unique window on what the civilizational development of western modernity could entail — an experiment in revolution worthy of protection and cultivation. This unfinished story is eminently exciting, and warrants being understood.

Chapter 7:
Making Sense of Maidan and Russia's War

The demonstration of people power that came to be known internationally as the "Euromaidan" and domestically as the "Revolution of Dignity" was largely an enigma to social scientists. As the variance in labelling suggests, Ukraine's revolution was multi-dimensional. In addition to toppling a corrupt regime, the demonstrators adopted the discourse and symbols of national self-determination (European integration was quickly sidelined); their actions reflected a communitarian ethic that seemed anarchic in its rejection of hierarchy (the protests were leaderless), but proved highly effective both during the protests, and in the mass mobilization of resources for defense in the face of Russian aggression. In the aftermath of the fall of the Yanukovych regime, the population faced dire economic conditions (e.g. threefold devaluation of the currency, large scale bank foreclosures), but Ukrainians endured this hardship without further rebellion. In 2013-14, and then throughout the years of Russia's war, Ukraine surprised many.

In this chapter, several authors' approaches to explaining the "Ukraine crisis" will be reviewed, and an alternative perspective presented. Prevailing narratives largely position Ukraine as a territory of struggle between external agents (e.g. Russia, the EU, NATO, the US) who played upon domestic cleavages within Ukrainian society to effect regime change in 2014, and subsequently to foster military conflict.[1] Historians substantiate these supposed cleavages with explanations of their apparent rootedness in an "objective" past that conditions the values and decisions of contemporary actors—both individual and collective.[2] Journalists and pundits, on the other hand, focus on the decisions and personality of leaders, particularly on one actor—Vladimir Putin—and his diabolical or brilliant (the adjective depends on political preference) role in advancing events in Ukraine, in the region, and further afield.[3]

The alternative view (presented here) posits the Ukrainian revolution as a revolution. As such, although its events occurred in an international context, and were therefore influenced both by external actors and historical circumstances, the locus of the agency effecting change is identified internal — within Ukraine. Our purpose is to elucidate the role of domestic Ukrainian agents in this revolution. As a participant observer of the Maidan protests, I cannot accept any representation of my experiences as having approximated those of a puppet fulfilling someone else's script. I do not imagine Ukrainian society as divorced or isolated from global social trends (quite the opposite), nor do I belittle the role of Russia (or specifically its President) in the eventual outcome of Ukraine's revolution, but I do argue that any description of the "Ukraine crisis" as an epiphenomenon of global structural (geo-political) discord, or simply as a playground either for Putin or for some ephemeral "West", leads to an incomplete and/or misconceived understanding of events and their significance.

Prevailing explanations

During the height of Russia's aggression, when discussions of events in Ukraine spread well beyond the country's borders, attempting to find an adequate paradigm to explain both Maidan, and the Kremlin's bellicose reaction to it, became popular among journalists and pundits, but was rarely broached by social scientists. One of the first (and few) excellent book-length analyses, Andrew Wilson's *Ukraine Crisis: What it Means for the West* (published in late 2014), included a valuable (though brief) chronicle of both the Maidan protests, and of the early stages of Russia's aggression in Crimea and the Donbas, but as the title implied, the book aimed to contextualize events for a *western* policy-making audience, rather than to delve deeply into the social phenomenon that was Ukraine's Revolution of Dignity.[4]

After Wilson's book, the analytical task was taken on (ironically) by Russia experts — generally former Sovietologists who presented Russo-centric narratives that largely grounded events in their supposedly historical antecedents.[5] Because the Cold War represented the most recent of historical contexts, a popular approach was to posit the

"Ukraine crisis" as fundamentally a clash between the West and Russia (i.e. as a "great power" contest). Accordingly, when Ukrainians were attributed agency at all, it was only in the context of their internal linguistic and political divisions which were seen as reflective of historical contingency (i.e. western Ukraine having been annexed to the USSR only after 1945; eastern and southern Ukraine being populated by a large ethnic Russian minority, and a majority of Russian-speakers; administrative control over Crimea having been transferred to the Ukrainian SSR from the RSFSR only in 1954). Perhaps unwittingly, these accounts seem to have supported Putin's reported position that Ukraine was "not really a country."[6] Logically, the population of such a country could make no claim to having effected a revolution on its own, but (ironically) this artificiality of the Ukrainian nation was then also seen as the root cause of the "civil war" — as the conflict in the Donbas was labelled.[7]

The "great power" Russo-centric narrative is frustrating to Ukrainians — particularly to those (like this author) who were active in the initial Maidan protests, and subsequently supported the grass-roots effort to mobilize resources for Ukraine's territorial defense. Most renowned among the Russia-watchers who belittled the role of domestic Ukrainian change agents (or relegated their role to "monist nationalists" and "radicals") in his account of the "Ukraine crisis" was Sovietologist Richard Sakwa. In the introduction to his *Frontline Ukraine: Crisis in the Borderlands*, he wrote:

> The groundwork of the Ukrainian conflict has been latent for at least two decades. It was laid by the asymmetrical end of the Cold War, in which one side declared victory while the other was certainly not ready to 'embrace defeat.'... This helps explain how Europe in 2014 has once again become the crucible of international conflict, harking back to an era that has so often been declared to be over. Today, Ukraine acts as the Balkans did in 1914, with numerous intersecting domestic conflicts that are amplified and internationalized as external actors exacerbate the country's internal divisions.[8]

In other words, according to Sakwa, if one is to understand events in contemporary Ukraine, questions (historical in the first place) must be asked in Washington, Brussels and Moscow. After-all, both the Maidan and the subsequent war in the Donbas, apparently, were "proxy conflicts" between the West and Russia – a continuation of the "unresolved" Cold War; Ukraine was merely the battleground – similar, supposedly, to the Balkans in World War One – a historically divided zone of contestation between great power interests.

The forms and foundations of this contestation have been variously identified. For example, according to E. Wayne Merry of the Woodrow Wilson Center, Maidan was the culmination of a decade-long struggle between the EU and Russia over effective control of Ukraine. [9] In pursuing its "traditional Great Power status" Russia saw itself as a suzerain of the "near abroad" – particularly the Slavic former republics of the USSR – Belarus and Ukraine – and devised the Eurasian Economic Union (which by 2013 included Russia, Belarus and Kazakhstan) as the primary vehicle for institutionalizing this sphere of influence. However, Russia's plans were countered in 2009 by the Eastern Partnership program of the EU: designed and implemented by Poland's Foreign Minister Sikorski and Swedish Prime Minister Bildt, this instrument of "soft power" included imposition of EU standards on many sectors of the neighboring countries' economies, and their acceptance of portions of the EU's Acquis Communautaire. From Moscow's perspective the Eastern Partnership was not as bad as NATO enlargement, but was nevertheless a mechanism for expanding the EU's sphere of influence, and as such conflicted with the Eurasian Economic Union. The EU's offer to Ukraine of an Association Agreement and accompanying DCFTA was thus seen as an encroachment on Russia, and such expansionism was bound to solicit a negative reaction from the Kremlin.

> In sum, the clash of EU and Russian policies in Ukraine transformed the long-simmering political crisis of that country into an international competition for influence and dominance. There was no inevitability to that clash; it was the product of policy choices. Both Brussels and Moscow conducted the competition without regard for its potential damage to Ukraine and without respect for its sovereignty. Thus, the EU and Russia share the responsibility for internationalizing the Ukrainian political crisis. However, Brussels initiated the competition,

as it sought to alter an existing status quo in Ukraine at Russia's expense whereas Moscow sought to preserve the status quo without compromising EU interests...[10]

Similar, more-or-less exonerating analyses of Russia's interventions in Ukraine are common in the social sciences literature. Some justify the Kremlin's aggression with an appeal to Russian political culture, which supposedly holds "great power status" as an endemic value.[11] Others echo the position of Sakwa, according to which the Maidan protests and the war in the Donbas were superficial expressions of a deeper structural conflict between the EU and Russia and/or between Russia and the "West" (NATO, the US, G7, etc.). These narratives posit Ukraine as the territorial battlefield, and its citizens as pawns in a larger international game, rather than as actors whose voices warrant attention. Accordingly, the key to understanding the "real" causes of the "Ukraine Crisis" lies in grasping its underlying structural causes — i.e. the material interests driving the policy choices of the world's power brokers.

Structural (Marxist) Realism

This approach to understanding events of international significance is called *structuralism*, and it derives its pedigree directly from Karl Marx. Marx identified class conflict as being the basis for all social relations and relegated all other social phenomena (including and especially ideas, cultural practices, symbols, and language) to the "superstructure" — an arena of "false consciousness" constructed by the dominant class of any society as a tool for reproducing its power. Thus, according to (particularly neo-Marxist) structuralists, what is visible is rarely (if ever) true.[12] For structuralists, the causes of events are always hidden. Explanations are to be found in a seemingly more fundamental, but inevitably masked, realm of material relations.

Sadly, the paradigm of structuralism has achieved near hegemonic status in the social sciences. True causes of events are believed to be found in underlying social relations that are rarely visible *prima facie*. As a result, more often than not, facts are interpreted in a way that is explainable through theory, rather than vice versa. For example, in international relations (particularly for adherents of the "realist" school),[13] real motives for policy choices and individual actions are said to be found in the material (power) interests of conflicting parties. Unarguably, these interests are hidden from view. The explanatory value of the immediately observable (e.g. what politicians actually say, how actors on the ground actually behave) is therefore questioned – particularly if/when a fit to preferred theory cannot be found.

Among analysts of Maidan and the Russian-Ukrainian war, the structuralist approach has gained significant popularity resulting in the proliferation of multiple pseudo-academic falsehoods. For example, when the Maidan protest movement was still in its infancy, few analysts (and even fewer regime officials) believed the demonstrations to be truly grass-roots phenomena: someone powerful had to be pulling the proverbial strings. When that hypothesis was proved patently wrong, analysis switched to searching for "nationalist radicals" who were somehow controlling the protests in an effort to take power, and then to create an ethno-nationalist Ukraine. Later, when a provisional post-Yanukovych government was formed of moderates (rather than nationalists) who faced overt Russian aggression in Crimea that was justified by President Putin in expansionist Russian *nationalist* terms, this fact was downplayed, and the "nationalist" narrative gradually waned.

"Analysis" of the early fighting in the Donbas led several authoritative commentators to conclude that the Kremlin's military intervention in Ukraine could be explained by Moscow's desire to control the northern Black Sea shelf natural gas and oil deposits off the coast of Crimea, and the newly discovered shale gas deposits of the western Donbas, centered around the town of Slovyansk. The fact that Putin's speech, given on 18 March 2014 on the occasion of the annexation of Crimea, justified Russia's actions in purely ideological (non-materialist) terms, and that the Russian President resorted to what amounted to a reinterpretation of historical facts[14] was somehow talked down. The same occurred after his announcement in August 2014 of the *No-*

vorossiya project for southeastern Ukraine, and the anti-western ideological pronouncements prominent in virtually all of Putin's public
appearances since the Munich Security Conference of 2007. The fact
that he repeatedly scoffed at western governments' imposition of sectoral and personal sanctions in the wake the Crimean annexation, and
"retaliated" with economic policies that hurt his own population in
the first place, was brushed off as political bluster. According to structuralist analysis, in each of these cases Putin was simply playing to the
electorate—perpetuating the false consciousness of the superstructure, as it were. His real motives must be different. After-all, according
to orthodox "realist" theory, all interests of international actors (particularly "great powers") are fundamentally material. Ideas are
merely a façade behind which the economic foundations of power
struggles hide—so says the dominant paradigm.

Axiomatically, according to "realists", states are rational actors
that perpetually pursue their national (material) interests. Their success in this great game is measured in their political power. Access to
resources, ability to spread economic, political and/or cultural hegemony over territory, capacity to influence the decision-making of
others—these are said to be the "real" motives for decision-making in
international relations. Because ideas (ideologies) are seen as window-
dressing for fundamental structural interests, values-based politics is
rejected as myth, and no concession is given to subjectivity (e.g. historical memory, political culture, irrational leadership). Neither is
grassroots agency, or the ability of idealistically motivated social
movements to effect change, taken seriously.

Realists contend that Russia's "soft" intervention in Ukraine's
political affairs prior to the collapse of the Yanukovych regime, and
then militarily in 2014 and thereafter, was justified by an apparent
threat of NATO expansion to include Ukraine. However, this argument (a repeat of the official Kremlin narrative) is based on a fallacy:
Ukraine's NATO membership became a marginally realistic option
for the country's political elites only *after* Russia's annexation of Crimea and invasion of the Donbas. Prior to 2014, domestic support for
NATO membership within Ukraine had ranged between 20% and
30% with over 2/3 of the population opposed.[15] Even in the midst of

Russian aggression in 2015, polls showed only 48% support for joining the alliance,[16] and it was only at the end of 2016 (after almost 3 years of war with Russia) that a majority of Ukrainians came to support their country's membership in NATO.

Yanukovych overtly rejected NATO membership, but prior to his election, successive Ukrainian leaders had promised a referendum on NATO if the alliance were to open its doors to Ukraine. In 2008, when pro-western President Yushchenko made a bid to receive a Membership Action Plan, the request was politely declined at the alliance's Bucharest summit: Germany and France (as well as several smaller member states) were not keen on infuriating Russia, and therefore the summit communique promised that NATO foreign ministers "will now begin a period of intensive engagement with both (Ukraine and Georgia) at a high political level to address the questions still outstanding pertaining to their MAP applications."[17] In the words of prominent political scientist Alexander Motyl: "Western policymakers have certainly been open to Ukraine's efforts to move westwards, but they have at best been consistently noncommittal about Ukraine's actually joining any key Western institutions such as the European Union and NATO."[18]

In addition to its being based on the false claim of Ukraine's westward orientation somehow posing an imminent threat to Russia, realist (structuralist) analysis of the "Ukraine Crisis" failed to provide any viable explanation for the masses of people gathered on the streets of Kyiv and other cities. The claim that a social movement numbering in the millions (including intellectuals, entrepreneurs, and educated white collar workers from a variety of Ukraine's regions), that was able to sustain continuous protest for several months in freezing temperatures, constituted a subversive plot orchestrated by the West or by radical nationalists (whose material interests were never explained), simply did not stand up to empirical scrutiny. Nevertheless, throughout the early post-Yanukovych period, the Russia-friendly narrative, according to which the Maidan had enacted a coup d'état (supposedly sponsored by the US and/or NATO), and the Kremlin's ensuing military aggression was termed a "civil war" remained prevalent in the western news media.[19] After-all, this story fit the dominant paradigm perfectly.

However, facts on the ground did not fit the paradigm. Denying agency to the most active segments of Ukrainian society may have been theoretically acceptable to a scholar writing in Washington, Berlin or Moscow, but on the ground this interpretation was patently wrong. To portray Maidan as having been a materialization of latent conflict between the West and Russia was to relegate the millions of people who supported the anti-Yanukovych movement to the status of puppets. Furthermore, to portray the stand-off between the regime and the protesters as a manifestation of ethno-linguistic cleavages that mapped onto regional politics, was belied by the fact that many (if not the majority) of Maidan participants were Russian-speaking. The same can be said of most of the volunteers who enlisted to fight in the Donbas, as well those who organized logistical support for Ukraine's military after the eruption of hostilities. The eastern and southern regions were well represented both on the anti-Yanukovych and on the anti-Russian sides. The "cleft country" hypothesis, according to which latent tensions became manifest in 2014, and then spiraled catastrophically into "civil war" in subsequent years was patently false.

Finally, to claim that liability for the downing of flight MH-17, and responsibility for the deaths of over 10,000 Ukrainian citizens and displacement of almost 2 million more, was somehow shared by the West, or caused by a "failed" Ukrainian state, was to absolve the Kremlin of guilt for invasion, illegal annexation, and continued military escalation in overt violation of supposedly agreed peace accords. In the words of RFE/RL commentator Brian Whitmore "… at the end of the day, one man is responsible for these people being dead, wounded or displaced… One man…"[20]

Putin

The Russian President is the one person who is never denied agency in any account of the "Ukraine Crisis". Indeed, the amount of ink

spent on psychoanalyzing Putin is astounding. His actions throughout the five-year period spanning 2013-18 were unpredictable and
highly unorthodox.

Whether Putin masterminded Russia's annexation of Crimea
and the separatist insurrection in the Donbas in advance, or whether
he took advantage of opportunities as they presented themselves, is
important to understanding the psychology of the Russian leader and
is a matter of some debate. According to the official Kremlin narrative,
the Russian President gave the "go ahead" to insert Special Forces into
Crimea during a "war cabinet" meeting on February 25. Apparently,
that meeting was held secretly in Moscow immediately after Putin's
return from Sochi where he had attended the closing ceremony of the
Winter Olympics. Only three of his closest advisors were present.[21]
Supposedly, the decision to invade Ukraine was taken that evening
spontaneously — as a reaction to the threat posed to "Russians and Russian-speakers" by Kyiv's pro-Maidan "junta." However, this version
of events is flawed: prior to the start of the Sochi games, Putin had
already ordered troop movements (numbering several hundred thousand soldiers, artillery, and tanks) in the southern and southwestern
military districts — i.e. along Ukraine's eastern border. Several of the
units involved were later moved into Crimea and ordered to seize key
infrastructure. Each unit had very specific instructions as to targets,
and the operation was obviously well rehearsed. It therefore seems
likely that Putin's Crimean operation was not spontaneous at all. The
Kremlin had *planned* its invasion of Ukraine well in advance.

Why? Why would the leader of one of the five permanent members of the UN Security Council, a signatory of multiple treaties and
agreements aimed at securing stability and peace in Europe, deliberately conspire to undermine his country's status as a pillar of the international order, and invade the sovereign territory of a neighboring
state? A theory that has been advanced by Elizabeth Wood of the
Woodrow Wilson Center[22] (the same theme has been echoed by Russian opposition politicians Gary Kasparov,[23] Ilya Ponomaryov,[24] and
the late Boris Nemtsov[25]) posits Vladimir Putin's power in Russia as
tied closely to "small quick wars" that increased his popularity and
fed his personality cult. The war in Chechnya (artificially ignited in

1999 by staged "terrorist" attacks in Moscow that were then blamed on Chechens), the war in Georgia in 2008, and the annexation of Crimea in 2014 all resulted in spikes in Putin's approval rating. During the initial Maidan protests, in the lead up to the Sochi Olympics, Putin's popularity was exceptionally low by Russian standards.[26] A "short victorious war" in Ukraine may have been devised to change that.

This theory is plausible with respect to Crimea, but it sheds little light on the motives for Putin's invasion of the Donbas. According to a document made public by Kyiv Post deputy editor Katya Gorchinskaya, plans to annex large parts of eastern and southern Ukraine were circulating in the Kremlin as early as December 2013.[27] The source or authenticity of this document has never been verified, but crucially, it shows the invasion plan as including provisions for the occupation of Kyiv. Another document (formulated as a policy recommendation), supposedly authored in early February 2014 when Yanukovych was still in office, was leaked by a Kremlin insider to Moscow's Novaya Gazeta a year later. Its author called for the deliberate destabilization of the Kyiv government by Russian agents so as to create a pretext for invasion by Russia's military: "to launch the process of the pro-Russian drift of Crimea and Eastern Ukrainian territories, it is necessary to create the events that would give this process political legitimacy and moral justification beforehand."[28] If one believes the authenticity of these leaks, Putin not only planned the dismemberment of Ukraine well in advance of Yanukovych's ouster, he may well have been responsible for the massacre of protesters on Maidan in late February 2014.

Such covert plans could not possibly have been part of a "short victorious war" scenario. These were part of a deliberate strategy of Russian territorial expansion. Years after the failed attempts by the Kremlin to foster armed rebellion in the eastern and southern oblasts (particularly in Odesa and Kharkiv), Ukraine's Prosecutor General's office released transcripts and audio files of intercepted telephone conversations between Russian agents in Ukraine in early 2014 and Putin's special advisor on Ukraine Sergey Glazyev.[29] The recordings suggested that a coordinating, if not leading, role was played by

Glazyev during the supposedly spontaneous anti-Kyiv protests in eastern and southern Ukraine that followed Yanukovych's flight to Russia. In addition to earlier published interviews by FSB Colonel Girkin, who commanded the Russian Special Forces operation in Slovyansk and Kramatorsk (Donetsk oblast) in April-May 2014,[30] these testimonies indicate that the Kremlin was directly orchestrating the post-Yanukovych civic unrest in the southern and eastern regions, and that Moscow had planned to annex much more Ukrainian territory than just Crimea. In fact, as political scientist Andreas Umland pointed out in the wake of the release of the "Glazyev tapes," Crimea seems to have been part of a broader Kremlin operation aimed annexing virtually half of Ukraine's territory.[31]

Throughout the first half of 2014, the Kremlin publicly maintained that Crimea had been "liberated" by "local self-defense forces" protecting themselves from "dangerous extremism, radical nationalism, and violent anti-Semitism."[32] Later the story changed, and Putin admitted to having ordered the Russian military to take control of key strategic targets directly.[33] However, even according to this revised narrative, the Kremlin asserted that Russian Special Forces were ordered into Crimea only *after* regime change in Kyiv, and only in response to the "obvious" threat "nationalists and fascists" posed to Russians and Russian-speakers on the peninsula. The Kremlin's expansionist plans required face legitimacy, but as events unfolded, this became increasingly problematic: plausible media reports of anti-Russian violence in Crimea and Ukraine's eastern oblasts were too few. The early March raids and forcible occupation of oblast administration buildings in the eastern cities of Donetsk, Kharkiv, and Luhansk by "local" pro-Kremlin demonstrators were supposed to have been opposed by "radical nationalists from Maidan," and video footage of anarchy and violence was supposed to have been transmitted worldwide. But none of this transpired. Despite being barricaded inside their bases by Russian troops, Ukrainian military personnel in Crimea did not fire their weapons. Television reports of large numbers of refugees from eastern Ukraine fleeing to Russia proved false. Maidan Self-Defense forces did not mobilize to fight the Russian "tourists" bussed in to eastern and southern Ukrainian cities to foment anti-Kyiv protests (see Chapter 5). Right Sector fighters did not descend on Donetsk or Kharkiv. This kind of peaceful restraint translated into an epic failure of the Putin plan to justify invasion on the basis of threats to the lives of Russians and Russian-speakers. The Ukrainian side did everything possible to avoid violence.

The fact that Putin initially claimed the soldiers in unmarked uniforms in Crimea were not Russian forces, and only admitted the obvious well after the operation was successfully completed, indicates that at the time the need for deniability was paramount. Similarly, the fact that Colonel Girkin acted relatively autonomously in Slovyansk and Kramatorsk in his efforts to spawn armed rebellion in April-June 2014, and that references to combat deaths or injuries of Russian soldiers in the Donbas were vehemently denied at the time by the Kremlin, suggests that Putin's decision-making during the later stages of the "Russian Spring" military operation in Ukraine was tactical and at least partly spontaneous.[34] The chaotic and poorly organized nature of the Donbas "uprising" (in contrast to Crimea) indicates that operational plans to annex this portion of Ukrainian territory were vague in 2014.[35]

It now seems likely that after the climax of the protests in Kyiv, Glazyev and Girkin (Putin's emissaries in the Donbas) were improvising within the broad framework of a previously planned (and gradually failing) scenario. In other words, the original *Novorossiya* plan had called for the legitimate President of Ukraine to ask for Russian assistance, but with Yanukovych too timid to address the February 2014 Kharkiv Party of Regions Congress (see Chapter 5), the Kremlin reverted to "plan B" — i.e. trying to foster rebellion through "hybrid" means: gradually escalating from insertion of special forces, to supplies of military hardware, and eventually to direct invasion. The back-up plan also failed. Moscow ended up with a mere 7% of Ukraine's territory (instead of the half Putin had planned for), and instead of being met with open arms by the Russian-speaking residents of Ukraine's east and south, the Kremlin now faced a belligerently defensive independentist neighbor on its western border.

Improvising *Novorossiya*

On 1 March 2014, the Federation Council of the Russian Federation (the country's highest legislative body) voted unanimously to support President Putin's request for authorization to deploy the Armed Forces of the Russian Federation onto the territory of Ukraine. This decision was widely interpreted as referencing the ongoing operation in Crimea — i.e. as a *post hoc* announcement that legalized what had already happened. But, the Council's decision may have been prepar-atory: covert operations aimed at fomenting separatism in the south-ern and eastern regions of Ukraine were just starting, and had they achieved their aim — occupation of local government buildings fol-lowed by oblast councils calling for Russian military assistance — the Russian Armed Forces would have invaded. The plan failed, and Putin was forced to settle for the creation of two rump "republics" in the eastern parts of Donetsk and Luhansk oblasts. But that was much later — in 2015.

In August 2014, the Russian President's plans were still germane. During a 4-hour televised "Dialog with Russians" aired to coincide with Ukraine's Independence Day celebrations, President Putin pub-licly laid out his vision of the territorial division of Russia's southwest-ern neighbor: "I'll remind you that this is *Novorossiya*. And it includes Kharkiv, Luhansk, Donetsk, Kherson, Mykolayiv, Odesa — they were not part of Ukraine during Tsarist times. All these territories were given to Ukraine by the Soviet government. Why this was done, God knows!"[36] Evidently, in the wake of the fall of the Yanukovych regime, Putin determined to "return" these territories to Russia.

Map 11:   *Novorossiya* as conceived by Putin in August 2014

Although publicly announced in August 2014, Putin's plan to create *Novorossiya* was likely hatched much earlier. Indeed, preparations for a large-scale military intervention into Ukraine seem to have begun well before the Maidan protests. For example, the "fictional" scenario underpinning the "Zapad-2013" military exercises held in Belarus 19-28 September 2013 (2 months before the start of Euromaidan!) involved Russian forces entering a "neighboring country" where "opposition forces" had created "illegal armed formations" that threatened violence against local ethnic Russians. At the time of the exercises, western analysts believed the "terrorists" in the scenario to have been a poor cover for NATO,[37] but according to long-time Ukrainian National Security Council Secretary Volodymyr Horbulin, the Zapad-2013 war game was a dress rehearsal for Putin's Crimean operation, and indeed for his invasion of eastern Ukraine.[38]

The theory according to which Russia's military intervention in Ukraine was pre-planned long before the Maidan protests maintains significant popularity in Ukraine. Many believe the Kremlin's hand was somehow pulling the strings of Ukraine's political scene even be-

fore the mass protests erupted. For example, according to Lviv publicist Taras Vozniak (editor-in-chief of "*Ji*" magazine), the overall script
of the Revolution of Dignity was largely pre-planned by the Kremlin.[39]
Understanding that Yanukovych's refusal to sign the EU Association
Agreement would provoke a popular reaction, Putin apparently
pushed his Ukrainian counterpart not only to refuse to sign, but also
to crack down hard on the demonstrations once they began. According to Vozniak, Putin needed violence in Kyiv to demonstrate to the
world that Ukraine was a failed state, and so ordered agents that he
had previously infiltrated into the Yanukovych regime to first organize the beating of students on November 30, and then to stage violence
against journalists and police in front of the Presidential Administration on 1 December 2013. In subsequent months, the Russian President
is said to have repeatedly called upon Yanukovych to crack down on
Maidan, and finally took matters into his own hands after the Ukrainian President refused to break-up his own country (Vozniak attributes
blame for the massacre in Kyiv's city center on 18-21 February 2014 to
Russian snipers—a claim that remains unproven).

This theory (and other variants)[40] seems to be based on an internal contradiction. On the one hand, the Russian President is portrayed
as a master strategist able to plan, anticipate, and engineer the behavior of large numbers of people, and to manipulate elites both in
Ukraine and in the West to his own benefit. Oddly however, his grand
strategic plan for breaking up Ukraine was foiled in the end by the
ineptitude of Yanukovych—his failure to condemn the "coup" in
Kyiv, and to announce the formation of an alternative Ukrainian state
during the Congress in Kharkiv under his own "legitimate" leadership—and by miscalculation as to the loyalties of Russian-speakers in
Kharkiv, Odesa, Dnipropetrovsk and throughout Ukraine's southeastern region. This seems inconsistent: on the one hand Putin is portrayed as a master puppeteer, worthy of the title Anti-Christ, and on
the other the actual outcome of events is explained as the result of
miscalculation.

Putin's greatest miscalculation seems to have been the result of
misunderstanding: in contrast to their portrayal by Russian historiography as a "brotherly people" Ukrainians proved themselves to be

fundamentally different from Russians. Despite often speaking Russian and claiming affinity to Russian culture, when presented with the prospect of political unity with Russia, the population of Ukraine's southeastern regions largely refused (the western and central regions wholeheartedly opposed). They did not rally behind an alternative leader, nor did they passively agree to be pawns in a geopolitical game between "great powers". They resisted. Their anarchic defiance was unexpected. The character and substance of this grassroots agency behooves explanation: these were nobody's puppets; they had a voice and they had values and interests that they believed worthy of armed defense.

Leaderless agency

Popular unrest and mass resistance are not new phenomena for Ukraine. In 1990, student protests in Kyiv's city-center forced the government of the Ukrainian SSR to implement concessions; in 2001, the "Ukraine-without-Kuchma" movement undermined the progress towards authoritarianism of the then in-post President; in 2004 large scale street demonstrations against voting fraud led to a repeat of the Presidential election run-off, and eventually to the loss of Ukraine's presidency by Yanukovych (who had been publicly favored by Putin) to Viktor Yushchenko.[41]

But the 2013-14 Maidan protests were fundamentally different from "Orange-style" election-based demonstrations, and from other Ukrainian "Maidans". In 2004, demonstrators in Kyiv had followed the classic "colored revolution" script:[42] they challenged a semi-autocratic regime (weakened by the reality of an election) through mass protests, organized by a united opposition, and led by a popular alternative leader. Indeed, this final component — the presence of a charismatic leader of the opposition — was a fundamental success factor of the Orange protests,[43] and has been identified as key to explaining the failure of similar election-based protests in Russia and in Belarus.[44]

However, the Revolution of Dignity was no Orange Revolution. Unlike the demonstrations a decade earlier, when "political/protest entrepreneurs"[45] carefully, and masterfully crafted the messages of the protests as a battle between "good" and "evil", the Revolution of

Dignity had no centralized advertising or PR structures. The imagery, slogans, and symbolism of 2013-2014 appeared spontaneously — often through a reconstitution of historical symbols for modern needs (see Chapter 8). Material demands were rarely voiced (despite the presence of an alternative elite on Maidan that represented a distinct economic status group — see Chapter 9). The protest demands were verbalized in idealistic terms: dignity, community, fairness, transparency, rights (see Chapter 10). The risks for the demonstrators was considerably higher because the Yanukovych regime was not contesting an election in 2013-2014, and therefore had no reason to hide its authoritarian essence. Few doubted that, unlike Leonid Kuchma in 2001 and 2004, Viktor Yanukovych was ready and willing to use force to disperse the crowds in Kyiv's city-center.[46]

Most importantly (and this is the most fundamental difference between the "Maidans" of 2004 and 2013-14), the Revolution of Dignity had no leader. Unlike Yushchenko, whose name was chanted nightly by the crowds gathered in Kyiv's city-center in 2004, the nominal political opposition leaders of 2013-14 — Yatseniuk, Klitschko and Tiahnybok — elicited marginally higher levels of trust from the protesters than Yanukovych and his closest entourage. Ironically, this anarchic aspect of the demonstrations proved key to their eventual success. The ability of representatives of the nominal political counter-elite to direct the will of the crowds was limited, and this made the protests both unpredictable and strong. Similarly, in the post-Yanukovych phase of the Revolution, lack of central command structure proved key to the success of the mass mobilization efforts against Russia's aggression in the Donbas (i.e. volunteer battalions and logistical supply efforts).

Past studies of social movements have generally focused on leadership as a key determinant of success.[47] However, recent analyses of such phenomena as Occupy, the Arab Spring, and Maidan (the 2016 protests in South Korea and Romania seemed to follow the same pattern), indicate that the importance of a clearly identifiable leader may have been overstated. On the contrary, one may differentiate between the traditional ("vertical") leadership of revolutionary movements of the past (i.e. those led by charismatic figures the likes of Lenin, Mao,

Gandhi, Che Guevara, and others), and the communitarian ("horizontal") model of leadership manifest in more recent protest actions.[48] We will return to this point in the context of the discussion of the Revolution of Dignity as a "post-modern" revolution (Chapter 10) because the heterarchical structure of both the Maidan protest camp, and of the volunteer battalions organized subsequently, seems to suggest a substantively new social phenomenon that warrants deeper inquiry.

Of course, to claim that the Maidan completely lacked leadership would be false. The fundamental feature of this protest was its lack of *consolidated* leadership: no single person commanded the protests, nor did a personified figure-head ever emerge from the movement. Instead, individuals banded together in small *ad hoc* groups for the fulfilment of a particular task e.g.: building barricades, preparing meals, organizing self-defense or the supply of clothing, fuel, etc. These groups were organized by local leaders who elicited authority from their immediate followers, but whose clout rarely extended beyond their personal trust network. The resultant structure of the movement was not completely "horizontal", but rather had multiple (hundreds if not thousands) of loosely connected local leaders, each eliciting loyalty from followers numbering from 5-6 to 100 persons (hence the "*sotnia*" or "hundred" designation given to the basic organizational unit of the Maidan). After the protests ended, the "weak ties" network[49] of local leaders was again manifest in community policing efforts (necessitated by the disappearance of formal police forces in several major cities, including Kyiv, in the wake of the February 18-20 shootings). Later, when hostilities began in the eastern regions, the defense of Ukraine's territorial integrity, and supplies of basic needs to the troops, were organized by local leaders linked together through informal networks rather than by more permanent hierarchical structures.

The "glue" that united this multiplicity of local leaders was ideational, and rarely personified. This fact should have made the structures temporary. Prior to Maidan, such communitarian (heterarchical) social movements had never been able to sustain protest for more than a few weeks. The Occupy protests dissipated less than a month after they started. The protests on Egypt's Tahrir Square lasted for 18 days, after which the army removed President Hosni Mubarak from office.

In contrast, the Ukrainian President tested the resolve of his ousters for over 3 months in much colder conditions than the Occupy movement or the protesters in Cairo had ever experienced.

The Ukrainian case seemed to point to a fundamental change in the way social movements organized and achieved their aims. Ironically, for a country that had traditionally been seen as having an underdeveloped civil society, Maidan organized and achieved success precisely through networked communitarian action. This grassroots mobilization (leaderless agency) and idealistic solidarity (collective action without material gain) were among the most striking achievements of Ukraine's Revolution of Dignity, and both require explanation. As will be argued further in subsequent chapters, the "glue" engendering solidarity was a grass-roots idea of "nation" (sacrosanct, but stripped of its traditional conceptual link to the state); the local leaders who organized resources and coordinated their efforts through heterarchical networks hailed from a new "creative" class of self-reliant urban bourgeois; the resultant phenomena reflect previously unobserved trends in organizational development that may well be of global civilizational importance.

Revolutionary idealism

To the non-specialist, a revolution is often associated with a momentary, usually violent change of government resulting from popular protest or rebellion. In fact, the technical term for such an event is "coup d'état" — a term used by Russian officials throughout 2014 (and thereafter) to discredit Ukraine's post-Yanukovych government given the questionable legal legitimacy of the former President's removal from office. Technically, a "revolution" is much more than a "coup d'état". A revolution involves rapid transformation of a society's political, economic, and social institutions — a process that is certainly accelerated by "revolutionary events" but is not limited to a single event. Any analysis of such rapid transformation (*qua* revolution) must be based on a *process* perspective. In the Ukrainian case, this process of transformation *began* with Yanukovych's departure, and is ongoing (i.e. the Revolution of Dignity should not be referred to in the past tense). The Maidan protests and the ouster of Yanukovych were not a *moment* of revolution, but rather the first stage of a much more fundamental process.

The argument presented here posits Ukraine's Revolution of Dignity not just as a social and political revolution, but as a "great revolution" — comparable in historical importance to the French or Russian revolutions, but whose events followed a sequence more like the American Revolution (1776-1789). Indeed, the American case is used for comparison because, firstly, as with Maidan, the period of "Terror" and/or ascension of a personalized tyrannical leadership figure (e.g. Robespierre or Stalin) during the later stages of the revolution's "lifecycle" did not materialize in the US case, and secondly, because the Ukrainian revolution's idealist core seems not (yet) to have become significantly contaminated by populist materialism. These arguments draw heavily on the work of two authors: Crane Brinton, and Hannah Arendt.[50]

In 1938 Crane Brinton first published what has come to be known as a "classic" study of revolutions. Revised in 1952 and 1965, his comparison of the English, American, French and Russian cases is still considered the seminal work on revolutionary "stages." *The Anatomy of Revolution* identifies a "natural lifecycle" of event trajectories that seemingly occur during revolutionary periods of history: from regime overthrow, to institution of a moderate post-revolt regime, to regime radicalization leading to the violent destruction of real or supposed "enemies of the revolution" (i.e. a "Reign of Terror"), and eventually to Thermidorian "cooling."

Brinton's schema is significant for the Ukrainian case because through its lens the Revolution of Dignity is seen as a *process* rather than an event. Accordingly, the Maidan protests and the ouster of Yanukovych represent the first stage in the postulated "natural" lifecycle of revolutionary development whereas the brief transition period under acting President Turchynov followed by Poroshenko's willy-nilly reform efforts correspond to the moderate post-revolt stage. Presumably this stage was to be followed by disillusionment and frustration leading to radicalization, and possibly to some form of "Reign of Terror" (i.e. the appearance of a Robespierre equivalent).

At time of writing, fears of Ukraine's revolutionary process descending into a Brintonian "Reign of Terror" had not materialized. No significant street protests occurred during Poroshenko's first term as President (at time of writing his election to a second term was far from a foregone conclusion), and although new parties calling for more radical reform did gain some popularity,[51] none called for political change through anything but peaceful means. The belief that disillusioned soldiers and volunteers would return to Kyiv after their tours of duty in the east, and would enforce street justice on political elites whose actions they deemed unworthy of the "values of Maidan" and/or the "memory of the Heaven's Hundred," was likely planted by the Kremlin as part of its information war against Ukraine,[52] rather than reflecting any real grassroots initiative. Throughout 2015 the meme of an inevitable future "Third Maidan" (i.e. where 2004 was identified as the "first", 2014 as the "second") was ever-present in the Ukrainian and international press,[53] and in February 2016, a short-lived protest under this banner did appear, but its main organizer later turned out to be a citizen of Russia who had previously supported the separatist "DNR" and "LNR" and had promoted the cause of Novorossiya in social media.[54] Nadia Savchenko, the captured Ukrainian military pilot who had been jailed by the Kremlin and later released, was charged in early 2018 with plotting a violent coup attempt aimed at toppling Ukraine's duly elected government, but revelation of her plans elicited more ridicule than support in popular discourse.[55]

The lack of support for radicalism during the years immediately following Yanukovych's ouster was surprising. The pace of transformation (objectively much faster than anything Ukraine had previously experienced, but still below expectations) implemented by Ukraine's new elites disappointed many. Forced by circumstances to focus their attention on combatting Russian military aggression, the post-Yanukovych leaders vacillated on many of the domestic reforms that the Maidan protesters had called for, concentrating instead on foreign affairs (securing western financial and diplomatic support) and military matters (including mobilization, supplying the troops, renewing equipment manufacturing). National defense was prioritized over domestic institutional reform, and so a memetic drift to "existential politics"[56] (i.e. subordinating political discourse and decision-making to the exigencies of warding off external threat) occurred.

By the end of 2016, the seemingly slow pace of domestic reform implementation (particularly in the judiciary, and in the enactment of anti-corruption initiatives)[57] finally led to a rise in public unrest. Protests were organized first in the Donbas: activists allied with the "Samopomich" party organized a blockade of rail lines leading into and out of the occupied territories of the "DNR" and "LNR", thus forcing an end to trade across the line of contact that was widely believed to be in the interests of corrupt high-level government officials. In mid-2017, small-scale protests were organized in Kyiv by Mikhael Saakashvili—the former President of Georgia, who had been granted Ukrainian citizenship by Poroshenko, and appointed Governor of Odesa in 2015. Saakashvili had fallen out with the Ukrainian President by 2016 and was later stripped of his citizenship while travelling outside of Ukraine (i.e. his passport was annulled). After forcing his way back into the country across the Polish border, Saakashvili organized a public crusade in November 2017 against what he termed "the corrupt Poroshenko" calling for the latter's impeachment.[58] However, even at their most numerous, the demonstrations organized by Saakashvili's Movement of New Forces were able to gather no more than 20 thousand people.

Despite the dire economic conditions endured by the Ukrainian population in the post-Yanukovych years, prevailing public discourse seems to have remained idealistic, and attempts by populists to shift the political agenda to material concerns failed.[59] Saakashvili's marginally successful 2017 protests focused on wages, tariffs, and pensions as *byproducts* of corruption (rather than on corruption as a social phenomenon *per se*), and so they aroused suspicion from the public rather than widespread support. After the former Georgian President's expulsion from Ukraine, the supposedly grassroots movement that he had organized quickly dissipated with no further protests forthcoming. In this respect, the course of events in Ukraine after the ouster of Yanukovych was quite surprising: despite multiple years of economic hardship, the coming to power of "radicals" seems to have been avoided. No equivalent to Stalin or Robespierre (nor even a Mao, Castro, Ortega, or a Franco) ever emerged from Ukraine's revolution.

As Hannah Arendt pointed out, the distinguishing characteristic of the American Revolution (i.e. what made it different from other "great revolutions") was the single-minded focus of its protagonists on the ideals that had brought about the initial overthrow of the ancien regime. A shift away from the novel principles that had inspired the original revolutionaries had resulted in both the French and Russian revolutions' discourse descending into populist materialism and led to the guillotine and tyranny. Thus, the lesson of the "great revolutions" was that a "leftward shift"—a move away from idealism towards materialist socio-economic demands—distorted the original romantic ideals of the revolutionaries and resulted in terror.[60] It would seem that as in the US case, in Ukraine, the discourse of independence (de-colonization) trumped the discourse of social engineering; although external threat slowed the pace of domestic reform, its reality seems to have provided some protection against radicalization. Thus, despite severe economic hardship and war, during the first four post-Yanukovych years, the revolutionary process (and its protagonists) seems to have remained lodged in idealism. A shift to populist discourse was in evidence in the pre-election campaigns of Yulia Tymoshenko (running for the Presidency in 2019, promising to reduce natural gas prices in half), and of actor-comedian Volodymyr Zelensky, but the incumbent President's message of "Language, Faith, Army" continued to approximate the "revolutionary canon" of Maidan. At time of writing, the eventual result of this electoral contest between materialism and idealism remained unknown.

Three-dimensional process

It should be clear to the reader by now, that the analysis of Ukraine's Revolution of Dignity presented in the balance of this book posits the Maidan and Ukraine's subsequent defensive war with Russia as a *process*. Furthermore, I argue that this process is intelligible through ideational, rather than through a materialist lens. As such, I reject the structuralist (especially "realist") approach that has led other authors to interpret the "Ukraine Crisis" as an epiphenomenon of some postulated geopolitical power play, and therefore to overemphasize the macro-level context of events at the expense of the actors on the ground. Ukraine's Revolution of Dignity was (and continues to be) effected by Ukrainians. Certainly, the persona and decisions of Russian President Vladimir Putin are key to understanding the course of events described here, but revolutions are by their very nature *social* processes, and their analysis should not be reduced to an account of individual decision-making.

To the extent that one accepts a developmental perspective, according to which societies are said to evolve along set paths, revolutions represent radical breaks in these paths. As Arendt observed, the discourse of revolutionaries, firstly, implies a restoration of the "proper" path of development for society—a historical correction of a society's developmental trajectory. Secondly, the revolutionaries' "pathos" centers around novelty: the break with the past is not just a correction, but also a new beginning—a new polity, new institutions, a new social context. Thirdly, revolutions are about ideas: novel senses, untested organizational forms, experimentation and discussion. In the next three chapters I elaborate a thesis that follows Arendt's threefold characterization. I present Ukraine's Revolution of Dignity as having been about three things:

1. National liberation—completion of the de-colonization process that began in 1991 but was never fully realized due to the enduring Soviet identity myth of "brotherly Slavic peoples". This aspect of the Maidan was most controversial during the early stages of Ukraine's Revolution because the nation-builders coopted symbolism rooted in the country's 1918-21 and 1939-52 insurgencies and wartime proclamations of Ukrainian independence. However, in the process of becoming "canonized" as symbols of the Maidan protests and subsequent territorial defense efforts, the portraits of historical figures, and the symbols (badges, logos, emblems) and slogans adopted from previous eras acquired radically different meanings from those of their original context. Whereas prior to the Revolution of Dignity, one might associate the semiotic markers of Ukrainian patriotism (e.g. the red and black flag of the OUN; portraits of WWII-era nationalist leader Stepan Bandera) with unacceptable forms of integral nationalism, during and after the Maidan protests, these iconic markers came to symbolize solidarity in resistance to foreign aggression.

2. De-feudalization—revolt against a thoroughly corrupt, neofeudal, oligarchic regime that had privatized and monopolized large sections of Ukraine's economy, and had created a regulatory environment that was hostile to both independent business and to foreign investors. In addition to this negative program, this aspect of the revolution included a very basic demand for safety—i.e. citizens should not be beaten and shot by police in the streets—and more complex demands for "voice" in decision-making which later were enacted through the cooption of new actors ("flexians") into Ukraine's post-Maidan government. The purview and effect of the Revolution of Dignity was far from uniform in this dimension: new social cleavages came to the fore which will define the country's political and socio-economic landscapes for years to come.

3. Novel values and practices — a declaration of "dignity" of the person through organization and interdependency. Independence square in Kyiv became a focal point for spontaneous organization (barricades, first aid services, supply of food and firewood); when called upon to defend the country, many from this volunteer movement refocused from supplying protesters to supplying the front while others enlisted for military service. For many observers, this spontaneous social process seemed hardly revolutionary, but it is precisely in these new forms of horizontal solidarity and active citizenship that Ukrainians have offered a unique contribution to the world's civilizational development. Indeed, it may be this third social process that the Kremlin found sufficiently threatening to warrant being crushed by military aggression.

These three dimensions of Ukraine's Revolution of Dignity will be explored in the three chapters that follow. We begin with the most basic (and perhaps most controversial) dimension: the view of Maidan and the subsequent Russian-Ukrainian war as moments of nation-building that resulted in the rapid construction of a new, coalesced polity.

Chapter 8:
A National Revolution

In early December 2013 there were many nights when I returned home late from Maidan. I would ride the long escalator down into Independence Square metro station (the subway in Kyiv's city center is exceptionally deep), and I would observe. One evening, as I waited for the train, a group of young ladies (in their mid-20's) descended the escalator singing Ukraine's national anthem. Within seconds several hundred people who had been waiting quietly on the underground platform stood at attention and sang. I stopped observing. I sang too. And then I cried tears of joy... This was Kyiv! No one ever sang the national anthem spontaneously here! That night, I addressed my Ukrainian Diaspora friends through Facebook with the following message:

> Please be patient! Ukraine is in the midst of a very real and very significant social revolution. This revolution for many Ukrainians involves a new conceptualization of their values and identities. This is a painful process that needs to occur through collective action, introspection, and without external intervention.

Later, Kyiv Post deputy editor Katya Gorchinskaya pointed out that when one came to the city-center regularly, one could not help but notice a gradual, but perceptible change in discourse, in symbols, in peoples' attitudes and actions towards each other. Katya (a Russian-speaker) famously called this process the "birth of a nation:"

> This is about a nation being born. Mutilated by years of misrule, impoverished by looting, it emerges slowly from the ruin. This process is massive, and we don't know how well this birth is going to go. But it's happening now and here, in Kyiv, and it's both painful and awesome. The only place to truly feel the pain and grandeur of this national awakening is to stand there right on Maidan.[1]

Although Kyiv's Independence Square was the focal point of Ukrainians' sudden realization of their nationhood, the wave of spontaneous

displays of patriotism that swept the country during the Maidan protests and in subsequent months was not limited to the capital. During
the heady months of 2014 the entire country turned blue and yellow —
literally — with the national colors hung on what seemed like every
building. Ribbons and flags were mounted on cars. Children painted
the railings of bridges in their towns and villages in blue and yellow.
Cars had tridents, embroidery, and the national colors decaled on
their hoods and trunks. Hundreds of millions of hryvnia were collected through crowd-funding efforts to pay for clothing, food, and
equipment for the front, and each dispatch was accompanied by a flag,
and by patriotic cards hand-made by school children. Although many
of the volunteer battalions adopted symbols that some observers
found objectionable (e.g. the Azov battalion's neo-Nazi *Wolfsangel*,
and the Right Sector's adoption of the red and black flag used during
WWII by the Organization of Ukrainian Nationalists — OUN), the ethnic origins of the fighters, and their language preferences, represented
a relatively typical cross-section of Ukrainian society.[2] These people
(men and women) came to the front to defend their country against a
foreign invader — Russia — and there was no doubt that the vast majority of their fellow citizens supported them, and honored their
valor.[3]

    In this chapter we examine the "national" dimension of
Ukraine's Revolution of Dignity. Many external observers interpreted
the symbolism and discourse of the protests, and the frequent displays
of patriotism in response to what was widely perceived as unwar-
ranted Russian aggression, as symptomatic of Ukraine's "radicalization" (and even a turn towards "fascism").[4] For Ukrainians however,
their adoption of symbols and slogans conceived by other freedom
fighters from their past were not a reflection of "nationalism", but rather of "patriotism". Whatever the label, the *idea of Ukraine* mobilized
millions to engage in collective action and sacrifice. Many of those
who did so, prior to the Maidan protests and the Russian invasions,
had never previously given their identity serious thought.

Birth of a nation

Throughout the country's post-Soviet history, Ukraine was said to be inherently divided between a Russian-speaking east centered in Donetsk, and a Ukrainian-speaking west centered in Lviv.[5] Given regional ethno-linguistic cleavages (reflected in electoral preferences — see Chapter 2), and supposed differences in identity, the vast majority of political analyses began with a presentation of the country as a union of two solitudes: nation-building policies were to be its "glue".[6] However, as eminent historian Yaroslav Hrytsak pointed out, the division of Ukraine between east and west, with Lviv and Donetsk representing polar opposites, was a heuristic simplification that grossly misinterpreted Ukraine's realities. This dichotomous Ukraine never really existed. In his words, "there are other regions that defy this dichotomy. Instead of the theory of "two Ukraines", I would suggest the metaphor of "twenty-two Ukraines" as a more accurate way of describing the Ukrainian cultural and political map."[7]

What became clear in the aftermath of Russia's invasions of Crimea and the Donbas was that in Ukraine, diversity does not necessarily entail division.[8] Contrary to historiographic myths propagated by Russian nationalist ideologues,[9] according to which the territory of Ukraine was actually inhabited by two ethnically and historically distinct peoples (Galician-Volynians in the west, and Russians in the east), by the end of 2014 it had become patently obvious that Ukrainians were one people, and proud of it. Internal differences between the country's regions turned out to be comparable to those in evidence in any large European country. After-all, a Bavarian speaking his/her local dialect will not be understood by a resident of Hamburg, but no one in Germany would seriously suggest that the north and south are somehow artificially joined by historical circumstance. The foundational glue of their "imagined community"[10] includes agreement on *national* symbols, values, history, and a common feeling of belonging to a bounded citizenry. This agreement does not negate allegiance and identification with one's region or hometown (or to a transnational identity e.g. "Europe"), but particularly in times of stress, it is their nation that 21st century Europeans identify with.

In the Ukrainian case, this feeling of belonging to a distinctly national community was amplified by the Maidan protests, and by Russia's invasions thereafter. In the table below, poll results from the summer of 2013 (before the start of Euromaidan) and those of the summer of 2014 (after Yanukovych's ouster) are compared. When asked "Who do you consider yourself in the first place?", the majority of respondents in both surveys answered, "A citizen of Ukraine". However, in the wake of the Maidan protests and the annexation of Crimea by Russia, the proportion choosing this option grew dramatically: from 50.4% to 64.6% nationally:

Region[11]	West		Center		South (not incl. Crimea)		East		Donbas		National average	
	2013	2014	2013	2014	2013	2014	2013	2014	2013	2014	2013	2014
Self-identification												
Resident of the village or town I live in	27.7%	14.5%	27.9%	14.4%	32.0%	25.1%	33.6%	13.8%	28.6%	16.0%	28.7%	16.1%
Resident of the region (oblast or group of oblasts) I live in	6.6%	6.7%	5.6%	2.7%	2.1%	5.1%	7.4%	5.1%	14.8%	22.6%	7.9%	8.0%
Citizen of Ukraine	55.9%	70.1%	56.3%	75.7%	41.4%	59.5%	48.1%	66.7%	41.7%	37.0%	50.7%	64.6%
Representative of my ethnic group, nation	3.2%	3.2%	2.4%	1.9%	3.9%	1.0%	0.9%	3.2%	0.3%	0.0%	2.0%	2.1%
Citizen of the former USSR	1.4%	0.3%	3.7%	2.7%	10.5%	5.6%	6.8%	8.6%	11.7%	19.3%	6.6%	5.5%
Citizen of Europe	2.3%	3.2%	1.2%	0.5%	1.1%	0.5%	1.2%	0.8%	0.3%	1.1%	1.2%	1.1%
Citizen of the world	2.6%	1.4%	2.1%	1.1%	2.8%	3.1%	1.8%	1.7%	1.8%	3.3%	2.4%	2.1%
Other	0.3%	0.5%	0.9%	1.0%	1.1%	0.0%	0.0%	0.0%	0.7%	0.5%	0.6%	0.5%

Table 3: Poll results of responses to the question "Who do you consider yourself to be in the first place?" Surveys taken 27 June – 28 July 2013 and 10-29 July 2014. N = 1800 in each survey. Margin of error = 3%[12]

Besides the obvious and striking increase throughout Ukraine (except in the Donbas) in the number of respondents identifying themselves firstly as Citizens of Ukraine (an indicator of increased national pride), the data also show a decline in regional and local city/town self-identification (again — except in the Donbas).[13] With respect to the Donbas, the data shows a dramatic rise in the number of respondents in this region identifying themselves as "Citizens of the former USSR", and of those answering "Resident of the region I live in." Given that the 2014 data are from one of the last polls taken before access to areas not controlled by the Ukrainian government became restricted, the rise in regional solidarity, and the increased identification of Donbas respondents with their Soviet past, are both significant indicators of local distinctiveness. We shall return to a discussion of the specificities of the Donbas identity later in this chapter.

On a national level, the data indicate that the Maidan protests and their immediate aftermath (i.e. Russia's annexation of Crimea and the first months of war) produced a new conceptualization of the identities of large numbers of Ukrainians throughout the country. This was a deeply personal process that involved introspection, participation in collective action, and sudden revelations as to the core of one's identity. It entailed individual and voluntary entry into a community of like others, much larger in scope than one's town or village or region. Rather than being taught or implanted by elites (as had been recommended by policy-analysts throughout the post-Soviet period), nation-building seems to have occurred organically from the bottom-up. Alternatively, one could argue that years of elite-led nation-building (i.e. "soft" Ukrainianization policies in education, media, official communications) finally bore fruit in 2014. Whatever the causal path, the phenomenon of identity introspection was suddenly evident in a very large number of people.

Often, the conscious decision to *be* Ukrainian involved a decision to *speak* Ukrainian. For example, on 22 December 2013, one month after the start of the Maidan protests, Sonya Koshkina, a respected Russian-speaking Kyiv journalist posted the following to her Facebook page (in Ukrainian): "More and more, I feel an internal need to speak Ukrainian. I stress — an internal need. I guess this is my own personal revolution. P.S. (continued in Russian): I haven't crossed the line yet, but I'm getting close." During the three years that followed this post, this author's observations suggest that the number of Ukrainian speakers in Kyiv increased dramatically.

On the other hand, although speaking Ukrainian in the capital may have become trendy, language use in other regions changed minimally. Three years after the Maidan protests, the Razumkov Center asked a national sample of Ukrainians what language they spoke at home: 55% of respondents said Ukrainian, and 41% said Russian (1% – "other" and 3% refused to answer).[14] This compared with 52% vs. 45% in an analogous survey in 2011. If one views language as an identity marker, then a 3-4% change nationally indicates minimal identity shift. However, when asked what language they considered their "native language" ("mother tongue"), the number of respondents answering "Ukrainian" rose in 2016 to 69% from 61% in 2011, and the number of respondents answering "Russian" declined from 36% in 2011 to 27% in 2016. In other words, more Ukrainian citizens identified Ukrainian as being their *native* language (a significant shift of 8-9%), while relatively fewer changed their daily linguistic practices. This reflects the dual function of language: on the one hand it is a means of communication, and in this dimension, Ukrainians seemed pragmatic (or lazy) with Russian remaining the language of everyday use for many (particularly in the eastern and southern regions), as it had been for many for decades. On the other hand, language is a marker of identity, and in this dimension significantly more Ukrainians in 2016 than 5 years earlier indicated (truthfully or otherwise) that Ukrainian was their *native* language.

Identity (r)evolution

Sonya Koshkina's "personal revolution" (cited above) reflected this shift in linguistic identity: she *almost* switched to Ukrainian in her daily interactions, and for her this near-change already represented a fundamental identity shift. For Sonya, *feeling* Ukrainian did not necessarily entail *speaking* Ukrainian in everyday interactions, but it did involve a public declaration of linguistic allegiance as part of her personal identity revolution. Reflecting upon his own personal revolution, President Poroshenko's first Chief of Staff, Borys Lozhkin (a Russophone native of Kharkiv), wrote the following in his memoires:

> If, prior to November 2013 someone had asked me "Who are you?", most likely, I would have answered "a manager." In March 2014, the airplane on which I was returning from a business trip landed at Boryspil (Kyiv's international airport). I was suddenly struck by everything I had reflected upon and felt during the previous winter, and something inside clicked. I felt myself Ukrainian. I can say for myself: Ukrainian identity is not something given once and for all. It's a process that was ongoing (in me) during the past decades, at first unnoticeably, and then suddenly it accelerated.[15]

During what seems like a previous lifetime, in January 1991, I travelled to the eastern Ukrainian (Soviet) city of Dnipropetrovsk from Canada as an exchange student. During the six months that I studied history there, I enjoyed playing a linguistic game with the locals: while walking along the main street (Karl Marx Prospekt) of this industrial city of just under one million inhabitants, I would stop random pedestrians to ask the time—in Ukrainian. In 9 out of 10 cases the reaction would be shock, and less than half would actually understand my question. At the time, Dnipropetrovsk was a city whose primarily ethnic Ukrainian population had become thoroughly russified. During the March 1991 all-Soviet referendum on renewal of the USSR, over 80% of the city's population voted in favor of preserving the Soviet Union as a "renewed federation" (82% at Dnipropetrovsk University where I studied). Six months later, these same voters cast their ballots in huge numbers in support for Ukraine's declaration of independence, but few really identified with the Ukrainian nation—theirs was primarily a vote *against* the USSR, rather than *for* an independent Ukraine. For many years after 1991, the blue and yellow flag continued to be considered mildly subversive and the trident was largely a foreign symbol in this heavily industrialized region that had been the birthplace of Brezhnev, and the home of the USSR's largest rocket factory.

Fast forward one generation. On 1 June 2014 I watched a news report about an officer from Dnipropetrovsk who had volunteered to serve in the Anti-Terrorist Operation in the Donbas. He had been wounded and was brought home for surgery and convalescence. His friends and comrades sent out a call for blood donors through social media. Within a few hours several hundred volunteers showed up, and the hospital's blood donor clinic was overwhelmed. The people in line spoke Ukrainian (loudly and proudly though with frequent errors in pronunciation and grammar); they sang the national anthem; they wore t-shirts with the trident, and many wrapped themselves in blue and yellow flags.

During subsequent months, the city of Dnipropetrovsk (officially renamed Dnipro in 2016 as part of Ukraine's "decommunization" policy)[16] became the *de facto* linchpin of Ukraine's defense against Putin's plans for the creation of Novorossiya. Although the role of Ihor Kolomoisky in turning this city into a fortress and central supply point for the front should not be underestimated, without support from the local population, Ukraine's third richest oligarch, and primary owner of the "Pryvat" financial industrial group would not have been successful in realizing his personal grudge against Putin.[17] Ukraine's eastern industrial hub continued its role as the central logistical center for the war effort well after Kolomoisky left the governorship in 2015. Furthermore, the city's Mechnikov hospital—and its Russian speaking Head Doctor, Dr. Sergey Rizhenko[18]—became staples of the national news throughout the war in the Donbas: whenever heavy shelling led to casualties, seriously wounded soldiers were evacuated there by helicopter for complex surgery. The doctors seemed to perform miracles.

Several observers have mused that Putin is to be thanked for making Ukrainians outside the Donbas and Crimea realize their nationhood,[19] but the process began well before Russia's (stealth and then overt) invasion. During the Maidan protests many activists reported having experienced a kind of identity reset: reflection, and purposeful decision-making as to their own definitions of "I". This process was in many ways spiritual (or felt as such), particularly in moments when newly identified "I"s found others (MANY others) who had just experienced the same introspective process.

Independentism

Ironically, Ukraine's identity revolution began as a declaration of unity with the European Union—a political project that was specifically designed to *downplay* what had been the tremendously destructive consequences of 20th century versions of nationalism on the continent. However, as argued in the final part of this chapter, the territorial, inclusive and present-focused version of Ukrainians' identity construct that emerged from the Maidan protests and subsequent defensive mobilization of volunteers, had very little in common with past European versions of ethno-linguistic (primordial) nationalism, and even less with the early 21st century pan-European political identity project of the EU. The territorial identity spawned by the Maidan protests and the experience of war was surprisingly inclusive of multiple languages and ethnicities. It was also non-etatist—often explicitly rejecting the state as a central institution of the nation. *Independence* was valued (expressed in the phrase "sovereignty and territorial integrity"), but not necessarily its instantiation in political structures.

Ukrainians' attitudes towards their country's independence has not always been unequivocal.[20] The Kyiv International Institute of Sociology first conducted a poll in 1991, on the eve of the referendum that led to the dissolution of the USSR, asking respondents as to their voting intentions (these data largely predicted the official results). The poll was repeated with the same question in 2006, 2011, and 2016.[21]

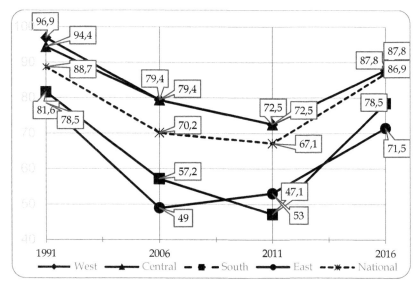

Figure 5:   Poll results showing support for Ukrainian independence. Comparative data for polls taken in 1991, 2006,
2011, 2016 by the Kyiv International Institute of Sociology (N=2040). Respondents were asked "If the referendum on Ukraine's independence were held today, how
would you vote?"[22]

As shown in the graph above, whereas the number of advocates of
independence clearly waned fifteen and twenty years after Ukraine's
separation from the USSR, by 2016 support for national self-determination had returned to 1991 levels throughout the country — most notably in the Russian-speaking regions of the east and south. In the
wake of the Maidan protests and Russia's invasion, Ukrainians
seemed to have become convinced as to the righteousness of their
founding choice twenty-five years earlier. As Steffen Halling and Susan Stewart of the German Institute for International and Security Affairs note:

> Surveys show that the Ukrainian population's emotional connection to
> the nation increased sharply in the course of 2014; one can certainly
> speak of an acceleration of the Ukrainian nation-building process.

> While pro-Ukrainian attitudes are more prevalent in the western, cen-
> tral and northern parts of the country than in the east and south, it
> should be noted that a majority of Ukrainians in all these areas identify
> with the Ukrainian state and support its independence. In fact, the
> strongest growth in pro-Ukrainian attitudes is found in the eastern
> parts of the country, where more than two thirds of the population
> now favor Ukrainian statehood. This underlines how regional differ-
> ences have as a whole declined in importance in the course of the crisis,
> and that despite regional specifics Ukrainian society is today more
> united than before.[23]

Universally, observers of post-Maidan Ukraine noted a significant decline in previously manifest regional divisions and an upsurge of *national* patriotism. Variously manifest in linguistic identification, affinity to symbols, re-evaluation of historical figures, reappraisal of holi-
days, etc., this process of identity reorientation involved emotional
soul-searching. Self-analysis of an individual's definition of "I" was of
necessity not an easy process. When this self-examination was followed by a realization that many others characterized themselves using the same (or very similar) interpretation of "I", the result was the
formation of a coalesced and very powerful "WE". The depth of this
personal revolution, and its uniqueness as a social phenomenon,
needs further explanation.

Development of discourse

Identity is intimately linked to jargon. Terminology reflects cultural
codes, mutually understood conceptual frames, communicative artefacts produced, exchanged, and understood by members of an in-
group. When new terminology is created—rapidly, to keep up with
fast-paced events—it is not inconceivable that a process of new identity creation is underway. When new terms are immediately understood and internalized by large numbers of people, a very special process of large-scale collective identity construction is in evidence. This
is precisely what seems to have transpired in Ukraine during the Maidan protests and during the early months of the conflict with Russia.

Sociolinguist Nadia Trach likened the evolution of discourse
around Maidan to a process approximating maturity: "By studying

the language of protest we witness Ukrainian society transforming from that of rebellious post-Soviet teenager into an entity that is grown-up, civic."[24] The first signs of this evolution were observable at the very start of the protests when the prefix "Euro" was added to the familiar (after the 2004 Orange demonstrations) place-of-protest term "Maidan".[25] The author of this innovation remains unknown, but the result was the establishment of a global brand that encapsulated the essence of the demands of the early protesters, and simultaneously caught the attention of the international press as an intriguing yet simple name for a complex political phenomenon. For many of those protesting (particularly after 1 December 2014), "Euromaidan" did not necessarily connote a specific demand to sign the EU Association Agreement. The "Euro" prefix symbolized a set of (imagined) values—life according to set rules, recognition of personal dignity, freedom to travel, study etc. Coupled with "Maidan", the resultant term encapsulated all of the place, the cause, the method, and the goal in a single identifier.[26]

Eventually however, the prefix "Euro" disappeared from domestic discourse surrounding Maidan. EU leaders' expressions of "deep concern" became the objects of ridicule, particularly when voiced in response to obvious aggression from Russia and/or loss of life. For example, a poster with the following words (in English) was initially shared on Facebook in late January as the first protester deaths were reported,[27] and then was posted on the wall near the entrance to the main post office on Kyiv's Independence Square:

> Dear European Union and United States of America!
> We no longer need your moral support. Act or fuck off!
> With Eurolove from EuroUkraine

Domestication of Maidan (its decoupling from the "Euro" prefix) was not only the result of disillusion with the lack of tangible assistance from Ukraine's western partners. It also reflected a positive tendency—evolution of the protest movement from one focused on a foreign policy document (effectively a free trade agreement) that was interpreted as carrying significant weight with respect to Ukraine's "civilizational choice," towards a primarily domestic movement engendering a distinctly Ukrainian struggle for self-identification, self-reliance, individual and collective dignity, and independent nationhood. In the words of the TaRuta folk-rock band "We were searching for Europe, but we found Ukraine."[28]

Several wordplays around the term *Maidan* appeared during the early "Sich" period of the protests (see Chapter 3), as the relevance of the "Euro" prefix declined. For example, in December 2013 a group of activists led by Yulia Tychkivska (nee Kocherhan) and rapper Oleksandr Polozhynsky organized an information center under the catchphrase "*Ne zlyy Maidan*" — a triple-meaning allusion that translates in the descriptive form as "Not a bad Maidan", in the instructive form as "Don't anger Maidan", and in the colloquial as "Don't betray Maidan" (in colloquial use "*zlyy*" means "flush" and implies betrayal — a reference to the political opposition leaders whom many of the protesters feared were actually in cahoots with Yanukovych).[29] In a testament to the national scale of Ukraine's revolutionary movement, in late 2013, people began referring to the local protest camps established in regional centers as "Maidans".[30] At approximately the same time, "Maidan" first came to be used as a verb in the context of "Let's maidan Yanukovych!" ("*Pomaidanemo Yanukovycha!*"), and demonstrators throughout the country came to identify themselves as "*maidanivtsi*" (adjectival noun), while their detractors called them "*maidauny*" (i.e. combined the term Maidan with Down — a reference to Down Syndrome). People caught up in the spirit of the protest movement became known as "*maidanuti*", and those who volunteered for public service in the aftermath of Yanukovych's ouster were said to be creating "internal Maidans" in their respective ministries. Universally, they were seen as carriers of "Maidan values" (*tsinnosti Maidanu*) — a term whose meaning varied over time, but initially and superficially meant valuing transparency, cooperation, idealism, patriotism, and service.

Unity of the nation was a central theme of the Maidan protests, and it became even more important during subsequent months when the threat of separatism loomed over many of the eastern and southern regions. The slogan "*Yedyna Krayina – Yedinaya Strana*" meaning

"One country", but written both in Ukrainian and in Russian, was broadcast in the top right corner of the screens of most Ukrainian television stations 24/7 throughout the summer of 2014. The burnt-out Trade Unions building on Kyiv's Independence Square was draped in a massive banner with these words, and several flash-mobs on social media were organized whereby normally Russian-speakers would write posts exclusively in Ukrainian, and Ukrainianophones would write in Russian.

A surprising source of solidarity and national pride was to be found among Ukraine's football ultras, including fans of Donetsk Shakhtar, Luhansk Zorya, and Kharkiv Metalist. During the protests they popularized the chant: "*Vid Luhanska do Karpat, fanat fanatu druh i brat!*" ("From Luhansk to the Carpathians, one fan for another is friend and brother"). Their message was a call for unity — i.e. a solidification of the in-group. Kharkiv's Metalist Ultras were later credited with authoring the "*Putin khuylo!*" ("Putin is a dickhead!") chant and song in March 2014 which defined the out-group with little uncertainty.[31] By the summer of 2014, the chant and associated song had gone viral on the internet, with Ukrainians around the world competing as to who could create the most creative rendition.[32]

The extraordinary social energy and collective creativity of 2014 (typical of revolutionary periods) resulted in terminology and discourse developing rapidly and in completely unpredictable ways. For example, whereas the greeting "*Slava Ukrayini!*" ("Glory to Ukraine!") and the requisite answer "*Heroyam Slava!*" ("Glory to the Heroes!") was once used only by marginal nationalist groups, during the Maidan, and especially in the context of the war with Russia, this greeting came to be adopted universally: pronounced at the end of President Poroshenko's speeches, and voiced by both Lithuanian President Dalia Grybovskaite and EU Commission President Donald Tusk in their addresses to Ukrainians on the occasion of the EU's granting them visa-free entry.[33] In August 2018, Poroshenko announced that "Slava Ukrayini!" would become the official greeting of the Armed Forces of Ukraine.

Misread symbols

One of the key aspects of the Maidan protests were their "national-liberationist" character, and therefore not surprisingly, symbols and slogans from previous independentist Ukrainian social movements (some of which had a controversial history) were eagerly adopted by the demonstrators, and later by volunteers who mobilized to support the war effort against Russia. In some cases, the line between righteous protest and territorial defense on the one hand, and extremism and military adventurism on the other became blurred. On the streets of Kyiv, the demonstrators wanted a change of government; they wanted to unseat a despot.[34] In the fields and trenches of the Donbas, the volunteer movement spawned by Russia's aggression was motivated by a similar ethos. Willingness to sacrifice for the sake of one's "nation" became the defining characteristic of both a Maidan revolutionary, and a Ukrainian volunteer defender.

But one might ask: why frame this patriotic ethos in nationalist rhetoric? Why fly red and black flags, and display portraits of WW2-era OUN leader Stepan Bandera — a figure who had been portrayed in Soviet historiography as an enemy of the Ukrainian socialist state, and was therefore divisive? One answer might involve reference to the OUN of the 1930's as one of the few organizations in recent history that propounded an independent Ukrainian state; the UPA (Ukrainian Insurgent Army) that the OUN spawned, fought both the Nazi and Soviet armies in equal measure (a fact that was downplayed by Soviet historians, generating a negative image of the insurgency in the central and eastern regions of the country). Although the details of particular military operations conducted by the OUN-UPA are highly controversial,[35] given the revolutionary situation of 2014 and thereafter, objective analysis of historical facts was completely irrelevant to the protesters on Maidan, and doubly so for most of the volunteers who took up arms to defend Ukraine's territorial integrity. For them Bandera and the OUN-UPA simply represented symbols of Ukrainian independentist struggle and were therefore a useful anchor for their own efforts.

However, this adoption of symbols from the past (their modernization) by the Maidan protesters, and later by volunteers mobilizing resources for Ukraine's territorial defense, caused significant controversy. Western journalists arriving in Kyiv in late 2013 or early 2014 — parachuted into a country they knew little about — would inevitably ask: is this a revolution, a rebellion, a sit-in, or a radical-right inspired conspiracy? The last characterization was clearly the "juicy story" most hoped to find, but many (i.e. those who bothered to objectively examine implanted stereotypes) were disappointed.[36] The first Euromaidan demonstrations were sparked by a Facebook post authored by Mustafa Nayem — an ethnic Pashtun journalist born in Kabul Afghanistan, who moved to Kyiv in his youth. The first tragic deaths on Hrushevskoho St. in January 2014 were of Serhiy Nigoyan, an ethnic Armenian who enjoyed reciting poetry by Shevchenko,[37] and of Mykhailo Zhysnevskiy, a Belarusian. Given these facts, any descriptions of the Maidan protests or of the subsequent war in the Donbas as clashes between ethno-linguistic identities were obviously false. Nevertheless, the portrayal of Ukraine's revolution as a "fascist coup" proved highly pervasive and sustained. In the words of journalist and commentator Oksana Forostyna "This approach is shallow but comforting: identity conflicts can be transferred to the domain of irrationality, which means we do not need to treat these tribes somewhere beyond the EU borders as comprehensible or driven by rational narratives."[38] Simplification does not require nuance. The fact that many of the Maidan activists and most of the volunteers who went to fight in the Donbas were Russian speakers (not ethno-linguistic Ukrainian nationalists) can be glanced over as a fact that adds superfluous complexity and can therefore be omitted from the presented narrative.

The above should not be interpreted as a claim that right-wing nationalism was not a factor in Ukraine's revolution. Certainly, supporters of the right-wing "Svoboda" party (led by Oleh Tiahnybok) were active in the Maidan protests, and nationalists/patriots (what one calls them depends on one's political preferences) were among those who condoned the use of violence against the Yanukovych regime. Indeed, the role of *Pravyi sektor* (the Right Sector led by Dmytro Yarosh) as an initiator of violence on 19 January 2014 on European Square, and then their role as autonomous combatants during the war in the Donbas is well documented. Notably however, candidates fielded by both groups gained a combined 6.5% of the popular vote in the October 2014 Parliamentary elections. Right-wing nationalism clearly did not enjoy national voter support, whereas the Maidan protests and the volunteer efforts aimed at defending the country, did.

On Maidan, and in the trenches of the Donbas, nationalist rhetoric and symbolism became the 'semiotic glue' for an *imagined community* formed and located in the *present* — not in the past. The protesters adopted the red and black of the OUN-UPA because it was a flag of resistance: after-all, Yanukovych, as President of Ukraine, used the traditional colors of the Ukrainian nation (blue and yellow), and so a different identifier was required.[39] The fact that the colors of the OUN-UPA were chosen as a symbol of bonding on Maidan was probably initiated by those right-wing nationalists ("Svoboda" and/or *Pravyi sektor*) present among the protesters who understood the flag's historical significance, but for the majority, the ideology of integral nationalism that had led to the creation of these symbols, was foreign. To claim that the Maidan or the volunteer battalions created in response to Russia's aggression in 2014 represented radical nationalist phenomena is equivalent to claiming that the images of American Presidents printed on US currency represent an acceptance by Americans of slavery — after-all, almost every one of these men, at one time, was a slave owner. A more nuanced approach would suggest that in the process of becoming "canonized", historical figures' factual biographies often become irrelevant to the nation that has adopted them as symbols. This is precisely what occurred in Ukraine during the Maidan: although the historical symbols of the OUN-UPA may have been introduced into public discourse by representatives of nationalist groups, as the transformation of these symbols into present-focused "semiotic glue" proceeded, followers of an exclusively ethnic conception of the Ukrainian nation became sidelined from public discourse.

Donbas and the southeast

Ukraine is a large country — the largest nation-state wholly within Europe. Not surprisingly, its regions differ. Unfortunately, these regional differences have rarely been the object of careful academic study[40] — a fact that has resulted in proliferated stereotype and misconception. As noted previously, one of the most tragic errors committed by analysts of Ukraine (and it would seem also by the Kremlin since Putin's proclaimed support for an imaginary "Novorossiya" was based on this error), was to equate choice of language for everyday interaction with identity and geopolitical preference. The portrayal of Ukraine as divided between two poles — one centered in Ukrainian-speaking Lviv, and the other in Russian-speaking Donetsk — represented an extreme case of oversimplification.[41] According to this stereotype, the south-central (e.g. Dnipropetrovsk), southern (e.g. Odesa and/or Mykolayiv), and eastern (e.g. Kharkiv) regions were portrayed as more moderate versions of the Donbas: whereas the electorates of Donetsk and Luhansk oblasts voted almost unanimously for the pro-Soviet Communist Party in the 1990's and thereafter for the pro-Russian Party of Regions, the other regions of the southeast displayed more plurality in political preferences, but nevertheless supported "orange" (pro-European national-democratic) forces only marginally. The reason for greater plurality in voting patterns outside of the Donbas (so it was believed) was that everyday use of Russian in these southeastern regions was not as all-embracing as in Donetsk and (especially southern) Luhansk oblasts. Given the highly significant statistical correlation between voting preference and language use,[42] Russian-speakers (a majority throughout the southeast, though not uniformly distributed) were deemed less loyal to Ukraine. This stereotype held until 2014.

In the wake of the Maidan protests it became clear that although Ukraine's largely Russian-speaking south-central industrial heartland (centered in the cities of Dnipropetrovsk and Zaporizhzhia), and the southern agricultural region (Kirovohrad, Mykolayiv and Kherson oblasts) predominantly voted for Yanukovych in 2004 and 2010, and for the Party of Regions in multiple parliamentary elections (including 2012), their electorates' geopolitical preferences were not pro-Russian. Whereas in Donetsk and Luhansk (and certainly in Crimea), anti-western and anti-Kyiv sentiment was relatively widespread, this was not the case (at least not to the same extent) in other southeastern oblasts. When prompted by circumstances to choose their geopolitical

orientation in 2014, most residents of Ukraine's southeast chose loyalty to the post-Maidan Kyiv government over Putin.

This geopolitical choice was not taken lightly. It was the result of
an identity revolution that swept the region in early 2014 — one in
which the image of the freedom-loving Cossack warrior proved an exceptionally strong identity marker for residents of Ukraine's southeast. To many this groundswell of historically rooted patriotism was
surprising because throughout the post-Soviet period, the Cossack
identity myth had been largely ignored in the discourse of memory
politics. To emotionally rouse their bases, Ukraine's politicians had
often appealed to differing interpretations of recent history (especially
WWII), but the Cossacks were generally left out of these debates:
Ukraine's steppe warriors were deemed archaic, outmoded, and/or
quaint, but uncontroversial. Whereas anti-nationalist rhetoric (propagated by the Communists and Party of Regions) was fostered in the
Donbas by local elites, and an anti-Soviet narrative was cultivated in
western Ukraine (not least by far-right groups such as "Svoboda"), the
memory politics of the south-central and southern regions were more
ambiguous. Their identity seemed to be rooted in an uncontentious,
uniquely Ukrainian, narrative of the Zaporozhzhian Cossacks that
was neither politicized, nor actively verbalized. In the geographical
Cossack heartland, the response to existential threat seemed almost
genetically programmed. Residents of Dnipropetrovsk, Kirovohrad
and Mykolayiv, may have been ambivalent as to who should be considered a hero in World War II,[43] but their regional identity — powered
by the Cossack mythomoteur — left no room for ambiguity as to what
should be done when their territory came under attack: of the approximately 90 volunteer battalions organized throughout Ukraine in
April-June 2014, seven originated in Dnipropetrovsk; Mykolayiv was
home to the 79th Airborne Brigade (sent into action in the Donbas in
July 2014), and later became home for the Ukrainian Marines (36th
Naval Infantry Brigade); Kirovohrad had been the base for Ukraine's
special operations training center, and also organized three volunteer
battalions in mid-2014.[44]

In Kharkiv and Odesa the populations' choices were equivocal.
Attempts to foster separatism in these cities failed, but for different

reasons than in the Cossack heartland regions of Dnipropetrovsk and/or Mykolayiv oblasts. The cities of Kharkiv and Odesa both have weak identity associations with Cossack history; their urban populations are largely descendants of Russian-speaking immigrants who settled in the agrarian Cossack region during the 200 years that preceded the formation of the USSR. In both cases, the urban centers are surrounded by Ukrainian-speaking villages and towns, and so language in these regions traditionally reflects rural/urban tension. However, during the Maidan protests, activist counter-elites emerged within the urban populations of both cities: in 2014, the traditionally passive Russophone working-class majority of Kharkiv was confronted by a suddenly active Ukraine-focused intellectual minority whose identity harkened back to the 1920's literary revival of the city (the informal leader of the Kharkiv Maidan was the Ukrainian writer Serhiy Zhadan); in Odesa, a similar ambivalence of identity was rooted in the city's history and image as a center of Ukraine's Jewish community — an image that ceased to reflect reality by the end of the 1990's due to mass emigration to Israel, but nevertheless left an indelible mark on the city's residents' self-perceptions. The existential threat to Ukraine, manifest in the violence in Kyiv, and then in the covert invasion of Crimea by Russia, resulted in the rise of pro-Ukrainian proto-elites in both Kharkiv and Odesa. They challenged these cities' established pro-Russian identity constructs, debunking the stereotype according to which Ukraine's predominantly Russian-speaking southeast universally leaned towards Moscow.

As a result, the *Novorossiya* project failed: the urban elites of Kharkiv and Odesa rejected the uncertainties of separatism, whereas throughout the rest of Ukraine's south-east, large majorities asserted their Cossack heritage to justify their distinctly Ukrainian identity. In the end, these supposedly pro-Russian regions spawned a new phenomenon: the Russian-speaking Ukrainian patriot. In the words of political scientist Volodymyr Kulyk, the Revolution of Dignity changed the geography of identity politics in Ukraine:

> (T)he main dividing line has shifted eastwards and now lies between the Donbas and the adjacent east-southern regions. Residents of the

latter have acquired a stronger and more anti-Russian Ukrainian identity, while in the former people increasingly prioritize the attachment
to their region or particular localities, coupled with a political and/or
cultural orientation towards Russia. For a decade after the Orange Revolution, Ukrainian society was characterized by the uneasy coexistence
of two roughly equal territorial 'halves' with their respective divergent
identities and policy preferences. Now the bulk of the population
seems to agree on the salience of national identity and main elements
of its content, including a pro-Western foreign policy...[45]

Asserting an eastward shift in Ukraine's regional identity divide
(though accurate) does not explain why such a shift occurred. Although it is now clear that anti-Maidan (and later pro-Russian) activism throughout eastern and southern Ukraine was instigated, financed, and organized by Russian agents in the region (see Chapters
5 and 6), clandestine operatives would not have been successful in
their efforts to sow unrest in the Donbas (and certainly Putin's "little
green men" would not have been successful in taking control of Crimea) if some level of support for separatism and/or joining Russia
were not forthcoming from the local population. Whereas the situation in Crimea is understandable—a majority of the peninsula's population was ethnically Russian; over 20 thousand Russian troops (and
their families) were permanently stationed there; pro-Russian political parties had operated openly and gained some support (although
minor) throughout the previous two decades—the sources of support
for separatism in the Donbas were not immediately obvious. What
made the people of the Donbas different from those of other regions
of Ukraine's southeast? Why did the wave of patriotism that swept
through all of mainland Ukraine in the wake of Putin's annexation of
Crimea, not affect the Donbas in the same way? Although it is now
clear that the "referenda" that supposedly legitimized the formation
of the breakaway "Luhansk People's Republic" and "Donetsk People's Republic" were shams, why in mid-2014, did some local leaders
(including police and SBU officers, mayors, city councilors) in the
Donbas overtly betray the Kyiv government whereas their counterparts in Dnipropetrovsk, Zaporizhzhia, Mykolayiv and Kharkiv did
not?

One possible answer refers to the differing historical roots of the various regions of Ukraine's south-east. Whereas the populations of the south-eastern oblasts outside the Donbas identified with an independentist Cossack past, this identity myth was not natural for the easternmost coal-mining region which had been settled much later (primarily in the late 19th and early 20th centuries). Several researchers of Ukraine's Donbas have concluded that the region's unique history as a frontier that attracted migrant "freedom-seekers and fortune hunters"[46] from all corners of the Russian Empire and (later) the USSR, generated a unique local culture characterized by insularity, mistrust of outsiders, and tolerance of crime. As politically incorrect as this hypothesis may sound, the Donbas identity seems to have differed from that of even its closest regional neighbors. According to one study of the coal basin's culture, "…spending time in prison (was seen as) an opportunity to enrich one's personal experience, especially in one's youth… (I)n the Donbass, serving a prison sentence is considered the equivalent of serving in the military."[47] The region's dependence on coal mining generated a strictly hierarchical culture whose representatives were characterized by "tough styles of behavior, respect for force, high value of labor culture, and a focus on issues of material well-being."[48]

A negative image of Kyiv had been fostered for years in the local Donbas media by elites who stripped legacy Soviet-era assets while blaming wage arrears and underinvestment on the central government.[49] Asset stripping reached epic proportions under the Yanukovych regime, and not surprisingly, after the change of government in Kyiv, many local officials feared prosecution. In 2014, mayors in towns like Slovyansk, Kramatorsk, Horlivka in Donetsk oblast actually led attacks against *their own* buildings. They feared prosecution by the revolutionary Kyiv government if local Yanukovych-era crimes were uncovered; feared losing access to income streams resulting from criminal/corrupt rent-extraction schemes. In Dnipropetrovsk, Mykolayiv, Odesa and Kharkiv corrupt elites (including former Party of Regions appointees) sided with the post-Yanukovych pro-Maidan government—likely not because they feared prosecution for corruption any less, but rather because they believed immunity deals and/or continued access to income streams could be negotiated more readily with Kyiv than with Moscow. In Donetsk and Luhansk oblasts, faced with the choice between loyalty to a pro-European post-Yanukovych government that promised rules-based administration (and possible prosecution), and the prospect of anarchic self-rule and banditry in nominally independent "people's republics", local elites in the Donbas chose the latter.[50] A significant portion of the population supported them—though not all. Tragically, within several months after the proclamation of the "DNR" and "LNR", anarchy resulted in a mass exodus of those Donetsk and Luhansk residents who had supported unity with Ukraine.[51] The de-populated and unrecognized "republics" of the Donbas came to be ruled by multiple criminal gangs supported (but not fully controlled) by the Kremlin.[52]

Russia's annexation of Crimea, and the events that led to the partial occupation of Donetsk and Luhansk oblasts, resulted in Ukraine losing approximately 7% of its territory. Identity conflict—stoked by Russian agents but supported by a small (compact) minority of pro-Russian citizens of Ukraine—was the root cause of this loss. However, had the previously accepted narrative, according to which Russian-speaking southeastern Ukrainians were said to crave closer ties with the Russian Federation been valid, the territorial loss would have been much greater.[53] To the surprise of many, Ukrainians in the country's southeast declared themselves Ukrainian: contrary to the Soviet-inspired myth of "brotherly peoples",[54] they avowed their difference from Russia. Their declared identity was neither linguistic, nor ethnic, nor (as seen below) "civic".

A newfound patriotism

Classical studies of the phenomenon of national identity (e.g. by Benedict Anderson, Anthony Smith, Ernest Gellner, etc.) suggest that nationalism evolved in Europe in one of two ways. In western Europe, pride in one's country developed according to an institutional ("civic") model whose nucleus was the state and its institutions (e.g. monarch, parliament, president, constitution, etc.). An alternative form of nationalism is said to have developed in Germany and in stateless Eastern European countries: a primordial identity based on a myth of common ethnic ancestry, focused on language, history, custom, etc. The brand of patriotism developed by Ukrainians during the Revolution of Dignity seems to fit neither conception. Although the Cossack mythomoteur was strong, this choice of historical myth was more based on a unifying territorial identification, than on an acceptance of a specific historiographic narrative. Plural and inclusive (i.e. in-group identification based neither on language, nor ethnic origin), Ukrainians' national pride seemed far removed from the ethno-nationalist ideology that spawned fascism and Nazism in the 20th century. On the other hand, the institutions of the state, which are said to form the core around which "western" national identities coalesced were almost universally weak in Ukraine.

Ukrainians are notorious for their consistently low levels of trust in government institutions.[55] Since independence, multiple polling agencies have repeatedly asked respondents whether they trust their government, Parliament, President, political parties, judges, police, army, security services, etc.[56] Despite short periods during which more respondents answered positively than negatively (usually immediately after elections) the balance of Ukrainians' trust in their state institutions has consistently been in deficit.[57] The army was a notable exception (trust levels rose dramatically in 2014 and thereafter), but when asked whether they trust the Armed Forces *command*, respondents' answers inevitably switched to "no". During the post-Maidan period, the only social institutions that consistently elicited trust were volunteers, the Church (denomination unspecified), and non-governmental organizations. Under such conditions, to claim that a "civic" form of national identity had formed during the Maidan protests and subsequent Russian invasions, would clearly be an overstatement.[58] Conversely, intense patriotism was in evidence throughout Ukraine during the post-Maidan years of defensive war with Russia, and the expression of such patriotism was not limited to Ukrainian-speakers, nor to ethnic Ukrainians. This was not an ethno-linguistic ("primordial") identity either. Indeed, discourse focused on "Ukrainian" as an ethno-linguistic category was patently rejected. The historical or political bases for this newfound Ukrainian identity were not immediately obvious.

The most striking aspect of Ukrainians' identity revolution was their refusal to ground identity in history. The discursive shift was logical and unifying: the wars of the past were controversial; the war of the present was clear-cut: Russia had attacked; Ukraine needed to be defended. During 4 years of hostilities spanning 2014-2018, almost 11 thousand Ukrainians lost their lives to the war — over 3,000 of these were servicemen killed defending their homeland. Throughout Ukraine, the dead were honored by passers-by kneeling on the street when military funeral processions passed. An additional 12 thousand Armed Forces personnel were wounded in battles with an aggressive enemy, and over 1.8 million citizens of Donetsk and Luhansk oblasts were internally displaced and resettled in other regions of Ukraine. These individuals (ever-present in the population — see Preface), and the graves of the sons, husbands, and fathers who paid the ultimate price defending Ukraine, generated a powerful foundation for common identity: even if it had not existed consensually in the past, it materialized and hardened quickly in the present. This shift to a present-focused identity represented a major — revolutionary — outcome of Ukraine's Revolution of Dignity.

A present-focused identity required a clear break with the past. In April 2015, the Verkhovna Rada adopted a package of laws mandating the removal of all remnants of communist rule from public places (i.e. Lenin statues and Soviet-era symbolism). The legislation also made the promotion of communist and fascist ideologies illegal, required the renaming of streets, villages, towns and cities with Soviet-era toponymics, and (controversially) equated the status of veterans of the World War II OUN-UPA nationalist movement to that of Red Army veterans. Public criticism of organizations and individuals who struggled for the cause of Ukrainian independence was declared "derision" and "humiliation of the Ukrainian people's dignity", and therefore illegal (the law did not specify punishment for infraction). Propaganda of both communism and national socialism (including displays of relevant symbolism) was outlawed.

The passage of this package of laws aroused opposition from scholars (both Ukrainian and foreign), concerned that its provisions would threaten objective historical research.[59] Later, the Polish Foreign minister sensationally declared that his country would veto any eventual EU accession request from Ukraine so long as Ukrainians continued to officially venerate the war-time leader Bandera.[60] Poland objected to the glorification of the OUN-UPA in particular, because this group had been accused of war crimes against Polish troops and civilians in the Volyn region in 1944.[61] Despite such high-level protests however, the implementation of the de-communization laws did not result in significant domestic resistance: in 2016 Dnipropetrovsk was renamed Dnipro; Kirovohrad became Kropyvnitsky; the names of 30 other urban centers and 955 villages were changed either by local-level decisions or by Parliament. A total of 1320 Lenin statues throughout Ukraine were dismantled in 2014-16.[62] Additionally, 1069 other Soviet-era monuments were torn down, and 51 493 streets were renamed. The de-communization initiative received some criticism from skeptics who questioned whether the expense of changing signs throughout the country was justified, but overall, Ukrainians welcomed the changes; some even enthusiastically. A nationally representative survey conducted in November 2016 found 48% of respondents supporting de-communization, 36% opposed, and 16% undecided.[63]

Ukraine's removal of Soviet-era monuments and renaming of toponymics contrasted sharply with the memory politics propagated by the "administrations" of the occupied territories of the Donbas and Crimea. Having fallen under the cultural umbrella of the Russian Federation, where Soviet heritage (including the persona of Stalin) was venerated, there, glorification of "Victory in the Great Patriotic War" was pompous and sacrosanct.[64] On the other hand, the Holodomor (Stalin's artificial famine), the one consensual 20th century identity anchor that Ukrainians universally commemorated—a tragedy that had decimated no less than 20% of the populations of the southeastern regions in 1932-33—was rejected by the Donetsk and Luhansk "republics". The contrasting commemorative contexts represented visible and tangible identity choices: whereas Russia and the occupied territories idolized the region's Soviet heritage (celebrating military victory, glory, and past grandeur), Ukrainians honored those who died innocently and tragically because of that Soviet legacy.

But the Holodomor did not form the core of Ukrainians' identity narrative after the Maidan,[65] nor did any other event or period in history. Given the controversial nature of Ukraine's historical narrative and of its varied linguistic tradition, and in the absence of trusted state institutions as points of cohesion, Ukrainians' spontaneous expressions of patriotism—a natural reaction when faced with existential threat—seemed to focus on the "institution" of *territory*, and its present need for defense. The *map* became one of the most publicly proliferated patriotic symbols to emerge from the early period of war with Russia: after 2014, displaying a map of Ukraine that included both the Donbas and in Crimea became an act of public defiance. The territory represented by the map was understood to be sacred. It was a place of birth and life (hence skepticism towards Ukrainians born and/or living abroad). It was life-giving (hence derision towards the term *"terytoriya"*, and its replacement with *"zemlya"* meaning "earth"). The slogan *"Zemlya Dobra"* (Land of Good) seemed to unite all Ukrainians, and although its meaning seemed banal to outsiders, it was this concept that both epitomized Ukraine for its citizens and united them in the cause of its defense. The contours of the country's internationally recognized borders were displayed prominently at state-sponsored events, on billboards, in schools, on company marketing materials, even on birthday and Christmas greeting cards. Companies who dared to display a map with Crimea shown as part of Russia, or missing from Ukraine, were vilified and their products boycotted.[66] Performances of artists who travelled to the occupied peninsula were boycotted throughout 2014-2018.[67] Russian products disappeared from Ukrainian store shelves because consumers refused to buy them. Russian retailers were largely pushed out.[68] Tolerance and inclusiveness remained mainstays of everyday interaction among Ukrainians, but a demand for recognition of dignity—particularly with respect to territorial integrity, as defined in the here-and-now, rather than in a mythical past—formed the core of the emergent national identity.[69]

For the citizens of a country forced into a defensive war, the symbolism of the map represented more than a geographic rendition of borders. The map symbolized "unity" — a discursive term that had represented a cliched dream in the past, became a very real declaration of political identity in the present. Given that such unity had never been experienced in Ukraine's post-Soviet history, its emergence — the "birth" of the Ukrainian nation — was truly revolutionary.

===

As noted in Chapter 7, revolutions are not events. Rather, they are processes that seem to conform to a somewhat uniform lifecycle, identified by Crane Brinton as involving revolt, rule of moderates, terror, and then thermidor. However, this schema is unidimensional: to follow the standard lifecycle, the revolution should be primarily about a single broad-based issue (e.g. the idea of "freedom" as suggested by Arendt,[70] or rectifying socio-structural disfunction caused by competition between social groups as suggested by Skocpol).[71] If Ukraine's Revolution of Dignity had been primarily an identity struggle led by "monist nationalists" (as suggested by Sakwa),[72] or indeed a "nationalist coup" followed by a domestic reaction to it by Crimean and Donbas separatists (as suggested by pro-Kremlin analysts), then applying a "lifecycle of revolutions" paradigm to its analysis one would foreshadow the likely appearance of a *nationalist* strongman on Ukraine's political scene several years after the ouster of Yanukovych. No such nationalist leader emerged, but facts on the ground suggest that at time of writing, Ukraine was undergoing a rapid open-ended transformation that was affecting more than just identity: the country's fundamental social structures were transforming. The latter (broadly termed) "class" aspect of the Revolution of Dignity, and its protagonists, will be examined next.

Chapter 9:
A Bourgeois Revolution

As outlined in the previous chapter, the phenomenon of mass patriotism on Maidan, and its near total manifestation throughout the country during the early years of the Russian-Ukrainian war that followed the protests, reflected a key *national* dimension of Ukraine's revolution. Its result was the constitution of an inclusive, multi-lingual and multi-ethnic "political" nation whose members strongly identified with patriotic symbols and a set territory deemed inviolable. However, Ukraine's Revolution of Dignity cannot be fully understood solely through the lens of nation-building (although without this lens, it cannot be understood at all). In addition to being a moment of national self-determination, the Maidan also spawned fundamental change in the country's political, economic and social structures. It was this dimension that made the protests, and the subsequent mobilization of resources for Ukraine's defense and domestic reform, unique phenomena in the country's post-Soviet history — different from previous social upheavals (e.g. the "Orange" protests),[1] and significant not only for the establishment of new forms of solidarity, but also for the institution of new governance structures and the foundations of a new economy. At time of writing (more than four years into the defensive war with Russia), Ukraine's domestic reset was far from complete: although significant aspects of the country's socio-economic and political structures had already been transformed, and substantial elite circulation had occurred, considerable work still needed to be done to complete the revolutionary agenda of Maidan.

New actors entered Ukraine's political class after the ouster of Yanukovych, effecting a fundamental transformation of the country's social and economic systems. As described further in this chapter, this new proto-elite came from Ukraine's urban private sector; they entered politics suddenly (often unexpectedly for themselves). Before the Maidan protests they had worked as managers, entrepreneurs, programmers, journalists, and university professors — members of Ukraine's nascent (and mostly unrecognized) "creative class."[2] Their socio-economic program was distinctly liberal — approximating what one might term "bourgeois"[3] — emphasizing self-reliance, entrepreneurship, civic activism, rational rule-based relations with the state, and valuing merit over ascription or connections. In the economic sphere, Maidan activists (generally younger than those who entered government) embarked on the creation of new entrepreneurial ventures, in sectors that had previously remained dwarfed by Ukraine's neo-feudal financial-industrial (oligarchic) groups. The result was a fundamental (truly *revolutionary)* transformation of Ukraine's socio-economic and political structures.

"Bourgeois" and "liberal"

According to the argument presented here, an important aspect of Ukraine's Revolution of Dignity was its "bourgeois" character. This choice of terminology requires some explanation. After-all in socio-economic terms many of those who slept in tents in Kyiv's city center during the winter months of 2013-14 could more accurately be called Ukraine's underclass — not bourgeois at all.[4] Our choice of designation stems from two demarcations of the term "bourgeois".[5] Firstly, Maidan activists (i.e. organizers, leading demonstrators, providers of material support) were almost exclusively urban dwellers (the term "bourgeois" is derived from the German "burger"). Although up to one third of Ukraine's population resides in rural areas, and an additional third live in settlements with populations under 50,000 (Ukraine has over 400 such towns where lifestyles are often more rural than urban in practice), representatives of this non-urban majority were generally not involved in the initial protests.[6] Even when "Maidans" erupted in multiple oblast centers (large cities), protest camps in rayon centers were exceptionally rare. Maidan (and anti-Maidan) was a distinctly large city (oblast center) social phenomenon — a fact that is likely to have long-lasting political aftereffects (see "New cleavages" below). During the post-protest phase of the Revolution of Dignity, volunteer soldiers and mobilized servicemen were drawn from all regions of Ukraine, and indeed many village and small-town residents were among the first to volunteer for military service. However, the grassroots organizational support network that fed, clothed, and armed the troops developed almost exclusively in large cities. Similarly, IDP aid and resettlement generally occurred in large urban centers.[7]

Secondly, the characterization of the Maidan as a "bourgeois" revolution refers to the professional backgrounds and values of its activists. The values that the Maidan (as a collective actor) stood for, and the economic and political reforms that its activists lobbied in the wake of the collapse of the Yanukovych regime approximated those generally associated with the bourgeoisie: self-reliance, innovation, limited government, entrepreneurial freedom, and meritocracy. These values represented the core beliefs of Ukraine's entrepreneurs, managers, artists, young academics, journalists, etc. who made up the majority of early Maidan protesters.[8] Paradoxically, they differed significantly from those of the Ukrainian majority. In the words of Kyiv-Mohyla Academy sociologists Sviatnenko and Vinogradov, who compared the results of a survey of Maidan activists taken in early December 2013 with representative data from Ukraine and several EU countries:

> The average Ukrainian and average protester on Maidan are situated on different ends of a trend line. That is why we are speaking about some sort of value or paradigm shift: compared to (the rest of) Ukraine, the Euromaidan (survey data) shows a "value shift," where instead of conservatism and dependence on state, the dominant value orientations are Universalism and Benevolence... a Euromaidaner, similar to a typical resident of Denmark, Finland, Germany, Sweden, Netherlands, and Belgium, can be characterized with high demand for openness to changes...The protester on Maidan is also characterized by a high degree of independence and non-conformism, courage to take responsibility, appetite for risk; (s)he is not in need of defense by the state, strongly expresses the need for novelty, creativity, freedom, and seeks fun and pleasure.[9]

As the protests dragged on in Kyiv, carriers of these "bourgeois" values (the capital's self-employed, entrepreneurs, and company managers) encouraged their subordinates to take leave of their jobs to demonstrate on Independence Square during working hours, and it was this bourgeoisie that financed much of the supply effort for the

Maidan camp. It was this bourgeoisie that formed the heart of the AutoMaidan—a very effective "cavalry" force of protesters who would
drive their midrange and upscale passenger vehicles to picket the
homes of regime representatives. After Yanukovych's flight, it was
this bourgeoisie that financed the volunteer battalions and rejuve-
nated Armed Forces whose (often rural and/or working class) soldiers defended Ukraine in the face of Russian aggression. And it was
members of this bourgeoisie who triumphantly entered the corridors
of power after the climax of the Maidan protests.

In January 2016, the Head of President Poroshenko's Administration Boris Lozhkin (a former businessman who had never held
political office before the Maidan protests) published a book entitled
"Fourth Republic" in which he presented Ukraine's brief period of independence during World War One as the country's first "republic",
existence in a state of limited autonomy within the USSR as the second, the post-Soviet Ukrainian state (1991-2014) as the third. He argued that Maidan represented the birth of a new state—the fourth republic. In his book Lozhkin muses much like a social scientist: "When
new rules are introduced and institutionalized, they are followed by
practices, from which grow new traditions and new values."[10] He then
continues:

> (These) new rules should ensure freedom of self-actualization for the
> active minority—entrepreneurs, managers, civic activists, creative pro-
> fessionals. They should ensure conditions under which no one will be
> able to take away the fruits of your efforts, forbid you from expressing
> your opinion—whether it be through mass action, or through a news-
> paper article, or through representation in politics. In this case, by
> guaranteeing the rights of the minority of the population (understand-
> ably, not everyone is ready to actualize their creative potential), the
> political system acts in the interests of the relative majority. If the
> hands of the active minority will be untied, we will have new jobs and
> growth of welfare for all other members of society.[11]

The Maidan protests launched a process of socio-economic transformation that was (and continues to be) sufficiently fundamental to the
social fabric of Ukraine to warrant being labelled "revolutionary"—a

transition from one "republic" to another. Furthermore, as demonstrated by the quoted passage from one of the prominent proponents of this new "republic", the revolutionaries put forth an ideology. Their political program emphasized freedom, self-reliance, and self-actualization — values that were antithetical to the neo-patrimonialism of Ukraine's oligarchic system.[12]

Notably, this ideology contradicted not only the paternalist ethic of the *ancien régime* (seen previously as all encompassing), but also clashed with the prevailing ideology of continental Europe (i.e. the "social market"). During the months immediately following Yanukovych's ouster, I met informally with Pavlo Sheremeta, the interim government's Minister of Economic Development.[13] In his words, the IMF functionaries who arrived in Kyiv in early 2014 to arrange bridge financing for the new government were shocked: in their history of dealings with developing countries, they had never encountered a government whose ministers were "more liberal than the IMF!" The term "liberal" in this context could well have been replaced with "libertarian" because the intent was to communicate a desire for drastically limiting the regulatory powers of the state. According to Ukraine's initial post-Maidan reformers, it was regulation that had historically led to massive corruption and had hindered the development of entrepreneurial ventures that were now to become the main drivers of the country's economy — a belief also reflected in the quote from Lozhkin's book cited above. When, in November 2014, investment bankers Natalia Jaresko (Finance Minister) and Aivaras Abramavicus (Economic Development Minister) took control of the economic bloc of the executive, the radical anti-etatist rhetoric of the initial post-Yanukovych government was toned down (likely for the sake of pleasing IMF advisors), but skepticism of the ability of the state to ensure social equity and economic growth remained widespread among Maidan activists.

Notably, the liberalism (libertarianism) of Ukraine's new "bourgeois" elite also represented a shift from materialism to idealism. Interviews with young firm founders whose start-ups appeared in 2014 or later[14] suggest that the intentions of most could be captured by the

classical Schumpeterian characterization of the entrepreneur as motivated by "the dream and the will to found a private kingdom."[15] In
other words, whereas accumulation of *material* possessions seems to
have been the primary measure of success of pre-Maidan business
owners (as reflected in the opulent lifestyle of Yanukovych-era political and business elites), in the wake of the protests and economic upheaval caused by Russia's aggression, a new generation of *idealistic*
(self-actualization oriented) start-ups appeared. And the values shift
seems not to have been limited to those choosing entrepreneurial careers: individuals entering politics in 2014 also seemed to exhibit an
idealistic mindset characteristic of their time and generation. For this
new political elite, the decision to participate in government meant
drastic income reduction. Having volunteered their time and effort,
they propagated a liberal reform agenda founded on self-actualization
and meritocracy because these were the foundational planks of their
ideology.

Elite renewal

Revolutionary social transformations typically lead to sudden entry
of new actors into a country's political elite. The Ukrainian case was
no different: the first post-Yanukovych government included several
ministers who had no previous political experience. Two came from
academia: Education Minister Serhiy Kvit was previously President of
Kyiv-Mohyla Academy; Pavlo Sheremeta, appointed Minister of Economic Development and Trade, was previously President of the Kyiv
School of Economics. Three were heroes of the Maidan protests:
Sports Minister Dmytro Bulatov had been kidnapped and badly
beaten in January 2014 in apparent retaliation for his role as organizer
of the AutoMaidan; Culture Minister Yevhen Nishchuk, an actor in
Kyiv's Ivan Franko National Theatre, was the "voice of Maidan",
speaking from the stage during the *viche* meetings, and at the height
of the sniper massacres; Health Minister Oleh Musiy was one of the
organizers of the Maidan First Aid Service. Several others were political appointees hailing either from Prime Minister Yatseniuk's Batkivshchyna party (e.g. Justice Minister Pavlo Petrenko, Social Policy
Minister Liudmyla Denysova, and Interior Minister Arsen Avakov),

or from "Svoboda" (e.g. Acting Defense Minister Ihor Tenyukh and Acting Prosecutor General Oleh Makhnitsky). Additionally, two non-aligned professionals were coopted into the first post-Yanukovych government: Andriy Deshchytsia (a career diplomat) was appointed Acting Minister of Foreign Affairs, and Oleksandr Shlapak (a banker) was picked for Finance Minister.[16]

After the October 2014 Parliamentary elections, several new faces joined the Cabinet. Most prominently, three non-citizens were granted citizenship in order to allow for their appointment to ministerial positions: Natalia Jaresko, a Diaspora Ukrainian from Chicago who had lived in Ukraine for over 20 years having managed a large investment fund, was appointed Finance Minister; Aivaras Abromavicus, a Lithuanian investment banker and long-time Kyiv resident, was appointed Minister of Economic Development and Trade; Oleksandr Kvitashvili, the former Georgian Minister of Health was appointed to Ukraine's Health Ministry. Three other Georgians were granted Ukrainian citizenship and appointed to positions in the law enforcement sector: Khatia Dekanoidze was appointed Chief of the new Ukrainian National Police; Eka Zguladze was asked to serve as First Deputy Minister of Internal Affairs; former Deputy Chief Prosecutor of Georgia David Sakvaralidze was appointed to an analogous post in Ukraine.[17] Also appointed were two men with no previous political experience, but considered to have strong reform credentials: Oleksiy Pavlenko, a former manager of a large Ukrainian agricultural concern, and former director of Ukraine's largest appliance retailer, was tapped for the Agriculture Ministry, and Andriy Pyvovarsky, another former corporate top-manager was appointed Minister of Infrastructure (Transportation and Communications). Former Kyiv-Mohyla Academy political science professor Rostyslav Pavlenko and former Microsoft Ukraine Managing Director Dmytro Shymkiv were appointed Deputy Heads of the Presidential Administration by Poroshenko.

The table below shows the backgrounds, birthdates and portfolios of a sample of the new post-Yanukovych political elite of Ukraine.

Name	Pre-political background	Year of birth	Role in government
Mustafa Nayyem	Ukrayinska Pravda journalist	1981	MP Poroshenko Bloc Founder of "Euro-optimists"
Serhiy Leshchenko	Ukrayinska Pravda journalist	1980	MP Poroshenko Bloc Anti-corruption campaigner
Ihor Lutsenko	Journalist; Kyiv city anti-corruption activist	1978	MP Batkivshchyna
Tetiana Chornovol	Journalist	1979	MP Narodnyi Front
Hanna Hopko	Anti-tobacco; Anti-corruption NGO activist	1982	MP Samopomich (excluded 2015) Chair of Foreign Affairs Committee
Svitlana Zalishchuk	Press Secretary of First Deputy PM; NGO activist	1982	MP Poroshenko Bloc Co-Chair Democratic Alliance Party
Inna Sovsun	University lecturer, NGO founder	1984	First Deputy Minister of Education until August 2016
Natalia Sevostianova	University lecturer, Parliamentary assistant	1986	First Deputy Minister of Justice
Viktoria Ptashnyk	Lawyer	1983	MP Samopomich (excluded 2015) Co-Chair Democratic Alliance Party
Alyona Shkrum	Lawyer	1988	MP Batkivshchyna
Rostyslav Pavlenko	University lecturer, political analyst	1976	Deputy Head of Presidential Administration
Dmytro Shymkiv	Managing Director of Microsoft Ukraine	1975	Deputy Head of Presidential Administration
Aivaras Abromavicus	Co-founder East Capital Investment Fund	1976	Minister of Economic Development and Trade—Dec 2014 to Apr 2016
Valeria Hontareva	Founder of ICU Holdings Investment Fund	1964	Head of the National Bank of Ukraine until May 2018
Natalia Jaresko	Founder of Horizon Capital and Western NIS Investment Funds	1965	Minister of Finance—Dec 2014 to Apr 2016

Oleksiy Pavlenko	Former Director of Rayz Agro-holding; Founder of Pharus Asset Management Investment Fund	1977	Minister of Agriculture—Dec 2014 to Apr 2016
Max Nefyodov	Former VP of Dragon Capital, Managing Director of Icon Private Equity Fund	1984	Deputy Minister of Economic Development
Oksana Markarova	Founder of ITT Investments	1970	Deputy Minister of Finance, Acting Minister of Finance from June 2018
Oleksandr Starodubtsev	Founder and Managing Director of "Otkrytiye" brokerage	1979	Director of the Department of Public Procurement at the Ministry of the Economy ("Prozorro") until Sept 2017
Andriy Pyvovarsky	Former head of investment banking at Dragon Capital; CEO of Continuum Group	1978	Minister of Infrastructure—Dec 2014 to Apr 2016

Table 4:   Backgrounds and roles of new post-Yanukovych elite members

During the political reset of 2014 (Presidential and Parliamentary elections) three distinct channels of elite recruitment emerged. Firstly, well-known opposition journalists and NGO activists were coopted into political party candidate lists (likely as vote boosters), and then became prominent in the Rada (several were eventually excluded from the factions whose lists they were elected on).[18] Specifically, in this category, one can identify Mustafa Nayyem and Serhiy Leshchenko (both former investigative journalists of the *Ukrayinska Pravda* website) included on the Poroshenko Bloc list, Ihor Lutsenko (a Kyiv-city activist and journalist) who was included on the "Batkivshchyna" list, and Tetiana Chornovol, elected on the People's Front list. All joined the "Euro-optimists" inter-factional parliamentary group in February 2015.

A second path to post-Maidan political prominence involved activism in Ukraine's NGO sector prior to 2013-14, and then vocal support for the Maidan protests once they developed. For example, Hanna Hopko, who was later to become Chair of the Parliamentary Committee for Foreign Affairs, gained prominence during the Yanukovych era as an anti-tobacco lobbyist and NGO anti-corruption crusader. She cooperated in her lobbying efforts with Lesya Orobets[19] — a vocal opposition MP in the 2012-2014 Parliament, and post-Maidan challenger for the Kyiv mayoral seat in May 2014.[20] Lesya was forced to quit politics for health reasons in late 2014, but during her tenure in Parliament, she was able to catapult several young activists to prominence, including Hopko and Vitaliy Shabunin — the head of Ukraine's Anti-Corruption Action Center watchdog NGO, and Dmytro Sherembey — Chair of the Patients of Ukraine NGO. Similar informal patronage was provided by Oleh Rybachuk — former Chief of Staff to President Yushchenko, and founder of the "Chesno" (Honest) NGO network which advocated transparency for politicians. After the Maidan protests, Rybachuk's former press secretary Svitlana Zalishchuk became a prominent MP and co-leader of the Democratic Alliance Party. Similar close association with a pre-Maidan prominent opinion-leader was in evidence in the naming of Inna Sovsun, a former Kyiv-Mohyla Academy lecturer and founder of the CEDOS think tank, as First Deputy by Education Minister Serhiy Kvit, and in the appointment of First Deputy Justice Minister Natalia Sevostianova — a young lecturer from Odesa Law Academy and former Assistant to Crimean Tatar leader Mustafa Dzhemilev.

The third source of recruitment for Ukraine's post-Yanukovych elite was the country's nascent western-oriented investment banking community. Although this recruitment mechanism was least publicized, its incumbents can be thanked for implementing some of Ukraine's most difficult (though controversial) economic reforms. Three prominent members of this group included Natalia Jaresko — co-founder of Western NIS and Horizon Capital investment funds and later Finance Minister; Aivaras Abramavicus — co-owner of East Capital Investment Fund and later Minister of Economic Development and Trade; and Valeria Hontareva — founder of ICU Holdings Investment Fund, and later Head of the National Bank. Also prominent were Max Nefyodov, Deputy Minister of Economic Development, and Oleksandr Starodubtsev, Director of the Department of Public Procurement at the Ministry of the Economy. Together, the latter two organized the award-winning "Prozorro" procurement system (one of Ukraine's most successful post-2014 reform projects)[21] which reportedly saved the state coffers over 24 billion UAH during the first two years after its launch in 2015.[22] Both the flamboyant Nefyodov and the reserved Starodubtsev worked in Ukraine's equity investment sector, and were colleagues at Dragon Capital[23] — the country's largest investment bank, involved in 1/3 of all equity investments — for several years prior to the Maidan. Infrastructure Minister Andriy Pivovarsky also worked at Dragon Capital for 7 years prior to his appointment to government in late 2014, while Deputy Finance Minister Oksana Markarova founded ITT Investments, a partner in several equity deals with Dragon Capital.

Whether the recruitment drive initiated by Presidential Administration Head Boris Lozhkin specifically targeted individuals with investment banking backgrounds for cooption into government is unknown. In late 2014, Poroshenko asked Lozhkin to enlist the services of several western recruitment firms, and then to personally oversee the selection process for key ministries.[24] As a former business owner,[25] the Head of the Presidential Administration would logically have preferred others who possessed professional managerial skills, but the choice of individuals with experience specifically in the financial sector (rather than in manufacturing and/or IT services) is notable. The post-Maidan government needed a financial rescue package from western donors (e.g. IMF, World Bank, EBRD, etc.), and was mandated to accelerate the implementation of the Association Agreement and DCFTA with the EU. This agenda required leadership positions to be occupied by individuals who had experience cooperating with western financial institutions and were themselves integrated into western business structures and networks. Such individuals represented a minority within Ukraine's business community prior to Maidan. Interestingly, these investment bankers' vision of Ukraine's economic development was less liberal than that of many domestic activists (including, it would seem, Lozhkin—the man ultimately responsible for their recruitment).

"Flexians"

In early 2016, once the fundamentals of the IMF stabilization program had been implemented,[26] and following a series of accusations of high-level corruption,[27] Prime Minister Yatseniuk was forced to resign. Jaresko, Abromavicus, Kvit, Pavlenko and Pyvovarsky lost their ministerial posts. Within several months, Lozhkin resigned from the Presidential Administration to head the National Investment Council, and several deputy ministers and high-level civil service functionaries resigned their posts as well (e.g. Dekanoidze, Zguladze, Sakvaralidze, Sovsun, Starodubtsev). Maidan activists who had been elected to Parliament remained in office, but with few colleagues able to implement reforms through high-level positions in the executive branch, a degree of depression consumed many.

Frustrations were vented during a semi-private event in Kyiv in November 2016 called "Reforms F*ck-up Night" where those who had recently resigned, reflected on their post-Maidan government experiences. They lamented the legacy elite's lack of political will for radical reform, and blamed the bureaucracy for stifling efforts to implement change.[28] In the words of Vlad Rashkovan (a former banker and university lecturer from Odesa who was appointed Deputy Governor of the National Bank in 2014): "when we entered government, we found the reform capacity of the various executive administrations and ministries to be close to nil."[29] Yanukovych-era government employees were trained to execute orders, but never to think or recommend action independently. As a result, the activists found few internal allies in the civil service. The idealistic maximalism with which they had entered government was dashed.

The Hroysman government which succeeded the cabinet of Yatseniuk in April 2016 included few flamboyant reformers. Most were career politicians who either had served as opposition MP's or had worked as civil servants during the Yanukovych period. The exception was Ulana Suprun—acting Minister of Health—an American doctor of Ukrainian descent who had come to the Maidan protests to volunteer, and then organized the "Patriot Defense" combat medical training initiative (providing first aid kits and training to military personnel), once hostilities in the Donbas started. Except for Suprun, the Hroysman coalition government was staffed with Ministers who were political appointees representing either the Poroshenko Bloc or the People's Front in Parliament. Yet despite low expectations, these ministers were able to achieve multiple policy breakthroughs including in the areas of education, health care, road construction, and decentralization (anti-corruption initiatives and judicial reform remained bogged down largely due to stalling from the Presidential Administration).[30]

The Hroysman government reform initiatives were often driven from behind the scenes by "advisors" — individuals who rarely claimed political limelight but were able to drive change through a relatively placid bureaucracy. Valerii Pekar, a former businessman who founded the "Nova Krayina" (New Country) NGO and served as advisor to PM Hroysman on civil service reform, presents a good example of such a behind-the-scenes player. Taras Kozak and Dmytro Sherembey, advisors to the Finance and Health Ministers respectively, were also able to use their NGO leverage to push through policy changes. This author was able to contribute to the reform of the system of educating and granting PhD's as a member of the National Erasmus+ Higher Education Reform Experts (HERE) Team, and Advisor to Ministers Kvit and Hrynevych.[31]

The role of such advisors as change agents seemed to approximate that of the "Flexian" described (critically) by Janine Wedel in her book *The Shadow Elite*:

> The mover and shaker who serves at one and the same time as business consultant, think-tanker, TV pundit and government adviser glides in and around the organizations that enlist his services… Such individuals are *in* these organizations (some of the time anyway), but they are seldom *of* them.[32]

Wedel's "flexians" are ultra-nimble players who move seamlessly among roles in the public and private sectors and academia/NGO's.

Their level of influence on policy suggests questions as to their accountability, and their interaction in close-knit networks arouses suspicion among those who are not part of their in-group. However, "flexians" are not lobbyists. They are volunteer policy advisors with regular access to in-post decision-makers. Rather than relying on bureaucracy, they use the structures of government to their advantage, and skillfully access media to "sell" their ideological message. Their affiliation with academic and/or NGO institutions legitimizes their programs, and thus serves to grease changes in organizations where status quo is the norm.

One can criticize the "flexian" phenomenon for its lack of transparency (as Wedel does), but faced with a despondent electorate, and the global rise of populism, the pragmatism of instituting reform from the shadows can well be understood. Furthermore, it would seem that in the early 21st century, a transformation of the traditional stratified social and political arrangements typical of the industrial era has been ongoing throughout western civilization. As Moses Naim has astutely pointed out, the "end of power" (the title of his book) seems to be a worldwide tendency manifest in many corporate, political, and social structures. Specifically, one can see a diminution of lasting authority emanating from hierarchical position or office, and its replacement by "influence".[33] In Ukraine this transformation became particularly evident after the Maidan protests due to the revolutionary atmosphere permeating the country; it seemed to reflect broader civilizational trends (e.g. horizontalization, popularization of self-reliant activism and de-institutionalization—see Chapter 10). In this context the appearance of "flexians" as the new movers and shakers within Ukraine's political structures is not surprising, but nevertheless interesting.

But the agenda of Maidan called for more than just a change of faces within elite circles. Ukraine's Revolution of Dignity was to bring about a shift in the organizational norms of society: from hierarchy to heterarchy; from large business to small; from industrial production to post-industrial services; from state-capture and asset-stripping to rules-based institution-building. The practices of previously dominant oligarch-controlled financial-industrial groups of Ukraine—organized strictly hierarchically and operating internally according to a tiered culture where formal rank often trumped expertise in decision-making—were to be replaced by the more horizontal cultures and structures of IT and service sector companies where teamwork and familial structures were preferred. At time of writing, transformation in this direction had commenced, but it remained an open question how long the revolutionary changes spawned by the Maidan (i.e. a complete reconstitution of the organizational practices of Ukrainian society) would take.[34]

If one limits analysis to the state apparatus, there is little doubt that in the wake of the violence on Maidan which culminated in Yanukovych's departure, authority structures throughout Ukraine self-dismantled. The revolutionaries—whether originating from the Maidan, or from the opposition parties, and whether formally in-post, or acting as behind-the-scenes "flexians"—universally called for the establishment of a rules-based meritocracy whose structure was much "flatter" (heterarchical rather than hierarchical) than the *de facto* ascriptive status pyramid of post-Soviet industrial society. Revolutionary change required the institutionalization of new rules and practices—i.e. to a dismantling of the clientelist relations that defined the "habitus" of the ancien regime. But first, the incumbents of that regime needed to be removed.

De-oligarchization

During the Yanukovych Presidency, seven identifiable groups were represented within the parliamentary faction of the Party of Regions (187 MP's), and each had delegated representatives to the executive branch. The following table identifies the key members of these "oligarchic" groups, and their fate after Yanukovych's ouster.

	Oligarchic group during Yanukovych regime	Post-Yanukovych
1	**Firtash group** Nominally led by Serhiy Tihipko (owner of TAS Group—a financial-industrial conglomerate) Forms base of support for Serhiy Liovochkin, Yanukovych's Presidential Administration Head until January 2014 Yuriy Boyko, Deputy Prime Minister responsible for energy, represents Firtash interests in relations with Russia.	- Tihipko: Presidential candidate in 2014, exits politics after receiving 5.2% of popular vote; owner of Universal Bank - Boyko: Elected to Parliament in 2014 (immune from prosecution); leader of Opposition Bloc faction - Liovochkin: Elected to Parliament in 2014 (immune from prosecution); member of Opposition Bloc faction
2	**Akhmetov group** Led in Parliament by Yuriy Voropayev (lawyer originally from Makiyivka Donetsk oblast) Represented in the Presidential Administration by First Deputy Head Irina Akimova (appointed on 17 January 2014 as the President's representative in the Cabinet of Ministers) Represented in Government by Deputy Prime Minister Oleksander Vilkul, Health Minister Raisa Bohatyriova, Economics Minister Prasolov, and Sports Minister Ravil Safiullin	- Voropayev: Elected to Parliament in 2014 (immune from prosecution); member of Opposition Bloc faction - Akimova: not politically active; living in Ukraine - Vilkul: Elected to Parliament in 2014 (immune from prosecution); member of Opposition Bloc faction - Bohatyriova: self-imposed exile in Russia; arrest warrant issued by Interpol - Safiullin: not politically active
3	**Kliuyev group** Led in Parliament by Serhiy Kliuyev Andriy Kliuyev Secretary of the National Security Council during the initial student beatings on 30.11.2013; appointed Head of the Presidential Administration in January 2014 Andriy Portnov—legal counsel of the Presidential Administration; considered author of 16 January "dictatorial" laws	- Both Kliuyev brothers in exile in Russia; abandoned business holdings in Donbas, but not in Crimea; EU sanctions imposed in 2014; Interpol arrest warrants issued - Serhiy Kliuyev was elected to Parliament in 2014, but stripped of his immunity in 2016; fled to Russia to avoid arrest - Andriy Portnov—sanctioned by EU in 2014 (lifted in Oct 2015); wanted by Ukrainian prosecutors; self-imposed exile

4	Yanukovych group	- Arbuzov, Lukash,
	Led by First Deputy Prime Minister Serhiy Arbuzov (appointed Acting PM in January 2014) Justice Minister Lukash, Interior Minister Zakharchenko, Revenue Minister Klymenko, and Prosecutor General Viktor Pshonka were all considered loyal to the Yanukovych "family".	Zakharchenko, Lebedev, Klymenko, and Pshonka, as well as Yanukovych and his two sons—all sanctioned by EU; all wanted by Ukrainian prosecutors; all in self-imposed exile in Russia; Viktor Yanukovych Jr. died in apparent automobile accident in 2016.
5	Ivaniushchenko group	- Ivaniushchenko accused of financing and organizing "titushky" thugs in Kyiv; criminal cases against him closed in February 2017 after an out of court settlement.
	Led by businessman and Party of Regions MP Yuriy Ivaniushchenko (nickname Yenakiyivsky) represented in the Azarov government by Agriculture Minister Prysiazhniuk	- Prysiazhniuk wanted by Ukrainian prosecutors; in self-imposed exile in Russia
6	Russian lobby	- Kolesnichenko moved to Sevastopol Crimea; in 2014 publicly declared that he is now a Russian citizen; ran for elected office in annexed Crimea—lost.
	Publicly represented by MP Vadym Kolesnichenko—co-author of controversial 2012 Language Law; co-author of January 2014 "dictatorial laws" Represented in Azarov government by Education Minister Dmytro Tabachnyk, Defense Minister Pavlo Lebedyev, SBU Head Oleksandr Yakimenko	- Tabachnyk in self-imposed exile in Israel - Lebedyev and Yakimenko in self-imposed exile in Russia; both were present at the Kremlin during Putin's Crimean annexation ceremony
7	Luhansk group	- Yefremov jailed in 2015 for aiding and abetting separatism in Luhansk oblast (trial pending)
	Led by Party of Regions Parliamentary faction leader Oleksandr Yefremov Represented in Azarov government by Social Services Minister Nataliya Korolevska	- Korolevska: Elected to Parliament in 2014 (immune from prosecution); member of Opposition Bloc faction

Table 5:   Party of Regions oligarchic groups pre- and post-Yanukovych

As shown in the above table, after the victory of the Maidan, all of the key representatives of the Russian lobby in the Party of Regions, and

the majority of the Kliuyev, Ivaniushchenko and Yanukovych oligarchic groups, were forced to leave Ukraine for fear of prosecution;
many were sanctioned by the EU and/or other western countries;[35]
several were elected to Parliament in October 2014 under the Opposition Bloc banner, and thus avoided prosecution (possibly temporarily). The more moderate groups within the former Party of Regions—
i.e. those members of the Yanukovych-era political elite financially
supported by Firtash and Akhmetov—fared better than hardliners.
But all lost their previously influential positions in power.

Besides being politically sidelined, practically all of Ukraine's
formerly all-powerful "oligarch" businessmen lost significant wealth
and economic influence in the wake of Yanukovych's ouster. The
value of the assets of Ukraine's richest individual—Rinat Akhmetov—
reportedly fell from a high of over 21 billion in 2012 to less than 4 billion during the first 2 years of war in the Donbas before rebounding
in 2017 to 6.9 billion.[36] Ihor Kolomoisky—considered Ukraine's 3rd
wealthiest oligarch together with his partner Hennadiy Boholiubov—
saw the state nationalize his bank (PrivatBank), and then file suit in
international courts seeking the arrest of 2.5 billion USD of his assets
both in Ukraine and abroad.[37] Another symbol of massive enrichment
through access to the corridors of power—Dmytro Firtash, whose gas
import business prospered under both Yushchenko and Yanukovych—was jailed in Vienna in anticipation of his extradition to the
US (or Spain) on bribery charges.[38] Similar fates awaited each of the
economic mainstays of the Yanukovych regime: the Kliuyev brothers
both fled from Ukrainian prosecutors to Russia, largely abandoning
their business holdings in the Donbas; Serhiy Kurchenko—the young
gas trader from Kharkiv who had been suspected of acting as a proxy-
owner for the Yanukovych "family"—also fled to Russia; his bank accounts in the EU and Switzerland were frozen.[39]

The obvious (and most controversial) exception to the post-
Yanukovych de-oligarchization trend was President Poroshenko,
whose net worth was estimated to have topped 1 billion USD for the
first time in 2017.[40] Furthermore, after the victory of the Maidan some
new oligarchs (e.g. Poroshenko ally Ihor Kononenko, and Yatseniuk
ally Mykola Martynenko) emerged—in each case causing huge public

outcry.[41] However, their enrichment through access to state resources amounted to tens of millions of dollars rather than billions. Without belittling the problem of persistent corruption in Ukraine, claims that its levels after the ouster of Yanukovych approximated those of the previous regime,[42] were outlandish.

In April 2017, assets and cash amounting to 1.5 billion USD allegedly belonging *personally* to Viktor Yanukovych were confiscated in Ukraine, and nationalized by court order.[43] The total amount of wealth extracted by the former President and his closest confidants in the course of 2010-2013 remains unknown, but according to former opposition MP Senchenko, up to 3 billion USD in cash was loaded onto special trucks and driven out of the palatial Mezhyhirya mansion in December 2013.[44] Oleh Makhnitsky, Ukraine's acting Prosecutor General, appointed immediately after the ouster of Yanukovych, sensationally announced in April 2014 that the former President's inner circle had been responsible for funneling up to 100 billion USD out of the country.[45] While this number is likely an overstatement, it is difficult to find a business owner or top manager in Ukraine who did not experience extortion and/or polite demands to "contribute informally" to local government "funds" under the previous regime. It was understood that only a portion of the collected cash was used locally. The rest—estimates vary in the range of 20-50% of collected amounts—was delivered to Kyiv.

On 4 April 2014 the political talk show ShusterLive broadcast a 3 minute video tour of the main building of the Ministry of Revenue, the government agency created in late 2012 by amalgamating the Tax and Customs agencies.[46] Minister Klymenko, a close confidant of Yanukovych, had overseen the construction of a closed area in the Ministry building which included a sauna, salt mine spa, private massage room, and boxing ring where no-rules fights were attended by top-level Ministry officials and members of the Yanukovych "family". The closed area also included a "safe-room" with thick metal doors, transparent furniture, and sound proofing. Apparently, this room was used for secret negotiations with owners of large businesses regarding profit distribution, false tax reimbursement claims, and kickbacks from state contracts.

The mechanics of wealth extraction by the Yanukovych regime were a poorly guarded secret prior to the eruption of the Maidan protests. Although business owners and managers understood that the bribes they paid regularly to tax, fire safety, and countless other state agency inspectors (including traffic police) were "shared" upwards through the state bureaucracy, the scale of the amounts of cash, and the extent to which the machine of graft was efficiently managed by the regime was not public knowledge. In the wake of events in late February 2014 when the President's formerly closed palatial residence in Mezhyhirya was suddenly opened to the public, it quickly became a symbol of the extent of the riches generated by the centralized "payments up" pyramid that the Yanukovych regime had constructed.[47] And the structure of graft did not serve the President exclusively. When the home of one of his most loyal vassals, Prosecutor General Pshonka, was raided by Maidan activists, the gaudy opulence on display (including paintings of the home's owner in the image of Caesar and Napoleon, Faberge eggs, golden chandeliers and candelabras) became an international sensation.[48] When the post-Yanukovych government ordered police to raid the home of former Energy Minister Eduard Stavitsky, they found 42kg of gold bars, and $4.8 million US in cash.[49] Two facts are striking in this case: firstly, Stavitsky had held his ministerial portfolios (Environment and Energy) from April 2012 until February 2014, so the discovered loot likely represented a personal accumulation requiring *less than two years* in high office; secondly, the former Minister did not flee Ukraine to Israel immediately after the climax of the Maidan protests (he left in early March), so the gold and cash discovered by police are likely to have represented only a small amount of his total booty — a stash that he had either forgotten, or was unable to take with him when running away.

Overthrowing the *ancien regime*

The composition of Ukraine's political elites obviously changed with the overthrow of Yanukovych and the Party of Regions. However, as Cambridge sociologist David Lane pointed out after the Orange protests of 2004, replacement of elites is a necessary, but insufficient pre-condition for calling historical events such as Maidan and its after-math, "revolutions":

> A maximalist definition of a social or political revolution requires ma-jor changes in the social and economic system consequent on the polit-ical transformation of the ruling elites by a new political class taking power… If the intentions of the insurgents are not subsequently real-ized in structural transformation, a political revolution cannot be said to have occurred. In this way we may distinguish a social/political revolution from a coup d'état consequent on public protest.[50]

The intentions of the Maidan revolutionaries were clear: they sought to replace the (post)Soviet system of corrupt neo-feudal clientelism that had been dominant in Ukraine after the USSR collapsed, with a "European" rules-based meritocracy. Yuriy Lutsenko[51] — a regular speaker on Maidan — said as much during the 1 December 2013 *viche* that gathered in Kyiv's city-center immediately after the student beat-ings: "Today, here, the Ukrainian Soviet Socialist Republic dies. This is its funeral!"[52] Lutsenko's words echoed the opinion of prominent intellectual Mykola Ryabchuk, who declared that after the collapse of the USSR, "the patrimonial nomenklatura system transformed (mu-tated) in Ukraine, into a patrimonial oligarchic one, but its patron-cli-ent, quasi-feudal essence did not change; the closed access regime, which makes impossible the development of a dynamic economy, ef-fective government institutions and full-fledged civil society, did not change."[53] The intent of the Maidan revolutionaries was to finally ef-fect this change.

In a process lasting over a decade, (beginning in the early 1990's), the apparatus of the Ukrainian state — its security, licensing, revenue collection and wealth distribution functions — had been gradually cap-tured by representatives of the former Soviet-era hierarchy ("Red Di-rectors") who allied themselves with "violent entrepreneurs"[54] who made their fortunes immediately after the USSR's collapse through racketeering and extortion (practices made possible by a weak state environment).[55] In other words, representatives of the Soviet-era no-menklatura (particularly from the eastern industrial regions), allied with outright crooks and bandits, took advantage of the weakness of nascent post-Soviet Ukrainian state institutions to *de facto* become the state — hence the term "oligarchy." The structures these "oligarchs" created were strictly hierarchical ("neo-patrimonial")[56] with state-embedded patrons offering protection and political advantages to clients (business owners) in exchange for loyalty and a share in profits.

In 2011, Russian academic Vladislav Inozemtsev described this oligarchic socio-economic and political system in Russia (which differed little from Ukraine at the time) as "neo-feudal":

> At every level of the hierarchy a certain degree of bribery and clientelist parochialism is not only tolerated but presupposed in exchange for unconditional loyalty and a part of the take for one's superiors. The system is based on the economic freedom of its citizens (consumers have choice), but cautious political restrictions on these freedoms generate the wealth of the biggest beneficiaries. There is a cascade of floors and ceilings to the restrictions on freedom, so it is a feudalism with more levels than the old kind. But it works fundamentally the same way: The weak pay tribute "up", and the strong provide protection "down."[57]

The neo-feudal oligarchic "habitus" (a term coined by French sociologist Pierre Bourdieu to denote values and behavioral practices accepted as standard by a group or community) involved three characteristics. Firstly, an ethic and discourse of materialism: for owners and managers of companies that formed part of Ukraine's financial-industrial groups, value was defined as the *tangible* output of business activities (i.e. production and/or construction); the universal measure of success was profit — no matter how begotten; the standard of personal worth was wealth — conspicuously demonstrated by one's material possessions. Secondly, the focus of capital accumulation activities was the state: oligarchic businesses were generally former state enterprises (privatized through insider deals and/or raided)[58] whose uncompetitive facilities required subsidies or guaranteed state contracts to operate; for the management of such companies, rent-seeking behavior was preferred to market competition. Thirdly, the structures of financial-industrial groups were strictly hierarchical and ascriptive rather than meritocratic; the primary criterion for appointments and upward mobility was personal loyalty, resulting in a territorial or regional dominance of personnel backgrounds.

During Ukraine's first two decades of independence, the economic power of the "oligarchs" was achieved first through non-transparent privatization of former state assets, and then consolidated through corporate raiding.[59] Eventually, individual "oligarchs" achieved monopoly status in their respective sectors, and sought to build both competitive barriers to outsiders (e.g. foreign investors), and to maximize profits from their enterprises by lobbying preferential tax regimes, subsidies, and regulated pricing schemes from the state. To support their lobbying efforts "financial-industrial groups" fielded representatives first to Parliament, then to the executive branch. No single group was ever able to monopolize the state completely, and so the function of the Presidential Administration in this system was to act as arbiter between the competing interests of big business.

This story has been retold repeatedly in the literature on post-Soviet Ukraine.[60] What has received much less attention is the story of Ukraine's 'de novo' or grass-roots entrepreneurship, and the autonomous (of the state) market sphere that emerged in parallel with the "oligarchic" system during the two decades preceding Maidan. Largely unnoticed by Ukraine watchers, concurrent with the economic crisis of 1998, an alternative economy—and concomitant "habitus"—began to gain strength. The transformation was both structural and cultural. Structurally, during the late 1990's Ukraine's GDP ceased to be dependent on industrial and/or agricultural production: over half of the economy became represented by services.[61] Although agriculture and the heavy industries of the east continued to provide the bulk of export revenues (offset by inflated hydrocarbon imports from Russia), increasingly, domestic wealth came to be the result of *intangible* production (services), with Kyiv and cities in the western regions becoming centers for such activities. In this 'de novo' entrepreneurial sector (i.e. where firm founders had not been involved in privatizing Soviet-era legacy assets), a "bourgeois" culture opposed to that of oligarchic companies developed: competitive, market-oriented, meritocratic, and with value placed on intangible assets (e.g. intellectual, cultural, social capital) on par with material possessions.

Ukraine's entrepreneurial sector spawned a new "class" in the late 1990's, composed first of small and medium business owners, and later (in select cases) representing quite substantial firms (1000+ employees). According to this author's calculations, at the turn of the millennium, up to 1/3 of Ukraine's employees worked in firms that had emerged 'de novo' since independence, and the share of such companies in the overall economy was growing.[62] The distinguishing characteristic of the entrepreneur-founders of these 'de novo' enterprises (interviewed by the author throughout the 2000's)[63] was their radical skepticism of the state as an institution, and their contempt for other business owners who had accumulated capital through insider privatization or other forms of interaction with the state. Furthermore, these owners exhibited an ethic of social responsibility that was neither paternalistic nor patrimonial, but rather reflected civic mindedness: they viewed Ukraine as the country in which they *lived*, nor merely as a territory on which to make profit.

Several analysts predicted that the new entrepreneurial sector would gain dominance over Ukraine's legacy oligarchy after 2004. That year, the architect of the "oligarchic" system, former Yuzhmash (Southern Machine Building) Rocket Factory Director Leonid Kuchma retired from the Presidency, and his post was filled (eventually) by Viktor Yushchenko, a banker who promised rules-based, broadly termed "European" socio-economic development, and a patriotic discourse that was new to Ukraine. Yushchenko's election campaign was generously funded by "moderate" oligarchs (e.g. Poroshenko) and especially by larger 'de novo' businesses. In some circles, the Orange protests came to be called a "revolt of millionaires against billionaires."[64] However, despite a noticeable shift in economic policy (e.g. increased FDI, spiked consumer lending, increased wages and pensions), "old" post-Soviet industrial economic practices remained dominant throughout the Yushchenko Presidency. Insider deals involving the Presidential Administration (e.g. on gas imports)[65] dashed the hopes of many for a complete shift to rules-based economic governance and a truly competitive market, but in other areas (e.g. in banking, retail, food processing, etc.) a tacit battle between the old Ukraine and the new continued throughout 2004-2009. The prize in the competition between the new and old economies was not necessarily material (although profit was the individual goal of the protagonists). The social contest was over the rules of capital accumulation. Two business elites competed over whose methods of enrichment would become legitimized.

British scholar Andrew Wilson famously noted that one of the reasons for the failure of the "Orange" protests to develop into a full-fledged socio-economic revolution in 2004 (i.e. resulting in structural change) was the weakness, at the time, of Ukraine's middle class.[66] By 2013-2014, entrepreneurs and managers of firms operating in Ukraine's services sector, together with journalists, academics, programmers, and other representatives of the country's "creative class" (a term that more accurately reflects the socio-economic status of Maidan activists than "middle class") were able to a form a critical mass of vocal and mobilized protest against the material excesses of the Yanukovych regime. After regime change in late February 2014, these same journalists, NGO activists, entrepreneurs, investment bankers, branch managers of western corporations, etc. entered the corridors of power, and for this new political elite, Maidan represented a watershed between a post-Soviet period of development and a new Ukraine. Throughout the previous 23 years of independence, members of Ukraine's "neo-bourgeois creative class" would have never even contemplated entering government, nor would they have been allowed to if they had tried. For them, the social lifts of Ukraine's "oligarchic democracy" had been largely closed. Idealistically, the (broadly termed) "bourgeois dream" of members of this new activist community (e.g. the "Euro optimists" inter-factional group in Parliament; the "Democratic Alliance" party, the "Reanimation Package of Reforms" and "Nova Krayina" NGO's) involved the creation of a state which guaranteed a level playing field for entrepreneurs and firms; one in which those with merit (talent, skills, drive, etc.) were able to

achieve success; one in which the state was neither partner nor predator with respect to the economy, but whose role in the private sector
was limited to that of impartial arbiter in case of dispute.

In the economic sphere, partly as a result of the sudden reorientation of Ukrainian firms' export markets from east to west (due to the
war with Russia), and also due to the abrupt diminution of the previous dominance of financial-industrial groups, Ukraine witnessed its
second (after the late 1990's) start-up boom after the Maidan.[67] Two
sectors may be identified as particularly entrepreneurial: export-ori-
ented information technology on the one hand, and consumer product
and service provision for the domestic market on the other. In the first
case, programmers and managers of outsourcing companies that had
been established during the 2000's to serve North American and EU
clients, used their accumulated experience and social capital to grow
their businesses rapidly, and to establish new companies that gradually shifted Ukraine's IT sector from project outsourcing to the provision of full-cycle technology services and (in some cases) ready products for western markets.[68] Outside the technology sector, sparked by
drastic devaluation of its currency (which suddenly made imports ex-
orbitantly expensive) Ukraine experienced an explosion of domestic
consumer product and service production. Examples included overnight delivery services, small businesses sewing clothes, manufacturing furniture, restaurants providing unique thematic ambiances, etc.

For the entrepreneurs who established these businesses, and the
consumers who purchased their offerings (i.e. "creative class" employees of Ukraine's "bourgeois" economy), the previously entrenched system of neo-feudal rents, hierarchical government, and
widespread corruption, was an affront to their basic values. Self-actualization, individual rights, transparency, rule-based government,
and perhaps most importantly, the *dignity* afforded by heterarchical
social structures (see Chapter 10), were principles for which in 2013-
14 they proved willing to make sacrifices. As it turned out, the price
to be paid for these principles (for many) amounted to 3 months of
private lives and careers put on hold, many terror-filled nights spent
manning barricades in sub-zero temperatures, and mobilization of all
possible resources for government reconstruction (reform) and armed

territorial defense after the climax of the Maidan protests. The self-reliance and collective solidarity that had characterized their "habitus" transferred organically to the volunteer battalions and grass-roots organizations created to supply the anti-Russian war effort and to provide relief to hundreds of thousands of people internally displaced by the fighting.

New cleavages

During Ukraine's first two post-Soviet decades, the resource extraction and processing sectors (coal, metallurgy), as well as energy and industrial manufacturing had become largely monopolized by business-owners who linked their wealth to direct and indirect state subsidies and to preferential tax regimes secured by lobbying government.[69] The enterprises that these "oligarchs" controlled were generally located in Ukraine's eastern regions (Donetsk, Luhansk, Dnipropetrovsk, and Zaporizhzhia oblasts) where the country's Soviet-era heavy industries had been located. These regions generated most of Ukraine's export revenues; they were heavily populated, generally Russian-speaking, and supported the Party of Regions or Communist Party. Conversely, the Ukrainian-speaking, relatively poorer western regions voted for "Orange" parties (i.e. Yushchenko's "Our Ukraine" or Tymoshenko's "Batkivshchyna").

However, during the decade preceding Maidan this stereotypical picture of Ukraine gradually changed: the economies of several cities in the western region began to grow — benefitting from an inheritance of Soviet-era educational centers that excelled in mathematics and engineering, and (ironically) from a dearth of industrial enterprises worth privatizing. For over two decades Lviv had not spawned a single national-level oligarch (unlike every other large Ukrainian city). This region had survived through entrepreneurship, and its 'de novo' firms (primarily in the IT and tourism sectors) had developed strong horizontal networks and organizational cultures well suited to a post-industrial economy. Their "bourgeois" ethos was reflected in everyday business practices: horizontal management, self-reliant entrepreneurship, civic activism, and rules-based relations with the state. At time of writing, the confrontation between this "habitus" and that of the "oligarchs" was far from resolved, but the legitimacy and viability of "bourgeois" practices had never been as strong in Ukraine in its post-Soviet history.

Ukraine's (ongoing) shift from an "oligarchic" to a "bourgeois" order was not sudden and was not spawned solely by Maidan. Prior to the outbreak of the protests, the economic base upon which the "oligarchs" had built their post-Soviet economic empires had already begun to shrink. Statistics are always difficult to judge in Ukraine because of its massive shadow economy (said to amount to up to 50% of total GDP during the Yanukovych period).[70] However, one thing is clear: individuals tend to migrate to areas where economic opportunities are prevalent, and quality of life can be secured. It is therefore notable that according to a UN Habitat 2012 study of the top 10 fastest shrinking cities in the world (!),[71] four were Ukrainian — all located in the eastern part of the country. Dnipro (formerly Dnipropetrovsk) topped the list as the city with the world's fastest rate of population shrinkage (decline of 16.78% projected for 1990-2025); Donetsk was number 3, and Zaporizhzhia — 4th in this global ranking. Because of Russian aggression, the downfall of Donetsk as an economic hub accelerated, but even prior to 2014, the structure of Ukraine's economy had begun to shift fundamentally. The heavy industries of the east were gradually losing both their attractiveness to the population and their significance as economic engines. The primary beneficiaries of this shift — at least in relative terms — were the cities of Kyiv and Lviv.

The magnetism of Ukraine's capital needs little explanation, but the rise of Lviv as an economic hub was a significant novelty that happened to coincide with the Maidan protests. Previously, the Ukrainian-speaking western city (and region in general) had been considered the poorest among Ukraine's major urban centers, with a population largely engaged in migrant work in Europe and/or subsistence activities. During the post-2008 years of overall economic decline and stagnation, Ukraine's IT sector (outsourcing, offshoring, gaming, etc.), largely centered in Lviv and Kyiv, uniquely experienced strong growth. Ukraine's software exports reached 2 billion USD in 2013 (topping 5 billion in 2018), and programmer and other IT service sector salaries averaged well over 1500 USD per month. Cumulative sector growth translated into consumer spending at the micro level which in turn resulted in small business job creation. The net result was dramatic improvement in the lifestyles of the populations of Kyiv and Lviv, and growth rates that outstripped those of the supposedly richer industrial cities of the east.

It is notable that the relative decline of the east, and improvement of living standards in the western and central regions did not magnify Ukraine's traditional political cleavage. On the contrary, shifts in regional economic might brought on by a decline in industrial production, and growth in post-industrial services (and a concomitant transformation of practices, including management relations, organizational cultures, volunteering, etc.), seemed to wither Ukraine's traditional electoral divide: during the two 2014 national elections (Presidential in April and Parliamentary in October — see Chapter 6), the regional cleavage that had defined geographic voting patterns for over 2 decades seemed to vanish. This political unity may well have been temporary — prompted by a patriotic reaction to Russian military aggression effected in the name of "protecting" the interests of Russian speakers who needed no protection, and by the complete discreditation of the once dominant Party of Regions (a result of the unmasking of Yanukovych's corruption and his lack of leadership during the Maidan protests). Or it may have been indicative of more fundamental structural transformations. Future elections (e.g. Presidential and Parliamentary in 2019) will be the test of whether the regional electoral cleavages that had plagued Ukraine for decades, and had largely reflected ethno-linguistic differences, return. It seems likely that other political cleavages will replace them.

In their 1967 seminal article on the subject of cleavages, political scientists Seymour Martin Lipset and Stein Rokkan, drew a link between the development of European political parties (i.e. national voting patterns), and their societies' historical experiences of revolutions.[72] Their claim was that three waves of revolution — involving the Church (Reformation), the Nation (dissolution of empires), and the economy (industrial revolution) — were experienced by European societies differently, and so left different legacies in the form of lasting electoral cleavages. In Ukraine in 2014, Yanukovych's ouster and Russia's aggression seemed to unite the country's regions, and to erase previous cleavages (i.e. the "national" cleavage was erased). But this was only part of the story of Ukraine's revolution. Socio-economic tensions between proponents of a closed, broadly termed "oligarchic" vision of development, and advocates of an "open-access order" (in the sense described by Douglass North and his colleagues)[73] that had previously remained hidden, became explicit.

Obviously, not everyone in Ukraine (before or after the protests) subscribed to the values professed by Maidan activists (and such disagreement had little to do with geopolitics, region or language). A "habitus" valuing self-reliant entrepreneurship, heterarchic social relations, meritocracy and civic activism may have been supremely attractive to residents of Ukraine's large cities — particularly the self-employed and/or IT professionals — but such values were largely foreign to the country's small town and rural residents. Although 69% of Ukrainians are said to live in cities, only 12% live in urban agglomerations of over 1 million residents.[74] Lifestyles in smaller cities — e.g. Vinnytsia, Ivano-Frankivsk, Rivne, Poltava, Sumy and Cherkasy — often approximate those of larger urban centers in some ways, but the smaller the urban center, the more its residents' lifestyles and values approximate those of the village. One may therefore conclude based on settlement type that no more than 25-30% of Ukraine's population could potentially be counted as "bourgeois" — in the sense of living an urban lifestyle, and possibly professing relevant values (and potentially expressing these in voting preferences).

Indeed, this estimate seems to correlate with polling data. According to a 2016 comprehensive study of Ukraine's "middle class" prepared by the Razumkov Center, 27% of respondents (N=10 054) identified themselves as belonging both to this "socio-economic stratum" and "class".[75] Interestingly, a larger number self-identified as belonging to the "middle class" (almost 50%), but when investigators controlled for other factors (e.g. education level, consumption capacity, friends and acquaintances from the relevant class/stratum, etc.) the proportion of respondents who actually adhered to a "middle class" lifestyle declined significantly. The authors concluded that

Ukraine's "middle class" consisted of a "core" (amounting to 14.2% of respondents) and "periphery" (numbering an additional 34.8%). The "core" included entrepreneurs, qualified professionals, managers, specialists, and others employed in creative service sector jobs.

In 2017, Denys Lavryk, an MA student in Sociology at Kyiv-Mohyla Academy applied the categorization of occupations developed by Richard Florida (the author of *The Rise of the Creative Class*) to the Razumkov data-set and concluded that 25.5% of the study's respondents were employed in jobs classified as being part of the "creative class".[76] Applying the same occupational categories to World Values Survey (WVS) and European Social Survey (ESS) data-sets from Ukraine, Lavryk identified the "creative class" as representing 29.8% and 22.1% of the respective samples. In each case, the "creative core" (as defined by Florida) represented roughly 11-13% nationally, with slightly higher numbers in Ukraine's western and central regions (17.4% and 15.7%) than in the east (11.5%) and south (10.3%)—a fact that may further explain the strength of the "bourgeois habitus" described above in these regions, and their amplified support for Maidan.

In coming years, Ukraine will surely develop new electoral cleavages. One dividing line is likely to be generational: between those who have internalized post-Soviet values and practices (i.e. what Russian publicist Oleksandr Zinoviev labelled the "homo Sovieticus"), and those who profess what we shall call in Chapter 10, a *post*modern ethic. A second divide will likely be formed between the urban "creative class" and the rural and small-town proletariat. In this contest, the country's emergent "neo-bourgeois creative class" will remain a quantitative minority, but it remains an open question whether the vision that representatives of this socio-economic stratum professed during and after the Maidan protests (i.e. the overthrow of Ukraine's established neo-feudal limited access "oligarchic" system) can be made attractive to the voting majority. In any case it seems unlikely that Ukraine's electoral geography will return to the contest between ethno-linguistic regions characteristic of the previous two decades.

The Maidan was not a contest for dominance between regions. The protest of Ukraine's "bourgeois" represented a culmination (or at least punctuation) of an evolutionary process of rebalancing contrasting economic models: one heavy industrial and/or agrarian and professing a hierarchic, neo-feudal habitus; the other—urban, young, globally connected, and engaged in the provision of "creative class" services. The latter will eventually succeed in fulfilling the "bourgeois" program of Maidan. But it is unclear when.

A new social system?

In retrospect, it is unlikely that the discourse of meritocratic, liberal self-reliance championed by Ukraine's Maidan revolutionaries was understood or espoused by the rest of the country's population. The protest activists who later became the drivers of post-Yanukovych reform represented an urban *minority* of Ukraine's population. However, as Hannah Arendt pointed out in her seminal study *On Revolution*:

> Even where the loss of authority is quite manifest, revolutions can break out and succeed only if there exists a sufficient number of men (sic.) who are prepared for its collapse and, at the same time, willing to assume power, eager to organize and act together for a common purpose. The number of such men need not be great...[77]

Arendt's observation points to an important ingredient of revolutionary transformation: a more-or-less organized programmatic counter-elite that is prepared first to destroy the hierarchical structures of the ancien regime, and then to reconstitute order in a new way. In Ukraine, there seems to have been no dearth of individuals prepared to take on this task: in early 2014 President Yanukovych was overthrown, and members of his inner circle were replaced—first by an interim administration consisting of former opposition politicians, and then through a series of elections in 2014 and 2015, with political newcomers. These newcomers sought to destroy the neo-feudal hierarchy of the Yanukovych regime within state structures, replacing these (perhaps temporarily) with horizontal network structures that originated on the Maidan. The central figures of the first Ukrainian government formed after the 2014 Parliamentary elections were western-oriented investment bankers (tasked with appeasing the IMF) and

idealistic Maidan activists (tasked with appeasing maximalist sentiments of recent protesters). Once the social mood calmed somewhat,
the key figures in the more opaque Hroysman government became
"flexians": individuals who held no formal office, but quietly advised
public officials on the implementation of key reforms.[78]

However, is it fair to say that the values these "bourgeois" activists who entered Ukraine's political class after the ouster of Yanukovych professed were *European?* Certainly, their ideas were antithetical to Putin's "managed democracy" — a concept that later expanded
into an ideological program that came to be known as "Russkiy Mir"
("Russian World"), and was flatly rejected by the vast majority of
Ukrainians.[79] But ironically, the liberal (approximating "libertarian")
economic ideology of Ukraine's new post-Yanukovych political elite
seemed also to conflict with the social market ideals dominant in the
EU. Maidan activists entering government sought to replace "oligarchic" neo-feudalism (neo-patrimonialism) with institutions that
would ensure meritocratic, open rules-based social mobility. To ac-
complish this, they sought to *reduce* the state's interventionist (administrative) capacity with respect to the economy (i.e. to chip away at the
uneven market relations that had led to the development of "oligarchy"). Such methods seemed difficult to square with the rational bureaucracy that ensures the "social market" system of the EU.

After the ouster of Yanukovych, Ukrainians seem to have begun
the construction of a "new system" — one that was neither European,
nor Russian (i.e. post-Soviet). The victory of Maidan catapulted new
elites into positions of power, but strangely, without completely re-
moving the mid-level bureaucracy of the previously in-post executive.
Top-level officials either fled the country or were removed through a
process of "lustration",[80] but the "system" largely remained unchanged. The *ancien regime* of Ukraine's oligarchs was certainly weakened, but the final outcome of the struggle between them and the
"neo-bourgeois" revolutionaries remained uncertain. What had become a certainty by the end of 2018 was that the economy of Ukraine
had changed unrecognizably. Dramatic currency devaluation had resulted in a drastic reduction of *per capita* GDP and had also led to migrant worker remittances becoming Ukraine's top foreign currency

generator.[81] Export markets had shifted away from Russia to the EU, and the structure of exports had transformed with volumes of incoming cash from sales of IT services, tourism and agricultural produce far outstripping revenues from trade in metals. The heavy industry of Ukraine's eastern regions which had previously been the basis for the oligarchs' economic power and political influence was trending towards catastrophic decline.

The "regime change" caused by the Maidan protests was not merely a change of faces. The ouster of Yanukovych affected the fundamental socio-economic fabric of the country: it transformed the legitimacy of wealth accumulation methods, shifting values away from production to creation; it altered the way in which productive activities were normally organized – shifting fashion away from hierarchy to heterarchy; it influenced values, introducing a non-materialist (ideational if not idealist "liberal") ethic of self-reliance to Ukraine's large urban centers. It transformed the fundamental institutions of government, and the way in which provision of services to citizens was organized at both national and local levels (e.g. policing, passport issuance, tax remittance, etc.). These changes were effected by Maidan activists who suddenly entered government offices after the ouster of Yanukovych – some as formal appointees, others as behind-the-scenes "flexian" advisors. The new elites came to positions of power having previously worked in the domestic entrepreneurial private sector, in Ukrainian branch offices of international corporations, or in the education and NGO sectors (i.e. few had been socialized in the hierarchical culture of Ukraine's oligarchic financial-industrial groups and/or post-Soviet civil service). Ukraine's revolutionary "flexians" professed a new "horizontal" culture: for them, social capital was more important than economic capital; meritocracy was the hegemonic ideology; the ideal was a society structured heterarchically (i.e. generally "flat" with leadership and authority appearing situationally). They implemented a program based on a right-of-center economic ideology: transparency, reduced subsidies, decreased levels of taxation, redundancies in the public sector.

This ideological program was not simply a philosophical import from the West. Indeed, the "bourgeois" ethic that seemed to drive the "creative class" Maidan activists was rooted in a domestic discourse that seemed to uniquely develop during Ukraine's Revolution of Dignity. The roots and possible consequences of this revolutionary discourse, and the contours of the new socio-economic and political systems that it may engender will be examined in the next chapter.

Chapter 10:
A Post-Modern Revolution

Revolutions are often viewed as inflection points: somehow after a revolution life is supposed to become radically different than it was before. Apparently, this is the main difference between a revolutionary period, and the "normality" of everyday life. Under normal conditions, social relations and practices (micro-level society) and political and economic institutions (macro-level) evolve gradually because they are underpinned by a relatively stable system of prevalent values and norms, which in turn are reinforced by a dominant discourse — terminology that is used in everyday life, with taken for granted meanings accepted by all. During a period of revolutionary transformation, the most enduring aspects of a social system — its ideational foundations — undergo accelerated transformation. Revolutions change prevalent ways of thinking, acting, and verbalizing. New ideas are generated, discussed, debated, and then piloted in new structures, organizations, initiatives, practices, and terms. For the protagonists it feels like a brave new world is being created by, before, and for them, and for the benefit of all humanity. In reality, the pace of transformation is often overestimated: during revolutionary periods, ideas develop faster than during non-revolutionary periods, but their institutionalization is necessarily more gradual than the pace at which members of the political elite are replaced.

In this chapter we examine the ideas (notions, values, philosophical concepts) underpinning what came to be known as Ukraine's Revolution of Dignity. Specifically, we will delve into the concept of "dignity" — a seemingly superficial demand of the Maidan protesters, and simultaneously a deeply philosophical concept. The choice of "dignity" as the signifying name for Ukraine's revolution was not random: the fact that demonstrators in Kyiv focused on this concept, I contend, reflected the leading-edge nature of the ideas they put forth. In this dimension Maidan represented no less than a disruption of western civilization.[1] Indeed, far from being a "backwater" event on the margins of Europe, Ukraine's revolution embodied ideas that may represent the future of civilizational development on the continent and beyond: a shift from individualism to personalism in social interaction; a transition from hierarchy to heterarchy in power relations; an attempt to horizontalize social relations — particularly with respect to institutionalizing "fairness" — which reflected a new cosmology, possibly reflective of more comprehensive trends affecting the development of European (western) civilization.

To be more specific, we argue here that Ukraine's Revolution of Dignity was an instantiation of a broader (ongoing and global) transformation of the ideas underpinning the socio-cultural system known as "modernity."[2] As the second decade of the 21st century ends, one can see evidence of this transformation throughout the western world: political institutions designed after WWII to guarantee peace in Europe and beyond have been openly questioned by the world's most powerful elites; global corporations, previously organized as hierarchical structures, have been outpaced by companies operating under a different organizational paradigm (e.g. Google, Facebook, Amazon); shifts away from mass consumption of material goods towards "experience" economies, sharing (including social media), and responsible purchasing seem to define the direction of development of individual consumption patterns — and the trend is neither short-term nor locally limited. This (nominally "post-modern" — i.e. ensuing the "modern" period) transformation of western civilization is fundamental. It affects ethics and norms of legitimacy, systems of organization and communication, dominant paradigms and institutions.

The term "post-truth" emerged in concert with the Maidan protests (although not because of them),[3] and reflected the global trend towards questioning the validity of accepted fact. Such a radical skepticism (and its use for insidious purposes by the Kremlin)[4] was only possible in the context of a global paradigmatic shift, symptomatic of a change that encompassed much more than Ukraine. Whether new organizational forms become institutionalized based on ideas spawned by Ukraine's revolution, and indeed what paradigms will become dominant in the new world that will result from this civilizational shift, is still unsure. But Maidan seems to have provided a (possibly momentary) telescopic view of socio-political life in the *post-modern*. Furthermore, it presented a challenge to Ukraine's (intellectual, if not political) elites: to seize the combined opportunity of the transformative moment, and their country's advantageous position on the periphery of European civilization, to create institutions that might eventually breathe life into these new ideas.

Civilizational shift

Maidan was not the birthplace of entirely new ideas, nor did the Ukrainian protests and subsequent Russian-Ukrainian war represent the start of a global transformation. The "Third Wave" civilizational phase shift, of which the Revolution of Dignity was a component, was detected much earlier, in other places, and in other (particularly technological) manifestations.[5] However, just as the Great Transformation from agrarian feudalism to industrial capitalism (described thoroughly by virtually every classical social scientist)[6] was punctuated by several political revolutions and wars in the course of its centuries-long progression, so too — according to the argument presented here — will history record Ukraine's Revolution of Dignity as one of the "great revolutions" that fostered the new ideas, values, social arrangements, and proto-institutions that defined social development in the era that followed industrial society (i.e. "modernity"). To explicate the argument, we must first examine what is meant by "civilizational shift". We will then examine the role of violent revolutions in such change and try to situate Ukraine's Revolution of Dignity in the civilizational development process.

Of the scholars whom social scientists see as the founding fathers of their disciplines (particularly sociology, but also political science), practically all had something to say about the 18-19th century shift of western (European) civilization from its traditional form to what came to be labelled "modernity." For Marx, the major feature of this shift was a transition from agrarian feudalism to industrial capitalism that involved the development of a new class system. For Weber, the key to understanding the civilizational shift was both structural (urbanization, rise of literacy, technology, available labor) and cultural (values changing due to the Reformation, spread of self-reliant entrepreneurship).[7] For Durkheim, the fundamental attribute of modernity was the newfound division of labor, and its consequent effect on interpersonal interaction and solidarity. For the American sociologist Talcott Parsons, the shift from traditionalism to modernity was characterized by a transition (among others) from preponderance of particularism in social relations to universalism, rule of law, equality of rights. Parsons also pointed out that shifts from ascription to meritocracy, and from collectivism to individualism occurred in parallel with industrialization, and so were an integral part of the transition from traditionalism to modernity.

Each of these classic scholars emphasized different aspects of a multi-facetted transformation of western civilization lasting over a century. Achieving "modernity" — the result of this civilizational makeover — involved urbanization, industrialization, the rise of consumerism, mass literacy and numeracy, the development of hierarchically organized and bureaucratically managed states (and companies) that ensured depersonalized application of legal norms, meritocratic stratification, replacement of absolutist monarchy with various forms of democratic governance, and consecration of the rights of the individual in written law. Notably, the confluence of these components of social organization did not appear through gradual evolutionary processes. Their development was intimately linked to various revolutions that affected the European continent in the post-Enlightenment era.

In the words of renowned sociologist S.N. Eisenstadt: "revolutions developed against the background of the major cultural and ideological trends which ushered in the cultural program of Western modernity, a program which became crystalized through these revolutions."[8] Thus, according to this most notable of scholars who studied the role of revolutions in the development of modernity, although the "great revolutions" (e.g. the American, French and Russian/Soviet) did not cause of the historical processes that culminated in 20th century Europe and North America in specific societal forms (i.e. industrial capitalism, welfare state institutions, liberal democracy, globalism, etc.), in retrospect, this process of civilizational development cannot have occurred without them.

Fast forward to the early 21st century: again western civilization seems to be undergoing fundamental transformation, this time from modernity (also labelled "industrialism" or "late capitalism") to some form of *post*-modernity (or "post-industrial" organization).[9] In 2016, the World Economic Forum declared the onset of a Fourth Industrial Revolution "characterized by a fusion of technologies that is blurring the lines between the physical, digital, and biological spheres."[10] Multiple authors have argued that the onset of a "wired world" in the 21st century has fundamentally changed the way products and services are produced, marketed, sold, and consumed. Political scientists have suggested that these changes will result in some form of "post-capitalism" and/or "post-democracy."[11]

Social attention to what Eisenstadt called "cosmological visions" — the ideational preconditions of social and political stability and/or change — obviously heightened at the start of the 3rd millennium, and under such conditions, normative debates as to the fundamentals of social order are to be expected. We live in a period when previously hegemonic ideas and formerly legitimate social and political institutions are openly questioned. According to Eisenstadt, it is not inconceivable that during such periods, reexamination of previously axiomatic political and social beliefs should be accompanied by political and social revolutions, and by violence — particularly in regions that are not at the core of the global political-economic system.

The American and French revolutions (the first occurred in a peripheral place; the second — in the heart of Europe) were rooted in a cosmology traceable to the Enlightenment. According to their protagonists, absolute monarchy was irrational: political order was to result from the application of rational principles, rather than from Divine right.

> The distinctiveness of the utopian visions which constituted the utopian core of the cosmologies of these revolutions lay not only in the transposition of the perennial themes of protest, of justice, liberty and the like into the central political arena... Closely related was also the

emphasis, rooted in the philosophy of the Enlightenment, in the attempts to bring the realm of reason into the political arena—a theme which could be found in the American and in a more radical way in the French Revolution. This distinctiveness lay also in the conception of society as an object which can be remolded according to such vision.[12]

Philosophers of the 18th century argued that in a post-monarchic order, political legitimacy was to be derived from codified rules, which in turn were to be derived from a recognition of the *individual* as sacrosanct. Therefore, instead of referencing the Divine as the root of social and political order, John Locke and Thomas Hobbes saw its constitution as the result of a "social contract" between sovereign individuals and the state to whom these individuals delegated a portion of their sovereignty. Political legitimacy was now to be derived from the individual, rather than from God.[13] The central organizing principle of the polity ceased to be the monarch, as representative of the Divine on earth, and now — logically — became the nation-state with its codified legal system, democratically elected rulers, separation of powers, etc.

However, despite their proclamation of "democratic" (or "republican") institutions as the ideal mechanisms for ensuring periodic rotation of elites (e.g. elections and separate legislative and executive branches) and "liberty" (voice) for the people, the paradigm of modernity instituted through (r)evolution remained hierarchical. In the wake of the immense social changes that swept Europe during the 18-19 centuries, opportunities for social mobility (i.e. status betterment) became available to a larger cross-section of the population, no longer being limited to those benefitting from ascription or the whims of a feudal lord. However, the structure of modern society still approximated a pyramid. Ideally, the basis for advancement was to be merit (however defined), but social status (class), nevertheless, remained a primary vertical analytical category that reflected the power-position of individuals with respect to one-another. Potentiality to employ force no longer determined one's power position; rather power stemmed from one's position within an organization (e.g. apparatus of state, corporation, institution).[14] To a greater or lesser extent (depending on the accepted role of the state as economic equalizer), by the mid-20th century, material wealth derived from career success within a hierarchical corporation had become *the* basis for measuring worth within the social structures of modernity.

In his analysis of the 1960's social movements in western Europe, Eisenstadt suggested that they foreshadowed the development of a different (broadly termed "post-modern") cosmology: "These transformations entailed the weakening of the definition of ontological reality as promulgated in the Enlightenment, which has been hegemonic in the classical period of modernity."[15] This first post-modern revolutionary movement seemed to emphasize the local over the macrosocial in politics, the collective over the individual in economics, and the ideal over the sensate (materialist) in ethics. Whereas late 18th century, post-Enlightenment, European intellectual development which spilled over into the American and French revolutions called for a pathos of liberty (i.e. individualism), the European uprisings of the 1960's seemed to foreshadow a shift towards networked solidarity, rejection of hierarchy ("horizontality"), and idealism over materialism.

In the early 21st century, social movements such as Occupy (2011), the Arab Spring (2012), the Ukrainian Maidan (2013-14), and then protests in Romania and South Korea in 2016-17 seemed to strengthen the trend. Firstly, technological breakthroughs in the form of smartphones and social media enabled a shift from traditional mass media (i.e. hierarchical dissemination of information from a single point to a mass audience) to more horizontal interaction.[16] In each of these movements, the protesters took full advantage.[17] Secondly, the common catalytic force for protest in each case was perceived corruption of entrenched elites, but the resultant demand was not for economic equality, but rather for "justice" in an ethical sense. More accurately, the demand was for "fairness" — i.e. a determination of rightfulness according to supposedly universal ethics (natural law) rather than through mere statutory legality — reflecting a shift to idealism, away from the rationalism of codified laws which (according to the protesters) could be (and were) applied unfairly by a wealthy and therefore powerful elite. These movements did not call for material equality per se. Instead they demanded a shift to collective governance whereby power would be a function of influence of person, rather than authority of office and/or power emanating from wealth. In each of these dimensions, as we shall see below, the protesters seemed to profess a new cosmology; an evolution of the paradigms underpinning modernity.

A "Revolution of Dignity"

Words and their meanings do not emerge randomly. In naming their revolution the "Revolution of Dignity," Ukrainians formulated a public declaration, and the fact that the name gained lasting popularity is a testament to its resonance. As a moniker that encapsulated the protesters' demands, the word "dignity" was addressed principally to a domestic audience, but its "shot was heard 'round the world." The multi-dimensional concept of "dignity" became a rallying cry for millions.

The concept of dignity has its roots in the Enlightenment and is often viewed as extension of the notion of individual rights—fundamental to the paradigm of western liberal democracy. As Harvard Professor Michael Rosen points out in *Dignity: Its History and Meaning*, the English word "dignity" traces its etymology to the Latin "*dignitas*" and is understood in the sense meant by Cicero in his "De Officio" (On Duties), as being a quality of honor, possessed by the "*optimi*" (best citizens) in a well-ordered society.[18] In traditional European (feudal) societies, only the landed gentry, were seen as "dignified" and therefore deserving of say in public discourse because of their believed link to the Divine. In other words, an individual was said to have dignity if he (inevitably it was "he") was said to deserve it through noble birth and requisite bloodline.

> "Dignity" originated as a concept that denoted high social status and the honors and respectful treatment that are due to someone who occupied that position. Terms to express similar conceptions exist in most languages, including ancient ones... There are four uses of "dignity" in the King James translation of the Hebrew Bible, although they

render three different Hebrew words. All three apparently also contain the sense of "elevation" or "majesty."[19]

In French, the word *"dignite"* traditionally denoted the privileges enjoyed by the aristocracy—until the French Revolution introduced the idea of universal rights.[20] Thus, the modern understanding of "dignity" as a term connoting a universal characteristic of the human condition, may be recognized (leaving Kant aside) as having been directly caused by the French Revolution. Increased democratization of western societies, and indeed their modernization, resulted in the assertion of dignity as a fundamental and universal human right in such 20th century legal documents as the Universal Declaration of Human Rights, the Geneva Convention, and the German *Grundgesetz* (Basic Law).[21] Two centuries after the French Revolution, Oxford Professor Jeremy Waldron observed: "the modern notion of human dignity involves an upward equalization of rank, so that we now try to accord to every human being something of the dignity, rank and expectation of respect that was formerly accorded (only) to nobility."[22]

However, the Ukrainian word *"hidnist'"* (commonly translated into English as "dignity") reflects a different conceptual category that has nothing to do with status, rank or privilege, and its etymology seems to have little in common with Ciceronian honor. According to the *Academic Dictionary of the Ukrainian Language* the word *"hidnist'"* has two meanings: 1) a set of traits that characterize a person's positive moral qualities; 2) comprehension by a person of their civic worth and civic responsibility.[23] In the first sense, the term refers to the inherent value of the person as a uniquely *moral* being capable of self-actualization, whereas in the second it implies the fundamentally *social* quality of human existence.[24] Neither of these definitions implies that *"hidnist'"* is an attribute of status. On the contrary, in the first sense, the term signifies a possession of virtue,[25] whereas in the second definition the term references a civic and/or societal (*"hromadske"*) context for the term. This seems most interesting, as it differs significantly from the conventional English or French (i.e. western) usage of the term "dignity"—if only because the Ukrainian term makes no allusion to hierarchy.

Given that western perceptions of Ukraine are often attenuated through the lens of Russia, some reference to the usage of terms in the Russian language may be useful. Conventionally, the Ukrainian word *"hidnist'"* is translated into Russian as *"dostoinstvo"*,[26] and the terms *"hidnist'"* and *"dostoynist'"* (both used in Ukrainian) are often claimed to be synonyms. The first is said to originate from the Polish *"godnosc'"* and the latter from the Russian *"dostoinstvo"*,[27] but the actual usage of the terms *"hidnist'"* and *"dostoynist'"* in Ukrainian indicates some nuance. Firstly, a bad person (lacking virtue) can be referred to as "nehidnyk" (lacking *"hidnist'"*),[28] but the equivalent antonymous noun does not exist for a person lacking *"dostoynist'"*. Secondly, when referring to a fundamental encroachment on the humanity of an individual, one references *"hidnist'"* (not *"dostoynist'"*): if a violation of that which is considered sacred in one's humanity occurs, a person is said to be stripped of their *"hidnist'"* (*"pozbavlena hidnosti"*).

Approximating the English "dignity", the term *"dostoynist'"* implies possession of status or rank whereas *"hidnist'"* seems to signify a more fundamental and universally human quality. The two are close, but not synonymous. A person may be *"dostoyniy"* (worthy) of respect or reward,[29] but this is not the same as *"hidniy"* (the adjectival form of the noun *"hidnist'"*). *"Hidnist'"* is an immutable quality of being human, universally possessed, and not subject to relativism (i.e. a person cannot have more/less *"hidnist'"*): in everyday usage one can be said to be *"hidniy"* or not, but without degree. On the other hand, *"dostoynist'"* is relative: the degree to which a person's virtuous qualities are actualized may be the subject of evaluation. But the basic quality of *"hidnist'"* may not be questioned. A person who is *"dostoyniy"* *deserves* recognition by others, whereas *"hidnist'"* implies a *right* or claim that is more fundamental and universal. In other words, *"hidnist'"* in the Ukrainian language seems to entail not only an inherent value possessed by the person (similar to the inherent "worth" or *"Würde"* that was the foundation of Kant's moral philosophy),[30] but also one that *requires respect from others for validation*. This claim to respect can be legitimately demanded by all who claim *"hidnist'"* – i.e. it does not require a status position or accomplishment, as is the case with *"dostoyniy"*.

For western scholars who have analyzed dignity in its various legal and philosophical usages, such a conceptual link between the concept of "dignity" (as *"hidnist'"*), and the *requirement that it be respected* is novel:

> In protecting the individual from degradation, insult, and contempt we are requiring that people act towards her in ways that are substantively respectful. To respect their dignity in this sense means to treat them *with respect* (italics in original) … (T)his is a very important point indeed. On the one hand, it gives content to the idea of human dignity-gives an answer to those who allege that there is nothing more to the idea of "dignity" than rhetorical wrapping paper for a set of substantive rights-claims. On the other, it implies that dignitary harms are harms of a special kind. What degradation, insult, and contempt have in common is that they are expressive or symbolic harms, ones in which the elevated status of human beings *fails to be acknowledged* [italics in original].[31]

Dignity–when recognized as the fundamental principle according to which society is organized–is both the principle that constrains the state from violating rights (i.e. a principle underpinning formal institutions), and the social force that constrains the individual from violating the rights of others (i.e. the foundation for informal institutions-conventions, social norms, moral rules). In other words, dignity is the principle that is actualized in the practice of respect. It was in this sense that the Maidan protesters *demanded recognition* (i.e. respect) for their individual and collective *"hidnist'"*.

From individualism to "Personalism"

As noted, the Ukrainian term *"hidnist'"* has two meanings: it refers to an inherent quality of a person (i.e. his/her unassailable value), and simultaneously connotes an ethical attitude (respect) of society to that person. In each of these dimensions, one can say that a person *possesses* *"hidnist'"*. Analysis of the "inherent dignity" of the person (the first definition) steers one in the direction of philosophical investigation: to the Aquinian doctrine of dignity as the reflection in humanity of the Creator, or to the Kantian categorical imperative from which universal ethical norms may be drawn. The second dimension leads us to the *social* aspect of the human condition: to the subject's self-identification within a community; to agency.[32]

This *social* aspect of the Ukrainian term *"hidnist'"* is most relevant to the present discussion of the novel senses produced on/by Maidan. Specifically: the protesters *demanded recognition* of their dignity. In this sense, dignity (*"hidnist'"*) was understood as an inherent potential of a person that could only be actualized in a relational logic: as an attitude of the individual towards society (i.e. comprehension of one's status as a citizen—member of the nation—and therefore of obligations towards others), and simultaneously as an orientation of society and the state towards the person (citizen). From this perspective, an individual may inherently possess dignity, but that in itself matters little unless that dignity is recognized by another. Thus, in the sense used by Ukraine's revolutionaries, dignity requires more than an individualistic conception of the subject: dignity is only possible within a *collectivity* of mutual respect.

This distinctively Ukrainian interpretation of the concept of dignity (*"hidnist'"*) deserves particular scrutiny. Its core seems to approximate the still underdeveloped strand of philosophy called "Personalism"—a worldview that emphasizes the centrality of the *socially-embedded person* as the starting point for moral and political reflection. Although not representing a clear school or doctrine, Personalism "emphasizes the significance, uniqueness and inviolability of the person, as well as the person's essentially relational or communitarian dimension."[33] This duality of the human condition is fundamental to Personalism: personhood subsumes individual dignity, but persons never exist in isolation, and interpersonal communion with others is fundamental to the human condition. As University of Notre Dame sociology professor Christian Smith explains:

> Humans literally cannot develop as persons without other persons with whom they share and sustain their personhood. To be a person is not to be an incommunicable self, distinct from other selves. It is also to be related to, communicating among, and in communion with other personal selves. Inherent to personalist understanding of the human being is a strong dimension of relational connection and solidarity.

> Only by living in communities of other personal selves can anyone be-
> come a distinct personal self.[34]

Central to the ethic of Personalism is the concept of transcendence. In
its theological interpretation (e.g. the writings of Karol Wojtyla—Pope
John Paul II),[35] personalist philosophy posits that every human has an
aptitude for "vertical transcendence"—an inherent orientation to
truth; a capacity to distinguish good from evil that is a manifestation
of the Divine image in which every human is believed by Christians
to have been created.[36] The Maidan protests certainly had a mystical
manifestation, but the feeling of humanity that was prevalent among
the protesters—and similarly reported by veterans returning from the
front—did not require affiliation to a particular faith. The ethic of Maidan (i.e. what Ukrainians refer to as the "values of Maidan" / "tsinnosti
Maidanu"), and indeed the ethic of defense in war, were both based on
a black/white absolutist appraisal of one's environment. Intellectually, in everyday interactions one may accept "grey", but in situations
of extreme stress and intense conviction, valuations defy conditionality: there is only good/evil; us/them; truth/lie.[37] The ability to make
such evaluative judgments in extreme situations is not a deficiency of
the human condition, but rather its essential virtue—that which defines the rational person; his/her inherent dignity. According to Personalist philosophy, this vertical transcendence is the basis for con-
science, self-determination (identity), self-control, and values.

In addition to theorizing the roots of humans' aptitude for moral
judgment, Personalism also proposes "horizontal transcendence" to
be a fundamental characteristic of the human condition. As the famous Personalist Emmanuel Mounier memorably quipped "I love,
therefore I am."[38] To be human means to organically combine individ-
uality and the mutual:

> On the one hand, personalism insisted on the person as an absolute
> whose nature could not be impinged in any way… On the other hand,
> the concept of person called for the most profound solidarity, drawing
> people together as one by the most deep and lasting bonds within
> themselves… It was only the notion of person as rooted in the trans-
> cendent which held these poles together.[39]

Personalists adamantly reject the post-Enlightenment development of philosophical thinking, according to which the *individual* was hallowed as the central figure of ethics, politics, and economics. Indeed, Personalists bemoan the fact that the sovereign individual—a being with inalienable *individual* rights and *individual* responsibilities—became the philosophical basis of modernity. Thinkers such as Hobbes, Locke, Rousseau and Marx all focused on the *well-being of the individual* as the aim of politics. Although each recognized—with differing emphasis—that individuals coexist in societies, living together according to some accepted system of rights, authority, and some form of solidarity, these fundamentally *social* aspects of the human condition were either downplayed (in the liberal tradition) or delegated to the state to regulate (in the socialist tradition). Sovereign individuals were seen as incapable of binding together without a mediating power to police their competing interests. Ideologs discussed how best to satisfy the material needs and wants of this sovereign individual (via free-market capitalism or state-guided socialism), but the fundamental tenet of individualism was never questioned.

During the 20th century it was this sovereign individual who became the central actor of consumerist industrial society—"modernity". To enable the ordered social interaction of these sovereign individuals, liberal philosophers devised the "social contract"—a concept that is antithetical to Personalism (as the late Pope John Paul II never tired of pointing out):

> For Hobbes and Locke… human beings are conceived in their natural state as having no intrinsic ties to other persons. The forces that drive them together to form a political community are the inconveniences of living without settled law and government. Although Hobbes' account of human nature is decidedly more pessimistic than Locke's, both conceive of the person as essentially an individual, all subsequent ties instrumental and utilitarian in nature. In their respective accounts of human nature, the individual is sovereign over himself and there is no sovereignty in the community at all. Political sovereignty is an artificial creation which occurs when individuals come together to make the social contract. In Hobbes' version, the surrender of individual sovereignty is total and the absolutist state, the Leviathan is created. Locke, on the other hand, insists that the transfer of sovereignty is limited.

The deeper issue however, is not the degree to which individual sovereignty is surrendered to create public sovereignty, but the very notion that sovereignty is created by such voluntaristic and individualistic acts in the first place. How can essentially private powers create public ones? As Aquinas had said centuries before, no private person can create a law. Lawmaking is a part of no man's nature and is therefore not an individual power that can be transferred to some artificial entity created by man. At the root of this erroneous thinking are the false assumptions that (a) individual, private contracts can create public rights, and (b) the common good is nothing more than an addition of private ones.[40]

For Personalists, to be human involves transcendence: the individual cannot exist without others, and the social is an integral part of the human condition. The shared essence of the person compels cohabitation in a community, and it is this community that is the basis for *public* sovereignty: "In this view, sovereignty is not so much a contract drawn up among individuals who are by nature autonomous, isolated, and unrelated, as it is a consensus arising from the unity of wills who seek to live in a community in pursuit of a common good."[41]

Article 5 of Ukraine's Constitution proclaims that "The people shall be the bearer of sovereignty, and the only source of power in Ukraine." It is notable that the term "people" (*"narod"*) is used in the singular — not referencing a collection of individuals, but rather an existential category *sui generis*. This seems to reflect an important tenet of Personalist philosophy, namely that *"community* is ontologically prior to the establishment of any political institution,"[42] and that political authority is derived from the community — a social union that consists of more than simply an aggregate of individuals. This fact could be considered peripheral (an interesting terminological anomaly of the Ukrainian Constitution) if one of the most prominent symbols of the Maidan protests had not been the Roman numeral "V" — a publicly expressive reference to Article 5. The protesters demanded that the *"hidnist'"* of the *"narod"*(people, *Volk*) be recognized and respected — a demand that seemed to reflect a phenomenological vision of collective sovereignty, engendered both in patriotic discourse, and in very concrete acts aimed at improving the *collective* wellbeing of so-

ciety. Sadly, a corollary effect of such (apparently) Personalist emphasis on collective sovereignty was rejection (or at least skepticism) of
any individual who aspired to a leadership role—a fact that attested
to the lack (as yet) of institutional expression of the values engendered
by the Ukrainian revolution.

The "person-of-Maidan" (and the volunteer fighter / aid pro-
vider / flexian government reform advisor) who declares his/her individual rights, but simultaneously recognizes collective responsibility to "the people" (i.e. a duty to help, defend, feed, and sacrifice for
others with no overt or assumed benefit in return) stands in sharp contrast to the Individual (writ large) of Hobbes and Locke, and therefore
diverges fundamentally from the basic tenets of "modernity". The
unique values complex generated and proliferated by the Ukrainian
revolution seems a strange mix of western individualism with respect
to rights, and Slavic collectivism with respect to responsibility.[43] It
may be interpreted as a cultural peculiarity of early 21st century
Ukraine, or as a product of social development, suggesting an evolution of ideas beyond those underpinning western modernity. Indeed,
it may be both.

A community of fairness

In the wake of the Maidan protests, Ukrainian Catholic University in
Lviv seems to have pinpointed a salient term relevant to the Revolu-
tion of Dignity in its phenomenological ("post-modern") dimension.
The slogan of UCU adopted in 2016 consisted of three words:
"*Svidchyty*" (to Witness), "*Sluzhyty*" (to Serve), and "*Spilkuvatysia.*" In
its official documents the university translated the third term into
English as "to Communicate", but the Ukrainian original is more nuanced. Although the etymology of the English word "communicate"
could (in principle) be traced to "commune", this would be a stretch.
Both the Oxford and Webster dictionaries define communication as
involving the exchange of information between individuals[44]—one
could add *sovereign* individuals. In contrast, the root of the Ukrainian
verb "*spilkuvatysia*" is "*spilka*" (union) or "*spilno*"—meaning "together". A more correct translation of this activity would be "socializ-

ing" or "sharing". The Ukrainian term refers to much more than information exchange, and indeed, exchange of information is designated as "*komunikatsiya*" rather than "*spilkuvannia.*"

This nuance is significant given the explosion in popularity of
words involving "*spilno*" in the wake of the Maidan protests.
SpilnoTV was a popular grassroots internet TV station streaming live
from Maidan during the protests. The primary vehicle for crowd-
funding (including volunteer initiatives aimed at supporting the war
effort, financing aid to IDP's and veterans) was called "*Spilnokosht.*"
Various civil society organizations included the word "*spil'nota*"
(community) into their self-descriptions or names. In mid-December
2013, the creative staff of one of Kyiv's advertising agencies created
the slogan "I am a Drop in the Ocean," and it became a powerful
meme in and around the protest camp. The metaphor spoke volumes:
it reflected the powerlessness of individual protest, and the massive
potency of collective action.

"Civil society" is a term used by social scientists to denote grass-
roots volunteer organizations that exist in democratic societies as
mechanisms through which citizens are able to both bond in solidary
groups and to express their political views (often bypassing or directly
pressuring traditional political structures).[45] Civil society seemed to
appear spontaneously on Maidan,[46] and the phenomena of civic activism and volunteering (both *ad hoc* and systemic), persisted after the
ouster of Yanukovych—largely as a reaction to Russia's military aggression. For Ukraine, the explosion of volunteering and civic activism in 2013-14 was a new social phenomenon. Whereas grassroots
philanthropy had been extraordinarily rare prior to Maidan, according to a poll conducted in late 2015 and 2016, 47% and 41.6% of respondents respectively, reported having provided aid in some form
to the war effort (the ATO), to displaced persons, to Donbas relief
funds, etc.[47] Whereas in 2012, only 21,4% of survey respondents reported having contributed to charitable funds and foundations, in
2015 that number rose to 41.4%;[48] the proportion reporting personal
engagement in volunteering grew from 10,2% in 2012 to 14% in 2016.
Observing both the novelty and broader significance of the sudden

appearance of grassroots community activism on a mass scale — especially during the early years of the Russian-Ukrainian war when mobilization of resources for defense became a near universal priority — eminent Ukrainian sociologist Yevhen Holovakha noted: "The phenomenon of volunteering has made Ukrainians happier... because for the first time in history, the Ukrainian concept of happiness now includes satisfaction from helping others... As a result, they now feel like full-fledged agents of social life."[49]

This optimism and positive determination to effect change at all levels of society represented a very real novelty of the Maidan experience[50] — particularly given the fatalism and pessimism of prevalent post-Soviet discourse with which it contrasted. As the slogan prominently posted at each entrance to the Maidan camp suggested, grass roots community activists set their sights high: "Please excuse the inconvenience: we're building a new country." During the three months of protest in the city center, not a single shop was looted, nor even a window broken on the capital's main thoroughfare (except the Trade Unions Building which was set ablaze by attacking regime forces). In the wake of Yanukovych's ouster, police presence effectively disappeared from the streets of most major cities (including Kyiv), but order was maintained by spontaneously organized community patrols. This author's subjective feeling (not confirmed empirically) was that traffic offenses and petty crime actually *decreased* during the immediate post-Maidan period. The atmosphere of revolution generated peaceful activism, and a spontaneous serenity.

The brave new world that the revolutionaries promised was to be both "fair" and "just" — uncorrupt, legitimate and righteous. This promise remained unrealized almost five years after the ouster of Yanukovych (multiple cases against corrupt officials were left unprosecuted), but the issue remained no less salient than immediately after the appalling massacre of the Heaven's Hundred. Russia's subsequent outrageous and illegitimate annexation of Crimea, together with Moscow's promotion of long-term violence and destruction in the Donbas, rendered calls for *"spravedlyvist'"* ("fairness") acute not just domestically: Ukrainians felt betrayed by the West whose political leaders had once promised protection in exchange for the former Soviet republic's voluntary handover of its nuclear arsenal. The fact that according to Paragraph 6 of the 1994 Budapest Memorandum, its signatories committed to "consult in the event a situation arises which raises a question concerning these commitments" – and certainly they did "consult" – left little consolation to Ukrainians. International agreements formally did not require the US, UK, France and China to intervene militarily on Ukraine's behalf when the country's borders were violated by Russia, but certainly it would have been *fair* ("*spravedlyvo*") to do so.

As is the case with "dignity", the Ukrainian word "*spravedlyvist'*" translates poorly into English. Its closest equivalent is "fairness", although most often it is rendered as "justice". This is a misnomer. In English (and in French) the term "justice" carries a legalistic connotation that reflects multiple centuries of judicial tradition: *justice* is achieved when, in accordance with due process, a judge arbitrates a dispute between two parties based on an interpretation of promulgated law. In contrast "fairness" ("*spravedlyvist'*") – a term which seems to approximate the Aristotelian notion of righteousness as a reflection of society's telos (agreed purpose)[51] – is secured not (necessarily) through the application of written law, but rather as a natural exigency of community. The term "justice" translates into Ukrainian as "*zakonnist'*" – "*spravedlyvist'*" refers to a moral (ethical) category, rather than a strictly legal concept. Ideally, "*spravedlyvist'*" is achieved through a "*pravova spil'nota*" (righteous community) that does not require a state, as the latter can be hijacked, whereas the community's "natural law" reflects the common good.[52]

Given the practical requirements of governance – i.e. the need for daily judgments of what constitutes the "common good" – the institutional arrangements of liberal democratic states (created within the civilizational paradigm of "modernity") include an impartial judiciary charged with securing the "rule of law." The Ukrainian language offers two possible translations of this English term: a) "*verkhovenstvo zakonu*" (meaning rule of *statute* law), and b) "*verkhovenstvo prava*" (meaning rule of *natural* law or "right" in the sense of *righteousness*). The contrast between "*pravo*" and "*zakon*" is similar to the French "*droit*" vs. "*loi*", or the German "*Recht*" vs. "*Gesetz*". The Ukrainian "*pravo*" approximates "*droit*" and "*Recht*" (i.e. natural law or "right-eousness") rather than statute. Ukraine's Constitution recognizes the primacy of "*verkhovenstvo prava*," and so one might rightfully ask a judge who is tasked with securing this version of the "rule of law", is (s)he to assume that what has been adopted by the legislator (i.e. stat-ute) is "*pravo*" (i.e. the instantiation of "*spravedlyvist'*" — fairness)? As became evident after the adoption of the "dictatorial laws" of January 16 (see Chapter 4), statute law may not always conform to "*pravo*." However, under circumstances when statute law is not the sole crite-rion of righteousness, it is unclear who is to be the arbiter of "*pravo*" and how "*spravedlyvist'*" (fairness) is to be achieved and/or institu-tionally assured.

The Ukrainian term "*spravedlyvist'*" implies the possibility of *nat-ural* justice that would include both a *feeling* of fairness and an objec-tive decision according to which "rights" ("*prava*") are restored if/when impinged. Spawned by a community of both protest and ac-tivism, the feeling that such righteous fairness was possible was pre-cisely what this author (and many others) experienced during the Maidan protests and their aftermath. The fact that "*spravedlyvist'*" was not achieved during the years after Yanukovych's ouster represented one of the main disappointments of the early years of the Revolution of Dignity.[53] During its next phase, the challenge faced by Ukrainians will be to find ways to institutionalize the communal "fairness" (nat-ural justice) of Maidan in new structures that will ensure both objec-tive justice (i.e. judicial impartiality, due legal process, and consequen-tial application of court decisions) and subjective feelings of trust in whatever dispute resolution system becomes implemented. This chal-lenge is equivalent to that faced by the US Founding Fathers who en-deavored to create the institutions of republican governance for the first time in the late 18th century.

Indeed, if the events of Ukraine's revolution are to become more than a footnote in the history of civilizational development, establish-ing (judicial) institutions that reflect the ideas of "*spravedlyvist'*" must become a programmatic goal of its next phase. One of the byproducts of "modernity" in western discourse seems to have been a conflation of the terms "fairness" and "justice" into a single concept: the "rule of law". Ukrainians have (perhaps accidentally) developed a differentiated concept—"*verkhovenstvo prava*"—and have enshrined this into their Constitution. Their contribution to civilizational development as part of the global movement to post-modernity may well be the instantiation of this concept into a novel and functioning institutional system, whereby a community ensures both its members rights and the common good.

Horizontalization

For those who experienced the phenomenon directly, Maidan had a kind of mystical quality: a feeling of spirituality was reported by numerous participants.[54] But mysticism surrounded not only the place, but also the concept that it represented. The word "*hidnist'*" captures one aspect of the protests (i.e. a demand for individual and collective dignity to be recognized and respected); "*spravedlyvist'*" (i.e. a belief in the possibility of a fair society) captures another. In both cases, the demands were transcendent. The protesters were not merely voicing demands, they were practicing their ideology in the protest camp, and in their daily lives outside. Mutuality, community, and belief in the possibility of a common good meant inclusiveness, and a consensual culture where no decision could ever be imposed. Their horizontal organization rejected any individual who would claim lasting authority within or over it because the collective was organized *heterarchically* with few lasting structures, and with authority roles that shifted according to situational need.

For the nominal political leaders (Yatseniuk, Klitschko, Tiahnybok), such overt rejection of institutionalized hierarchical relations by the protesting masses posed a massive management problem—felt repeatedly throughout the protests when effective control over the crowds was lost and comprehended pointedly on the night of February 20 when the Maidan snubbed the accord that the opposition leaders had just signed with Yanukovych (see Chapter 4). A similar management problem was faced by Ukraine's top military commanders during the summer of 2014 and into 2015: for many on the frontlines, compliance with orders was not consequential of their receipt. The volunteer battalions of the National Guard (and the Right Sector Volunteer Corps) were in fact created because of widespread distrust of the chain of command of the Ukrainian Army (see Chapter 5). Internally, these battalions were managed as consensual units whose leaders were respected only when they shunned the trappings of rank.[55] Among the men, although the ideal of defending one's country was venerated, a clear differentiating line was drawn between "*krayina*" (country) and "*derzhava*" (state). Patriotism meant love of country; in many cases (tragically), it also meant hatred of the state. In countless interviews from the frontlines, one heard the same: the enemy is despised, but the general staff is hated more: "At least the enemy is predictable—they are trying to kill you. With the brass you never know."[56]

The words of Ukraine's frontline defenders may have sounded anarchic, but they reflected a paradigm that seemed to be deeply rooted in the revolutionary discourse of Maidan, according to which personal freedom was valued above all else. From mid-2016 to mid-2018, the burned-out Trade Unions Building on Independence Square in Kyiv was draped with a massive banner proclaiming "Freedom is our Religion!".[57] For Ukraine's revolutionaries and territorial defenders, this freedom included the right of assembly, freedom of speech, and personal liberty to manage one's affairs. By extension, the freedom of the "nation" was also valued—although in this case, "freedom" referred to a more philosophical category: a collective of equals, a broad-based community of like-minded others who are necessarily skeptical of the hierarchical structures of the state. The conceptual link to the mythomoteur of the Zaporizhian Cossacks was plainly visible here.[58] Indeed, during a closed meeting that this author attended at the Presidential Administration in August 2015, Poroshenko lamented that during the retreat from Debaltseve in January, he as Commander-in-Chief of the Armed Forces, had had to deal with over 25,000 incidents of desertion and/or dereliction of duty. That evening Ukraine's President lamented: "I can tell you, this kind of *Otamanshchyna* is very difficult to manage."[59]

On the other hand, in post-Yanukovych civilian life, the energy of horizontal activism was harnessed locally in very constructive ways. Under the banner of "dignity", inclusive education was introduced for the first time in Ukrainian schools.[60] Maidan activists became involved in community associations that pressured city administrations to install bicycle paths and parks, advocated changes to hospital rules that allowed parents access to intensive care facilities where their children were being treated,[61] organized local flat owners to create management companies for their apartment blocks, which in turn advocated energy efficiency.[62] During the parliamentary election of October 2014—held in the wake of the Maidan protests—the "Samopomich" party (the name translates as "Self-help") gained significant voter support with a slogan that it had borrowed from Ukrainian Catholic University: "*Viz'my i zroby!*" which roughly translates into "Pick it up, and do it!" (paraphrasing the Nike advertisement "just do it!").

According to accepted social science (and its reflection in management theory), a prerequisite for effecting change in an organization or society is leadership. Someone must take responsibility, and more importantly, to be effective (particularly in revolutionary times), this leader must be charismatic. But the protesters in Kyiv in 2013-14 had no leader! Although the three leaders of the opposition parties (Klitschko, Yatseniuk, Tiahnybok) were listened to when they rose to the Maidan stage, each of their appearances represented a battle for hearts and minds, rather than an oration to converted followers. For example, in early February 2014, when Yatseniuk pronounced that he was ready to make the ultimate sacrifice for the sake of the victory of Maidan, his phrase "*kulia v lob*" (bullet in the temple) became a satirical badge of ridicule. Instead of eluding respect, the image of Klitschko covered in white powder after having been sprayed by a fire extinguisher during clashes on Hrushevskoho St. in January were circulated in social media with the caption "snowman boxer".

The greatest challenge to the three leaders' authority on Maidan came on February 21, from Volodymyr Parasiuk, a previously unknown "*sotnyk*" (self-defense unit commander), who hopped onto the stage during the evening gathering, grabbed the microphone from Vitaliy Klitschko, and in a highly emotional outburst told the crowd that his "*sotnia*" flatly rejected the EU-brokered agreement that the three opposition leaders had just signed, and that if Yanukovych was not ousted by 10am the following morning, he and his followers would storm the Presidential Administration building with firearms. Parasiuk's speech was greeted with tumultuous applause by the crowd while the three nominal opposition leaders quietly retreated from the stage. A year later, when Parasiuk was elected to Parliament, he was made to feel the full force of Ukrainians' skepticism of those who presented themselves as "leaders" in an institutionalized hierarchy — his speeches in Parliament, and fiery orations during rallies outside, were greeted with skepticism if not ridicule.

The Maidan protesters (and Ukrainians in general) were openly skeptical of any individual who attempted to ascend to the status of "leader". Maidan embodied a horizontal "*spil'nota*" (community) that previously was believed (by social scientists) to be effective only in uniting individuals with similar interests (e.g. in organizations such as clubs or fraternities), but not in effecting real change. Such social configurations were certainly not capable of driving fundamental social revolution. In this respect Maidan, presented an apparent structural similarity to other protest actions occurring almost contemporaneously (e.g. Occupy, Arab Spring, Candlelight protests in South Korea, etc.). The common characteristic of each of these protest actions was skepticism, if not outright rejection, of the principle of hierarchy by the protagonists. These social movements attracted thousands of supporters willing to take to the streets to demonstrate their disagreement with a particular political issue or institutional arrangement (usually the catalyst for protest seems to have been a perceived corrupt practice in government), and each was nominally leaderless.

Paradigm shift

The significance of the rejection of hierarchy, and the appearance of heterarchical collectives ("*spil'noty*") as effective political forces driving Ukraine's Revolution of Dignity is not to be underestimated. Horizontalization seems to represent one of the symptoms of the ongoing fundamental shift in western civilization from "modernity" to "postmodernity": whereas during the industrial era, change required a charismatic leader (entrepreneur, political visionary, etc.), in the early

21st century, it would seem that humanity has witnessed multiple protest movements that have patently *rejected* those who would position themselves as leaders. This observation should not be understood to mean that personal leadership is no longer relevant for social action or organizational cohesion. However, these movements demonstrate an evolution of the leadership paradigm that may have broader structural consequences.

Specifically, whereas as Max Weber observed, modernity involved the "institutionalization of charisma" (i.e. transference of the charismatic authority of the leader-persona to an office or rank within an institutionalized hierarchy or organization),[63] both the Maidan protests and the subsequent spontaneous organization of volunteer battalions and logistical organizations suggest a *post*modern trend towards heterarchy and situational leadership—though not the disappearance of charisma as such. Whereas Weber saw charisma as the "quality of an individual personality,"[64] on Maidan we witnessed the *charismatic idea* existing and spreading independently, without attachment to individual personality. Throughout the events of Ukraine's Revolution of Dignity, the individual leader-persona was distrusted, but the common ideal (differently verbalized) was supremely charismatic—i.e. inspirational and compelling to action. In this logic, the principle of charisma (i.e. compelling attractiveness) remained operative, and indeed was the glue of the collective, but rather than being embodied in the leader, devotion and loyalty were instilled in the ideals of the group, and action—both individual and collective—was driven by an idealism that prevailed over material interests.

This phenomenon of *idealism* (embodied in the *charismatic idea*) is key both for understanding the individual actions of Ukraine's Maidan activists during the protests and in the years after Yanukovych's ouster, and for appreciating the global significance of the events that began in Kyiv in late 2013. The Maidan protests did not coalesce around material demands. The materialist discourse of Yanukovych (e.g. his televised musings on the costs of EU Association, and the concomitant losses from broken trade ties with Russia—see Chapter 3) was hardly relevant to the protesters. The Maidan protests erupted because Yanukovych visibly demonstrated contempt for fundamental values that many in Ukraine believed to be sacrosanct (e.g. the values-complex that many associated with "Europe", and more basically rules-based government). On the opposite side, the annexation of Crimea occurred because the Putin regime sought to boost the Russian President's popularity by fostering the idea and *values of nationalism* (i.e. the "Russian World"). The war in the Donbas began because of a *clash of ideas* (identities), and then was fed by the same idea of Russian greatness (embodied in three principles: Orthodoxy, Russian exceptionalism and Autarchy).[65] In no case can the motives of the protagonists of each of these events be rationally explained with reference to their material interests. They were driven by ideas.

Given the noted similarities between the Maidan protests and social movements in other countries that appeared at roughly the same time, one might well postulate the shift from materialism to idealism observed during Ukraine's Revolution of Dignity (i.e. both during the Maidan protests and in Moscow's subsequent aggression) as reflecting a broader trend. Throughout, motives and justifications for action were verbalized in ideational (i.e. non-materialistic) terms. One might therefore be forgiven for seeing these events as reflecting a more comprehensive civilizational shift from the "sensate" materialism characteristic of the modern period, to some form of *post*modern idealism as predicted by the eminent sociologist Pitirim Sorokin.[66]

Based on extensive research on historical cycles of fashion in art, philosophy, social relationships (including political structures), and culture (including discourse), Sorokin postulated that civilizations change over time according to a pendular pattern that cycles between the dominance of sensate and ideational value systems. According to Sorokin, cynicism is the final stage before the violent shift of the direction of civilization's pendulum. A decline of sensate culture — when problems appear in the way a civilization's cultural superstructure is logically integrated — is accompanied by a rise in the social importance of ideas over possessions and artefacts, increased emphasis on spiritual rather than material ends, heightened soul-searching at the expense of time and effort spent on accumulation.[67] In Sorokin's view, western civilization entered a period of crisis (characterized by passage from an "active sensate" to a "passive sensate" phase) after the end of WWII. With the advent of "alternative facts" and the use of information as a weapon (with obvious lies broadcast on mainstream networks as news), it would seem that, at least in some respects, by the second decade of the 21st century, this crisis had resulted in the degeneration of modernity into a "cynical sensate" phase.

> During a sensate period, all aspects of life are dominated by a materialistic world view, and economic and scientific activities flourish, particularly during the "active" sensate phase. During the "passive" phase hedonistic values prevail, and in the final "cynical" state the sensate mentality negates everything including itself. Ideational periods, in contrast, are spiritually oriented, and social relationships are familistic rather than contractual... When civilizations shift from one of the "supersystems" to the other, there is a stormy period of transition marked by increases in the intensity and magnitude of wars and revolutions...[68]

Superficially, Ukraine's Revolution of Dignity seems to have demonstrated the symptoms of a nascent idealistic value system. Social relations during the Maidan protests and in the volunteer movement (both in the battalions and in aid organizations) were familistic (heterarchical) and driven by idealism. After the ouster of Yanukovych this idealism transformed, but the discourse of Maidan never shifted towards materialism: discussions of economic hardship, growing inequality, and/or increasing poverty never gained mobilizational strength. When Russia invaded, the charismatic idea of Ukraine's revolution became crystalized in patriotism: a notion that compelled action in the form of enlistment in volunteer battalions, support for territorial defense, self-sacrifice in public service in the cause of state-building and reform. Patriotism, in turn, spawned the *idea* of anti-corruption. Whereas territorial defense and public service were actions compelled by an external threat to the twin concepts of "fairness" and "dignity" (interpreted collectively as affronting the nation), the drive to rid the state apparatus of shady practices that resulted in the enrichment of individuals many would consider undeserving (i.e. in the institutionalization of non-meritocratic social structures) was the result of the application of these ideas to domestic politics. In both cases we see the driving force of collective and individual actions (some more successful, others less so) being the non-embodied, depersonalized, leaderless *charismatic idea*.

The appearance of a powerful leaderless agency in the Maidan movement, its ability to spawn and make charismatic new (or at least redefined) ideas such as dignity and patriotism, and the capacity of both the Maidan protests and the subsequent volunteer movement for longevity in heterarchical structures, are all elements that point to an underrecognized significance of Ukraine's revolution—indicative of its having represented (at least) a punctuation event in a larger story of civilizational transformation. This civilizational shift was predicted by Sorokin (among others):

> In accordance with my diagnosis and prognosis in the original four-volume edition of this work published in 1937-41, the central process for the last few decades has consisted in a) the progressive decay of sensate culture, society and man; and b) the emergence and slow growth of the first components of the new—ideational or idealistic—sociocultural order... This struggle between the forces of the previously creative but now largely outworn sensate order and the emerging, creative forces of a new—ideational or idealistic—order is proceeding relentlessly in all fields of social and cultural life.[69]

Sorokin stressed that his analyses of historical data on systems of art, philosophy, law and social relationships did not reveal any period when a pure sensate or pure ideational culture had been completely dominant.[70] Nevertheless, he stressed that his exceptionally broad empirical base indicated a shift in emphasis was ongoing. He predicted the transition would be accompanied by violence and revolution: social, political and economic institutions based on a sensate (material) paradigm that had been designed to ensure the wellbeing of the *sovereign individual* would have to be replaced with some form of new (ideational—perhaps collectivist) institutional order.

Institutionalizing novelty

In this chapter we have portrayed Ukraine's Revolution of Dignity as a punctuation mark in the historical shift of western civilization from a modern to "post-modern" (sensate to idealist; individualist to personalist) stage of development. Our purpose was to demonstrate that the ideas engendered by the Maidan carried global significance, and although it is an axiom of world history that new senses that develop in local conditions may have broader civilizational connotations, whether this will be the case with Ukraine's Revolution of Dignity remains to be seen. For now, it is noteworthy that the newly embodied idealism of the Maidan (and of the volunteers who mobilized to counter Russian aggression in the aftermath of the protests) seems highly relevant to the broader themes of civilizational transformation identified by various observers of macro societal trends.

Idealism seems to be characteristic of the early stages of the lifecycle of all revolutions—regardless of the developmental phase they transgressed. In revolutions that spanned the transition from premodern to modern civilizations, ideational demands for "life, liberty, and property" (i.e. meritocracy and secularism) set the revolutionaries apart from representatives of the ancien regime, whose cosmology emphasized ascriptive hierarchy (legitimized through the Church), and conservative propriety (validated by custom and scripture). The American and French Revolutions both began with modest demands: as Hannah Arendt pointed out, "nothing more was originally intended than reforms in the direction of constitutional monarchies".[71] In the Ukrainian case, the protests also began with a modest demand: to sign the EU Association Agreement. But then confrontation with a resistant regime radicalized the movement. In the US case, the revolutionary lifecycle led to the birth of a new "foundational" ingredient: the institutionalization of individual liberty as a basic right and principle of the organization of the American political system as enshrined in the US Constitution. The idea of the sovereign individual then became a sacred foundational component of modern political systems throughout western civilization. In the Ukrainian case (reflecting the modern-to-postmodern essence of the Maidan), the buzzword became "dignity"[72] and its underlying philosophical "personalist" current.

The Ukrainian revolution did not depose a monarch. Formally, the principles of democratic governance had all been established by the country's 1996 Constitution (amended in 2004), and these institutional arrangements, though temporarily hijacked by Yanukovych who sought to use the Presidency as a means of personal enrichment, constrained his efforts. After Yanukovych's ouster, the formal arrangements typical of a modern democratic state, including separation of powers, regular elections, a representative and empowered Parliament, and an accountable executive (i.e. institutions born primarily during the American revolution) continued in Ukraine with minimal adjustment. But in parallel, the Revolution of Dignity gave birth to significant novelty. Beyond traditional debates focused on finding balance between the legislative and executive branches, Ukraine's revolutionaries highlighted problems in structuring the judiciary—a major step forward in the agenda of institution building. Put differently, rather than asking "who will rule and how?" the key question that emerged from Maidan can be paraphrased as "who will judge?" and furthermore "according to what standard?". The global significance of this shift in debates can be summed up as follows: whereas the revolutions of modernity concerned themselves with establishing accountable governance (i.e. institutions through which power would be legitimately exercised in a non-ascriptive, but yet hierarchically organized polity), Ukraine's Maidan asked the quintessentially postmodern question: who will be the legitimate arbiter of conflict in a horizontally organized polity?

As noted in Chapter 7, revolutions are not events. They may involve accelerated social change, but even if hurried, the process of revolution takes time. Furthermore, this process seems to proceed according to a defined lifecycle, where discourse (i.e. the relevance of questions asked, the topics and forms of debate) appears to affect both the speed and path of development of the revolutionary process. Thus, whereas at time of writing (almost five years after the ouster of Yanukovych), Ukraine's revolution had progressed through the first two stages ("regime overthrow", and "rule of moderates"), progression to or avoidance of the third (i.e. "terror") seemed dependent on how political discourse within Ukraine's political class would be elaborated. The real challenge of Ukraine's revolutionaries (Maidan activists, war veterans, new political elites) in the coming years—if what Arendt called the "leftward shift" that led to a Reign of Terror in the French and Russian Revolutions was to be avoided (as occurred in the American case)—would be to institutionalize the *idealism* of the Revolution of Dignity. To this end, major questions need to be answered:

1. How can a large community (a nation) be managed horizontally? Can the principle of heterarchy be extended to the state apparatus? Clearly decentralization was one of the major achievements of Ukraine's post-Yanukovych reforms (see Chapter 6), but can a large and diverse nation-state be governed long-term with a fluid hierarchy?

2. How do the principles of "fairness" and "dignity" become institutionalized in local and national communities, and (most importantly) in the economy? How can companies and community organizations realize the power of horizontal leadership in new management structures? How can organizations created under a "modern" paradigm shift to the "post-modern"?

3. In what way should the aspiration of "*spravedlyvist'*" (fairness) become institutionalized in Ukraine's judicial system? Given the demand for natural justice, and the overwhelming skepticism of society towards formal legal institutions (including statute law), how is "fairness" to be judged? How shall a society of natural justice be established?

A great deal has been written by eminent authors[73] about the importance of institutions for political stability and economic growth. No doubt, flourishing liberal democracies are founded on stable "rules of the game" that are both formalized in laws, and informally supported through norms, ethics and social conventions. And these in turn are enforced directly by the state or indirectly by organizations that legitimize and/or socially proscribe particular behavior. Few today question the institutionalists' emphasis on the importance of establishing such a system as a prerequisite of a society's prosperity. However, fewer still provide recipes on how such institutions are to be established in the context of civilizational change. Specifically, how does one deal with the legacy of suboptimal institutions? How does one balance between establishing formal institutions "top-down" and the "bottom-up" latency of informal practices that often contradict the most well-intentioned reform effort? What is the sequence for establishing sustainable institutions? Is culture always a drag on social change? What if the civilizational context on which "modern" political institutions were established, changes: can one create "post-modern" institutions immediately, or must the revolutionary "steam" cool before one can start? These questions are likely to remain open for some time. Their delineation here serves to add to the agenda of Ukraine's revolutionary process rather than to complete it.

The transformation of Ukraine, and of western civilization as a whole, is not a task that will be completed quickly. In the end, the country's renovation (i.e. the fulfilment of the agenda of Maidan) will involve the persistence of the old together with appearance of the new. In other words, the future will be messy and hybrid. Delineating the contours of this future for both Ukraine and the broader region will be the task of the next and final chapter.

Chapter 11:
Moving Forward

In 2013-14, what started as a small-scale protest under the "Euro-maidan" banner turned into a catalyst of massive and mind-bog-glingly rapid social change both domestically in Ukraine, and interna-tionally in Europe and beyond. The impact of the initial demonstra-tions could have been negligible had the Yanukovych regime allowed the protests to simply fizzle out. Instead, "Berkut" riot police were or-dered to attack peaceful students in the dead of night. That act sparked demonstrations that brought hundreds of thousands of peo-ple into the streets, and closed Kyiv's city-center for 3 months. When the Ukrainian President was finally forced to flee, his Russian coun-terpart launched two invasions: one resulting in the illegal annexation of Crimea, and the other in continuous low-level artillery battles last-ing over 4 years across a virtually immovable front-line in the Donbas. Putin then flexed his muscles in Syria and engaged in multiple clan-destine operations in western countries aimed at influencing electoral processes (including in the US), and at murder using chemical weap-ons (in the UK). It would seem the catalyst of these subsequent dra-matic events was a miscalculation: in the dead of night, on 30 Novem-ber 2013, in a very peripheral European capital, a thuggish Ukrainian regime attacked a peaceful student demonstration.

The above chain of events is not necessarily a causal chain. Mai-dan did not cause Russia's invasion of Ukraine, nor were Ukrainians responsible for Putin's covert aggression against the West. However, a degree of connectedness seems to be in evidence. If not for Russian aggression, it is highly unlikely that Ukraine's population would have experienced the level of political mobilization and patriotic solidarity manifest throughout the country during the months and years follow-ing the overthrow of Yanukovych. Neither would the contrast be-tween the competing socio-economic models proposed by post-Soviet Russia and the EU (neo-feudal kleptocracy vs. rules-based govern-ance) have been displayed with such starkness to a young urban Ukrainian bourgeoisie. If not for the outbreak of hostilities in Kyiv, followed by actualization of a very real external threat from Russia, it is unlikely that Ukrainian society would have generated the novel senses that were perhaps the greatest contribution to civilizational development emanating from Maidan and the subsequent Russian-Ukrainian war. Such senses seem to be a hallmark of revolutionary change and are rarely born during periods of relative social stability.

The Russia problem

During the months and years following the mass killings of protesters in the center of Kyiv in February 2014, the world order — the European civilizational context (i.e. the complex of ideas, norms, practices) based on which hegemonic cultural, political and economic institutions functioned in the West for many decades — experienced a shock. When Russia invaded, and then annexed the sovereign territory of its neighbor, the institutions of Europe (EU, NATO, OSCE), which were supposedly designed to ensure peace and prosperity, were undermined: a state actor with nuclear weapons, which seemingly aspired to global power status, and which had been part of the foundation of the international system (including the UN Security Council), had violated that very system's basic agreements and institutions. The apparent catalyst of the crisis amounted to a dispute over a what amounted to a trade deal with a country (Ukraine) that few Europeans (and fewer still Americans) could place on a map of the world.

In early 2014, Kyiv's demonstrators provided exciting material for visiting journalists: young activists (some called them "extremists") throwing Molotov cocktails at well-armed riot police translated into juicy imagery for western commentators. But the Maidan protests were largely of peripheral interest to the outside world: more of an enthralling show in a far-away land than an event that had obvious and immediate significance to a global audience. That changed when Putin ordered his Special Forces into Crimea. By annexing the peninsula, Russia directly violated Article 4 of the UN Charter.[1] What's more, it violated the 1994 Budapest memorandum — a document signed by Russia, the US, UK, France, and China, according to which each country promised to respect Ukraine's territorial integrity in exchange for that country giving up its nuclear weapons. As Andreas

Umland, Senior Fellow at the Institute for Euro-Atlantic Cooperation in Kyiv, pointed out, Russia's actions in Crimea effectively voided the Nuclear Non-Proliferation Treaty (NPT) which Ukraine had signed, and which western leaders considered part of the foundation of the global security system:

> If an NPT signatory can't even be kept safe from one of the treaty's five guarantors, then what is the value of banning the spread of nuclear weapons? What nation with no deterrence potential or a close alliance with a nuclear power can now count on the inviolability of its borders? If a Security Council member can enlarge its territory at the expense of a neighboring country without much punishment, the NPT turns into a vehicle for the official nuclear powers to advance their own agendas.[2]

Russia's annexation of Crimea, and its military intervention in the Ukrainian Donbas, certainly heightened global interest in the Kremlin's role in international affairs. Prior to 2014, western policy-makers seemed to be content in believing that Russia's limited economic power translated into minimal real influence on the international stage: despite periodically rattling its nuclear sabre, Moscow's actual global clout was waning. US and EU policy-makers turned to other priorities; academic career opportunities in "area studies" gradually diminished. The western world became comfortable in its belief that although "the end of history" had not yet arrived, Russia was no longer a special case worthy of special attention. Unlike Islamic extremists who lived (and died) by different rules than the rest of the world, after the collapse of the USSR, Russians (and their elites) became basically "like us".

This state of affairs changed dramatically during the Kremlin's military escapade in Syria where it became evident to western political elites that Russia was neither "like us" nor "with us". In September 2015, immediately after having addressed the UN General Assembly in New York, and having met with US President Obama, President Putin ordered aerial bombardments of anti-Assad forces in Syria. In the words of Sovietologist Robert van Voren (writing in 2015):

> Syria is to Putin what Ukraine was a year ago: a means to exert power, a means to show his country he is the boss, a means to show that the

decadent West is incompetent, denigrated and unable to meet the challenges of today. Together with Assad he can do what he likes to do:
bomb away anybody who stands in his way.[3]

Despite the Obama administration's belief that Russian forces would
be caught in a "quagmire" in Syria, Putin was able to maintain air su-
periority over the country throughout 2015-16, and by indiscrimi-
nately bombing the city of Aleppo, succeeded in keeping his vassal,
the Syrian President, in power—in spite of US administration insistence that Assad must go. Furthermore, in Syria, Russia gained a stage
on which to demonstrate the technical prowess of its weaponry—particularly in October 2015 when the Kremlin launched a cruise missile
attack on Syrian targets from ship-based launch facilities in the Cas-
pian Sea over 2000 km away.

Having been able to largely ignore Russian aggression in Georgia in 2008 and having voiced "deep concern" over Moscow's invasion of Ukraine in 2014, western policy-makers were no longer able to
acquiesce to seeing Russia as a "regional power", only flexing its limited muscle in the post-Soviet space. Putin's Syrian intervention
proved that Russia needed to be dealt with seriously. Indeed, this was
likely the intended goal of the deadly display of the Kremlin's projec-
tive capabilities: to draw the US to the negotiating table where Russia
would be treated as an "equal". As US military expert Joseph Micallef
pointed out, the "resurgence of Russia" was in fact part of Vladimir
Putin's foreign policy "bluff":

> Russia's aggressive posture in recent years, primarily since 2008, is not
> the result of growing Russian strength but a gambit to hide growing
> Russian weakness. It's as if, starting in 2008, the Kremlin decided that
> reasserting Russia's status as a great power was more important than
> maximizing economic growth, investment and development. Indeed,
> as the economic wellbeing of the average Russian family has declined,
> the Kremlin's answer has been to emphasize its success in restoring
> Russia's international status regardless of the fact that in doing so it
> has further aggravated the economic downturn…[4]

As the above quote demonstrates, after the Kremlin's intervention in
Syria, Western policy-advisors' economy-centered blinders seem to
have finally come off. Most in the West had falsely assumed that in

the modern world, global military (and political) power was a function of economic might, but for the Russians it was never "the economy, stupid".[5] For this reason, imposing economic sanctions as a response to the Kremlin's illegal annexation of Crimea and military intervention in the Donbas proved largely ineffective. Putin's foreign policy agenda was/is not motivated by economic concerns, and this fact requires a rethink of western foreign policy instruments vis-à-vis the Kremlin—particularly since few in the West have an appetite for all-out war with Russia.[6]

Indeed, many would prefer to placate the Kremlin, despite evidence of Moscow's outrageous behavior on the international scene since 2014: limited military aggression in the Donbas and Syria, covert operations with chemical weapons in the UK, hacking of computer systems and dissemination of fake news in the US, France and Germany. In each case, the Kremlin denied its responsibility, thereby delaying response. And while western investigators built a case against Moscow, the global political agenda moved on. As commentator Peter Dickinson pointed out in 2018:

> Since Russian troops began seizing government buildings in Crimea four years ago, the international community has become accustomed to encountering new acts of Russian aggression on an almost daily basis. Whether it is masked men in eastern Ukraine, a chemical weapons attack in the English countryside, or an attempted coup in the Balkans, the process is more or less the same—faced by a fresh round of accusations, the Kremlin denies everything and declares, "You can't prove it was us." If the evidence pointing toward Russia is particularly damning, Moscow then insists that those involved were non-state actors operating entirely independently of the government... This is how Putin's Russia wages war, by attacking in a myriad of different directions while carefully maintaining a semblance of plausible deniability that leaves its victims partially paralyzed and unable to respond effectively to an enemy they cannot conclusively unmask... One of the reasons Putin's strategy of plausible deniability is so effective is because virtually nobody in the West seems to appreciate the scale of Russian hostility toward the post-Cold War world or the Kremlin's readiness to resort to acts of aggression... Above all, nobody wants to acknowledge the dire reality that a state of war—albeit hybrid war—already exists between Russia and the entire democratic world.[7]

In this global war, Ukraine remains the frontline — both figuratively and literally. However, this conflict was/is not simply a geopolitical battle over territory, nor was/is it simply a manifestation of the Kremlin's desire to assert the "great power" status of Russia on the world stage. The multi-faceted reality of the conflict (its "hybrid" character)[8] manifest in the use of both traditional military might (both overt and covert forces) in conjunction with subversive activities such as hacking, targeted dissemination of fake news via alternative mass media and/or via Twitter, "trolling" commentary on newspaper websites and social networks, indicates that the practice of warfare has entered a new phase of development. Just as the onset of "industrial warfare"[9] over a century ago reflected changes in technology (transportation, communication, mass production), political identity and solidarity structures (nation-states, multi-national alliances), ideologies and political practices (socialism, capitalism, democracy), so too does the appearance of "hybrid war" reflect a fundamental change in human civilization. Putin's war is ideological in nature because it reflects a civilizational split — not in the sense of Huntington (i.e. reflecting primordial cleavages between cultures with differing religious traditions), but rather reflecting differing visions of the next phase of human development.

To illustrate his vision of human development, in his 2014 public speeches, Russian President Putin often referenced three of his favorite philosophers from the 19th and 20th centuries: Nikolai Berdyaev, Vladimir Solovyov and Ivan Ilyin. Others in Kremlin circles referenced the writings of Russian ultra-nationalist Alexander Dugin who proposed "Eurasianism" as a solution to the "decadence" of the West.[10] In each case, Russia's aggression was justified and framed in messianic terms. The frightening (and highly threatening) tendency was cogently captured by NY Times commentator David Brookes:

> To enter into the world of Putin's favorite philosophers is to enter a world full of melodrama, mysticism and grandiose eschatological visions... Three great ideas run through this work. The first is Russian exceptionalism: the idea that Russia has its own unique spiritual status and purpose. The second is devotion to the Orthodox faith. The third is belief in autocracy. Mashed together, these philosophers point to a

Russia that is a quasi-theocratic nationalist autocracy destined to play a culminating role on the world stage… (T)hese philosophers had epic visions of Russia's role in the world. Solovyov argued that because Russia is located between the Catholic West and the non-Christian East, it has a historic mission to lead the way to human unification. Russia would transcend secularism and atheism and create a unified spiritual kingdom. "The Russian messianic conception," Berdyaev wrote, "always exalted Russia as a country that would help to solve the problems of humanity…" In his 1948 essay, "What Dismemberment of Russia Entails for the World," Ilyin describes the Russian people as the "core of everything European-Asian and, therefore, of universal equilibrium…" All of this adds up to a highly charged and assertive messianic ideology… Russia is now involved in a dispute in Ukraine that touches and activates the very core of this touchy messianism.[11]

It is in the interests of the West to counter or at least contain such an expansionist Russian messianism. In this context, in the local theatre of conflict represented by Ukraine, the least objectionable solution seems to involve acquiescence to a "frozen conflict" in eastern Ukraine, and formalization of the status of Crimea as an "occupied territory". Such a condition will not necessarily end local hostilities on Europe's eastern frontier (and it certainly will not re-establish Ukraine's territorial integrity in the short term), but it will limit the spread of military conflict beyond the established line of contact in the Donbas.[12] Furthermore, notwithstanding the enormous cost of defending Ukraine's eastern border from continued Russian aggression, military defense is clearly more desirable to the Ukrainian nation than its disintegration in a reconstituted Russian empire. On the other hand, "freezing" the status quo between Ukraine and Russia — although representing the least bad solution in the short term — is unlikely to become permanent. Ideologically enthused elites who admire the writings of long-dead philosophers that promoted Russian exceptionalism and imperialism currently rule Russia, and these elites' political interests are served by fostering Russia's territorial and cultural expansion at the expense of Ukraine (and of the West). However, these elites are not permanent. The persona of Vladimir Putin is currently venerated (even revered) by the Russian population, and a cult of personality has been created around the Russian President in popular culture that presents him as the sole guardian against an apocalyptic degeneration of the country into chaos.[13] But Putin is not immortal.[14]

Furthermore, Kyiv is now prepared to foot most of the bill to defend itself against Moscow's aggression. The Ukrainian army, a force that according to former acting President Turchynov, had been capable of fielding a mere 6000 battle-ready troops at the height of the Kremlin's operation to annex Crimea in March 2014, grew to number over 250 thousand active duty personnel in 2018, with an additional 180,000 in operational reserve. Many of the country's former volunteer, and now professional soldiers and reservists were battle-hardened and/or received training from western advisors. Although NATO members had provided Ukraine with only minimal weaponry, diplomatic and humanitarian support had been plentiful both from western governments and from the Ukrainian diaspora throughout the world. Problems with logistics and supply were resolved. From the standpoint of defensive military capability, Ukraine seemed capable of withstanding further Russian advance, and its political class seemed united in the belief that further solidification of the country's defensive capabilities—given the long-term existential threat posed by Russia—should remain a top priority for many years to come.

Russia's war in Ukraine can have no end except the destruction of Ukraine has an independent state—a condition that Ukrainians have demonstrated as being unacceptable. Alternatively, it may end with the disintegration of the Russian Federation—a process that is unlikely to be ordered and/or peaceful.[15] In this context, since 2014, the exemplar of Israel has increasingly been referred to in domestic media and elite discourse as instructive for Kyiv. Throughout several decades after its establishment in 1948, the state of Israel received extensive military, economic and political support from its western allies (particularly the US), and as a result developed into a unique, well defended, civilizational outpost in an inherently hostile environment.[16] A similar project now needs to be set out for Ukraine. Western governments must realize that Ukraine matters to them—not just as a frontline state countering Russia's geopolitical ambitions, but as a civilizational outpost that demonstrates to the world that (broadly termed) "western" modernity and postmodernity (i.e. a developmental trajectory based on national self-determination, that involves rules-based government, prosperity derived from effort and meritocratic social relations, respect for international law and diplomatic rules, domestic tolerance and openness consequent on a recognition of the dignity of the person) can be constructed and is worthy of defense under threat.

In his opening address to the May 2014 "Thinking with Ukraine" conference, organized in Kyiv by renowned Yale University historian Timothy Snyder, former literary editor of *The New Republic* and award-winning author of several books on Jewish themes, Leon Wieseltier, addressed the gathering of some of the world's most respected scholars of the humanities and social sciences with the following words:

> The Ukrainian desire to affiliate with the West, its unintimidated preference for Europe over Russia, is not merely a strategic and economic choice; it is also a moral choice, a philosophical choice, a societal decision about ideals, a defiance of power in the name of justice, a stirring aspiration to build a society and a state that is representative of some values and not others... Ukraine is testing the proposition that people who speak different languages can live together in a single polity. That proposition is one of the great accomplishments of modern liberalism. Putin repudiates it. He shrinks nationalism into tribalism. His view, in the name of which he claims territory and steals territory, is that people who speak different languages cannot live together and should not live together; that sameness is preferable to difference, and homogeneity to diversity; that languages, and therefore cultures, are monolithic and insular and exclusive, and that this insularity and exclusiveness should be expressed in the organization of societies and states, so that like will live only with like and like will be governed only by like; that intolerance and conflict are legitimate corollaries of cultural pride; that the mingling of languages and cultures is not enriching to an individual and a nation but depleting, not a refreshment of identity but a threat to its purity. But you know better; and with you, we know better.[17]

Ukraine is important for the West. Certainly, it is also important to Russia, but for Europe and North America, Ukraine matters not for mythical geopolitical reasons. Ukraine matters because it represents a battleground between two civilizational paradigms—no less significant than the ongoing paradigmatic battle between ISIS and Al Qaeda on the one hand, and western civilization on the other. Ukraine matters not merely as territory, nor even as a keystone of moral responsibility whose sovereignty the world's major powers once vowed to respect in exchange for its de-nuclearization. Ukraine matters because it represents a nascent future for the West—a civilizational experiment involving a new form of revolution.

War of narratives

Throughout 2014-16 (and in some cases thereafter), events in Kyiv, Crimea and the Donbas were analyzed by western journalists and academics under the general rubric "Ukraine crisis". This label was highly misleading and incorrect. Firstly, it suggested that the "crisis" was primarily a domestic Ukrainian problem—a narrative inspired by the Kremlin which persisted in portraying the ouster of Yanukovych as a coup d'état, the Ukrainian government elected afterwards as a "fascist junta", and the conflict in the Donbas as a "civil war".[18] Although the Ukrainian revolution certainly was reflective of a domestic agency (as described extensively in this book), the "crisis" after late-February 2014 was fueled externally by Russia. Indeed, given the messianic ideology proclaimed by Russian elites as justification for military aggression, one might question whether the focal point of "crisis" was perhaps in Russia, rather than in Ukraine.

More significantly however, the portrayal of Ukraine as being in "crisis" suggested that events occurring there (i.e. Russia's invasion) had a potential completion date. In fact, when Putin's forces invaded Crimea, and later when Russia annexed the peninsula and intensified its subversive activities in the Ukrainian south-east—massing troops and firing rockets across the border, and later inserting troops that would fuel an ongoing tank and artillery war on Ukrainian territory—the Kremlin demonstrated that it did not recognize the right of Ukraine to exist as a sovereign state. Russia's military intervention in

Ukraine was/is not a war for territory, political control, or geopolitical assertion. Official Russian historiography (regularly touted by its political and even religious elites)[19] denies the separateness of Ukraine; Vladimir Putin is infamously reported to have stated to President George Bush that "Ukraine is not a real country"[20] and he repeatedly referred to Ukraine as a "territory" rather than a separate state throughout 2014-16. Later, Russian Orthodox Church Patriarch Kirill (a close Putin ally) vehemently opposed the granting of autocephaly (independence) to the Ukrainian Orthodox Church when a *"Tomos"* (decree) was offered by the Ecumenical Patriarch of Constantinople, causing a schism within Orthodoxy that has global ramifications.[21]

Russia's position with respect to Ukraine was/is untenable and can have no possible resolution. The existential threat to Kyiv from Moscow was/is permanent. If the West sees Ukraine's long-term survival as a sovereign state as being of value — if for no other reason than to demonstrate the validity and relevance of international diplomatic norms and agreements such as the NPT — then infrastructural support (i.e. assistance in defense, diplomacy, and access to markets) must be offered to Ukraine for years to come. Furthermore, we must stop treating the conflict in and over Ukraine as a regional dispute over spheres of influence, or even as a proxy war reflective of a larger geopolitical struggle.

After the Maidan protests it became cliché to state that the world had transformed. The West entered a "post-truth" era[22] where political spin degenerated into a battle of narratives based on "alternative facts." "Active measures" — a term derived from Soviet-era intelligence discourse[23] — were employed by Russia's hacking and propaganda machines to undermine government institutions and to misinform and divide the citizenry of the liberal democratic states that the Kremlin identified as its adversaries.[24] This practice of manipulating media messages with outright falsifications had roots in the Soviet period,[25] but after 2014, the Kremlin seems to have crossed some illusory boundary set by the journalism profession by overtly fabricating news stories. The web resource Stopfake.org (based at Kyiv-Mohyla Academy and launched by activists from the university's Journalism School) has been particularly vigilant and effective at uncovering

Kremlin lies, misuse of images, and dissemination of deliberately fictional stories in its quest to inculcate a narrative in the global public that discredits Ukraine and serves Russia's strategic ambitions.[26] According to Peter Pomarantsev, author of the award-winning *Nothing is True and Everything is Possible: The Surreal Heart of the New Russia,* this practice represents "a new form of conflict (that) emerged in 2015."[27]

A key weapon in this "hybrid" war became the prevailing narrative. Thus, if the world could be convinced that Ukraine was a failed state ("the most corrupt nation in Europe" according to The Guardian),[28] or that it had become a bastion of fascism where right-wing extremists ruled the government,[29] western support for Kyiv could be discredited. The symbolism of the Revolution of Dignity provided an easily manipulated backdrop for the Kremlin-supported narrative: the Maidan protesters and later many of Ukraine's volunteer battalions coopted the flag and slogans of the WWII-era OUN-UPA; they established structures and practices that paralleled those of the 16-18 century Cossacks (including haircuts and clothing). A romantic interpreted these symbols as modernized references to a historical mythomoteur; a parodist saw filth and backwardness, and a tendency to whitewash a problematic past. The fact that these historical symbols had become present-focused, and that Bandera (the OUN leader), the red and black flag, and the greeting "Glory to Ukraine!" (all formerly associated with integral nationalism) had lost their original ideological ingredient,[30] and had become symbols of *patriotic* struggle against aggression in a defensive war against Russia, was not easily understood by a non-specialist audience.

As for the war in the Donbas, Moscow's narrative presents an easily understood—and grossly simplified—sequence of events: according to the Kremlin, in early 2014, right-wing Ukrainian nationalists in Kyiv overthrew the legitimately elected Yanukovych, and then the former President's heartland revolted against the new "fascist" government; months later, Moscow moved to assist its local compatriots in their struggle for linguistic rights and their desire to identify with Russian/Soviet historiography. There is a problem with this narrative however: Crimea does not fit. Crimea was annexed by Russian troops immediately after Yanukovych's ouster—without any prior "struggle for linguistic rights" on the peninsula. Here, the narrative of "internal conflict" or "civil war" does not apply.

In their official statements, Russian officials (Putin, Lavrov, Churkin and others) have consistently perpetrated an interpretation of Ukraine's "crisis" as an internal issue and have deliberately separated Crimea from the Maidan-Donbas story. In fact, this is a single spiral of violence: beatings and shootings on Maidan (likely supported by the Kremlin), followed by Russian invasion and annexation of Crimea, followed by Kremlin-sponsored protests in Ukraine's southern and eastern regions, movement of Russian military equipment (initially) and troops (later) into the Donbas, and escalating violence thereafter. These events form a continuity, and persistent Russian agency in the chain is undeniable.

Prevailing narratives affect policy—as seen in the direct link between the portrayal of the conflict in the Donbas as a "civil war", and the policy discourse of western governments with respect to sanctions against Russia on the one hand, and the Minsk peace process on the other. Thus, the prospective end goal of the Minsk Accords, the work of the tri-lateral contact group, the Normandy format negotiations, etc. was to agree some form of accommodation between the Ukrainian government and Russia-backed "separatists". However, the premise behind this goal was a narrative, according to which dissatisfaction in the Donbas with the post-Yanukovych government in Kyiv (specifically on language policy), eventually boiled over into mass protests in the region in March-April 2014. The "separatists" were said to have been a domestic ("native") phenomenon that only later was supported by Russia (first indirectly, and then directly militarily). However, as increasingly mounting evidence suggests (e.g. the Glazyev tapes), the "Russian Spring" in Ukraine's eastern regions in 2014 was artificially manufactured by the Kremlin. Consequently, the basis for demanding concessions from Kyiv must now be seen as questionable. But the implanted narrative persists.

The narrative presented in this book—one that ascribes agency to the brave Ukrainians who effected Yanukovych's ouster (numbering in the millions—far more than the "extremists" claimed by Moscow), who demonstrated astonishing levels of spontaneous cooperation, self-sufficiency, individual and collective patience in the face of extreme hardship, both during the Maidan protests and in countering Russian aggression in the years that followed—has received exceptionally little attention in the western press. Even more difficult to understand and proliferate is the notion that the idealists of Ukraine's revolution—in a place that few in the West could identify with—would be able to offer the world new civilizational principles: "*spravedlyvist'*" (natural justice or "fairness"), "*hidnist'*" (individually realized / collectively recognized "dignity"), and a distinctly *post-*modern application of Personalism.

If the Maidan was about the emergence of a new social paradigm—one where (perhaps idealistically, as with any ideology) the "good" is defined as respect for Persons and their inter-relations, and the "evil" is represented by a de-personalized system—then the current conflict between the West and Russia (in which Ukraine is commonly seen as the battleground, but not itself an actor) seems to have little to do with Ukraine's Revolution. The war between Russia and the West (currently limited to low level combat in a limited theatre, and to the diplomatic, espionage, informational, and cyber realms, but conceivably capable of degenerating into a global conflagration) is a battle of systems, not Persons. And that is not what Maidan was about. By de-personalizing (intellectualizing) events, we de-emphasize the narrative of Maidan and Ukraine's defensive war against Russian aggression as a revolution of identities, social groups and ideas, and we therefore risk missing their essence: the genuinely inspiring achievements of their protagonists.

Summing up the Revolution

For me, and for many others who spent many days and nights absorbed by the Maidan phenomenon, what occurred during the protests in Kyiv (before the massacre on 18-21 February) can only be described as magical.[31] And this feeling of magic was not simply a biproduct of personal involvement in collective action. Although the purpose of our mass gathering was protest, and the central demand was for the corrupt "oligarchic" system that had become cemented under Yanukovych to be dismantled, this movement was also about social construction: about building something new on the ashes of the old; escaping the decisions that had trapped Ukrainians in a post-Soviet historical trajectory, and placing the country on an alternative (broadly termed) "European" path. The "magic" was reinforced by the fact that our uprising was a grassroots phenomenon, occurring not at the behest of elites, but rather despite their efforts. The flag, the anthem, the symbols, the slogans, poems, lyrics, graffiti, and bumper stickers — all of it was effected spontaneously, genuinely, emotionally, and righteously. At least in this respect Maidan represented a profound social revolution, the magnitude of which we would comprehend only much later. At the time we understood only that we were partaking in the "birth of a Nation."

Then Russia invaded. If support for the Maidan protests, and the concomitant feeling of grass-roots national naissance, had been initially (primarily) a western and central Ukrainian phenomenon, in the aftermath of the annexation of Crimea, and of the Kremlin's aggression in the Donbas, Ukrainian patriotism became a truly national sensation. Citizens of Dnipro, Mykolayiv, Kharkiv, Odesa, and other cities in Ukraine's south and east visibly displayed their choice of identity in defiance of the "*Russkiy mir*" ideological program propagated by the regions' minority Putin supporters. Although the separatist ambitions of some of the latter were genuine, *post-hoc* evidence shows that much of the pro-Russian public fervor was sponsored and animated surreptitiously by the Kremlin. In a development that surprised many, the overwhelmingly Russian-speaking majority of the population in Ukraine's eastern and southern regions publicly and vehemently declared their allegiance to Ukraine: many volunteered their time and money to help establish defenses against the aggressor, and to help those fleeing the violence that had fallen upon their homes; others signed up for military service, risking (and in some cases sacrificing) their lives. With these acts they seemed to confirm the (re)naissance of the Ukrainian nation that had been self-evident in Kyiv during the protests. Ukraine's revolution truly had (so it seemed) corrected the country's historical trajectory and had erased the previous regional differences that had apparently defined Ukrainians' political preferences and supposedly divergent identities.

However, the mass patriotism that I experienced during the Maidan protests, and then later when travelling to the south and east of the country, was not as all-encompassing as it seemed: Ukraine's rural and small-town residents, as well as the urban working class, were engaged in the revolution only peripherally. Although the war effort mobilized soldiers and volunteers from across the spectrum of socio-economic strata, and representatives of Ukraine's rural and semi-rural population certainly contributed, the true grassroots leaders of the revolution hailed from the country's understudied and underrecognized urban creative class: entrepreneurs, journalists, academics, and white-collar managers. They formed the core of the Maidan movement. It was their anti-neo-feudal, broadly termed "bourgeois" program that formed the dominant "liberal" discourse of Ukraine's revolution. For these new entrants into the political elite, Ukraine's revolution represented a watershed between a post-Soviet period of development and a new Ukraine. Their "habitus" differed dramatically from that of the evolved "homo sovieticus"[32] on which the pre-Maidan oligarchic system had been based: they were plugged-in to social networks and new media, and they cultivated trendy images rather than craving distinguished or sacrosanct authority; for them, social capital was more important than economic capital; meritocracy was the hegemonic ideology, but the ideal was a society structured heterarchically. Their organizations (companies and NGO's) had long-since introduced flatter management structures: their managers and leaders were no longer prepared to "buy" legitimacy in exchange for paternalistic loyalty.[33] They craved the creation of a state which guarantees a level playing field for entrepreneurs and firms; one in which those with merit (talent, skills, drive, etc.) would be able to achieve success; where the state would be neither partner nor predator with respect to the economy, but whose role in the private sector would be limited to that of impartial arbiter in case of dispute. Before the Maidan protests, they had achieved significant career success in the non-oligarchic sector of the economy; they now seized the opportunity to implement real systemic reform, filling (often to their own surprise) government positions or acting as behind-the-scenes "flexian" reform drivers in various government agencies.[34]

All revolutions (and the Ukrainian case was no exception) seem to involve abrupt removal of an oppressive government by individuals who nominally position themselves as revolutionaries (i.e. profess transformative romantic ideals or at least promise regime change), but who according to their socio-economic status, are actually break-away members of the established elite. As evidenced by the very gradual implementation of domestic reforms during the immediate post-Yanukovych period, the Ukrainian case seemed to differ only marginally from the historical model: faces changed, but vested interests remained (mostly) vested. At time of writing, the outcome of the revolutionary transformation of Ukraine from a neo-feudal "oligarchy" to a rules-based meritocracy that replicated Maidan activists' "bourgeois" habitus, remained unknown. What had become clear by this time (late 2018) was that Ukrainians' appetite for change, and their willingness to endure hardship for the sake of a nominally attractive, but uncertain future, had waned over time. The euphoric "magical" social mood—a condition spawned by activism and (at least for a while) capable of self-replication—eventually faded into cynicism.

Renowned social psychologist Serge Moscovici once observed that after their initial "big bang", revolutionary societies inevitably "cool":

> Here the contrast is between a revolutionary or anomalous society, resulting from a big bang, and normal society, which is formed once the forces behind the explosion have cooled down and the innovations that provoked it have become commonplace. The first kind of society is distinguished by the ebullience of its members and the creative urge they display. Favored by a state of collective over-excitement, historical and moral energies are released; these change the course of society, which had been assumed to be as little variable as the trajectory of a planet... Such a society, however, reduced to its essentials and lived only from the inside, can only be short-lived... Insofar as the day-to-day functions of administration, production and exchange must be carried on and the demands of daily life respected, it is these which

once more assume the preponderant role... In this sense (in time) society becomes normal...[35]

Ukraine did not return to "normality" immediately after the victory
of the Maidan protests. On the contrary, the country's polity gained
national self-identification (a fact that in itself constituted an identity
revolution); the financial-industrial groups and their oligarch-owners,
although not yet bankrupt, lost their previous ability to dictate the
policies of the state without question (due to having lost their previously exclusive access to cash flows — be it from gas (Firtash), electricity generation and distribution (Akhmetov), banking (Kolomoisky),
steel exports (Pinchuk)); the previous dominance of eastern region
based industrial production in the structure of GDP was replaced by
services (including IT outsourcing), small-scale manufacturing, and
farming — a fact that balanced Ukraine's regional political economy;
institutions tasked with fighting corruption and maintaining the impartial monopoly of the state on the use of force were finally established (though not necessarily yet made effective). All these results
were evidence of significant reform having been implemented by the
country's leaders.[36] Furthermore, partly due to the exigencies of war
(i.e. the need to organize and volunteer), Ukraine experienced the
birth of a truly autonomous civil society — skeptical of political institutions, but capable of regularly influencing decision-making.[37]

   Despite popular expectations (domestic and international) of a
complete "reboot of government", the pace of reform implementation
in the post-Yanukovych years pleased few. The protagonists of the
Revolution of Dignity had promised a new Ukraine, but despite the
best efforts of many, this new country had not (yet) materialized. Put
simply, this is a story of excessive expectations not being fulfilled. The
Maidan agenda had called for total reconstruction of Ukraine's social,
political and economic institutions — a task that surely required more
than 4-5 years. Sadly however, disillusionment in the pace of transformation (and war fatigue) resulted in neglect of the significance of the
events that had catalyzed the process — i.e. the original Maidan phenomenon.

Objectively, more was done to transform Ukraine during the four years that followed Yanukovych's ouster, than had been accomplished during the previous 23 years of independence. Among the achievements of the Maidan activists who entered Kyiv's corridors of power one can identify the following twelve transformations:

1. Rejuvenation of the Ukrainian Armed Forces: from a poorly equipped and ineffective force that relied on volunteers to provide basic foodstuffs, clothing, and fuel when first confronted with Russian aggression in 2014, to an Army that numbered over 250,000 active troops in 2018, and an additional 180,000 in operational reserve — all well-equipped, battle hardened, and engaged in a program of continuous training and upgrading of military capabilities in concert with Ukraine's western allies.[38]

2. Police reform: from a thoroughly corrupt and poorly trained national force that had been known for its corrupt practices (e.g. traffic infractions were routinely resolved with bribes) to a citizen-friendly law enforcement service with new uniforms and hybrid patrol cars (provided by the Japanese government as part of an emissions trading scheme under the Kyoto Protocol). Although the first phase of reform — focused on traffic police and local constabularies — was successfully rolled out in 2015-2017, improvements in police management and transformation of the prosecution service were stalled.[39]

3. Introduction of electronic public procurement and reduction of central government corruption: from a state where kickbacks and insider deals added an estimated 50% to government procurement expenditures, to receipt by Ukraine's new Prozorro e-procurement system of the 2016 World Procurement Award.[40] Although other avenues for syphoning state funds into private hands had not been completely closed, by 2017 the previously pervasive corrupt enrichment schemes involving central government procurement had been eradicated.

4. Drastically reduced energy dependency on Russia: whereas Ukraine had been completely dependent on Russian gas for home heating and industry (amounting to 40% of total imports for over 2 decades), by 2017 the country's natural gas imports from Russia had been reduced to nil. Throughout the country's post-Soviet history, gas imports had generated massive incomes from corrupt schemes for oligarchs and were the foundation for Kyiv's economic dependence on Moscow.[41]

5. Macro-financial renewal including reform of the domestic banking sector, and intensification of cooperation with international financial institutions: from a condition when over half of Ukraine's banks were *de facto* mechanisms for insider lending, and the country's sovereign bonds were considered junk, to a condition where Ukraine had returned to international credit markets, restored its foreign reserves to non-critical (3 month import) levels, and had closed over half its banks for non-performance. The system clean-up included nationalization of Ukraine's largest financial institution, PrivatBank, for which stress testing had identified a 5.5 billion USD shortfall in finances.[42] Controversially, as a result of the clean-up, over 65% of Ukraine's banking sector had become state-owned, and intensified cooperation with the IMF and World Bank had increased the country's sovereign debt levels from approximately 40% of GDP in 2013 to almost 80% of GDP in 2018.

6. Structural reorientation of the economy: from reliance on energy-intensive commodity exports to service sector growth, including intensified development of IT-outsourcing and product development companies. This reorientation was highly painful for the eastern industrial regions of Ukraine which lost their previously hegemonic position as primary providers of export revenues, but the overall result was a more balanced regional political economy. On the other hand, restructuring was a gradual process, and so GDP growth in 2016-18 was moderate, and had not yet recovered the economic loss of 2014-15.

7. Decentralization: from a policy of increasing centralization implemented as part of the "administrative reforms" of the Yanukovych regime, to Ukraine's municipalities receiving significant increases in their spending powers and revenues, and amalgamation of communities resulting in increased effectiveness of local government.[43]

8. Educational reform: from a teacher-centered Soviet-style system of 11-year education with limited institutional autonomy for schools and universities, to the introduction of a 12-year student-centered system designed in line with European Standards and Guidelines for Educational Quality Assurance.[44] The "New Ukrainian School" reform was launched in 2018, after a year of retraining for almost 20,000 first-grade teachers; a new National Agency for Higher Education Quality Assurance was launched the same year. Both reforms were considered belated.

9. Health Care reform: from an inefficient system notorious for providing poor quality care with hospital staff regularly requiring bribe payments for service, to a system where state financing "follows the patient", and hospital management (institution- and district-level) will be re-engineered.[45] These reform initiatives proved highly controversial in 2017-18, but given the catastrophic condition of Ukraine's medical facilities and patient care, and the scale of the challenge of their transformation, even the initial drive to have citizens register with a family doctor was seen as a positive step towards improving the system.

10. International travel: from a state where Ukrainians were required to apply for demeaning visas to visit EU countries and
then to purchase expensive air tickets from a national carrier
with limited routes, to a visa-free regime for 90-day visits and
an explosive expansion of airports and routes, including access to three low-cost airlines flying regularly to/from the
country's major cities; improved high speed international rail
service to Poland from Lviv and Kyiv.

11. Improved infrastructure: from a road network in catastrophic
condition and infrastructure repair regularly costing outrageous sums due to skimming, theft and corruption, to visible
high-quality reconstruction of Ukraine's almost 170,000 km of
roads (budgets of over 1.2 billion USD allocated yearly in
2017-18), and new rail links (e.g. Kyiv-Boryspil airport) completed ahead of schedule and under budget.[46]

12. Cultural policies aimed at de-communization, de-russifica-
tion, and nation-building: from a condition of virtual monopoly enjoyed by Russian-language media (radio, television,
newspaper), and minimal local cultural production within
Ukraine (music, programming, films overwhelmingly imported from Russia), to a significant increase in locally produced Ukrainian-language content due to institution of quo-
tas on radio and television. In parallel, the state has actively
promoted reorientation of memory politics away from glori-
fying Soviet cultural symbols (in fact, banning them) to celebrating a distinctly Ukrainian identity—without restricting
expression by minorities.

These transformations, effected by Ukraine's post-Yanukovych governments (led by Prime Ministers Yatseniuk and Hroysman), were
largely informed by the desire voiced commonly by the Maidan protesters: to live in a "normal" country (see Chapter 3). The results were
mixed—all of the above were still "works in progress" four years after
the ouster of Yanukovych—but nevertheless admirable. Much was
achieved in the area of reforming state services (health care, medicine,
police), building national institutions (army, language and culture)

and infrastructure (roads, railways, airports); painfully, the economy was sanitized and returned to (albeit gradual) growth, and a cursory clean-up of previously pervasive corrupt schemes was performed. Despite repeated calls for increasing the pace of transformation, the reform accomplishments were highly impressive.

However, despite the generally positive appraisal of the reform drive outlined above, the unreformed judicial branch remained a glaring "hole" in the puzzle of Ukraine's institutional transformation. The Supreme Court was supposedly reformed in 2017, but several the new appointees to the country's top bench were unable to explain the sources of their past incomes and were therefore not recommended for appointment by the oversight committee. They were appointed anyway. An anti-corruption agency, an investigative bureau, and a specialized anti-corruption prosecutor and anti-corruption court were created by legislation, but their effectiveness was disappointing.[47] According to the 2016 Law on Justice, the judicial branch gained greater independence, and was supposed to be cleansed of corrupt judges—a noble intention that was irregularly implemented.

The reason Ukraine's judicial reform seemed to stall was twofold: 1) vested interests within the system fought to retain their privileged positions and avoid prosecution for previous misdeeds, and 2) the system itself was subject to reform rather than complete reconstruction, as had been called for by the agenda of Maidan. Ukraine's revolutionaries had demanded the creation and legitimization of a judicial system that would guarantee "fairness" as well as "justice", and this simply could not be done within existing approaches to (re)structuring the judicial branch. The next stage of transformation required shifting discourse beyond building a "normal" country (i.e. modifying an existing western model) towards constructing a vision of a desired institution that would reflect the conceptual novelties generated by Ukraine's Revolution of Dignity.

Agenda for the future

Rather than ending with Maidan, Ukraine's revolution *began* with Yanukovych's departure. Thereafter (2015-2018), came a period of moderate reform with some successes and some failures, but with the buoyancy and activism of the Maidan protests and their immediate aftermath eventually becoming replaced with an overall social malaise. As discussed in the opening chapter, according to Crane Brinton's classic *Anatomy of Revolution*, one should have expected a period of "terror" (e.g. house-cleaning a la Robespierre or Stalin) to result from such disillusionment with moderate reform. Yet, at time of writing, the rise of radicalism had thus far been avoided in Ukraine.

The history of "great revolutions" reveals that the "terror" stage — although representing the next logical step in a typical lifecycle of revolutions, having spectacularly developed in both the French and the Russian cases — was avoided in the American case.[48] The 13 colonies that became the United States were able to elude the violent reaction to the disappointments of moderation seemingly because there, *revolution was accompanied by a war of independence* that lasted for 7 long years. In this aspect (and in others), the Ukrainian and US cases seem similar. The persistent existential threat posed by the former metropole, and the discourse of independence (i.e. the paramount need to protect a set territory and its people against renewed subjugation) resulted in consolidation and solidarity which enabled avoidance of radicalization. From this perspective, Russia's invasion of Ukraine in 2014 and its continued aggression since then, may (ironically) have been a blessing.[49]

However, at time of writing, Ukraine's revolutionary lifecycle still risked degenerating into radicalism and bedlam (as per the classic lifecycle). The next stage of revolution would be Ukraine's point of bifurcation: would the country's political elites succumb to the "social question" (as Hannah Arendt called the leftward discursive shift from idealism to materialism that led to the guillotine in France and terror in Russia),[50] or would ideational development, and the institutionalization of conceptual innovations remain their priority? The first option was easier: populism presented attractive electoral opportunities for political leaders who were not driven by ethical principles. The second option was more difficult and of necessity needed to be led by an intellectualized (i.e. visionary rather than careerist) political elite. In the US example, the Founding Fathers set to work on institutional-

izing the ideas of their revolution (i.e. republican government, separation of powers, institutionalized liberty) immediately after the
ouster of the ancien regime in 1776; the result was series of documents:
The Declaration of Independence, Articles of Confederation, the Fed-
eralist Papers, and eventually the US Constitution. In France, the Gi-
rondins failed to establish a functioning republican government, and
were ousted by the radical Jacobins who promised "compassion" and
substantive equality for the "sans-culottes" — with tragic consequences.

In Ukraine, by mid-2018 the need to place political system design
at the top of the political agenda had become obvious. Yulia Tymoshenko — the opposition leader who had been jailed by Yanukovych
and released immediately after his ouster — announced that constitutional reform would be a fundamental plank of her 2019 campaign for
Ukraine's Presidency.[51] Incumbent candidate Poroshenko also tabled
amendments to the country's Constitution: these were aimed at en-
shrining decentralization and Ukraine's strategy of eventually joining
NATO and the EU into the country's basic law.[52] However, both candidates' proposals (both were frontrunners in opinion polls at time of
writing) focused on amending the institutional arrangements of *governance* (i.e. domestic decision-making and/or foreign policy direction). Neither proposed a fundamental (conceptual and/or institutional) overhaul of the *judicial* system — a clear societal demand that
had emanated both from the Maidan protests and from the dearth of
prosecutions of those responsible for the February 2014 massacres in
Kyiv and Yanukovych-era crimes. Social perceptions of persistent
elite corruption and *de facto* immunity fueled popular discontent with
Ukraine's incumbent elite, but discussions of *how "spravedlyvist'"*
could be achieved (i.e. what institutional design was desirable for
Ukraine's judicial branch) had not yet been formulated by any of the
candidates or parties vying for power in the country's 2019 electoral
contests.[53]

Sadly, by the time of the start of the official campaign in late 2018,
candidate Tymoshenko's message had shifted away from idealism to
a populist (materialist) discourse: billboards and advertisements
throughout the country proclaimed her promise to cut natural gas

prices by no less than half as part of her proposed "New Economic Course" for the country.⁵⁴ President Poroshenko on the other hand, based his re-election campaign on replaying his administration's achievements in strengthening the army, promoting Ukrainian language rights, and inaugurating the Autocephalous Orthodox Church of Ukraine. Establishing an independent Ukrainian church, legitimately separated from the Moscow Patriarchate (i.e. with a *Tomos* granted by the Ecumenical Patriarch of Constantinople on 6 January 2019), was declared by Poroshenko to be equivalent in importance to Ukraine's 1991 declaration of independence, and a step towards the country's prospective membership in NATO and the EU.⁵⁵ For many Ukrainian voters this correspondence may have rung true, but whether their numbers were to be sufficient to secure Poroshenko's re-election, at time of writing, remained unknown.

It would seem that instead of using the Presidential and Parliamentary campaigns of 2019 to flush out new institutional arrangements whose public discussion would eventually be required, the agenda of Ukraine's elites (and electorate) was destined to remain focused on personalities, and their ability either to improve the material conditions of average Ukrainians (i.e. materialist-populist programming), or to counter the country's continued existential threat from Russia (i.e. an identity and security-focused discourse). In such a condition the risk of following the French revolutionary path (rather than the American) in Ukraine remained high. On the other hand, Ukraine's intellectual elites — those who inevitably would be charged with institutionalizing the ideals of "*spravedlyvist'*" (fairness) and "*hidnist'*" (dignity) in new governance structures, particularly in the judicial branch — enjoyed unprecedented support from a socio-economic group with compatible values and interests. Representatives of the country's new bourgeois "creative class" regularly lamented their inability to field a consolidated party that could viably compete in electoral contests, but the eventual emergence of such a political force — allied with the country's intellectuals and possibly with veterans of the war with Russia — seemed inevitable. Whether such a party would succeed in countering the degradation of Ukraine's political discourse into materialist-populism remained unknown, but given the stakes,

and the opportunities presented by the Revolution of Dignity to establish institutional novelty (both in Ukraine and more broadly), such
a *post*modern political force was both desirable and highly anticipated.

As argued in Part II of this book, Ukraine's Revolution of Dignity
represented a threefold socio-political transformation, and each of its
characteristics reflected those Hannah Arendt once attributed to
"great revolutions"[56] Specifically, the Maidan protests and the subsequent defensive war with Russia:

1. represented a dramatic *moment of completion* for a previous
    historical era (some would frame this process as correction of
    a developmental trajectory that had been hijacked by a
    (post)Soviet variant of "Great Russian" colonialism); the iden-
    tity revolution, experienced *en masse* by Ukrainians during the
    Maidan protests and (especially) during the early the mobili-
    zation effort to counter Russia's aggression, represented the
    end of a process of nation-building: the Ukrainian political na-
    tion had finally arrived;

2. connoted a *new beginning* (a transition or inflection point) both
    in the minds of the revolutionaries, and in a broader sense for
    Ukraine's polity—specifically with respect to the accepted
    system of power relations and wealth distribution. A new eco-
    nomic model had emerged from the "bourgeois" Maidan's re-
    bellion against Yanukovych's corrupt "neo-feudal" regime;
    supported by an incipient urban "creative class" the country's
    new political and economic elites seemed intent on transform-
    ing socio-economic practices, and establishing the dominance
    of their (meritocratic, rules-based, heterarchic) "habitus";

3. produced and conveyed *novelty*—particularly in the senses
    and concepts that were elucidated on Maidan but were likely
    to reverberate far beyond Ukraine's borders well into the fu-
    ture. Specifically, the Ukrainian revolution involved mass
    mobilization in support of such *post*modern (broadly termed)
    "liberal" values as dignity, self-reliance, natural justice
    ("*spravedlyvist'*"); the challenge of the revolutionaries in the
    next stage was to engender these concepts in lasting institu-
    tions.

In each of these three dimensions, at time of writing, the Maidan agenda remained unfinished. The natural evolution of Ukrainian society into a recognizable European polity with a right-left socio-economic foundation forming the basis for political party rivalry (i.e. with an "urban creative class" party competing on the right, and an "industrial-agrarian" party on the left) was interrupted artificially by the Kremlin. Putin's military aggression, framed as a defense of ethnic Russians and Russian-speakers (whose linguistic freedoms were supposedly threatened by Kyiv's "nationalists"), returned Ukraine's political agenda to the question of identity and security. According to widely accepted perceptions of the country's previous political reality, this forced step backward should have laid bare latent ethno-linguistic cleavages that had supposedly made the country susceptible to breakup. But much to the surprise of both domestic and international observers (and one suspects to Putin's chagrin), deep identity cleavages did not materialize in the wake of Maidan. Support for separatism in the southern oblasts (Odesa, Mykolayiv, Kherson) was muted at best, and immediately stifled by local elites in the primarily Russian-speaking east-central industrial heartland of Dnipropetrovsk (Dnipro) and Zaporizhzhia.[57] Instead of catalyzing the creation of "Novorossiya" throughout southeastern Ukraine, Putin was only able to grab 7% of the country's territory, and in the process fueled the establishment of a consolidated Ukrainian identity: a "territorial nation" that revered the sacred integrity of the country's internationally recognized borders.[58]

Territory is clearly important to any nation-state, but the extent to which borders were sanctified by Ukrainians in response to Russia's aggression was largely unprecedented. Furthermore, Ukrainians' version of patriotism explicitly rejected the *state* as a central institution of the nation. Instead, the essential nucleus of their new Ukrainian identity became the *map*. Years into the Russian-Ukrainian war, one may question the objective importance of the eastern Donbas and of Crimea to Ukraine: both were depressed regions prior to Russia's invasion, and their reintegration if allowed by Russia would certainly be a drag on Ukraine's economic development. But the symbolism of territory (as embodied in the map) trumped economic calculation: the dream of regaining integrity within the country's internationally recognized borders rallied (and continues to rally) Ukrainians to support the war effort, acting as a powerful symbolic mobilizer.

Ukraine emerged from the Maidan protests and from the experience of defensive war with Russia as a political nation inclusive of multiple languages and ethnicities, and this in itself represented a massive achievement of Ukraine's Revolution of Dignity. The challenge faced by the country's elites during the next phase of transformation was to channel the activism of Maidan constructively, and to maintain the nation's patriotic fervor while building new institutions — without succumbing to the temptation of securing short-term electoral victories through populism. The sacrifices of those who fell for the twin causes of personal and national dignity, generated a powerful claim on Ukrainians to continue their domestic revolution. To imagine even the possibility of failure would be to underrate the global significance of their country on the international stage, to deny the domestic agency of its Maidan activists and Donbas war volunteers, and to discard the potential influence footprint of Ukraine's Revolution of Dignity on western civilization.

Afterword

Academic social scientists may criticize this book for its one-sidedness. I likely will be reproached for having "mythologized" the Maidan protest movement, and for having presented a black-and-white narrative, according to which the revolutionaries were (almost) exclusively "good" and the Yanukovych regime was (almost always) "evil". Similarly, I will be censured for painting Putin's Russia as unequivocally aggressive, murderous, expansionist, and backward. The criticism is well taken: this book and its author are both (now) products of an intensely experienced period of revolution and war, and for me the "other side" (i.e. the Yanukovych regime and/or the Kremlin) have become the equivalent of a Tolkien-like Mordor where human life is cheap, and Orwellian opposites define reality. Mythologizing events under such circumstances is natural.

On the other hand, as the popular writer Yuriy Andrukhovych pointed out while accepting the 2014 Hannah Arendt Prize for Political Thought "Post-modern consciousness presumes reconciliation and excludes a black-and-white approach."[1] Many non-participant observers of Ukraine's Revolution of Dignity will consider my approach excessively color-blind. As with most globally significant processes, understanding the multiple facets of Ukraine's revolution and its global aftermath is no easy task, and the narrative that I have presented here is a subjective one. I have told the story as I saw it from the inside. I do not claim academic distance.

For observers from outside Ukraine, Maidan was a huge surprise: revolutions of this magnitude and global importance are not supposed to occur in peripheral countries. Only weeks before the Vilnius Summit (where Yanukovych was scheduled to sign the EU Association Agreement), many in Europe, and indeed throughout the world, had written off Ukraine as hopelessly divided, utterly corrupt, and effectively a backward client state of Russia.[2] Then suddenly Ukraine topped the world's headlines: millions were protesting on the freezing wintry streets of its capital city, apparently demanding integration with the European Union. Within weeks of the start of the first peaceful protests on Independence Square, the French philosopher and playwright Bernard-Henri Levy was calling Kyiv "the capital of Europe" while US Senators visiting the Maidan in December 2013[3] were proclaiming that "Ukraine will make Europe better, and Europe will make Ukraine better." Given that Ukrainians had elected a twice sentenced criminal as their President in 2010 (freely and fairly, though by the narrowest of margins), and had repeatedly expressed skepticism as to their country's prospects of EU integration when asked in polls to choose between the EU and the alternative Eurasian Economic Union promoted by Moscow, one could be forgiven for being somewhat perplexed by the sudden mass protests in Kyiv—catalyzed by a change of policy on what amounted to a trade deal, and with demonstrators waving EU flags.

Fast forward six months: Ukraine's highly unpopular President has fled the country; the Crimean peninsula (formerly an Autonomous Republic, but part of the sovereign territory of Ukraine) has been *de facto* annexed by Russia following a covert military operation aimed at gaining control of key strategic targets; government buildings in the eastern region of Donbas (consisting of Donetsk and Luhansk oblasts) have been occupied by Russian-backed separatists, and arms and materiel are pouring across the Russian-Ukrainian border in regular convoys; clashes between pro-Moscow and pro-Kyiv demonstrators in the southern port city of Odesa, and the eastern metropolis of Kharkiv have resulted in severe injuries and deaths.

Clearly, Yanukovych's flight was far from the end of the story of Ukraine's revolution. By mid-summer 2014, Russian forces were directly engaged in fighting on Ukrainian territory: on July 17 a surface-to-air missile (BUK) fired from a Russian mobile launcher parked near the town of Torez in occupied Donetsk oblast, shot down a Malaysian Airlines passenger plane from its cruising altitude of over 10 km above ground, killing all 298 passengers and crew; Russian ground troops (equipped with tanks, "Grad" multiple rocket launchers, and heavy artillery) engaged the Ukrainian regular army and volunteer battalions in direct fighting near Ilovaysk, Donetsk oblast, and shelled Ukrainian personnel from across the border in Luhansk oblast.

Ukraine's western partners—most notably Germany and France—engaged Russia in negotiations in an effort to establish a ceasefire, and some semblance of a peace process. Meanwhile, Poland, Lithuania, Canada, and the US sent non-lethal equipment and military trainers to Ukraine to help build up the country's defenses. The United States vociferously condemned Russia's aggression in the UN Security Council and led the international community in imposing economic and political sanctions against the Kremlin, effectively isolating Moscow while providing generous financial assistance to Kyiv. By the autumn of 2014 Russia was officially proclaimed an adversary of NATO, and Ukraine remained the center of European security concerns throughout 2015-2016 (discussed extensively by both Presidential candidates during the US election campaign), taking a back seat only to Islamist terrorism.

In this book we have sought to both chronicle and contextualize Ukraine's Revolution of Dignity—a string of events that began in the central square of Kyiv (Maidan), but quickly spread to other regions of the country, eventually leading to regime change, and to violent aggression on the part of Russia. In the immediate aftermath of events in Ukraine's capital, the Kremlin responded to its loss of effective control over its former quasi-client government in Kyiv by illegally annexing Crimea, and by fostering war in the Donbas. The international order as it had been constituted in the wake of the collapse of the USSR almost 25 years earlier (according to which international borders in Europe were deemed inviolable) was unilaterally wiped out, precipitating an institutional crisis within the UN, and renewed animosity between the West and Russia. During the ensuing two years, tensions spread beyond the local eastern European theatre to include direct Russian military intervention in Syria, and subversive activities in multiple NATO and EU member states. The international institutions that previously ensured peace and prosperity in Europe were never to be the same.

However, political transformation (regime change, shifting borders, reappraisal of trans-national institutions) captures only one aspect of the events that began in Ukraine in late 2013. The Revolution of Dignity represented a "civilizational break"[4] between modernity and a new order that is yet to be named or defined. It would seem that this disruption involved multiple dimensions of the Western "habitus": firstly, a re-evaluation of the bases on which humans form communities (i.e. a possible resurgence of the importance of "nation" as a nucleus for solidarity, but with a horizontal, territorial, rather than state-centered structure); secondly, a reassessment of the foundations of wealth (and therefore appearance of new forms of stratification, management methods and "heterarchical" structures, and new social cleavages); and thirdly, appearance of new ideas and senses based on integration of concepts previously deemed contradictory (such as "collectivist individualism" in the form of personalism; non-materialist meritocracy, etc.). Although these phenomena did not necessarily originate in Ukraine, they seem to have become accentuated by Maidan.

In the analytical section of this book (Part II), we attempted to make sense of Ukraine's Revolution of Dignity—to understand the domestic agency that led to global consequences. But intellectualizing events can leave them dehumanized and dry. And so, in Part I we presented a chronicle of the trials and experiences of the participants of Maidan: of the protest activists, of the volunteer defenders of Ukraine's territory, of the reformers who forfeited careers to build a new country. But words on paper rarely reproduce the emotions of events realistically: the psychological effect of having lived them cannot be conveyed adequately without significant empathy from the reader. In time, emotional wounds heal, but the passion of sacrifice fades as well…

My friend Lyubomir Markevych who, like me, has Canadian roots, and has lived in Kyiv for more than two decades, posted the following to his Facebook page at the start of Easter weekend 2014:

> I've been in Kyiv throughout all the killings beginning in January. This evening I decided to walk down Hrushevsky street, a parallel street to Institutska, where the killings began a month earlier on January 22. It's much quieter here with fewer people milling about and I like it this way. I can't really explain why I'm compelled to come here this evening. I know its Friday, not just any Friday, but Good Friday… I know I'm looking for closure, but I can't find it. I feel compelled (…there's that

word again) to return to the scene of the crime of January 22 and subsequent days. My emotions are frayed and tormented. Memories of leisurely cappuccinos on this street clash with more recent memories of snipers, blood and stretchers carrying out the dead and wounded. I can't reconcile it. It's much too raw and still too early.

When the spring of 2014 arrived, those of us who had lived through the Maidan protests thought we had lived a lifetime during the previous 4-5 months. In early December 2013 my wife and I had watched in awe as hundreds of people (maybe thousands—we weren't counting) in Kyiv's city center spontaneously built barricades from snow and ice—seemingly with no guidance as to what each person should be doing and how, but building nevertheless; we laughed (a reflection of pride, confidence in victory, and patriotism all wrapped together) when we first heard the announcement from the Maidan stage: "Dear Kyivans! Please don't bring us any more food—we have more than we can eat". In January, I witnessed a balaclava-clad piano player playing Chopin less than 10 meters from a line of armed riot police, and for the first time I saw my city, my beloved Kyiv, descend into violence and burn. In February, I saw a "Berkut" officer stepping out from behind the Stella (monument) on Independence Square to shoot a young man running through the "no-man's land" between protesters and riot police; I cried like I have never cried before when the coffins of the Heaven's Hundred were brought forth to the tune of "Plyve Kacha", and then carried away on their final journey to the sound of thousands chanting "Heroes do not die!". At the end of February, we celebrated—we won! Sure, the Crimean thing was outrageous, but at the end of the day, Yanukovych had fled, and Ukraine could now rebuild.

But the Russian invasion dragged on. Despite several unilateral and (supposedly) negotiated multilateral ceasefires, the evening news continued to be filled with stories of the dead and wounded. Meanwhile foreign news broadcasts filled with overt disinformation and fakes: apparently Ukraine was a country where nationalists and fascists regularly killed Russian-speaking children… Putin-apologists such as New York University professor Stephen Cohen, who provided frequent commentary on the "Ukraine crisis" on CNN and other US news networks in 2014-15, seemed to pop up in the most unlikely places. Thankfully, several other area specialists have seen Russia's actions in Ukraine for what they are: military aggression against a sovereign neighbor whose people want nothing more than to live normal lives, and to be proud of their country. Hopefully this book will contribute to setting the record straight.

The significance of Ukraine's revolution to global civilizational development is yet to be fully appreciated. The demonstrations in Kyiv were a unique phenomenon for 21st century Europe. The core of the protests was fundamental dissatisfaction with a deeply corrupt political regime that had ordered the beating of students and journalists. The symbol of change that the protestors adopted was the "lighthouse" of the EU, but *en route* to proclaiming their right to a dignified existence, Ukrainians also learned to organize; to act collectively; to become a civil society. In the process they became a nation; they recalibrated their economy; they generated novel interpretations of foundational ideas, and these may yet become important for the development of western civilization.

Ukrainians called the events of 2013-14 the "Revolution of Dignity". This label is both profound and accurate. It reflects the deeply philosophical reality of the Maidan experience. During those three months of peaceful protest each of us individually, and all of us collectively, came to understand what it truly means to be a Person. As a Christian, I understand that this is how it should have been: "As a spiritual being, the human creature is defined through interpersonal relations. The more authentically he or she lives these relations, the more his or her own personal identity matures. It is not by isolation that man establishes his worth, but by placing himself in relation with others and with God." (Pope Benedict XVI — Caritas in Veritate).

In his account of a similarly "spiritual" revolution in Poland, Timothy Garton Ash recalled a worker with a pale face and dirty jacket in Poznan calling the Solidarity movement in 1980-81 "a revolution of the soul."[5] Maidan was just such a "revolution of the soul" for Ukrainians — a time and place to discover one's personhood; to connect with others; to declare and defend one's beliefs. And to understand (nay feel) that millions of others believe exactly as you do.

A drop in the ocean. A tide of civilizational change.

Notes

Acknowlegments

1   Kimmel, Michael S. (1990) *Revolution, a Sociological Interpretation*. Philadelphia: Temple University Press, p. viii

Preface

1   "Thoughts from Kyiv" were republished by http://ukiedaily.com, by http://circusbazzaar.com.

2   Scholarly works that justify Russian aggression in Ukraine based on the myth of imminent NATO expansion eastward include Sakwa, Richard (2014) *Frontline Ukraine: Crisis in the Borderlands,* London: I.B. Tauris, and others.

Chapter 1 — Introduction

1   Like many residents of Ukraine's capital, throughout the winter of 2013-14, I made a point of going to Independence Square during evening hours on weekdays (between 18:30 and 22:30 every night, crowds would swell to several thousand – regardless of temperature), and especially on Sundays to attend the regular "viche" rallies when numbers would top 100 thousand. Several nights were spent in philosophical discussion in the city center while trying to grab warmth from a fire burning in a barrel, and waiting for the sun to rise. During the weeks before the protests degenerated into violence, I participated in brainstorming sessions organized by "Hromadskyj Operatyvnyj Shtab" (HOSh) – an informal strategic thinktank which gathered the leaders of the various groups of demonstrators spontaneously organizing on and around Maidan. I also gave lectures as part of the "Open University of Maidan". In the months that followed Yanukovych's ouster, I became a member of the "21 November Initiative Group" (2111.org.ua) and served as Advisor to the Minister of Education and Science. I would like to think that my role in Ukraine's revolution was that of participant and observer, but on several occasions the distinction between these roles was not maintained.

2   Gorchinskaya, Katya (20 Feb. 2016) "Birth of a Nation" *Kyiv Post*. Ref: www.kyivpost.com/article/opinion/op-ed/birth-of-a-nation-333459.html

3   "Журналісти встановили подробиці втечі Януковича з України" (21 April 2014) *Ukrayinska Pravda*. Ref: www.pravda.com.ua/news/2014/04/21/7023153/

4   Despite repeated Kremlin denials, Russian Special Forces were present in Slovyansk (the epicenter of the supposed Donbass "insurgency") in May-June 2014. This fact was admitted by the commander of the subversives, GRU Colonel Girkin (alias "Strelkov"), in November 2014 — see "Girkin says he and his special ops team started conflict in Donbas" (20 Nov. 2014) *UNIAN Information Agency*. Ref: www.unian.info/politics/1011888-girkin-says-he-and-his-special-ops-team-started-conflict-in-donbas.html

5   Case, Sean (21 Dec. 2016) Putin's *Undeclared War: Summer 2014 – Russian Artillery Strikes Against Ukraine* Bellingcat Report. Ref: www.bellingcat.com/news/uk-and-europe/2016/12/21/russian-artillery-strikes-against-ukraine/

6   Two years after the incident, the Bellingcat Investigation Team, identified Russia's 53rd Anti-Aircraft Missile Brigade as the unit most likely responsible for the downing of Flight MH17. See Romein, Daniel (23 Feb. 2016) *MH17 – Potential Suspects and Witnesses from the 53rd Anti-Aircraft Missile Brigade* Bellingcat Rebort. Ref: www.bellingcat.com/news/uk-and-europe/2016/02/23/53rd-report-en/

7   Akkoc, Raziye and Winch, Jessica (28 Aug. 2014) "Ukraine-Russia Crisis: August 28 as it happened" *The Telegraph*. Ref: www.telegraph.co.uk/news/world news/europe/ukraine/11060959/Ukraine-Russia-crisis-Ukraine-invaded-by-Russian-forces-says-Petro-Poroshenko-live.html

8   Kim, Lucian (Nov. 2014) "The Battle of Ilovaisk: Details of a Massacre Inside Rebel-Held Eastern Ukraine" *Newsweek Magazine*. Ref: www.newsweek.com/2014/11/14/battle-ilovaisk-details-massacre-inside-rebel-held-eastern-ukraine-282003.html

9   Viktor Kovalenko, a journalist who emigrated to the US after having served as a volunteer in the Ukrainian military, saw action near Debaltseve. He published his recollections of the battle in a personal blog. See: Kovalenko, Victor (19. Dec. 2016) "Debaltseve Diary 22: Counter Attack At Lohvynove" Kovalenko Blog. Ref: https://viktorkovalenko.wordpress.com/category/battle-of-debaltseve/

10   Extensive military training by Canadian advisors was provided in Yavoriv in western Ukraine. For full background, see: Fuhr, Stephen (Dec. 2017) *Canada's Support to Ukraine in Crisis and Armed Conflict: Report of the Standing Committee on National Defense* House of Commons, Canada. For background on U.K. military assistance see: Mills, Claire (20 May 2015) *U.K. Military Assistance to Ukraine* House of Commons Library Briefing Paper, Number SN07135.

11   The flight of Serhiy Kluyev–the brother of Yanukovych confidant Andriy Kluyev–caused an uproar in the press given that it seemed to have been facilitated by the Prosecutor General's office.

12   For example: Sakwa, Richard (2014); Kalb, Marvin (2015) *Imperial Gamble: Putin, Ukraine and the New Cold War,* Washington: The Brookings Institution. These works and others that adopt a similar paradigm are critically reviewed in Chapter 7.

13   Kimmel (1990), p. 8

14   Eisenstadt, Shmuel N. (2006) *The Great Revolutions and the Civilizations of Modernity.* Leiden, Boston: Brill.

15   Eisenstadt, Shmuel N. (2003) *Comparative Civilizations and Multiple Modernities,* Leiden, Boston: Brill.

16   The full transcript of Levy's speech was published in a blog hosted by *Huffington Post*. Lévy, Bernard-Henri (18. Feb. 2014) "Kiev's Independence Square — Where Europe Hangs in the Balance" *Huffington Post Blog*. Ref: www.huffington post.com/bernardhenri-levy/kievs-independence-square_b_4808629.html

17   In *On Revolution* (1963), Hannah Arendt pointed out "the word 'revolution' meant originally restoration… The revolutions of the seventeenth and eighteenth centuries, which to us appear to show all evidence of a new spirit, the spirit of a modern age, were intended to be restorations…" (p. 34) The aims of initial protagonists of the French and American revolutions was to "restore an old order of things that had been disturbed and violated by the despotism of absolute monarchy and the abuses of colonial government." (p. 35).

18   In a popular interview, TV producer Kateryna Makarevych, who emigrated from
     Russia to Ukraine, seems to have coined the term "Mordor" with reference to con-
     temporary   Russia   (see: http://patrioty.org.ua/blogs/deistvytelno-mordor-
     spovid-emihrantky-z-rosii-118897.html). In January 2016, likely thanks to a joking
     hacker, users of Google Translate noticed that when asked to translate "Russia"
     from Russian into Ukrainian, the program would respond with "Mordor"; enter-
     ing the word "Lavrov" in Ukrainian would return "sad horse" in Russian and
     "Russians" translated into "occupiers". This story was reported by *Ukrayinska
     Pravda* on 5 January 2016. See: www.pravda.com.ua/news/2016/01/5/7094522/
19   Pekar, Valerii (21 April 2014) "Границы и дороги: Судьба Украины в мировом
     контексте" *Hvylya.net*. Ref: https://hvylya.net/analytics/society/granitsyi-i-
     dorogi-sudba-ukrainyi-v-mirovom-kontekste.html
20   When the Association Agreement was finally signed in June 2014, the event was
     peripheral news in Ukraine. For an analysis of the event and its repercussions see
     former US Ambassador Steven Pifer's blog: "Poroshenko Signs EU-Ukraine Asso-
     ciation Agreement" *Brookings Institution* (2014). Ref: www.brookings.edu/blog
     /up-front/2014/06/27/poroshenko-signs-eu-ukraine-association-agreement/
21   Arendt argued that the primary reason the French Revolution degenerated into
     violence and terror was because its progenitors de-emphasized the imperative of
     freedom in favor of "the social question" – i.e. the imperative of economic oppor-
     tunity and/or equality – see Arendt (1963).
22   Volodymyr Ishchenko, a self-proclaimed Ukrainian leftist and follower of the
     Skocpol thesis, published several articles in 2014-2015 denouncing western gov-
     ernments for supporting "right wing radicals on the Maidan" and for "propping
     up the oligarchic post-Yanukovych regime of Ukraine." In his view the Revolution
     of Dignity was not a revolution at all. See: Ishchenko, Volodymyr (28 Feb. 2014)
     "Ukraine has not experienced a genuine revolution, merely a change of elites" *The
     Guardian*.   Ref: www.theguardian.com/world/2014/feb/28/ukraine-genuine-
     revolution-tackle-corruption
23   Arendt (1963), pp. 34-35
24   See Umland, Andreas (11 Nov. 2016) "The Glazyev Tapes: Getting to the root of
     the Conflict in Ukraine" *European Council on Foreign Relations Commentary*. Ref:
     www.ecfr.eu/article/commentary_the_glazyev_tapes_getting_to_the_root_of_
     the_conflict_in_7165
25   See for example: "Russia's motives in Ukraine" (2014) *Strategic Comments*, 20:4, viii-
     ix; Deyermond, Ruth (27 April 2014) "What are Russia's real motivations in
     Ukraine? We need to understand them" *The Guardian*. Ref: www.theguardian.
     com/commentisfree/2014/apr/27/russia-motivations-ukraine-crisis;   Shoichet,
     Catherine E. (7 Aug. 2014) "What is Putin's endgame in Ukraine?" *CNN*. Ref:
     https://edition.cnn.com/2014/08/07/world/europe/russia-putin-ukraine-endgame/.
26   For analysis suggesting the Kremlin's goal in Ukraine to be the restoration of Rus-
     sia as a "great power" see: Adelman, Jonathan (19 April 2016) "Thinking the Un-
     thinkable: Russia has Re-Emerged As a Great Power" *Huffington Post Blog*. Ref:
     www.huffingtonpost.com/jonathan-adelman/thinking-the-unthinkable-_2_b_
     9720304.html; and Courtney, William and Jensen, Donald (21 March 2016) "Rus-
     sia's Great Power Future" *The Rand Blog*. Ref: www.rand.org/blog/
     2016/03/russias-great-power-future.html; and Gvosdev, Nikolas (2006) "Because
     it is: Russia, the Existential Great Power" *The National Interest*. Ref:
     www2.gwu.edu/~sigur/assets/docs/major_pow-
     ers_091407/Gvosdev_on_%20Russia.pdf

27   See for example "The Third Coming? Is Maidan 3.0 possible, and what would it look like?" (17 Dec. 2015) *Ukrainian Week*. Ref: https://ukrainianweek.com /Politics/154194. Several attempts to organize protests under the auspices of a "Third Maidan" were also reported throughout 2016, but these seem to have been rooted in Kremlin-sponsored subversive activity—see: "Russian troll farms behind campaign to topple Ukrainian government" (11 Oct. 2015) *StopFake* Ref: http://www.stopfake.org/en/tag/third-maidan/

28   For a western view on the problem see Abrams, Neil A. and Fish, M. Steven (13 June 2016) "Dethroning Ukraine's Oligarchs: A How-To Guide" *Foreign Policy*. Ref: http://foreignpolicy.com/2016/06/13/dethroning-ukraines-oligarchs-a-how-to-guide/

29   Brinton, Crane (1938) *The Anatomy of Revolution*. New York: Prentice-Hall, p. 24.

30   For a review of the Nadiya Savchenko story see: Shandra, Alya (30 March 2018) "The Rise and Fall of Nadiya Savchenko" *Euromaidan Press*. Ref: http://euro-maidanpress.com/2018/03/30/the-rise-and-fall-of-nadiya-savchenko/

31   This seems to be the intention of Onuch, Olga and Sasse, Gwendolyn (2016) "The Maidan in Movement: Diversity and Cycles of Protest" *Europe-Asia Studies*, vol. 68, pp. 556-587.

32   This is the intent of the Kremlin-inspired narrative promulgated by such western commentators as Prof. Stephen Cohen. For a list of his articles on the topic see: http://jordanrussiacenter.org/author/scohen/

33   Lane, David (2008) "The Orange Revolution: 'People's Revolution' or Revolutionary Coup?" *British Journal of Politics and International Relations* vol. 10, pp. 525-549.

34   The term "internal Maidan" seems to have been coined by deputy Prosecutor General David Sakvaralidze. See Musayeva, Sevhil (2 March 2016) "Давид Сакваралідзе: У нас внутрішній Майдан в системі прокуратури" *Ukrayinska Pravda*. Ref: www.pravda.com.ua/articles/2016/03/2/7100854/

35   "В Україні зростає протестна активність громадян – дослідження" (20 March 2013) *День*. Ref: www.day.kiev.ua/uk/news/200313-v-ukrayini-zrostaie-protestna-aktivnist-gromadyan-doslidzhennya

36   Budjeryn, Mariana and Rohrback, Robin (eds.) (15 Feb. 2014) "From Maidan the Camp to Maidan the Sich: What changed?" *Euromaidan Press*. Ref: http://euro-maidanpress.com/2014/02/15/from-maidan-the-camp-to-maidan-the-sich-what-changed/#arvlbdata

37   An excellent explanation of the legal issues pertaining to the post-Yanukovych government's legitimacy were published in a blog form here: http://www.david-morrison.org.uk/ukraine/why-ukrainian-regime-illegitimate.htm

38   I am indebted to my former MBA student, and now good friend Valerii Pekar (a serial entrepreneur and Maidan activist) for initially articulating this threefold characterization.

39   This perspective is typified by the work of Sakwa (2014), but also by analysts of the Woodrow Wilson Center—see Chapter 7.

40   Pomeranz, William E. (2016) "Ground Zero: How a Trade Dispute Sparked the Russia-Ukraine Crisis" *Roots of Russia's War in Ukraine*, Washington: Woodrow Wilson Center Press.

Chapter 2 — Antecedents of Revolution

1   This argument has been repeated extensively. For examples see: Arel, Dominque (1994) "Language and Group Boundaries in the Two Ukraines" paper presented at conference on "National Minorities, Nationalizing States, and External National Homelands in the New Europe," Bellagio Study and Conference Center, Italy, August 1994; Zimmerman, William (1998) "Is Ukraine a Political Community?" *Communist and Post-Communist Studies* vol. 31, no. 1; D'Anieri, Paul (2002) "Introduction: Debating the Assumptions of State-led Nation building in Ukraine" in Kuzio, Taras and D'Anieri, Paul (eds.) *Dilemmas of State-led Nation building in Ukraine*, Westport, London: Praeger; Hrycak, Alexandra (2006) "Institutional Legacies and Language Revival in Ukraine" in Arel, Dominque and Ruble, Blair (eds.) *Rebounding Identities: The Politics of Identity in Ukraine and Russia*; D'Anieri, Paul (2007) "Societal Divisions and the Challenge of Liberal Democracy in Ukraine" in *Understanding Ukrainian Politics: Power, Politics, and Institutional Design*, Armonk, London: M.E. Sharpe.

2   To determine language preference interviewees were asked in a mixed Ukrainian-Russian sentence (with alternating words in each language) which language they preferred to use to answer the survey.

3   Western region: Volyn', Rivne, Lviv, Ivano-Frankivsk, Ternopil, Zakarpattya, and Chernivtsi oblasts; West-Central: Khmelnytsky, Zhytomyr, Vinnytsia, Kirovohrad, Cherkasy, Kyiv oblasts and Kyiv city; East-Central: Dnipropetrovsk, Poltava, Sumy, and Chernihiv oblasts; South: Odesa, Mykolayiv, Kherson, Zaporizhzhia oblasts and A.R. Crimea; East: Kharkiv, Donetsk, and Luhansk oblasts.

4   Khmelko, Valeriy "Ethno-Linguistic Structure of Ukraine: Regional Features and Tendencies of Change during Independence" — Data from 2003 surveys N=22462

5   See Kuzio, Taras and D'Anieri, Paul (eds.) (2002) *Dilemmas of State-led Nation building in Ukraine*, Westport, London: Praeger.

6   The language of choice in the central regions of Ukraine is "Surzhyk" — a "creole" mixture of Ukrainian and Russian — see: http://kiis.com.ua/materials/articles_HVE/16_linguaethnical.pdf.

7   Forostyna, Oksana (2015) "Poaching, Simmering and Boiling: the Declining Relevance of Identity Discourse in Ukraine" in Wilson, Andrew (ed.) *What Ukrainians Think*, European Council on Foreign Relations.

8   Taras Kuzio ((2010) "Nationalism, identity and civil society in Ukraine: Understanding the Orange Revolution" in *Communist and Post-Communist Studies*, vol. 43, pp. 285–296) claims that the process of national awakening was central to the Orange Revolution protests. However, as Michael McFaul ((2007) "Ukraine Imports Democracy: External Influences on the Orange Revolution" *International Security*, vol. 32, no. 2, pp. 45–83), David Lane (2008), and Andrew Wilson (2005) have shown, the protest antecedents were much more complex.

9   Wilson, Andrew (2005) *Ukraine's Orange Revolution*, Yale University Press.

10   Wilson, Andrew (2005) *Virtual Politics: Faking Democracy in the Post-Soviet World*, Yale University Press.

11   This portrayal was personally painful to Yushchenko whose father had been interned in a Nazi concentration camp during WWII.

12   Pifer, Steven (14 May 2015) "Putin and Ukraine's east/west Divide" *Brookings Institution.* Ref: www.brookings.edu/blogs/order-from-chaos/posts/2015/05/14-putin-russia-divide-pifer

13   On 3 December 2004 Ukraine's Supreme Court ruled that pervasive cases of electoral fraud during the second round of voting made a just determination of the will of the people impossible. A repeat second round was ordered. It was witnessed by large teams of international observers sent from (among others) Canada and Poland.

14   This term originates from France—from the Presidential-Parliamentary system on which the Ukrainian system is modelled. It describes the situation when the in-post Prime Minister and President represent competing political parties.

15   Falconbridge, Guy, Dobrowska, Anna, Gray, Stephen (30 April 2014) "Toppled 'mafia' President cost Ukraine up to $100 billion, prosecutor says" *Reuters.* Ref: www.reuters.com/article/us-ukraine-crisis-yanukovich-idUSBREA3T0K820140430

16   See Chapters 5-7 of Kuzio, Taras (2017) *Putin's War Against Ukraine: Revolution, Nationalism and Crime,* Toronto: Chair of Ukrainian Studies.

17   Yanukovych's administrative reform consisted of a series of Decrees (№ 1085/2010 "On the optimization of the central bodies" and № 370/2011 "On the issue of optimization of the central bodies") issued (ironically) in fulfilment of a reform plan financed by Akhmetov's "Foundation for Effective Governance" and developed by the prestigious consulting company McKinzie. The plan was supposedly aimed at harmonizing the public sector with European governance structures, delineating the functions of a Ministry (policy), Agency (execution), and Inspection (control). In reality, it centralized government giving the President enormous powers.

18   Wilson, Andrew (2014) *Ukraine Crisis: What it Means for the West,* Yale University Press, p. 50.

19   Harding, Luke (27 April 2010) "Ukraine Parliamentary Vote on Black Sea fleet erupts in fist fight" *The Guardian.* Ref: www.theguardian.com/world/2010/apr/27/ukraine-parliament-fight-eggs

20   Sanford, Daniel (11 Oct. 2011) "West condemns Ukraine over Yulia Tymoshenko jailing" *BBC.* Ref: www.bbc.com/news/world-europe-15263475

21   A 5-floor building with a helicopter pad on the roof was built in a park in downtown Kyiv, ostensibly for use during for the Euro-2012 football championship.

22   In his hometown of Yenakieyevo, the name Yanukovych elicited harsh reactions a mere year after his election—see street interviews: www.youtube.com/watch?v=2nW79V58TCw. However, this criticism did not translate into anti-Yanukovych votes in the region.

23   Author's research presentation, University of Glasgow "Will Ukraine's political regime change soon?" (Feb. 2013).

24   Yanukovych first mentioned building the "Honka" mansion in Mezhyhiriya while on a visit to Germany. See Leshchenko, Serhij (31 Aug. 2010) "Німецький будинок Віктора Януковича" *Ukrayinska Pravda.* Ref: www.pravda.com.ua/articles/2010/08/31/5346144/ and Leshchenko, Serhij (8 June 2012) "Yanukovych, the luxury residence and the money trail that leads to London" *Open Democracy.* Ref: https://www.opendemocracy.net/od-russia/serhij-leschenko/yanukovychs-luxury-residence-and-money-trail-that-leads-to-london

25   Mishchenko, Mascha (3 Feb. 2011) "Податковий Майдан: влада намагається знищити і площу, і тих, хто на неї вийшов?" *UNIAN Information Agency.* Ref: www.unian.ua/politics/456163-podatkoviy-maydan-vlada-namagaetsya-znischiti-i-ploschu-i-tih-hto-na-neji-viyshov.html

26 "Соціологи зафіксували рекордну кількість протестів з 2009 року – дослідження" (2009) *UNIAN Information Agency*. Ref: http://press.unian.ua/pressnews/980748-sotsiologi-u-berezni-zafiksuvali-rekordnu-kilkist-protestiv-z-2009-roku-doslidjennya.html

27 "Українські музиканти про мовний закон" (5 July 2012) *BBC*. Ref: www.bbc.com/ukrainian/entertainment/2012/07/120705_singers_language_law_oz

28 According to a survey taken in 2012, over 60% of Ukrainians (regardless of region) believed that at a local level, police violence was pervasive—see Zaikina, Zhanna (2012) "Protection From Torture And Other Ill-Treatment" in Bushchenko, Arkadiy and Zakharov, Yevhen (eds.), *Human Rights in Ukraine* Kyiv: Ukrainian Helsinki Human Rights Union. Ref: http://helsinki.org.ua/index.php?id=1362722817

29 "Протетстні настрої населення: останні тенденції" (11 June 2013) *Democratic Initiatives Foundation*. Ref: https://dif.org.ua/article/protestni-nastroi-naselennya-ostanni-tendentsii

30 "Падающая башня" (27 June 2013) *Корреспондент* No. 25.

31 "Електоральні настрої населення України, березень 2013" (15 March 2013) *Kyiv International Institute of Sociology*. Ref: www.kiis.com.ua/?lang=ukr&cat=reports&id=148&y=2013&m=3&page=1

32 "Колесніков розповів емісару ЄС про незмінність європейського курсу України" (26 Oct. 2011) *Gazeta.ua*. Ref: http://gazeta.ua/articles/politics/_kolesnikov-rozpoviv-komisaru-es-pro-nezminnist-yevropejskogo-kursu-ukrayini/406569

33 When Yanukovych was asked in Austria about the government's decision to cease preparations for the signing of the EU-Ukraine Association agreement, he is reported to have said: "Ukraine has proceeded and will continue to proceed along the path of Eurointegration" (Koshkina, 2015:24).

34 Zinchenko, Oleksandr (17 Feb. 2015) "Щоденник Майдану. Про що ми тоді думали" *Istorychna Pravda*. Ref: www.istpravda.com.ua/articles/2015/02/17/147354/

35 In a poll conducted in October 2013, the Party of Regions enjoyed a mere 20% support nationally (heavily concentrated in the eastern oblasts), Batkivshchyna polled 19.4%. Klitschko's Udar Party enjoyed 14.8% support, while the Communists polled 7% and Svoboda—5%. Almost one third of respondents either refused to answer or said they would not take part in elections. For detailed polling data from 2010 to 2013 see: www.razumkov.org.ua/ukr/poll.php?poll_id=115

36 I missed Mustafa's initial "call to arms" in Kyiv due to a teaching assignment at Lviv Business School.

37 Van Zon, Hans (2001) "Neo-patrimonialism as an impediment to economic development" *Journal of Communist Studies and Transition Politics* vol. 17, issue 3, pp. 71-95.

38 Koshiw, Jaroslav V. (2002) *Beheaded: The killing of a journalist*, Artemia Press Ltd.

39 For a description of the "Ukraine without Kuchma" protests see: Mykhelson, Oleksandr (11 March 2011) "The First Revolution – 10 years later" *Ukrainian Week*. Ref: http://ukrainianweek.com/Politics/19091

40 Onuch, Olga (2014) *Mapping Mass Mobilizations*, Palgrave Macmillan, Ch. 3.

41 Wilson, Andrew (2005) *Ukraine's Orange Revolution*, New Haven: Yale University Press.

42 In June 2016, during a conference in Euro College Natolin (Warsaw) which aimed to find commonality between Ukraine's three revolutions, the organizers suggested the presence of a continuum: 1) Maidan was always the central focal point, and the tactic was occupation; 2) Each subsequent Maidan has put forth increasingly universalistic demands—evolving from the very specific demand for military service within Ukrainian SSR to a universal claim of "dignity"; 3) Each major Maidan was preceded by minor protests in the same place—Ukraine without Kuchma in 2001 preceded the Orange Revolution in 2004; the 2010 Tax Maidan preceded the 2013 Euromaidan.

43 "Huge Ukraine rally over EU Agreement delay" (24 Nov. 2013) *BBC*. Ref: www.bbc.com/news/world-europe-25078952

44 Author's translation of interview with O. Turchynov in Koshkina, Sonia (2015) *Майдан: Нерассказанная история*, p. 38.

45 See "Михайло Винницький про ЄвроМайдан". Ref: www.youtube.com/watch?v=xS5x4FbZnc8

46 "На Євромайдані розпочалася бійка: мітингувальники розтрощили автомобіль з "прослушкою" СБУ" (25 Nov. 2013) *ТСН*. Ref: http://tsn.ua/politika/na-yevromaydani-vlashtuvali-provokaciyi-nevidomi-z-simvolikoyu-batkivschini-pochalasya-biyka-322003.html

47 Wilson, Andrew (2005)*Ukraine's Orange Revolution*, New Haven: Yale University Press

48 According to Ukrainian law, the right to strike is guaranteed only to individuals who are employed, and so the student action could not officially be called a "strike."

49 Video of Kvit's statement is here: www.youtube.com/watch?v=UFsDsktuqGU

50 "10 днів, які змінили Україну: 26 листопада" (26 Nov. 2014) *BBC*. Ref: www.bbc.com/ukrainian/politics/2014/11/141121_10_days_in_november_2013_26_az

51 For a synopsis of Yanukovych's interview on the eve of the Vilnius summit, see: www.youtube.com/watch?v=MqS_dw-maCM. Full version: www.youtube.com/watch?v=GGMwGv04u0E

52 Until the last minute, EU leaders sought to convince Yanukovych to sign. See Gotev, Georgi (29 Nov. 2013) "Ukraine, EU dig in heels as Vilnius summit opens" *Euroactiv*. Ref: www.euractiv.com/section/europe-s-east/news/ukraine-eu-dig-in-heels-as-vilnius-summit-opens/

Chapter 3—Maidan Becomes "Sich"

1 During the 18-19 centuries, the term "Moskal'" referred to a soldier of the Russian imperial army. During the early 20th century, it came to be used by Ukrainians as a demeaning term for all Russians. However, the term is not as insulting as, for example, "Katsap".

2 Farion had been vocal in her condemnation of what she saw as "russification" policies instituted by the Yanukovych regime. She gained notoriety in the wake of her visit to a Lviv nursery school where she was filmed scolding children for calling themselves Masha and Dasha—the Russian diminutives of Maria and Daria.

3 I was employed as a "chronicler" (political commentator) by Savik Shuster appearing regularly on the Monday-Thursday evening broadcasts of the ShusterLive talk show throughout 2008-2009. In early 2010, the "chronicler" format was discontinued.

4   The full 29 November 2013 program can be viewed here: www.youtube.com/
    watch?v=y8Fp5kcj98o

5   For details on the incident with Yatseniuk and the sound system see Koshkina
    (2014), pp. 56-60.

6   "Попов сообщил ГПУ, что выполнял распоряжения Клюева" (14 Dec. 2014)
    Zerkalo Nedeli. Ref: http://zn.ua/POLITICS/popov-soobschil-gpu-chto-vypolnyal
    -rasporyazheniya-klyueva-135077_.html

7   The term "yolka" means Christmas tree in Russian, but the word achieved notori-
    ety after a televised speech by Yanukovych, during which he could not recall the
    Ukrainian word "yalynka", and after a 10 second pause, used the Russian equiva-
    lent. See: www.youtube.com/watch?v=sYRjvs3Y-Wk

8   Koshkina (2015), pp. 74-85.

9   Koshkina (2015), pp. 67-68.

10 Supporters of the Euromaidan movement abroad gathered on December 1 in many
    world capitals to demonstrate their support for Ukraine's eurointegration, and
    many EU leaders continued to believe this issue to be salient.

11 A popular slogan born that weekend was "Yanukovych pid aresht!" This was a
    play on words: pronounced correctly it was a call for Yanukovych to be arrested,
    but the phrase sounds very similar to "piderast"—a demeaning term for a homo-
    sexual.

12 Zubko later became Minister of Infrastructure and Deputy Premier in the first two
    post-Yanukovych governments.

13 Koshkina (2015), p. 89—author's translation from Russian original.

14 Strazhnyy, Oleksandr (2016) *Maidan: Podiyi – Svidchennia – Mentalitet*, Kyiv: Dukh
    i Litera, p. 46.

15 Koshkina (2015), p. 90—excerpt of interview with O. Turchynov.

16 Arsen Avakov, the opposition MP from Kharkiv who later became Minister of the
    Interior, kept the napkin as a souvenir—photo in Koshkina (2015), p. 128.

17 I attribute this description of the situation to Valerii Pekar (personal conversa-
    tions).

18 The incident with the tractor was stopped by Petro Poroshenko. This act of bravery
    was the first of several that would propel Poroshenko's rise from opposition MP
    to eventual election as Ukraine's President.

19 "Корчинський після штурму Банкової виїхав до Росії, а покловник Беркуту
    міг займатися провокаціями" (5 Dec. 2013) *TCH*. Ref: http://tsn.ua/poli-
    tika/korchinskiy-pislya-shturmu-bankovoyi-viyihav-do-rosiyi-a-polkovnik-
    berkutu-mig-zaymatisya-provokaciyami-323778.html. According to Andrew Wil-
    son "Dmytro Korchynsky had a long tradition of working for Kremlin organiza-
    tions and speaking at pro-Putin summer camps in Russia." Wilson (2005), p. 69.

20 Kyrychenko, Vladyslav "Black side of the Maidan" (2015) in Mukharsky, Antin
    (ed.) *Майдан: (р)еволюція духу*, Kyiv: Nash Format.

21 Koshkina (2015), p. 98.

22 Koshkina (2015), p. 100.

23 Kirichenko (2015), pp. 51-56.

24 Wilson (2014), p. 70.

25 On 10 December the units broke out of their surrounded Vasylkiv quarters.

26 Strazhnyy (2016), p. 8.

27 Koshkina (2015), p. 102.

28 Ukraine's Constitution limits the number of times a confidence motion in the gov-
    ernment can be tabled in Parliament to once per session. The in-force version of the

Constitution (i.e. the 1996 text that Ukraine reverted to after 2010), allowed the President to dismiss the government at any time.

29   Strazhnyy (2016), pp. 153-154.
30   Among those charged was Valerii Garagutz, a journalist from Dnipropetrovsk, who was accused of assaulting 70 (!) Berkut officers. In fact, Valerii had been knocked unconscious by a "Berkut" officer while trying to provide first aid to an injured colleague. He lay on the December pavement face down for several hours—see Koshkina (2014), p. 99.
31   Strazhnyy (2016), p. 68.
32   BBC estimated up to 2 million, but this seems somewhat overstated.
33   Strazhnyy (2016), pp. 68-80.
34   Koshkina (2015), pp. 133-141.
35   Ashton, Catherine (2014) "Message by EU High Representative Catherine Ashton to Maidan protesters" European Commission. Ref: http://europa.eu/rapid/press-release_SPEECH-13-1060_en.htm
36   "John McCain tells Ukraine protesters: 'We are here to support you!'" (15 Dec. 2013) *The Guardian*. Ref: www.theguardian.com/world/2013/dec/15/john-mccain-ukraine-protests-support-just-cause
37   Koshkina (2015).
38   "Дві третини Киян підтримують Євромайдан" (19 Dec. 2013) *Ukrayinska Pravda*. Ref: www.pravda.com.ua/news/2013/12/19/7007755/
39   Journalists immediately contacted the EU ambassador in Kyiv, who clarified that no such requirement had ever been tabled in any negotiation, and that visa regimes and national legislation on marriage were not related.
40   Shymkiv took leave from Microsoft at the start of the protests—a fact that some interpreted as a PR stunt. Later, Mr. Shymkiv was to become Deputy Head of the Poroshenko Administration responsible for reforms.
41   I am proud that in both of these cases, the support to Maidan was provided by business owners who had previously completed the MBA program that I directed at Kyiv-Mohyla Business School.
42   Wilson (2014), p. 74.
43   Strazhnyy (2016), p. 91.
44   The VUM initiative continued in January when Ukrainian House on European Square was occupied by Maidan activists, and the stage near Lyatsky Gate was dismantled. After Yanukovych's ouster, VUM moved its activities to an online format (vum.org.ua), offering courses for civic activists.
45   See: www.facebook.com/mychailo.wynnyckyj/timeline/story?ut=60&wstart=1385884800&wend=1388563199&hash=3472839685389271950&pagefilter=3
46   www.facebook.com/OleksandrStarodubtsev/posts/1076587359038498
47   Strazhnyy (2016), p. 95.
48   The NOM was later renamed into the "All-Ukrainian Assembly "Maidan" (Vseukrayinske obyednannia "Maidan").
49   Wilson (2014), p. 75.

Chapter 4 — Descent into Violence

1   Evidence of the direct involvement of Yanukovych's Chief of Security Konstantyn Kobzar in Chornovol's beating was found in Mezhyhiriya after the President's ouster. See: Wilson (2014), p. 77

2   "Тетяна Чорновіл пробралася в Межигір'я" (27 Aug. 2012) *TVi* . Ref: www.you tube.com/watch?v=PisHecewK_k

3   Chornovol, Tetjana and Lutsenko, Ihor (25 July 2013) "Царські справи – нове "Межигіря" для Януковича в Криму" *Ukrayinska Pravda*. Ref: www.pravda. com.ua/articles/2013/07/25/6994933/

4   Interfax Ukraine "Svoboda demands to qualify beating of Ilyenko as attempted murder" (4 Jan. 2014) *Kyiv Post*. Ref: www.kyivpost.com/article/content/ukraine-politics/svoboda-demands-to-categorize-beating-of-mp-ilyenko-lawyer-kizin-as-attempted-murder-334661.html

5   Grytsenko, Oksana (23 Jan. 2014) "Kidnapped activist Verbytsky found dead; activist Lutsenko describes abduction" *Kyiv Post*. Ref: www.kyivpost.com/article/content/euromaidan/kidnapped-activist-verbytsky-found-dead-activist-lutsenko-describes-abduction-335401.html.

6   Marson, James (31 Jan. 2014) "Missing Ukraine Protester Turns Up Badly Bruised" *The Wall Street Journal*. Ref: www.wsj.com/articles/missing-ukraine-protester-bulatov-turns-up-1391158592

7   Rybak's request to be barricaded was confirmed by Poroshenko. Koshkina (2015), p. 167.

8   "16 січня рік тому – як це відбувалося, і які мало наслідки" (16 Jan. 2015) *24TV*. Ref: http://24tv.ua/16_sichnya_rik_tomu_yak_tse_vidbuvalosya_i_yaki_malo_naslidki_n532318

9   The President's Press Secretary Darka Chepak, and the head of the Strategic Research Institute, Andriy Yermolayev, among others, were also dismissed that day.

10 The signatories included Vyacheslav Brioukhovetsky (former President of Kyiv-Mohyla Academy), Yaroslav Hrytsak (renowned historian), Serhiy Zhadan (poet), Yosyf Zisels (human rights activist), Myroslav Marynovych (Soviet dissident), Aleksandr Paskhaver (economist), and Myroslav Popovych (philosopher).

11 Koshkina (2015), p. 176.

12 Pravyy Sektor's proclaimed political goal was the creation of a "Ukrainian totalitarian nationalist state". Their initial proclamations (early January 2014) rejected the legitimacy of both the Yanukovych regime, and of the parliamentary opposition leaders. They ridiculed Maidan as a "song and dance festival", and they called on all young people who wished to be heroes to join them with molotov cocktails on Hrushevskoho St. to "destroy the regime's dogs."

13 Koshkina (2015), p. 188.

14 Strazhnyy (2016), pp. 183-185.

15 The bullets were identified as the type used for apprehending vehicles by puncturing their tyres. Koshkina (2015), p. 184.

16 Strazhnyy (2016), interview with Berkut officer, p. 188.

17 Wilson (2014), p. 84.

18 Koshkina (2015), pp. 191-194.

19 Koshkina (2015), pp. 186-187.

20 Koshkina (2015), p. 195.

21 Strazhnyy (2016), p. 202.

22 Sindelar, Daisy (27 Jan. 2014) "Who are Ukraine's 'Ultras'?" *RFE/RL*. Ref: www.rferl.org/a/ukraine-protests-sports-fans-euromaidan/25244357.html

23 Strazhnyy (2016), p. 203.

24 Koshkina (2015), p. 200.

25 On Saturday January 20, Akhmetov's System Capital Management (SCM) issued a statement condemning the use of force to resolve Ukraine's political crisis.

26 During a speech at the Yalta European Strategy conference in 2013, Yanukovych described Ukraine as "squeezed between two large monsters: the EU and Russia." The Lithuanian President, Dalia Grybauskaite, forcefully reminded her Ukrainian counterpart that "the EU is not a monster."

27 Gorchinskaya, Katja (21 March 2014) "Putin's original plan for Ukraine" *Kyiv Post*. Ref: www.kyivpost.com/article/opinion/op-ed/putins-original-plan-for-ukraine -340233.html

28 Koshkina (2015:183-184) suggests that the murders of Nigoyan and Zhesnevsky on January 20 were possibly "ritual killings" aimed at aggravating the situation—i.e. stimulating mass violence, and an appropriate regime reaction.

29 On February 4, Polish Foreign Minister Radoslav Sikorski warned of "apocalyptic" consequences if a peaceful resolution to the stand-off with Maidan could not be found. This was echoed by US Assistant Secretary of State Nuland on 6 February after her meeting with Yanukovych.

30 To demonstrate his displeasure with the actions of Yanukovych, on 29 January Putin ordered an increase in tariffs on Ukrainian imports to Russia from 5% to 40%, effective immediately.

31 Strazhnyy (2016), p. 212.

32 Violent clashes had occurred during the previous weeks in various regions of Ukraine, and "titushky" thugs continued to roam the streets of Kyiv, brutalizing passers-by suspected of being Maidan supporters, destroying their property (including burning cars), but the epicenter of the protests seemed to be gradually calming.

33 Koshkina (2015), p. 228.

34 Strazhnyy (2016), p. 241. Koshkina (2015), p. 247.

35 Koshkina (2015), p. 264.

36 Koshkina (2015), p. 270.

37 Koshkina (2015), p. 254.

38 "Під'їзди до Києва блокують, машини перевіряють, люди їдуть лісами" (19 Feb. 2014) *Ukrayinska Pravda*. Ref: www.pravda.com.ua/news/2014/02/19/ 7014696/

39 Koshkina (2015), p. 281.

40 According to subsequent investigations by Hromadske TV, the Conservatory shooter was Ivan Bubenchik. See: Gorchynskaya, Katja (26 Feb. 2016) "He Killed for the Maidan" *Foreign Policy*. Ref: http://foreignpolicy.com/2016/02/26/he-killed-for-the-maidan/

41 Video of the Berkut retreat: https://www.youtube.com/watch?v=IWzI9V3WSnc

42 For example: "Kyiv – Bloody Battle on Maydan". Ref: www.youtube.com/watch? v=U4GbDgN7emM

43 "No justice one year on for those killed in Kiev's Maidan Square" (20 Feb. 2015) *Financial Times*. Ref: www.ft.com/content/fbc442ec-b844-11e4-86bb-00144feab7de

44 Katchanovski, Ivan (5 Sept. 2015) "The 'Snipers' Massacre' on the Maidan in Ukraine". Available at SSRN: https://ssrn.com/abstract=2658245 or http://dx. doi.org/10.2139/ssrn.2658245

45 MacAskill, Ewen (5 March 2014) "Ukraine crisis: bugged call reveals conspiracy theory about Kiev snipers" *The Guardian*. Ref: www.theguardian.com/ world/2014/mar/05/ukraine-bugged-call-catherine-ashton-urmas-paet

46 A "Postanova" is a one-time legislative order that has the force of law but need not be signed by the President.

47 "Agreement on the settlement of crisis in Ukraine – full text" (21 Feb. 2014) *The Guardian*. Ref: www.theguardian.com/world/2014/feb/21/agreement-on-the-settlement-of-crisis-in-ukraine-full-text

48 "Сікорскі, вмовляючи Раду Майдану, сказав, що інакше всі помруть" (21 Feb. 2014) *Ukrayinska Pravda*. Ref: www.pravda.com.ua/news/2014/02/21/7015576/

49 That announcement marked the birth of Dr. Ulana Suprun's initiative called "Patriot Defense" which later transformed into a program of training in combat medicine for Ukraine's Army and volunteer battalions.

50 Klitschko later apologized both for shaking hands with Yanukovych and for negotiating a deal with him but justified his actions as having been aimed at maintaining peace: "Кличко вибачився перед Майданом і готовий вимагати від Януковича піти" (21 Feb. 2014) *Ukrayinska Pravda*. Ref: www.pravda.com.ua/news/2014/02/21/7015611/

51 Parasiuk's speech may be viewed here: www.youtube.com/watch?v=M01BVoOfJL8

Chapter 5—Climax and Recoil

1 "Янукович вилетів до Харкова" (21 Feb. 2014) *Dzerkalo Tyzhnia*. Ref: https://dt.ua/POLITICS/yanukovich-viletiv-do-harkova-138060_.html). That night, many (including me) tracked what seemed to be Yanukovych's plane on flightradar24.com until 4:30 am Kyiv time when it landed in the Arab Emirates. The aircraft circled Dubai and then diverted to Fujairah airport. According to later reports, Yanukovych's second wife (with whom he lived in Mezhyhiriya in a common-law relationship, while remaining officially married to his first wife, Liudmyla), and their young child were onboard. But according to Kharkiv oblast governor Mykhailo Dobkin, Yanukovych's common-law wife arrived with him to Kharkiv that night (Koshkina 2015:315). The contents of the airplane flying from Kyiv to the Arab Emirates on February 21-22 remains unknown. The evacuation of valuables (including large amounts of cash) from Mezhyhiriya was completed as Yanukovych departed, so it is possible that the purpose of the flight to Fujairah was to secure possessions rather than persons.

2 "Калетник втік до Росії" (22 Feb. 2014) *Espresso TV*. Ref: http://espreso.tv/news/2014/02/22/kaletnyk_vtik_do_rosiyi

3 "Верховна Рада повернула Конституцію 2004 року" (21 Feb. 2014) *UNIAN Information Agency*. Ref: www.unian.ua/politics/887883-verhovna-rada-povernula-konstitutsiyu-2004-roku.html

4 "Полное интервью Януковича". Ref: www.youtube.com/watch?v=LNh-fup8KK0

5 "Янукович: я не збираюся у відставку" (22 Feb. 2014) *Ukrayinska Pravda*. Ref: www.pravda.com.ua/news/2014/02/22/7015766/

6 Later this claim was called untrue by Speaker Rybak who had travelled with Yanukovych to Kharkiv: "Рибак спростував заяву Януковича, що у нього стріляли" (23 Feb. 2014) *Tyzhden'*. Ref: http://tyzhden.ua/News/102979

7 The Kivalov-Kolesnichenko Law on Languages was ruled unconstitutional (contravened by Article 10) by Ukraine's Constitutional Court in 2018.

8 Wilson (2005).

9 Koshkina (2015), p. 310.

10   Quote from Koshkina (2015:319). The morning after his departure, the Mezhyhiriya guards opened the grounds to Maidan activists and journalists. Their im-
pressions were broadcast through live streaming: "Журналістів пустили в
резиденцію Межигір'я" (22 Feb. 2014) *LB.ua*. Ref: http://ukr.lb.ua/news/
2014/02/22/256622_zhurnalistov_pustili_rezidentsiyu.html

11   Koshkina (2015), p. 321.

12   According to the story recounted by Vladimir Putin in the film "Crimea: Return
Home", Russian Special Forces attempted to extract Yanukovych from Ukrainian
territory when his cortege reached the Sea of Azov (presumably either in Donetsk
or Zaporizhzhia oblast) but was unsuccessful.

13   Carcetti, Tommy (19 Feb. 2015) "One year ago today, Victor Yanukovych began
packing his valuables in preparation for leaving Ukraine" — video:
www.democraticunderground.com/10026247627

14   "Депутати з'їзду в Харкові перебирають владу на Південному сході та в
Криму" (22 Feb. 2014) *Ukrayinska Pravda*. Ref: www.pravda.com.ua/news/
2014/02/22/7015713/

15   The US Foreign Assistance Act (1961): "restricts assistance to the government of
any country whose duly elected head of government is deposed by military coup
or decree." Similar legislation exists in multiple EU countries. See: Fisher, Max (3
July 2013) "Law says U.S. is required to cut aid after coups. Will it?" *The Washington
Post*. Ref: www.washingtonpost.com/news/worldviews/wp/2013/07/03/law-
says-the-u-s-is-required-to-cut-aid-after-coups-will-it/

16   "Допа і Гепа втекли в Росію" (22 Feb. 2014) *Ukrayinska Pravda*. Ref: www.pravda.
com.ua/news/2014/02/22/7015803/

17   According to NATO estimates, in late February 2014 over 150,000 Russian troops
were placed on alert on the border with Ukraine. See: Strange, Hannah and Oli-
phant, Roland (26 Feb. 2014) "Ukraine revolution: 150,000 Russian troops on alert
as U.S. warns Putin" *The Telegraph*. Ref: www.telegraph.co.uk/news/
worldnews/europe/ukraine/10662187/Ukraine-revolution-Protesters-in-stand-
off-in-pro-Russian-Crimea.html

18   Interview with Serhiy Pashynsky, Acting Head of the Presidential Administration
in Berezovets, Taras (2015) *Анексія: Острів Крим, хроніки «гібридної війни*, Kyiv:
Bright Star Publishing, p. 38.

19   Charbonneau, Louis (4 March 2014) "Russia: Yanukovych asked Putin to use force
to save Ukraine" *Reuters*. Ref: www.reuters.com/article/us-ukraine-crisis-un/russia-
yanukovich-asked-putin-to-use-force-to-save-ukraine-idUSBREA2224720140304

20   "Буде хаос: Глазьєв лякає Україну перспективою розколу у разі підписання
УА" (24 Sept. 2013) *Bigmir.net*. Ref: http://news.bigmir.net/ukraine/754290-Byde
-haos-Glazev-lyakae-Ykrainy-perspektivou-rozkoly-y-razi-pidpisannya-YA

21   Interview with Dmytro Bilotserkivets, Crimean "Udar" party youth wing activist,
and native of Sevastopol, in Berezovets (2015), p. 48.

22   Veselova, Victoria (24 Feb. 2016) "Севастополь-2014: як почалася окупація
Криму" *RFE/RL Krym:Realiyi*. Ref: https·//ua.krymr.com/a/27570900.html

23   Williams, Phil and Picarelli, John (March 2001) "Organized Crime in Ukraine:
Challenge and Response" *Trends in Organized Crime*, vol. 6, Issue 3-5, pp. 100-142.

24   Berezovets (2015), p. 41.

25   Interview with Turchynov in Berezovets, p. 86 — author's translation from Ukrainian

26   Berezovets (2015), p. 94.

27 Aksionov claimed that his candidacy had been submitted by the "legitimate President of Ukraine," but when asked about this during his 28 February press conference from Rostov-on-Don, Yanukovych denied having submitted Aksionov's
name for confirmation to the Crimean Parliament.

28 According to Berezovets (2015:52) Aksionov's gang was called "Salem"—apparently named after the cigarette brand. Speaker Konstiantinov headed the "Consol"
construction company whose reputation for illegally buying building permits was
preceded only by its reputation for defaulting on bank loans and investor prepay-
ments.

29 In a televised film recounting Crimea's "Return Home" (first aired on 8 March
2015) President Putin admitted as much, boasting that it was on 27 February that
he first ordered Russian Special Forces into action on the peninsula. For a summary
of the film see Wynnyckyj, Mychailo (18 March 2015) "Crimea: the Road to the
Homland. The Putimentary" *Circus Bazaar*. Ref: www.circusbazaar.com/crimea-
the-road-to-the-homeland-the-putimentary/

30 Interview with Dmytro Tymchuk, in Berezovets (2015), p. 56.

31 The appeal was supported by 246 Parliamentarians. Deputies elected from consti-
uencies in the Autonomous Republic of Crimea did not vote in favor.

32 The Agreement required the guarantors of Ukraine's sovereignty and territorial
integrity to consult one another if a breach should occur. According to strict legal
procedures, the US, UK and others did not violate the agreement: in the aftermath
of Russia's aggression, the UN Security Council discussed the issue at length.

33 "Statement by the President on Ukraine" (28 Feb. 2014) *The White House*. Ref:
https://obamawhitehouse.archives.gov/the-press-office/2014/02/28/statement
-president-ukraine

34 For map of facilities occupied by Russian forces see "Составлена карта
расположения российских войск в Крьму" (1 March 2014) *Glavred*. Ref:
http://glavred.info/politika/sostavlena-karta-raspolozheniya-rossiysk-voysk-v-
krymu-272674.html

35 "Совет Федерации разрешил Путину ввести войска на Украину" (1 March
2014) *Lenta.ru*. Ref: https://lenta.ru/news/2014/03/01/sovfed/

36 "Аксьонов став прем'єр міністром Криму з порушенням закону – указ
Турчинова" (1 March 2014) *24TV*. Ref: https://24tv.ua/aksonov
_stav_premyerministrom_ar_krim_z_porushennyam_zakonu__ukaz_turchi-
nova_n415262

37 "Тимчук назвав кількість зрадників в окупованому Криму" (6 Nov. 2017)
Segodnia. Ref: https://ukr.segodnya.ua/regions/krym/tymchuk-nazval-kolichestvo-
predateley-v-okkupirovannom-krymu-1069850.html. Later, Turchynov provided details on numbers of defectors from the SBU, Border police, and Internal Affairs—
see: "З усіх силовиків Криму під час окупації Україну не зрадили менше 20%
- Турчинов" (27 Feb. 2017) *TCH*. Ref: https://tsn.ua/politika/z-usih-silovikiv-
krimu-pid-chas-okupaciyi-ukrayinu-ne-zradili-menshe-20-turchinov-887945.html

38 The Ukrainian military had been neglected by successive governments for decades, and especially during the Yanukovych Presidency.

39 "Юлій Мамчур: армія за рік навчилася вважати Росію агресором" (3 March
2015) *BBC*. Ref: www.bbc.com/ukrainian/politics/2015/03/150302_yulii_mamchur
_interview_vc

40 For a video report of the event, see: www.youtube.com/watch?v
=DPXV2XOhmoU

41 "Курсанти, які співали в Криму гімн України, стали лейтенантами в Одесі" (26 Feb. 2016) *Ukrayinska Pravda*. Ref: www.pravda.com.ua/news/2016/02/26/7100403/

42 Ensign ("Praporshchyk") Serhiy Kokurin was killed in Simferopil on March 18 during a firefight with Russian forces storming the Ukrainian Naval facility where Kokurin was on guard duty.

43 "Ukraine Crisis: 'Illegal' Crimean referendum condemned" (6 March 2014) *BBC*. Ref: www.bbc.com/news/world-europe-26475508

44 "В Севастополі за відокремлення проголосували 123% населення" (17 March 2014) *Texty.org.ua* Ref: http://texty.org.ua/pg/newtextynewseditor/read/52528/V_Sevastopoli_za_vidokremlenna_progolosuvaly_123_naselenna

45 "Динаміка ставлення населення України до Росії та населення Росії до України, яких відносин з Росією хотіли б українці" (4 March 2014) *Kyiv International Institute of Sociology*. Ref: www.kiis.com.ua/?lang=ukr&cat=reports&id=236

46 Gregory, Paul R. (5 May 2014) "Putin's 'Human Rights Council' Accidentally Posts Real Crimean Election Results" *Forbes*. Ref: www.forbes.com/sites/paulroderickgregory/2014/05/05/putins-human-rights-council-accidentally-posts-real-crimean-election-results-only-15-voted-for-annexation/#68c0ebd5f172

47 Dreyfuss, Bob (19 March 2014) "Full text and analysis of Putin's Crimea speech" *The Nation*. Ref: www.thenation.com/article/full-text-and-analysis-putins-crimea-speech/

48 Croft, Adrian (2 April 2014 "Russia could achieve Ukraine incursion in 3-5 days - NATO general") *Reuters*. Ref: https://uk.reuters.com/article/uk-ukraine-crisis-breedlove/russia-could-achieve-ukraine-incursion-in-3-5-days-nato-general-id UKBREA310J820140402

49 Gregory, Paul R. (7 April 2014) "Putin's Attack On East Ukraine Began Today: What This Means For Europe And The US" *Forbes*. Ref: www.forbes.com/sites/paulroderickgregory/2014/04/07/putins-attack-on-ukraine-began-today-what-this-means-for-europe-and-the-us/#145ab06b5617

50 Kazansky, Denis (26 Sept. 2014) "Привид «ХНР» - з підвалу на базар" *Tyzhden'*. Ref: http://tyzhden.ua/Society/119962

51 During Anti-Maidan demonstrations in Kharkiv in March, several (supposedly local) protesters were caught on camera asking for directions; they mistook a local theatre for the oblast administration building.

52 Chekalkin, Dmitry (7 Dec. 2014) "How Russia invaded Ukraine as told by FSB colonel Girkin" *Euromaidan Press*. Ref: http://euromaidanpress.com/2014/12/07/fsb-colonel-girkin-tells-details-of-how-russia-invaded-ukraine-in-twice-censored-interview/

53 Shtepa would later be removed from office by the "separatists" and replaced by the "people's mayor" Vyacheslav Ponomarev. In 2015 Shtepa was charged by the Ukrainian state for inciting separatism.

54 "У Донецькій області почалась анти-терорестична операція – Турчинов" (15 April 2014) *Ukrayinska Pravda*. Ref: www.pravda.com.ua/news/2014/04/15/7022458/

55 "Ukrainian troops in control of Donetsk Oblast's Kramatorsk airfield, Ukrainian deputy prime minister says several hundred Russian troops in Ukraine" (16 April 2014) *Kyiv Post*. Ref: www.kyivpost.com/content/ukraine/turchynov-anti-terrorist-operation-has-begun-in-northern-donetsk-343563.html

56 Sergatskova, Kateryna (15 April 2015) "Глава уряду самопроголошеної Донецької народної республіки: 'Зараз мені ніколи займатися МММ'" *Ukrayinska Pravda*. Ref: www.pravda.com.ua/articles/2014/04/15/7022531/

57 Amoss, Howard (30 April 2015) "'There was heroism and cruelty on both sides': the truth behind one of Ukraine's deadliest days" *The Guardian*. Ref: www.theguardian.com/world/2015/apr/30/there-was-heroism-and-cruelty-on-both-sides-the-truth-behind-one-of-ukraines-deadliest-days

58 Because the masked men seemed to not know their way around (i.e. they were not Odesa natives), police officers led the pro-Russian demonstrators through the streets of the city. See: www.youtube.com/watch?v=ixWRe49o7XY

59 Cohen, Tamara (25 March 2014) "G8 becomes the G7 as leaders kick Russia out: It's not a big problem, says Putin's foreign minister" *Daily Mail*. Ref: www.dailymail.co.uk/news/article-2588490/G8-G7-leaders-kick-Russia-Its-not-big-problem-says-Putins-foreign-minister.html

60 Borger, Julian and Luhn, Alec (17 April 2014) "Ukraine Crisis: Geneva talks produce agreement on defusing conflict" *The Guardian*. Ref: www.theguardian.com/world/2014/apr/17/ukraine-crisis-agreement-us-russia-eu

61 Birnbaum, Michael, Kunkle, Fredrick and Denyer, Simon (7 May 2014) "Putin calls for postponement of separatists' referendum in eastern Ukraine" *Washington Post*. Ref: www.washingtonpost.com/world/europe/putin-calls-for-postponement-of-separatists-referendum-in-eastern-ukraine/2014/05/07/a041c261-b47f-47ae-8f33-51ef9d1b92c8_story.html?utm_term=.83ad4195e7ad

62 Blair, David (7 May 2014) "Ukraine Crisis: Vladimir Putin urges separatists to postpone referendum" *The Telegraph*. Ref: www.telegraph.co.uk/news/worldnews/europe/ukraine/10814402/Ukraine-crisis-Vladimir-Putin-urges-separatists-to-postpone-referendum.html

63 "Після втечі Януковича в скарбниці залишилося 108 133 гривні 65 копійок. Документ" (11 March 2017) *Censor.net*. Ref: https://censor.net.ua/ua/news/431546/pislya_vtechi_yanukovycha_v_skarbnytsi_zaly-shalosya_108_133_gryvni_65_kopiyiok_dokument

64 Kramer, Andrew E. (2 March 2014) "Ukraine Turns to Its Oligarchs for Political Help" *The New York Times*. Ref: www.nytimes.com/2014/03/03/world/europe/ukraine-turns-to-its-oligarchs-for-political-help.html

65 During the spring and summer of 2014, Kolomoisky turned Dnipropetrovsk (officially renamed Dnipro in 2016) into a fortress. All roads into the city were equipped with an electronic system of vehicle checks, and personnel were deployed to man checkpoints. Volunteer battalions were organized, equipped and funded – a fact that became problematic once the Ukrainian Armed Forces had been rebuilt by the end of 2015.

66 "Віденська зустріч Порошенка з Фірташем тривала 28 годин – ЗМІ" (8 June 2015) *Dzerkalo Tyzhnia*. Ref: https://dt.ua/POLITICS/videnska-zustrich-poroshenka-z-firtashem-trivala-28-godin-zmi-175216_.html

67 "Рада зробила перший крок до розширення автономії вищої освіти" (8 April 2014) *IPress.ua*. Ref: http://ipress.ua/news/rada_u_pershomu_chytanni_progolosuvala_za_zakon_pro_vyshchu_osvitu_58759.html

68 Wynnyckyj, Mychailo (6 Sept. 2014) "Thoughts from Kyiv on Higher Education" *UkieDaily*. Ref: http://ukiedaily.com/thoughts-kyiv-60-08-2014-higher-education/

69 Starodubtsev, Oleksandr (20 Sept. 2016) "Історія реформи публічних закупівель". Ref: https://prozorro.gov.ua/news/istoriya-reformy-publichnyh-zakupivel

70 Savytsky, Oleksandr (7 Nov. 2015) "Довгий шлях з міліції в поліцію" *DW*. Ref: https://p.dw.com/p/1H1hB
71 Walker, Edward W. (31 May 2014) "Interpreting the results of Ukraine's presidential election" *Eurasian Geopolitics*. Ref: https://eurasiangeopolitics.com/2014/05/31/reading-the-results-of-ukraines-presidential-election/
72 "Порошенко: АТО має тривати не місяці, а години" (26 May 2014) *Ukrayinska Pravda*. Ref: www.pravda.com.ua/news/2014/05/26/7026737/?attempt=1
73 On 23 August 2018 Poroshenko publicly apologized for having unduly raised expectations among Ukrainians as to the prospects of ending the war quickly. See: "Порошенко вибачився за слова «АТО триватиме кілька годин" у 2014-му" (23 Aug. 2018) *Radio Svoboda*. Ref: www.radiosvoboda.org/a/news-poroshenko-pro-ato-za-hodyny/29448775.html
74 "Donetsk militants send 34 pro-Russian separatist bodies to Russia—leader" (30 May 2014) *Kyiv Post*. Ref: www.kyivpost.com/article/content/war-against-ukraine/donetsk-militants-send-34-pro-russian-separatists-bodies-to-russia-leader-350016.html

Chapter 6—War and Reform

1 Finnin, Rory (28 March 2014) "A divided Ukraine: Europe's most dangerous idea". Ref: www.cam.ac.uk/research/discussion/a-divided-ukraine-europes-most-dangerous-idea
2 Transcript of the National Security and Defense Council meeting 28 February 2014, p. 31. See: "Стенограма засідання РНБО України у зв'язку з початком російської агресії в Криму" (22 Feb. 2016) *Ukrayinska Pravda*. Ref: www.pravda.com.ua/articles/2016/02/22/7099911/
3 "15000 police 'defected to Donbas separatists'" (16 Oct. 2014) *UNIAN Information Agency*. Ref: www.unian.info/politics/996995-15000-police-defected-to-donbas-separatists.html
4 Blair, David (14 June 2014) "Ukraine: rebels shoot down plane carrying 49" *The Telegraph*. Ref: www.telegraph.co.uk/news/worldnews/europe/ukraine/10899657/Ukraine-rebels-shoot-down-plane-carrying-49.html
5 "Указ Президента «Про часткову мобілізацію»"—see: http://zakon2.rada.gov.ua/laws/show/303/2014
6 Goralska, Agnieszka (18 May 2015) "Report: Volunteer battalions. Origin, operation, controversies" *Open Dialog Foundation*. Ref: https://en.odfoundation.eu/a/6448,report-volunteer-battalions-origin-operation-controversies
7 Tytysh, Halyne and Zhartovska, Maria (5 Feb. 2015) "Айдар: історія одного добровольчого батальйону без купюр" *Ukrayinska Pravda*. Ref: www.pravda.com.ua/articles/2015/02/5/7057488/
8 "Підмога в Іловайськ в середу ввечері так і не надійшла – Семенченко" (27 Aug. 2014) *Ukrayinska Pravda*. Ref: www.pravda.com.ua/news/2014/08/27/7035978/
9 Karatnycky, Adrian (30 Dec. 2014) "Warlords and armed groups threaten Ukraine's rebuilding" *Washington Post*. Ref: www.washingtonpost.com/opinions/the-rise-of-warlords-threatens-ukraines-recovery/2014/12/30/a23b2d36-8f7b-11e4-a412-4b735edc7175_story.html
10 In the aftermath of the scandal over control of UkrNafta (a corporation majority owned by the state, but effectively controlled by the Pryvat group), Kolomoisky

was dismissed from the post of governor of Dnipropetrovsk oblast by President Poroshenko.

11 Taub, Amanda (20 Feb. 2015) "Pro-Kiev militias are fighting Putin, but has Ukraine created a monster it can't control?" *Vox.* Ref: www.vox.com/2015/2/20/8072643/ukraine-volunteer-battalion-danger

12 Boyd-Barrett, Oliver (2017) *Western Mainstream Media and the Ukraine Crisis: A Study in Conflict Propaganda*, London, New York: Routledge.

13 In March 2014, Crimean media propagated hysteria among the local Russian-speaking population of the peninsula with false claims that Right Sector fighters were on their way to effect ethnic cleansing. In April, after a firefight near Slovyansk, Russia's LifeNews accused Right Sector fighters of terrorizing local Russian-speakers in the Donbas. As evidence they showed what supposedly was Dmytro Yarosh's business card, apparently found at the scene together with a WWII era German machine gun and night vision goggles; the business card was said to have survived unscathed while the body of its carrier had been burned unrecognizably. The accusation was so preposterous that the meme "vizytka Yarosha" went viral among Ukrainian internet users, as a symbol of the country's indestructibility—see: "Визитка Яроша стала хитом Интернета -фото" (20 April 2014) *ipress.ua.* Ref: http://ipress.ua/ru/ljlive/vyzytka_yarosha_stala_hytom _ynterneta__foto_60762.html. Yarosh later admitted that the driver of the exploded car was in fact a member of Right Sector, but confirmed the business card was a fake—see: "Визитка Яроша оказалась правдой" (22 April 2016), Korrespondent. Ref: https://korrespondent.net/ukraine/3673500-vyzytka-yarosha-okazalas-pravdoi.

14 In 2015 several incidents suggesting that local Right Sector leaders in Ukraine's regions were involved in illicit and/or criminal activities became public – in particular in Mukachevo, TransCarpathia, where Right Sector fighters seemed to be involved in significant contraband trade. See: Romaniuk, Roman and Murayeva-Borovyk, Sevgil (13 July 2015) "Мукачівський трикутник. Контрабанда, Правий сектор та закляті друзі" *Ukrayinska Pravda.* Ref: www.pravda.com.ua/articles/2015/07/13/7074291/

15 "Частина бійців "Правого сектора" увійде до складу СБУ" (20 Aug. 2015) *Dzerkalo Tyzhnia.* Ref: https://dt.ua/UKRAINE/chastina-biyciv-pravogo-sektora-u-viyde-do-skladu-sbu-182310_.html

16 Matiash, Michael (14 Oct. 2017) "Українське волонтерство – явище унікальне. Йому завдячуємо суверенітетом" *UkrInform.* Ref: www.ukrinform.ua/rubric-society/2324579-ukrainske-volonterstvo-avise-unikalne-jomu-zavdacuemo-suverenitetom.html

17 See site of Ministry of Information Policy of Ukraine: "Volunteer Organizations" https://mip.gov.ua/en/content/volonterski--organizacii.html

18 Zarembo, Kateryna (15 Feb. 2018) "How volunteers both strengthened and weakened the Ukrainian state after Euromaidan" *Euromaidan Press.* Ref: http://euromaidanpress.com/2018/02/15/how-volunteers-both-strengthened-and-weakened-the-ukrainian-state-after-euromaidan/

19 Kuzio, Taras (2017) *Putin's War Against Ukraine*, Toronto: Chair of Ukrainian Studies.

20 Gordon, Michael R. (13 June 2014) "Russia Has Sent Tanks to Ukraine Rebels, U.S. Says" *The New York Times.* Ref: www.nytimes.com/2014/06/14/world/europe/russia-has-sent-tanks-to-ukraine-rebels-us-says.html

21 "Сили АТО дали відсіч бойовикам, які атакували Луганський аеропорт" (9 July 2014) *Ukrayinska Pravda*. Ref: www.pravda.com.ua/news/2014/07/9/7031453/

22 "11 июля 2014 года. Российская армия убила 37 украинскьх военньх под Зеленопольем" (12 July 2015) *Censor.net*. Ref: https://censor.net.ua/resonance/343516/11_iyulya_2014_goda_rossiyiskaya_armiya_ubila_37_ukrainskih_voennyh_pod_zelenopolem

23 "США обпублікувала докази обстрілів України з території РФ" (28 July 2014) *BBC*. Ref: www.bbc.com/ukrainian/politics/2014/07/140728_kerry_lavrov_shelling_zsh.shtml

24 Investigation by the Dutch Safety Board — see: www.government.nl/topics/mh17-incident/investigation-by-the-dutch-safety-board

25 Bellingcat "MH17 – The Open Source Investigation Three Years Later" (July 2017). Ref: www.bellingcat.com/wp-content/uploads/2017/07/mh17-3rd-anniversary-report.pdf

26 Romein, Daniel (23 Feb. 2016) *MH17 – Potential Suspects and Witnesses from the 53rd Anti-Aircraft Missile Brigade* Bellingcat Rebort. Ref: www.bellingcat.com/wp-content/uploads/2016/02/53rd-report-public.pdf

27 Lysytska, Maryna (7 Aug. 2014) "Nalyvaychenko says separatists intended to shoot down Russian passenger plane" *Kyiv Post*. Ref: www.kyivpost.com/article/content/war-against-ukraine/nalyvaychenko-said-that-separatists-intended-to-shoot-down-russian-passenger-plane-359765.html?cn-reloaded=1

28 "Google Earth shows how Russians crossed border to create Ilovaysk massacre" (28 Jan. 2015) *Ukraine@War*. Ref: http://ukraineatwar.blogspot.com/2015/01/google-earth-shows-how-russians-crossed.html

29 "Border guards retreat as two columns of Russian tanks enter Ukraine" (28 Aug. 2014) *Fox News*. Ref: www.foxnews.com/world/2014/08/28/ukraine-rebel-leader-reportedly-admits-thousands-russians-fighting-with.html

30 Kim, Lucian (4 Nov. 2014) "The Battle of Ilovaysk: Details of a Massacre Inside Rebel-Held Eastern Ukraine" *Newsweek*. Ref: www.newsweek.com/2014/11/14/battle-ilovaisk-details-massacre-inside-rebel-held-eastern-ukraine-282003.html

31 The Russians promised a corridor if the Ukrainian forces disarmed. The surrounded battalions refused to give up their weapons, arguing that they were on Ukrainian soil, and would not yield to the demands of invaders.

32 Tynchenko, Yaroslav (7 Nov. 2014) "Іловайськ – цифри і факти" *Tyzhden'*. Ref: http://tyzhden.ua/Society/122995

33 "Українська влада уточнює кількість вбитих під Іловайськом" (3 Sept. 2014) *BBC*. Ref: www.bbc.com/ukrainian/politics/2014/09/140903_ilovaisk_situation_results_vc.shtml

34 "Результати розслідування Іловайської трагедії" (14 Aug. 2017) *Prosecutor General's Office of Ukraine*. Ref: www.gp.gov.ua/ua/news.html?_m=publications&_t=rec&id=213793

35 Tynchenko (2014).

36 Hladka, Kateryna et. al. (2017)*Volunteer Battalions*, Kharkıv: Folıo, p. 144.

37 Pavliuk, Alina (5 Sept. 2016) "Іловайська трагедія 2014 р.: події та відповідальність", Ukrainian Helsinki Human Rights Union. Ref: https://helsinki.org.ua/wp-content/uploads/2016/09/Yllowaysk_UGSPL-1.pdf

38 During the run-up to the invasion by Russian regular army troops which culminated in the battle of Ilovaysk, Zakharchenko and Plotnitsky were promoted: on 14 August the latter replaced Valeriy Bolotov as supreme leader of the "LNR",

while the former replaced Alexander Borodai as "Prime Minister" of the "DNR". Unlike their predecessors, both Plotnisky and Zakharchenko were Ukrainian citizens.

39   "Full transcript: Remarks by Ambassador Samantha Power, U.S. Permanent Representative to the United Nations, at a Security Council Session on Ukraine" (28 Aug. 2014) *Washington Post*. Ref: www.washingtonpost.com/world/full-transcript-remarks-by-ambassador-samantha-power-us-permanent-representative-to-the-united-nations-at-a-security-council-session-on-ukraine/2014/08/28/b3f579b2-2ee8-11e4-bb9b-997ae96fad33_story.html?utm_term=.1a17418267d9

40   The original protocol (in Russian) is available on the OSCE website. Ref: www.osce.org/ru/home/123258?download=true

41   During a meeting attended by the author on 10 February 2016 in the Presidential Administration, Poroshenko lamented that he had had to deal with over 27 thousand cases of dereliction of duty in and around Debaltseve in early 2015.

42   "Источники среди военных рассказали подробности об авиаударе под Дебальцево" (9 Feb. 2015) *UNIAN Information Agency*. Ref: www.unian.net/war/1042061-istochniki-sredi-voennyih-rasskazali-podrobnosti-ob-aviaudare-pod-debaltsevo.html

43   Kovalenko, Oksana (18 Feb. 2016) "Дебальцевський плацдарм. Невідомі подробиці операції та переговорів в Мінську" *Ukrayinska Pravda*. Ref: www.pravda.com.ua/articles/2016/02/18/7099435/

44   Although "all for all" was not respected, large numbers of prisoners and captives were released by both sides. Similarly, the withdrawal of heavy weaponry was accomplished selectively. Throughout 2015-2018 skirmishes along the front continued – particularly in the hotspots of Shyrokino (near Mariupol), Pisky (near Donetsk Airport) and Shchastia (Luhansk oblast).

45   "Law on special self-government procedures in certain districts of Donetsk and Luhansk regions takes effect in Ukraine" (20 Oct. 2014) *Interfax-Ukraine*. Ref: https://en.interfax.com.ua/news/general/229474.html

46   See Arendt (1963), p. 145.

47   "Grenade Attack Outside Ukrainian Parliament Kills National Guardsman" (31 Aug. 2015) *ViceNews*. Ref: https://news.vice.com/article/grenade-attack-outside-ukrainian-parliament-kills-national-guardsman

48   Coman, Julian (12 Nov. 2017) "On the frontline of Europe's forgotten war in Ukraine" *The Guardian*. Ref: www.theguardian.com/world/2017/nov/12/ukraine-on-the-front-line-of-europes-forgotten-war

49   "Порошенко: Наша армія буде однією з найсильніших у Європі" (22 Aug. 2018) *Gordon.ua*. Ref: https://gordonua.com/ukr/news/politics/-poroshenko-nasha-armija-bude-odnijeju-z-najsilnishih-v-jevropi-317573.html

50   "Volker: Russia has more tanks in the Donbas than western Europe combined" (26 July 2017) *UAWire*. Ref: https://uawire.org/news/volker-russia-has-more-tanks-in-the-donbas-than-in-western-europe-combined

51   Sharkov, Damien (26 Aug. 2016) "Ukraine claims rebels heavy vehicles increase tenfold" *Newsweek*. Ref: http://europe.newsweek.com/ukraine-claims-rebels-heavy-vehicles-increase-tenfold-493822

52   Akimenko, Valeriy (22 Feb. 2018) "Ukraine's Toughest Fight: The Challenge of Military Reform" *Carnegie Endowment for International Peace*. Ref: https://carnegieendowment.org/2018/02/22/ukraine-s-toughest-fight-challenge-of-military-reform-pub-75609

53 Gould, Joe (2 Aug. 2015) "Electronic Warfare: What US Army Can Learn From Ukraine" *DefenseNews*. Ref: www.defensenews.com/home/2015/08/02/electronic-warfare-what-us-army-can-learn-from-ukraine/

54 Bonenberger, Adrian (1 July 2015) "Ukraine Can Defeat the Separatists" *Forbes*. Ref: www.forbes.com/sites/realspin/2015/07/01/ukraine-can-defeat-the-separatists/#69349d3c4576

55 Grant, Glen (31 Jan. 2017) "How Ukraine can build an army to beat Putin" *Kyiv Post*. Ref: www.kyivpost.com/article/opinion/op-ed/glen-grant-ukraine-can-build-army-beat-putin.html

56 During the early 2016 government reshuffle resulting from Yatseniuk's resignation, Groysman moved to the Prime Minister's office, and Parubiy took over as Speaker, with Poroshenko loyalist and former Yushchenko Press Secretary Iryna Herashchenko elected First Deputy Speaker of Parliament.

57 Reports are available here: http://reforms.in.ua/ua/storinka/zvity

58 These data are quoted from "Моніторинг сприйняття реформ у суспільстві: підсумки першого року" prepared in 2015 and 2016 by *TNS Ukraine* for the *National Reforms Council*. Retrieved from http://reforms.in.ua/ua/report/all

59 IMF support was eventually renewed in December 2018, but only after early adoption of the state budget (in November rather than at the end of the year).

60 "IMF Survey: Stabilizing Ukraine's Economy" (2 Sept. 2014) *International Monetary Fund*. Ref: www.imf.org/external/pubs/ft/survey/so/2014/car090214a.htm

61 The nationalization of PrivatBank was decided during a late-night meeting of the Cabinet of Ministers with the participation of President Poroshenko and NBU Governor Hontareva.

62 Fitzgeorge-Parker, Lucy (1 Nov. 2017) "Defusing PrivatBank: a very Ukrainian nationalization" *Euromoney*. Ref: www.euromoney.com/article/b15fd8q5l9v8y4/defusing-privatbank-a-very-ukrainian-nationalization

63 Janssen, Kim (20 Dec. 2017) "Ukrainian oligarch with ties to Manafort and wanted in Chicago gets holiday reprieve" *Chicago Tribune*. Ref: www.chicagotribune.com/news/chicagoinc/ct-met-firtash-1221-chicago-inc-20171220-story.html

64 Olearchyk, Roman (6 Jan. 2018) "Court freezes $820m of oligarch's assets" *Financial Times*. Ref: https://www.ft.com/content/1a92bacc-f155-11e7-ac08-07c3086a2625

65 Cohen, Josh (26 Feb. 2018) "Ukraine still needs an anti-corruption court" *Atlantic Council*. Ref: www.atlanticcouncil.org/blogs/ukrainealert/ukraine-still-needs-an-anti-corruption-court

66 For example, the US State Department (see: "Committing to the Fight Against Corruption in Ukraine" (4 Dec. 2017) *U.S. Department of State*. Ref: www.state.gov/r/pa/prs/ps/2017/12/276235.htm), the IMF (see "IMF warning sparks Ukraine pledge on corruption and reform" (10 Feb. 2016) *Financial Times*. Ref: www.ft.com/content/44c1641e-cff7-11e5-831d-09f7778e7377), and Transparency International (see: "Transparency International Urges the Prosecutor General to take Constructive Criticism Less Emotionally" (25 May 2017), Transparency International. Ref: https://ti-ukraine.org/en/news/transparency-international-urges-the-prosecutor-general-to-take-constructive-criticism-less-emotionally/)

67 "Association Implementation Report on Ukraine" Joint Staff Working Document (14 Nov. 2017), European Commission, Brussels. Ref: https://eeas.europa.eu/sites/eeas/files/association_implementation_report_on_ukraine.pdf

68 Presentation "Horizon Capital: An Investor's perspective" (Dec. 2015), p. 8 – Source of statistics is UkrStat.

69   Aslund, Anders (12 Jan. 2018) "Why Ukraine's economy will not take off in 2018" *Kyiv Post*. Ref: www.kyivpost.com/article/opinion/op-ed/ukraines-economy-will-not-take-off-2018.html.

70   "В Україні прискорилося зростання ВВП" (14 Aug. 2018) *Segodnya*. Ref: https://ukr.segodnya.ua/economics/enews/v-ukraine-uskorilsya-rost-ekonomiki-gosstat-1162879.html

71   "Споживчі ціни в Україні знижуються – Держстат" (10 Aug. 2018) *Segodnya*. Ref: https://ukr.segodnya.ua/economics/enews/potrebitelskie-ceny-v-ukraine-snizhayutsya-gosstat-1161765.html

Introduction to Part II

1   Aslund, Anders (2009) *How Ukraine became a market economy and democracy*, Washington: Peterson Institute for International Economics.

2   Wilson, Andrew (2005) *Orange Revolution*.

3   Wesslau, Fredrik (19 Oct. 2016) "Putin's Friends in Europe" *European Council on Foreign Relations*. Ref: www.ecfr.eu/article/commentary_putins_friends_in_europe7153 and Shekhovtsov, Anton (2018) *Russia and the Western Far Right: Tango Noir*, London, New York: Routledge.

4   Sorokin, Pitirim (2010) *Social and Cultural Dynamics: A Study of Change in Major Systems of Art, Truth, Ethics, Law and Social Relationships*, New Brunswick: Transaction Publishers.

5   Arendt (1963).

Chapter 7 — Making Sense of Maidan and Russia's War

1   For example: Sakwa, Richard (2014) *Frontline Ukraine: Crisis in the Borderlands*, London: I.B. Tauris.

2   Kalb, Marvin (2016) *Imperial Gamble: Putin, Ukraine, and the New Cold War*, Brookings.

3   For example: Gessen, Keith (22 Feb. 2017) "Killer, kleptocrat, genius, spy: the many myths of Vladimir Putin" *The Guardian*. Ref: www.theguardian.com/world/2017/feb/22/vladimir-putin-killer-genius-kleptocrat-spy-myths and Bildt, Carl (11 May 2017) "Putin is not the geopolitical genius the world makes him out to be" *Washington Post*. Ref: www.washingtonpost.com/news/global-opinions/wp/2017/05/11/putin-is-not-the-geopolitical-genius-the-world-makes-him-out-to-be/?utm_term=.9875ee1cbbe6 and McFaul, Michael A. (23 Oct. 2015) "The Myth of Putin's Strategic Genius" *The New York Times*. Ref: www.nytimes.com/2015/10/23/opinion/the-myth-of-putins-strategic-genius.html

4   Andrew Wilson is Senior Policy Fellow at the European Council on Foreign Relations.

5   Kalb (2016) exemplifies the "history explains all" approach to analyzing Maidan and the subsequent Russian-Ukraine war.

6   These words were reportedly uttered by Putin to US President George W. Bush when the two met at the 2008 NATO summit in Bucharest.

7   Wilson, Andrew (June 2016) "The Donbas in 2014: Explaining Civil Conflict Perhaps, but not Civil War" *Europe-Asia Studies*, vol. 68, no. 4, pp. 631-652.

8   Sakwa (2014), pp. 2-3.

9   Merry, E. Wayne (2016) "The Origins of Russia's War in Ukraine" in *Roots of Russia's War in Ukraine*, Washington: Woodrow Wilson Center Press.

10   To be fair, Merry continues: "responsibility for the militarization of the competition—for the resort to covert and overt war—is not shared. That responsibility rests exclusively with Moscow." (p. 42).

11   Trudolyubov, Maxim (2016) "Russia's Grand Choice: To be feared as a Superpower, or Prosperous as a Nation?" in Merry, E. Wayne *Roots of Russia's War in Ukraine*, Washington: Woodrow Wilson Center Press.

12   According to the Frankfurt School tradition of Critical Theory, outward appearances of social phenomena hide their true essence.

13   Alexander Motyl pointed out: "Realists can be found on the right (Henry Kissinger and Nikolas K. Gvosdev), on the left (Stephen F. Cohen and Michel Chossudovsky), and in the center (John J. Mearsheimer and Stephen M. Walt)." See: Motyl, Alexander (Jan./Feb. 2015) "The Surrealism of Realism" *World Affairs.* Ref: www.worldaffairsjournal.org/article/surrealism-realism-misreading-war-ukraine

14   See Kalb (2016), Chapters 3 & 4.

15   Vorobiov, Ievgen (13 Aug. 2015) "Surprise! Ukraine Loves NATO" *Foreign Policy.* Ref: http://foreignpolicy.com/2015/08/13/surprise-ukraine-loves-nato/

16   "Підтримка вступу до НАТО досягла рекордного рівня – опитування" (16 Oct. 2015) *Ukrayinska Pravda.* Ref: http://www.pravda.com.ua/news/2015/10/16/7085112/

17   "Bucharest Summit Declaration" (3 April 2008) *NATO.* Ref: http://www.nato.int/cps/en/natolive/official_texts_8443.htm

18   Motyl (2015).

19   Thankfully, these falsehoods were not hegemonic. In February 2016, a group of prominent academics presented the EU Foreign Affairs Commissioner Frederica Mogherini with a report entitled "From Hybrid Peace to Human Security: Rethinking EU Strategy Towards Conflict" (13 April 2016) *Human Security Study Group.* Ref: https://europa.eu/globalstrategy/en/file/424/download?token=VFwH62WJ. The authors argue: "Twentieth-century nation states were based on a clear distinction between inside and outside. Typical outside instruments were state-to-state diplomacy or economic and military coercion. Typical inside instruments are the rule of law, politics, and policing. In today's complex, contested and connected world, outside instruments do not work; they backfire and make things worse. Human security is about extending the inside beyond the EU." (p. 3)

20   Whitmore, Brian (22 Feb. 2017) "The Daily Vertical: The Human Cost of Putin's War" *RFE/RL.* Ref: www.rferl.org/a/daily-vertical-ukraine-war-putin-human-cost/28324855.html

21   Alexander, Harriet and Kravtsova, Yekaterina (20 March 2014) "Vladimir Putin held secret meeting to agree Crimea annexation weeks before referendum" *The Telegraph.* Ref: www.telegraph.co.uk/news/worldnews/vladimir-putin/10712866/Vladimir-Putin-held-secret-meeting-to-agree-Crimea-annexation-weeks-before-referendum.html. This narrative was repeated by Putin in the "documentary" film "Crimea: Return Home".

22   Wood, Elizabeth A. (2016) "A Small Victorious War? The Symbolic Politics of Vladimir Putin" in Merry, E. Wayne *Roots of Russia's War in Ukraine*, Washington: Woodrow Wilson Center Press.

23   "Putin Needs Wars to Legitimize His Position" (10 Nov. 2015) *Spiegel Online.* Ref: www.spiegel.de/international/world/garry-kasparov-interview-putin-needs-wars-a-1061942.html

24   Romanenko, Yuriy (12 Jan. 2017) "Илья Пономарев: Россия может атаковать страны Балтии, чтобы развалить НАТО" *Hvylia*. Ref: http://hvylya.net/ interview/geopolitics2/ilya-ponomarev-rossiya-mozhet-atakovat-stranyi-baltii-chtobyi-razvalit-nato.html

25   Prior to his murder, Boris Nemtsov announced his intention to publish documentary evidence of Putin's direct involvement in planning and executing the invasion of Ukraine. Nemtsov's protégé later published a portion of the murdered opposition politician's planned publication.

26   Birnbaum, Michael (5 March 2016) "How to Understand Putin's Jaw-droppingly High Approval Ratings" *Washington Post*. Ref: www.washingtonpost.com/world/ europe/how-to-understand-putins-jaw-droppingly-high-approval-ratings/2016/ 03/05/17f5d8f2-d5ba-11e5-a65b-587e721fb231_story.html?utm_term=.2d9a9d013 200

27   Gorchinskaya, Katja (21 March 2014) "Putin's Original Plan for Ukraine" *Kyiv Post*. Ref: www.kyivpost.com/article/opinion/op-ed/putins-original-plan-for-ukraine -340233.html and Rothrock, Kevin (22 March 2014) "Putin's Alleged "Ukraine Annexation Plan" Surfaces Online" *Global Voices*. Ref: https://globalvoices.org/ 2014/03/24/putins-alleged-ukraine-annexation-plan-surfaces-online/

28   Withnall, Adam (25 Feb. 2015) "Russia's Roadmap for Annexing Eastern Ukraine Leaked from Putin's Office" *Independent*. Ref: www.independent.co.uk/news /world/europe/russias-roadmap-for-annexing-eastern-ukraine-leaked-from-vladimir-putins-office-10069203.html and Nemtsova, Anna (25 Feb. 2015) "Putin's Secret Ukraine Plan 'Leaked'" *The Daily Beast*. Ref: www.thedailybeast.com/articles /2015/02/25/russia-s-great-ukraine-conspiracy-revealed.html

29   "English translation of audio evidence of Putin's advisor Glazyev and other Russian politician's involvement in war in Ukraine" (29 Aug. 2016) *UAPosition*. Ref: http://uaposition.com/analysis-opinion/english-translation-audio-evidence-putins-adviser-glazyev-russian-politicians-involvement-war-ukraine/

30   Chekalkin, Dmitry (7 Dec. 2014) "How Russia Invaded Ukraine as told by FSB Colonel Girkin" *Euromaidan Press*. Ref: http://euromaidanpress.com/2014/12/07 /fsb-colonel-girkin-tells-details-of-how-russia-invaded-ukraine-in-twice-censored-interview/

31   "The PowerVertical Podcast: The Tale of the Tape" (26 Aug. 2016) *RFE/RL*. Ref: www.rferl.mobi/a/27948433.html — see minute 21 and thereafter.

32   These words were used by Putin to describe the situation in Crimea during his 5 March 2014 press conference.

33   See Putin's interview in the "documentary" film *Crimea: the road to the homeland*. First broadcast 8 March 2015.

34   Ioffe, Julia (Jan.-Feb. 2018) "What Putin Really Wants" *The Atlantic*. Ref: www.theatlantic.com/magazine/archive/2018/01/putins-game/546548/

35   Rogue United Russia MP Ilya Ponomaryov claimed that the whole Novorossiya project was a spontaneous operation effected by Colonel Strelkov and approximately 50 former Special Forces officers who came to Slovyansk in March-April 2014 to stoke unrest; apparently Putin was informed of their initiative after it had been launched.

36   Chronicle of Putin's comments on Novorossiya: Shapoval, Ekaterina (1 Sept. 2014) "Путин и Новороссия: хроника признаний" *Hubs*. Ref: http://hubs.ua/ authority/putin-i-novorossiya-19881.html

37   Blank, Stephen (4 Oct. 2013) "What Do the Zapad Exercises Reveal?" *Eurasia Daily Monitor* vol. 10 Issue 177. Ref: https://jamestown.org/program/what-do-the-za-pad-2013-exercises-reveal-part-one/

38   Horbulin, Volodymyr (18 Feb. 2016) "Тези до другої річниці російської агресії проти України" *Ukraine Crisis Media Center*. Ref: http://uacrisis.org/ua/40347-gorbulin-tezy. According to sources, Viktor Pinchuk–former President Kuchma's son-in-law and organizer of the Yalta European Strategy conference–warned Sweden's Carl Bildt in April 2013 of Russia's coming military aggression in Ukraine, but was ignored.

39   Vozniak, Taras (25 Nov. 2014) "Паралельні сценарії подій 2013-2014 pp." *Ji Magazine*. Ref: http://ji-magazine.lviv.ua/anons2014/Voznyak_Paralelni_scenarii_podij_v_Ukraini.htm

40   According to Prosecutor General Yuriy Lutsenko, documentary evidence exists of Yanukovych's treasonous complicity with Putin's plans to invade Ukraine during the Maidan protests, see: Kostyk, Vladimir (22 Jan. 2017) "Путін планував напад на Україну ще під час Майдану – Луценко" *Presa Ukrayiny*. Ref: http://uapress.info/uk/news/show/159108. Former Putin advisor Andrey Ilarionov claimed to have heard the Russian President voicing his intention to annex Ukrainian territory at least three times, see: Dekhtaryenko, Artjom (29 Jan. 2016) "У Кремля было три попытки захватить Крым—экс-советник Путина Андрей Иларионов" *Apostrof*. Ref: http://apostrophe.ua/article/politics/2016-01-29/u-kremlya-byilo-tri-popyitki-zahvatit-kryim---eks-sovetnik-putina-andrey-illarionov/3063

41   For a complete account see Wilson (2005).

42   The "colored revolutions" script seems to have been broadly described by Gene Sharp in *From Dictatorship to Democracy* (1994, East Boston: Albert Einstein Institution)—a work that many of the Orange leaders professed to having received training on. See for example Kaskiv, Vladyslav, Chupryna, Iryna and Yevhen Zolotariov (2007) "It's Time! Pora and the Orange Revolution in Ukraine" in Forbrig, Joerg and Demeš, Pavol (eds.) *Reclaiming Democracy: Civil Society and Electoral Change in Central and Eastern Europe*, German Marshall Fund.

43   McFaul (2005) identified 5 success factors of the Orange Revolution. Similar factors are enumerated by Kuzio, Taras (2007) "Comparative Perspectives on the Fourth Wave of Democracy" in Forbrig, Joerg and Demeš, Pavol (eds.), *Reclaiming Democracy: Civil Society and Electoral Change in Central and Eastern Europe*.

44   Brazhko, Illia (2014 "The Factors Behind Electoral Revolutions in the Postcommunist World") MA Dissertation, Department of Political Sciences, Central European University.

45   Shukan, Ioulia (2011) "Orchestrating a Popular Protest Movement to Conduct a Revolution" *Orange Revolution and Aftermath: Mobilization, Apathy and the State in Ukraine*, John Hopkins University Press, pp.76-109.

46   When interviewed in November 2016 in Russia, Yanukovych admitted that he regretted not having acted more decisively to quell the protest movement by force. See: Nechepurenko, Ivan (15 Nov. 2016) "Ukraine's Ex-Leader Regrets Not Breaking Up Protest That Led to His Fall" *The New York Times*. Ref: www.nytimes.com/2016/11/25/world/europe/yanukovych-ukraine-maidan-protests-russia.html?_r=0 and "Yanukovych Regrets Not Cracking Down on Maydan with Troops" (25 Nov. 2016) *LB.ua*. Ref: https://en.lb.ua/news/2016/11/25/2442_yanukovych_regrets_cracking_down.html

47   For example: Snow, David (ed.) (2004) *The Blackwell Companion to Social Movements*, Malden, Oxford, Victoria: Blackwell Publishing.

48 Oleinik, Anton and Strelkova, Olga (2015) "The relocation of a repertoire of collective action: Maidan 2013" *European Journal of Cultural and Political Sociology*, vol. 2, issue 2.

49 Granovetter, Mark (1983) "The Strength of Weak Ties: A Network Theory Revisited", Sociological Theory, vol. 1, pp. 201–233.

50 Crane Brinton would not have approved of his work and Arendt's being cited as providing complementary analytical frameworks. In the Bibliographical Appendix to *The Anatomy of Revolution* he described Arendt's *On Revolution* as "emotional, intellectual, full of existentialist despair, poles apart from the approach attempted in this book." (1963:291).

51 For example, the Anti-Corruption Forum led by former Georgian President and later Odesa governor Mikhael Saakashvili, and the "Ukrop" party financed by oligarch Ihor Kolomoysky.

52 "Russian troll farms behind campaign to topple Ukraine's government" (11 Oct. 2016) *Stopfake*. Ref: www.stopfake.org/en/tag/third-maidan/

53 Kazanskyi, Denys (17 Dec. 2015) "The Third Coming? Is Maidan 3.0 possible and what would it look like?" *The Ukrainian Week*. Ref: http://ukrainianweek.com/Politics/154194

54 Samokhvalova, Lana (14 Feb. 2016) "The Russian organizers of a "Third Maidan" in Ukraine" *Euromaidan Press*. Ref: http://euromaidanpress.com/2016/02/14/the-russian-organizers-of-a-third-maidan-in-ukraine/

55 "Savchenko to Ruban discussing terror plot: "I propose a coup. They need to be removed physically – all at once" (22 March 2018) *UNIAN Information Agency*. Ref: www.unian.info/politics/10052489-savchenko-to-ruban-discussing-terror-plot-i-propose-a-coup-they-need-to-be-removed-physically-all-at-once.html

56 Mälksoo, Maria (2006) "From Existential Politics Towards Normal Politics? The Baltic States in the Enlarged Europe" *Security Dialogue*, vol. 37 no. 3, pp 275–297.

57 Rogozin, Leonid (1 Aug. 2018) "Four Years After Its Revolution, Ukraine is Still a Mess" *Bloomberg Businessweek*. Ref: www.bloombergquint.com/businessweek/ukraine-reforms-stall-as-economy-lags-and-corruption-lingers#gs.0ycbcs

58 "Thousands of Saakashvili supporters stage protest against Ukraine president" (10 Dec. 2017) *Reuters*. Ref: www.reuters.com/article/us-ukraine-protests-saakashvili/thousands-of-saakashvili-supporters-stage-protest-against-ukraine-president-idUSKBN1E40NV

59 Vyshlinsky, Hlib (12 June 2017) "Why populism isn't Ukraine's Number One Enemy" *Atlantic Council*. Ref: www.atlanticcouncil.org/blogs/ukrainealert/why-populism-isn-t-ukraine-s-number-one-enemy

60 Arendt (1963), pp. 173-174.

Chapter 8 — A National Revolution

1 Gorchinskaya, Katja (11 Dec. 2013) "Birth of a Nation" *Kyiv Post*. Ref: www.kyivpost.com/article/opinion/op-ed/birth-of-a-nation-333459.html

2 According to a 2016 study of the linguistic preferences of Ukraine's soldiers, 73% of those serving in the ATO called Ukrainian their "native language" (the national average was 55%). When asked which language they spoke at home, 55% of soldiers said Ukrainian compared to 43% for non-ATO participants: "73% учасників АТО назвали рідною мовою українську - опитування" (7 June 2016) *Ukrayinska Pravda*. Ref: www.pravda.com.ua/news/2016/06/7/7111025/

3   A spontaneous custom appeared whereby funeral processions for fallen Ukrainian soldiers would be lined with people kneeling in an act of reverence. This practice became widespread during the first three years of the war with Russia. See: www.youtube.com/watch?v=c3m0ras2AbU

4   Motyl, Alexander (2 March 2015) "Is Ukraine Fascist?" *Huffington Post Blog*. Ref: www.huffingtonpost.com/alexander-motyl/putin-calls-ukraine-fasci_b_6600292 .html

5   Kuzio, Taras (ed.) (1998) *Ukraine: State and Nation-Building*, London, New York: Routledge.

6   Polese, Abel (2011) "Language and Identity in Ukraine: Was it Really Nation-building?" *Studies of Transition States and Societies*, vol. 3, no. 3; Zhurzhenko, Tatiana (2014) "A Divided Nation? Reconsidering the Role of Identity Politics in the Ukraine Crisis" *Die Friedenswarte*, vol. 89, no. 1-2.

7   Hrytsak, Yaroslav (2011) *Страсті за Націоналізмом*, Kyiv: Krytyka.

8   Marples, David (22 Feb. 2014) "Ukraine—Divided or Diverse" *Current Politics in Ukraine*. Ref: https://ukraineanalysis.wordpress.com/2014/02/22/ukraine-divided-or-diverse/

9   For example, Dugin, Alexander (8 March 2014) "Letter to the American People on Ukraine" *Open Revolt!*. Ref: http://openrevolt.info/2014/03/08/alexander-dugin-letter-to-the-american-people-on-ukraine/

10 This term was coined by Benedict Anderson (1983) whose seminal work on national identity was entitled *Imagined Communities*, London: Verso.

11 West includes: Volyn, Zakarpattya, Ivano-Frankivsk, Lviv, Chernivtsi, Ternopil, Rivne oblasts. Center includes: Vinnytsia, Khmelnytsky, Zhytomyr, Kyiv, Kirovohrad, Sumy, Poltava, Cherkasy, Chernihiv oblasts. South includes: Mykolayiv, Odesa, Kherson oblasts. East includes: Dnipropetrovsk, Zaporizhzhia, Kharkiv oblasts. Donbas includes Donetsk and Luhansk oblasts.

12 Polls taken by Socis. Results published in Haran, Olexiy and Bekeshkina, Iryna (eds.) (2017) *Трансформації суспільних настроїв в умовах протидії агресії Росії на Донбасі: регіональний вимір*, Kyiv: Stylos.

13 This is striking, given that in 2005 (Razumkov Center poll conducted 20-27 December 2005 N=2009) 38.7% of Ukrainians reported identifying themselves firstly with their town or village, 20.4% with their region, and only 30.7% as Citizens of Ukraine.

14 N=2015 representative of all regions of Ukraine except Crimea and occupied areas of Donbas, margin of error 2.3%. See: "69% громадян вважають українську рідною мовою – опитування" (16 Dec. 2016) *Censor.net*. Ref: https://censor.net. ua/ua/news/419747/69_gromadyan_vvajayut_ukrayinsku_ridnoyu_movoyu_ opytuvannya

15 Lozhkin, Boris (2016) *Четверта Республіка*, Kharkiv: Folio, p. 77.

16 The Soviet-era city name had been a combination of Dnipro (the name of the river) and Petrovsky—named after Grigorii Petrovsky, People's Commissar of the NKVD in 1917-1919, and later one of the officials responsible for the Holodomor of 1932-33.

17 On 3 March 2014, during his first press conference as governor Kolomoisky referred to Putin as a "small sized schizophrenic". Ref: www.youtube.com/ watch?v=RYwntgDPZDo. Putin responded the following day during his own meeting with journalists calling Kolomoisky a "bandit".

18 As Head Doctor of the Mechnikov Hospital in Dnipro, Ryzhenko briefed journalists daily on the state of newly arrived wounded soldiers. Although his demeanor

was always calm, his hatred for the enemy who had inflicted harm on Ukraine's fighting men was clear in every spoken word. In April 2017, "STB" television aired a four-part documentary series featuring Dr. Rizhenko entitled "Likarnya №1". Ref: http://vikna.stb.ua/ua/episode/likarnya-1-persha-seriya-spetsproektu-vikon/

19   Kuzio, Taras (29 Oct. 2015) "Ukraine says thank you to Vladimir Putin" *Financial Times*. Ref: http://blogs.ft.com/beyond-brics/2015/10/29/ukraine-says-thank-you-to-vladimir-putin/ and Dickinson, Peter (15 Feb. 2017) "Multiculturalism is the Answer to Ukraine's Identity Crisis" *Atlantic Council*. Ref: www.atlanticcouncil .org/blogs/ukrainealert/multiculturalism-is-the-answer-to-ukraine-s-identity-crisis

20   Wilson, Andrew (1996) *Ukrainian Nationalism in the 1990's: A Minority Faith,* Cambridge University Press.

21   The surveys were conducted in October 2006, June 2011 and in August 2016. A nationally representative sample of respondents in each poll (N=2040) was constructed with a maximum margin of error of 3.3%. The 2016 poll did not include respondents from Crimea or the occupied regions of the Donbas.

22   Data available: "Зміни у ставленні громадян до суверенітету України" (June 2011) *Kyiv International Institute of Sociology*. Ref: http://kiis.com.ua/img/pr_img/20110822_nezalezhn/indep.pdf and "Україна -25: досягнення та поразки (громадська думка)" (22 Aug. 2016) *Democratic Initiatives Foundation*. Ref: http://dif.org.ua/article/ukraini-25-dosyagnennya-ta-porazki-gromadska-dumka

23   Halling, Steffen and Stewart, Susan (March 2015) "Identity and Violence in Ukraine: Societal Development since the Maidan Protests" *Stiftung Wissenschaft und Politik Comments*. Ref: www.swp-berlin.org/fileadmin/contents/products/comments/2015C19_hln_stw.pdf

24   Trach, N. "Razom Syla!: Rytoryka ukrayinskoho sprotyvu" (2015), Kyiv: Klio, p. 17. (my translation from Ukrainian original)

25   The word "Maidan is of Turkish origin. After 2004 it was coopted into Ukrainian as both a place (Independence Square in Kyiv), and a concept: a representation of peaceful anti-establishment protest.

26   For the early Euromaidan protesters, being "European" meant living a certain lifestyle:
"Euromaidan is — passing a driver's test without cheating"
"Euromaidan is — planting a flower next to the entrance to your apartment building"
"Euromaidan is — cleaning up after your dog in the park"
"Euromaidan is — installing licensed software on your computer"
These playful slogans adorned posters and stickers displayed throughout Kyiv in late 2013.

27   Bociurkiw, Michael (19 Feb. 2014) "Ukraine: Doing Nothing is the worst of all options" *Huffington Post*. Ref: www.huffingtonpost.com/michael-bociurkiw/ukraine-western-intervention_b_4813267.html

28   See: http://taruta.com.ua/index.php/en/

29   Popular memes created by volunteers during the early Maidan protests included "Yanukovych PidAresht" (a play on words that literally means "Arrest Yanukovych", but sounds very similar to "Yanukovych is a fag") and "Bimba" (meaning bomb, but with "o" replaced with an "i" thereby ridiculing the misplaced vowels common in Prime Minister Azarov's attempts to speak Ukrainian).

30   Zelinska, Olga (Fall 2015) "Who were the Protestors and What Did They Want?: Contentious Politics of Local Maidans Across Ukraine, 2013-2014" *Demoktratizatsiya: The Journal of Post-Soviet Democratization* vol. 23, No. 4, pp. 379-400.

31   The identification of Putin as *the* symbol of the outgroup was also reflected in the slogan "Putin idy na yukh!" — a verse seemingly calling for the Russian president to go south ("yug"), but actually a play on letters because "yukh" in Russian spelled backwards means "penis".

32   Syndelar, Daisy (18 June 2014) "'Putin Khuilo!' Ukraine's obscene patriotic rallying cry" *The Atlantic.* Ref: www.theatlantic.com/international/archive/2014/06/putin-khuilo-ukraine-obscene-patriotic-rallying-cry/372991/

33   During the 2018 FIFA World Cup in Russia, the star Croatian defender Domagoj Vida recorded a message after his semi-final win, thanking his fans at Dynamo Kyiv where he played professionally, and ended the video with "Slava Ukrayini!".

34   In early December, a rap tune put together by comedian Michael Shchur "Vitya — tse perebor" (Viktor — this is over the top) went viral on Maidan, and was quickly popularized throughout Ukraine.

35   Historian Ivan Katchanovski has chronicled the wartime transgressions of the OUN-UPA in numerous articles and publications.

36   In early February 2014 I attended a roundtable session in Ukrainian House during which the various portrayals of Maidan in the western press were discussed. When an English journalist tried to argue that the portrayal of Svoboda and the Right Sector as radical right organizations was justified, very emotional reactions were sparked in the audience. According to the Ukrainians taking part in the discussion, their version of "nationalism" had little if anything to do with the horrendous ideology of 20th century fascism: national self-identification and patriotism should not be confused with xenophobia or fascism.

37   Taras Shevchenko is Ukraine's national poet. Videos of the Jesus-looking Nihoyan reciting "Boritesia, poborete!" ("Fight and you will prevail") became symbols of the patriotic mood that characterized the Maidan in December-January.

38   Forostyna, Oksana (2015) "Poaching, Simmering and Boiling: The Declining Relevance of Identity Discourse in Ukraine" in Wilson, Andrew (ed.) *What Does Ukraine Think?* European Council on Foreign Relations, p. 27.

39   After the ouster of Yanukovych, the blue and yellow flag returned to its rightful place as the primary symbol of national unity; the red and black was used either as an identifier of "Pravyy Sektor" or by volunteer groups supplying troops in the Donbas. It was referred to by fighters in the volunteer battalions as the "flag of war" whereas the national colours were called the "flag of the nation at peace".

40   Notable exceptions include Herlihy, Patricia (1991) *Odessa: a History*, Harvard Ukrainian Research Institute; Kuromiya, Hiroaki (1998) *Freedom and Terror in the Donbas*, Cambridge University Press.

41   Hrytsak, Yaroslav "Історія двох міст: Львів і Донецьк у порівняльній перспективі"and Sereda, Viktoriya (2007) "Regional Historical Identities and Memory", in Hrytsak, Yaroslav, Portnov, Andrii and Susak, Victor (eds.) *L'viv–Donets'k: sotsiial'ni identychnosti v suchasnii Ukraïni* (special issue of *Ukraïna Moderna*), Kyiv: Krytyka.

42   Arel, Dominique and Khmelko, Valeri (1996) "The Russian Factor and Territorial Polarization in Ukraine" *The Harriman Review*, 9, 1–2; Pirie, Paul S. (1996) "National Identity and Politics in Southern and Eastern Ukraine" *Europe-Asia Studies*, 48, 7; Wolczuk, Kataryna (2007) "Whose Ukraine? Language and Regional Factors in the 2004 and 2006 Elections in Ukraine" *European Yearbook of Minority Issues*, 5.

43 Throughout the 2000's, debates surrounding conflicting narratives of World War II were used by competing elites as weapons in electoral contests: Were the OUN-UPA heroes? What was the legacy of the Red Army? Were Ukrainians and Russians brotherly peoples? For more on these debates, and their deliberate aggravation by populist elites seeking electoral support see Zhurzhenko (2014).

44 In both Mykolaiv and Kirovohrad, the Lenin statues that had stood in the city-centers were dismantled in February 2014. The main square in Kirovohrad ceased to be called "Kirov Square" and became "Heroes of Maidan Square" (the city itself was renamed Kropyvnytsky as a result of de-communization). In Mykolaiv, Lenin Square became "Unity Square".

45 Kulyk, Volodymyr (2016) "National Identity in Ukraine: Impact of Euromaidan and the War" *Europe-Asia Studies*, vol. 68 no. 4, p. 607.

46 Kuromiya (1998).

47 Osipian, Arabat and Osipian, Alexandr (Fall 2006) "Why Donbas Votes for Yanukovych: Confronting the Ukrainian Orange Revolution" *Demokratizatsiya,* vol. 14, no. 4, p. 498

48 Kuzio, Taras (May 2015) "Rise and Fall of the Party of Regions Political Machine" *Problems of PostCommunism*, vol. 62, no. 3.

49 Van Zon, Hans (2007) *The Rise of Conglomerates in Ukraine: The Donetsk Case*, New York: Taylor & Francis.

50 For example, in April 2014 oligarch Akhmetov was accused of providing financial support for the occupation of administrative buildings in Donetsk (see: "Джерело: донецькими і луганськими сепаратистами керують люди Ахметова" (7 April 2014) *Tyzhden'*. Ref: http://tyzhden.ua/News/106965).

51 According to the UNDP, approximately 1.8 million Ukrainian citizens were displaced as a result of the war in the Donbas – the vast majority migrated to Ukraine, not to Russia.

52 See Girkin interview: "Igor Strelkov's Revealing Interview" (27 Dec. 2017) *Digital Research Forensic Lab*. Ref: https://medium.com/dfrlab/igor-strelkov-girkins-revealing-interview-acf44b22b48

53 Russian nationalist ideologue Alexander Dugin, clearly expected the "artificial country of Ukraine" to split into two parts quite naturally. He said as much in his "Open Letter to the American People". Ref: http://openrevolt.info/2014/03/08/alexander-dugin-letter-to-the-american-people-on-ukraine/

54 Anastasia Dmytruk—a native of Nizhyn, Chernihiv oblast—writes poetry in Ukrainian and in Russian. In March 2014, reacting to Russia's annexation of Crimea, she wrote "Ми никогда не будем братьями". The poem quickly went viral, and several weeks later was put to music. An English translation was posted to Facebook: www.facebook.com/knellera/posts/290782174430944

55 Chabanna, Marharyta (2014) "Trust in Political Institutions: Preconditions and Consequences for Democracy" *Magisterium: Political Studies,* Issue 58.

56 For example: "Довіра громадян до органів влади та базовихсоціальних інститутів" (2007) *National Institute of Strategic Studies*. Ref: http://old.niss.gov.ua/Monitor/april08/6.htm and "Найбільше українці довіряють волонтерам, церкві і армії" (23 Oct. 2017) *Dzerkalo Tyzhnya*. Ref: https://dt.ua/UKRAINE/naybilshe-ukrayinci-doviryayut-volonteram-cerkvi-i-armiyi-257833_.html and "Ставлення громадян України до суспільних інститутів, електоральні настрої" (April 2017) *Razumkov Center*. Ref: http://razumkov.org.ua/uploads/socio/Press0417.pdf

57   "Довіра до соціальних інституцій та груп" (15 Jan. 2015), *Kyiv International In-stitute of Sociology.* Ref: http://kiis.com.ua/?lang=ukr&cat=reports&id=579

58   Kulyk, Volodymyr (2016) "National Identity in Ukraine: Impact of Euromaidan and the War" *Europe-Asia Studies*, 68:4, 588-608

59   Marples, David (April 2015) "Open Letter from Scholars and Experts on Ukraine re. the so-called 'Anti-Communist Law'" *Krytyka.* Ref: https://krytyka.com/en/articles/open-letter-scholars-and-experts-ukraine-re-so-called-anti-communist-law

60   "МЗС Польщі: З Бандерою Україна не ввійде в Європу" (4 July 2017) *UNIAN Information Agency.* Ref: www.unian.ua/politics/2009359-glava-mzs-polschi-z-banderoyu-ukrajina-ne-uviyde-v-evropu.html

61   During his meeting with President Duda of Poland in Kharkiv in 2017, Poroshenko attempted to smooth relations by promising a bi-lateral research initiative to objec-tively investigate the role of the OUN-UPA in these events.

62   "В Україні декомунізували майже тисячу міст і сіл. Інфографіка" (27 Dec. 2016) *Tyzhden'.* Ref: http://tyzhden.ua/News/181868

63   Support was highest in the western regions and declined as one moved south and east. Support for de-communization correlated with education level, and inversely correlated with age (i.e. older respondents were likely to oppose the initiatives): "Как украинцы относятся к процессу декоммунизации" (20 Nov. 2016) *Noviy Format.* Ref: https://nf.dp.ua/2016/11/kak-ukraintsy-otnosyatsya-k-protsessu-dekommunizatsii/

64   Sasse, Gwendolyn and Lackner, Alice (2018) "War and identity: the case of the Donbas in Ukraine" *Post-Soviet Affairs*, vol. 34, issue 2-3, pp. 139-157.

65   During the Yushchenko presidency, 2005-2010, an attempt was made to establish the Holodomor as a defining event for Ukrainians' identity—paralleling the Holo-caust for Jewish identity.

66   For example, in late 2015, Coca Cola portrayed a map of the Russian Federation with Crimea in its New Year's advertisement ("Unhappy New Year for Coca-Cola as it upsets first Russia, then Ukraine" (5 Jan. 2016) *The Guardian.* Ref: www.theguardian.com/business/2016/jan/05/new-year-coca-cola-upsets-russia-ukraine). The ad placement prompted a call for a boycott of the company's products and led to an apology.

67   Ukraine was nearly sanctioned by the organizers of the Eurovision Song Contest for refusing to allow the Russian contestant to compete in Kyiv in 2017 after she had performed illegally in Crimea.

68   Nekrashchuk, Aleksandra (6 Dec. 2016) "Игра на вылет: российские ритейлеры уходят из Украины" *Liga.Business.* Ref: http://biz.liga.net/all/fmcg/stati/3555535-igra-na-vylet-rossiyskie-riteylery-ukhodyat-iz-ukrainy.htm

69   Ukrainians' post-Maidan identity construct was also closely tied to the idea of cit-izenship: all individuals, regardless of language or ethnicity, *born* on the territory of present-day Ukraine were considered Ukrainian. My personal experience of seeking acceptance as a Ukrainian illustrates the post-Maidan identity construct. I speak Ukrainian fluently. My parents were born in what is now Ukraine (but was then Poland), but were brought to Canada as children by their refugee parents dur-ing WWII. I was raised in a diaspora environment which entailed learning Ukrain-ian history, immersion in cultural traditions, and exclusively speaking Ukrainian at home. I have lived in Ukraine permanently for over 15 years, but when a Ukrain-ian citizen learns that I was not born in Ukraine, I am immediately categorized as "not-fully-we". Inevitably, the conversation shifts to the question of citizenship,

and the fact that I have not yet received this badge of belonging merely confirms my interlocutor's suspicion. Paradoxically, friends who are Jewish or Russian, but born in Ukraine (including those who speak no Ukrainian) are often considered *more* Ukrainian than I.

70   "The end of rebelion is liberation, while the end of revolution is the foundation of freedom... The basic misunderstanding lies in the failure to distinguish between liberation and freedom; there is nothing more futile than rebellion and liberation unless they are followed by the constitution of the newly won freedom" (Arendt 1963:142).

71   Skocpol (1979).

72   Sakwa (2015).

Chapter 9 — A Bourgeois Revolution

1   Cambridge sociologist David Lane called the "Orange Revolution" of 2004 a "popular coup d'état" rather than a revolution because Ukraine's fundamental social fabric transformed only minimally (see Lane, David (2008) "The Orange Revolution: 'People's Revolution' or Revolutionary Coup?" *British Journal of Politics and International Relations*, vol. 10, pp. 525-549). As argued in this chapter, this time was different.

2   This term was coined by Richard Florida in *The Rise of the Creative Class* (2002) New York: Basic Books.

3   McCloskey, Deirdre (2006) *The Bourgeois Virtues: Ethics for an Age of Commerce*, University of Chicago Press.

4   For a detailed description of the underclass phenomenon see Kyrychenko, Vladyslav (2014) "Black side of the Maidan" in Mukharsky, Antin (ed.) *Майдан: (р)еволюція духу*, Kyiv.

5   Instead of "bourgeois", one could characterize the core of the Maidan protest movement as "middle class", but the classification of socio-economic strata in Ukrainian society according to a traditional "working", "middle" and "upper" class scale is problematic — see: Rachok, Anatoliy (2016) *Середній клас в Україні*, Kyiv: Razumkov Center. Ref: http://razumkov.org.ua/uploads/article/2016_Seredn_klas.pdf

6   By January 2014 poor small town residents came to form the core of those camped in Kyiv's city center. However, very rarely did they carry the practices of the Maidan home to their towns.

7   "Profiling and Needs Assessment of Internally Displaced Persons (IDPs)" (17 Oct. 2014) *UNHCR*. Ref: https://reliefweb.int/report/ukraine/profiling-and-needs-assessment-internally-displaced-persons-idps-17-october-2014

8   Sviatnenko, Sviatoslav and Vinogradov, Alexander (2014) "Euromaidan Values from a Comparative Perspective" *Social, Health, And Communication Studies Journal*, 1(1), 41-61. Ref: https://journals.macewan.ca/shcsjournal/article/view/251

9   Sviatnenko & Vinogradov (2014), pp. 50-51.

10   Lozhkin (2016), p. 74.

11   Lozhkin (2016), p. 76.

12   Van Zon, Hans "Political Culture and Neo-Patrimonialism Under Leonid Kuchma" (2005) *Problems of Post-Communism*, vol. 52 no. 5, pp. 12-22.

13   Pavlo was the founding Dean of Kyiv-Mohyla Business School where I lectured 2003-2014. He resigned from his Ministerial post in September 2014.

14   Interview research currently being conducted by Sviatoslav Sviatnenko, a PhD student at Kyiv-Mohyla Academy supervised by the author.

15   Schumpeter, Joseph A. (1934) *The Theory of Economic Development*, 1911, p. 93. Schumpeter's characterization of the entrepreneurial motive continues: "Then there is the will to conquer; the impulse to fight, to prove superior to others, to succeed for the sake, not for the fruits of success, but of success itself... Finally, there is the joy of creating, of getting things done, or simply of exercising one's energy and ingenuity."

16   This ministerial configuration was essentially a compromise between two groups: Maidan activists on the one side, and Svoboda and Batkivshchyna party bosses on the other. Vitaliy Klitschko's "Udar" party declined to put forth candidates for ministerial positions in the immediate aftermath of Yanukovych's ouster, but its members became the core of the later Poroshenko bloc which won a plurality of seats in the October 2014 parliamentary elections. During the 2014 Parliamentary elections Svoboda was unable to gain enough support to enter the Rada under proportional representation rules, while Yatseniuk, whose executive team left the Batkivshchyna party to form the People's Front, unexpectedly retained the Prime Minister's post.

17   In 2015, President Poroshenko also granted citizenship to former Georgian President Mikhael Saakashvili, appointing him Governor of Odesa oblast. Saakashvili's citizenship was controversially revoked in 2016 after his resignation from the governorship. He later attempted to organize an opposition movement against Poroshenko.

18   Hanna Hopko and Viktoria Ptashnyk were excluded from the Samopomich faction in 2015.

19   Churanova, Olena (17 Dec. 2012) "Україна – палити в громадських місцях заборонено" *Voice of America*. Ref: https://ukrainian.voanews.com/a/ua-smoking/1566681.html

20   Ms. Orobets came in 2nd in the May 2014 vote for Kyiv mayor, losing to Vitaliy Klitschko. I am proud to have been a part of her election campaign.

21   "Ukraine's Prozorro e-procurement system wins another international award" (2017) *UNIAN Information Agency*. Ref: www.ukrinform.net/rubric-economy/2201918-ukraines-prozorro-eprocurement-system-wins-another-international-award.html

22   "Гройсман повідомив скільки вдалося заощадити завдяки Прозорро" (23 May 2017) *Slovo i Dilo*. Ref: www.slovoidilo.ua/2017/05/23/novyna/polityka/hrojsman-povidomyv-skilky-vdalosya-zaoshhadyty-prozorro

23   Dragon Capital was founded by Tomas Fiala, a Czech native. Goldman Sachs has been a minority shareholder in the company since 2000.

24   Lozhkin (2016), p. 37

25   In June 2013, Lozhkin sold his publishing concern (UMH Group) which included the Ukrainian version of Forbes magazine to Serhiy Kurchenko, the front-man of Yanukovych's business empire.

26   See series of IMF Technical Assistance Reports published in February-March 2016, including "Ukraine: Technical Assistance Report—Reforming the State Fiscal Services" (18 March 2016) *IMF*. Ref: www.imf.org/en/Publications/CR/Issues/2016/12/31/Ukraine-Technical-Assistance-Report-Reforming-the-State-Fiscal-Services-43698

27   Economic Development Minister Aivaras Abramavicus tendered his resignation after publicly accusing President Poroshenko's close friend and MP Ihor Kononenko of attempting to influence economic policy for his own personal gain—see "Statement by the Minister of Economic Development and Trade of Ukraine Aivaras Abromavicius" (3 Feb. 2016) *Ministry of Economic Development and Trade of Ukraine*. Ref: www.me.gov.ua/News/Detail?lang=en-GB&id=f13fa574-3e1b-4eca-b294-f9e508910e01&title=StatementByTheMinisterOfEconomicDevelopmentAndTradeOfUkraineAivarasAbromavicius

28   Pavlyuk, Svyatoslav (30 Nov. 2016) "Державна служба вимагає специфічних знань. Помилка реформаторів" *Maidan.org.ua*. Ref: https://maidan.org.ua/2016/11/derzhavna-sluzhba-vymahaje-spetsyfichnyh-znan-pomylky-reformatoriv/

29   Personal conversation with the author.

30   Rusakova, Svitlana et. al. (22 May 2017) "First Year of Groysman Government: Which Ministries Worked Better than Others" *VoxUkraine*. Ref: https://voxukraine.org/2017/05/22/first-year-of-groysman-government-which-ministries-worked-better-than-others/

31   The HERE team is funded by the EU through the Erasmus+ program. It consists of 15 University academics from various regions of Ukraine. In 2016, two members of this team were appointed to high-level positions within the Ministry of Education, while others continued to exert significant influence on policy. Similar EU-funded structures were established in other ministries in the post-Maidan period with "bourgeois" "flexian" activists at their core.

32   Wedel, Janine R. (2009) *Shadow Elite: How the World's New Power Brokers Undermine Democracy, Government and the Free Market*, New York: Basic Books, p. 1.

33   Naim, Moisés (2013) *The End of Power*, New York: Basic Books.

34   Such reconstitution of organizational practices (and with it class structure) is a sine qua non requirement for these processes to be called a "revolution" according to Marxists.

35   In late February 2014, Austria, Luxemburg and Switzerland froze the bank accounts and assets of the Kliuyev brothers, Yanukovych and his sons, and several other members of the former President's inner circle. The EU froze the bank accounts of Yanukovych, Pshonka, Zakharchenko, Tabachnyk, Bohatyriova and other (total of 17 persons—see: "ЄС заморозив рахунки Януковича і ще 17 чиновників" (6 March 2014) *BBC*. Ref: www.bbc.com/ukrainian/business/2014/03/140306_eu_sanctions_ok.shtml). Some sanctions were lifted by the EU in 2015 or later.

36   Grytsenko, Oksana and Sukhov, Oleg (20 Oct. 2016) "Rinat Akhmetov: Too Big to Tame" *Kyiv Post*. Ref: www.kyivpost.com/ukraine-politics/rain-shine-guys-always-got-shiny-dime.html

37   "UK court freezes $2.5bn of Ukraine oligarch's assets" (15 March 2018) *Financial Times*. Ref: www.ft.com/content/4bc2f436-e5d9-11e7-8b99-0191e45377ec

38   Walker, Shaun (21 Feb. 2017) "Ukrainian businessman Dmytro Firtash arrested after extradition ruling" *The Guardian*. Ref: www.theguardian.com/world/2017/feb/21/austria-grants-us-request-to-extradite-ukrainian-mogul-dmytro-firtash

39   Grey, Stephen et. al. (12 Dec. 2014) "Special Report: How a 29-year-old Ukrainian made a killing on Russian gas" *Reuters*. Ref: www.reuters.com/article/us-russia-capitalism-kurchenko-specialre/special-report-how-a-29-year-old-ukrainian-made-a-killing-on-russian-gas-idUSKBN0JP1KO20141212

40 "Статки Порошенка зросли до 1 мільярда – ТОП-100 найбагатших українців" (26 Oct. 2017), *Dzerkalo Tyzhnia*. Ref: https://dt.ua/POLITICS/statki-poroshenka-zrosli-do-1-milyarda-top-100-naybagatshih-ukrayinciv-258205_.html/

41 Kononczuk, Wojziech (Aug. 2016) *Keystone of the System: Old and New Oligarchs in Ukraine*, Warsaw: Ośrodek Studiów Wschodnich im. Marka Karpia, Centre for Eastern Studies.

42 Outrageous claims as to the equivalence of corruption levels under Poroshenko and Yanukovych were common in both the domestic and western press throughout 2015-2018. For example: Bullough, Oliver (6 Feb. 2015) "Welcome to Ukraine, the most corrupt nation in Europe." *The Guardian.* Ref: https://www.theguardian.com/news/2015/feb/04/welcome-to-the-most-corrupt-nation-in-europe-ukraine

43 "Ukraine Begins Confiscating $1.5 Billion Yanukovych Allegedly Stole" (29 April 2017) *RFE/RL.* Ref: www.rferl.org/a/ukraine-confiscates-money-yanukovych-allegedly-stole/28458549.html

44 "Цінності і гроші з Межигір'я Янукович вивозив спеціальними банківськими КАМАЗами – депутат" (15 Nov. 2017) *Expres.ua.* Ref: http://expres.ua/news/2017/11/15/271946-cinnosti-groshi-mezhygirya-yanukovych-vyvozyv-specialnymy-bankivskymy

45 Faulconbridge, Guy et. al. (30 April 2014) "Toppled 'mafia' president cost Ukraine up to $100 billion, prosecutor says" *Reuters.* Ref: www.reuters.com/article/us-ukraine-crisis-yanukovich-idUSBREA3T0K820140430

46 "Міністерство доходів і зборів. Шустер Live 04-04-2014" (4 April 2014) *Shuster-Live.* Ref: www.youtube.com/watch?v=_6sW1tSb298

47 "In pictures: Inside the palace Yanukovych didn't want Ukraine to see" *The Telegraph.* Ref: www.telegraph.co.uk/news/worldnews/europe/ukraine/10656023/In-pictures-Inside-the-palace-Yanukovych-didnt-want-Ukraine-to-see.html

48 "Ukraine revolution: A tour of former prosecutor general Viktor Pshonka's house" *The Telegraph.* Ref: www.telegraph.co.uk/news/worldnews/europe/ukraine/10660562/kiev-ukraine-maidan-russia-war-clashes-protest-wounded-yanukovych-europe-police.html?frame=2833482

49 "Ukraine police find 42kg of gold in home of ex-energy minister" (22 March 2014) *Reuters.* Ref: www.reuters.com/article/ukraine-crisis-corruption-idUSL6N0MJ0CL20140322

50 Lane (2008), p. 529

51 Lutsenko had been one of the leaders of the Orange Revolution. He was jailed by Yanukovych on trumped up charges, and later was appointed Prosecutor General by Poroshenko.

52 "У Києві хоронять УРСР – Луценко" (1 Dec. 2013) *Voice of America.* Ref: https://ukrainian.voanews.com/a/1801174.html

53 Ryabchuk, Mykola (11 April 2017) "Чи справді українське суспільство кардинально змінилося після Євромайдану?" *Zbruc.* Ref: https://zbruc.eu/node/64655

54 Volkov, Vadim (2012) *Силовое предпринимательство XXI век*, St. Petersburg: European University Press.

55 Rotberg, Robert (2003) "Failed States, Collapsed States, and Weak States: Causes and Indicators" *State Failure and State Weakness in a Time of Terror,* Washington: Brookings Institution.

56 Bielashko, Sergei (Fall 2015) "Roots of Political Turmoil in Post-Soviet Ukraine" *New England Journal of Political Science*, vol. 8, no. 1

57 Inozemtsev, Vladislav (March 2011) "Neo-Feudalism Explained" *The American Interest*. Ref: www.the-american-interest.com/2011/03/01/neo-feudalism-explained/

58 The practice of raiding ("reyderstvo") was common throughout the 2000's: a court order would be obtained (usually through corrupt means) according to which, due to some supposed infraction against the rights of minority shareholders, the decisions of previous shareholder meetings would be declared null and void, and new executive management would be appointed. This new management would enable the transfer of controlling interest (often with the use of force) from one shareholder to another. For details see: "Поняття рейдерства та його суспільна небезпечність" *Pozov.com.ua*. Ref: www.pozov.com.ua/ua/rejderstvo_ua.html

59 Matuszak, Sławomir (Sept. 2012) *The Oligarchic Democracy: the Influence of Business Groups on Ukrainian Politics*, Warsaw: Centre for Eastern Studies.

60 Aslund (2009); Kuzio (2015); Wilson, Andrew (2005) *Virtual Politics: Faking Democracy in the Post-Soviet World*, New Haven: Yale University Press.

61 Chaika, Yuliia M. (2013) "Галузеві трансформації економіки України" *Naukoviy visnyk poltavskoho universytetu ekonomiky I torhivli*, No. 4 (60).

62 Wynnyckyj, Mychailo (2003) *Institutions and Entrepreneurs: Cultural Transformation in the 'de novo' market sphere of Post-Soviet Ukraine*, PhD Dissertation, University of Cambridge.

63 In 2001, I conducted 53 interviews with 'de novo' founders in Kyiv, Lviv and Donetsk as part of my dissertation research. Thereafter, beginning in 2003, I taught courses in Kyiv-Mohyla Business School, where many of my students were 'de novo' business owners. I was part of the team that founded the Presidents' MBA program (exclusively for business owners) in 2007.

64 Freeland, Chrystia (27 Jan. 2012) "Reuters Magazine: The One Percent War" *Reuters*. Ref: www.reuters.com/article/us-chrystia-freeland-the-one-percent-war/reuters-magazine-the-one-percent-war-idUSTRE80Q02920120127

65 Balmaceda, Margarita (2008) *Energy Dependency, Politics and Corruption in the Former Soviet Union*, London, New York: Routledge, p. 128.

66 Wilson (2014:39). The term "middle class" is problematic in the Ukrainian case because the spending habits of those included in this category are often far from middle class levels by western standards. However, as a "values category" the term is valid.

67 Hulli, Enis (22 Aug. 2017) "Ukraine: The Next Start-up Nation" *startupgrind*. Ref: https://medium.com/startup-grind/ukraine-the-next-startup-nation-d81e0b7cffcc

68 For examples see: Abrosimova, Kate "Interview: Ukraine May be the Next Start-up Nation" *Yalantis*. Ref: https://yalantis.com/blog/ukraine-can-become-next-startup-nation-interview-yevgen-sysoyev-ukrainian-investor/ and Ternovyi, Dmytro (29 Nov. 2018) "10 Ukrainian Start-ups that are Revolutionizing the Tech Industry" *Ignite*. Ref: https://igniteoutsourcing.com/publications/best-ukrainian-it-startups/

69 Hawrylyshyn, Oleh (2017) *The Political Economy of Independent Ukraine: Slow Starts, False Starts, and a Last Chance?*, Palgrave Macmillan.

70 Vinnichuk, Igor and Ziukov, Serhii (2013) "Shadow Economy in Ukraine: Modelling and Analysis" *Business Systems and Economics*, vol. 3, no. 2, pp. 141-152.

71 2012-13 UN Habitat ranking of cities with populations over 750 thousand in 1990: http://mirror.unhabitat.org/pmss/listItemDetails.aspx?publicationID=3387. In a similar study with a time range of 2005-2014, two Ukrainian cities were ranked in the global Top-10 shrinking cities: Makeyevka (Donetsk oblast) and Dnipro. See:

"Shrinking cities: population decline in the world's rust-belt areas" (16 June 2017) *Financial Times.* Ref: www.ft.com/content/d7b00030-4abe-11e7-919a-1e14ce4af89b

72   Lipset, Seymour M. and Rokkan, Stein (1967) "Cleavage Structures, Party Systems, and Voter Alignments" *Party Systems and Voter Alignments: Cross-National Perspectives,* The Free Press, pp. 1-64.

73   North, Douglas C. et. al. (2007) *Limited Access Orders in the Developing World: A New Approach to the Problems of Development,* Policy Research Working Paper, No. 4359, World Bank, Washington, DC.

74   See World Bank statistics on Ukraine. Ref: https://tradingeconomics.com/ukraine/rural-population-percent-of-total-population-wb-data.html

75   Rachok, Anatoliy et. al. (2016) *Middle Class in Ukraine: prevalence and relevance of the notion,* Kyiv: Razumkov Center.

76   Lavryk, Denys (June 2017) "The Creative Class in Ukraine in the Context of Revised Modernization Theory", dissertation prepared in fulfilment of the requirements of the Master's of Sociology degree, National University "Kyiv-Mohyla Academy".

77   Arendt (1963), p. 117.

78   Among the most prominent of these were the former Head of Poland's Central Bank, Leszek Balcerowycz, and the former Deputy PM and Minister of Finance of Slovakia, Ivan Miklos — both individuals with strongly liberal reputations and reformist credentials. Ref: http://old.kmu.gov.ua/kmu/control/en/publish/article?art_id=248986947&cat_id=244314975

79   Based on the work of Putin's favorite philosopher, Ivan Ilyin, one can deduce that this program was based on three key ideas: 1) Russian exceptionalism; 2) Orthodoxy; 3) Nationalist autocracy. See Brooks, David (3 March 2014) "Putin can't stop" *The New York Times.* Ref: www.nytimes.com/2014/03/04/opinion/brooks-putin-cant-stop.html?smid=fb-share

80   "Ukraine: Lustration of Government Officials Started" (29 Oct. 2014) *Global Legal Monitor,* Library of Congress. Ref: https://www.loc.gov/law/foreign-news/article/ukraine-lustration-of-government-officials-started/

81   International Organization for Migration, *Migration as an Enabler of Development in Ukraine,* Kyiv, 2016.

Chapter 10 — A Post-Modern Revolution

1   Whether Ukraine can rightfully be included in "western" civilization is a matter of some dispute. According to Huntington (*Clash of Civilizations,* 1996), the country is "cleft" between European culture (i.e. a Catholic-Protestant tradition) that is supposedly dominant in the western regions, and Orthodoxy in the east. However, this characterization is clearly inaccurate because the rite of the eastern (Greek) Catholics of Ukraine's western oblasts is closer Orthodoxy than to Roman Catholicism. Furthermore, if Huntington's cleavage were accurate, the frontline of the Ukrainian-Russian war should run through Zhytomyr and Khmelnytsky oblasts, rather than almost 1000 km to the east.

2   According to Eisenstadt (2003, 2006), modernity itself may be regarded as a civilization. Furthermore, the version of modernity of Europe and North America is one of various possible variants of civilizational development.

3   "Word of the Year 2016 is…" *English Oxford Living Dictionairies.* Ref: https://en.oxforddictionaries.com/word-of-the-year/word-of-the-year-2016

4   For example: "Defensive Disinformation as decoy flare: Skripal and Flight MH17" (27 March 2018) *EUvsDisinfo*. Ref: https://euvsdisinfo.eu/defensive-disinformation -as-decoy-flare-skripal-and-flight-mh17/

5   In the 1970's Alvin Toffler first popularized the idea that humanity was on the verge of a "Third Wave" of development—a new post-industrial revolution that would replace the mass-production based economic order with an "information age." The literature on "post-industrial society" (a term coined by Alain Touraine, and popularized by Daniel Bell) has since grown extensively. The labels "knowledge economy" and "information society" seem to signify the same developmental phenomenon, namely a shift to tertiary sector employment, wealth creation through creative services rather than industrial manufacturing, and shifting consumer preferences.

6   Braudel, Fernand (1979) *Civilization and Capitalism, 15th-18th century*, New York: Harper and Row; Polanyi, Karl (1944) *The Great Transformation*, New York: Farrar and Rinehart; Weber, Max (1905) *The Protestant Ethic and the Spirit of Capitalism*.

7   For an excellent summary of Weber's argument see Randall Collins (Dec. 1980) "Weber's Last Theory of Capitalism" *American Sociological Review,* vol. 45, no. 6, pp. 925-942.

8   Eisenstadt (2006), p. 38.

9   The term "post-modern" is used here solely as a designation referencing an age that succeeds the contemporary "modern" period. From the perspective of the early 21st century we understand little as to the outcome of the ongoing institutional transformations currently affecting "western" (i.e. "globalized" with some regional variations) civilization. To characterize the coming new age while it is still in its infancy would be equivalent to branding modernity as the age of the steam engine. Certainly, at the start of the industrial revolution, when levels of sociopolitical upheaval were equivalent to those witnessed today, and steam power was the driver of economic change, this may have seemed like an accurate characterization. But at the time few predicted the invention of the internal combustion engine, and fewer still foresaw the development of nuclear power. Similarly, to characterize the coming *post* modern (or "post-industrial") system as "knowledge capitalism" (e.g. Burton-Jones, Alan (1999) *Knowledge Capitalism*, New York: Oxford University Press) or as a "network society" (e.g. Bard, Alexander and Soderqvist, Jan (2002) *Netocracy: the New Power Elite and Life After Capitalism*) is myopic. At the end of the second decade of the 21st century we are witnessing the full extent of the ongoing transformation: it will affect technology, warcraft, consumption, production, government, education, health, wealth and many other aspects of the human condition. The best we can do for now is simply to agree that it will follow the current phase which we have come to call modernity.

10   Schwab, Klaus (2016) *The Fourth Industrial Revolution*, New York: Crown Publishing.

11   Mason, Paul (2015) *Postcapitalism*, London: Allen Lane; Crouch, Colin (2004) *Post-Democracy*, Cambridge: Polity Press.

12   Eisenstadt (2006), p. 14

13   This shift away from other-worldly legitimation also resulted in a "revaluation" of material consumption as a means to happiness (if not necessarily salvation)—see McCloskey (2006), pp. 20-30

14   See Galbraith, John K. (1983) *Anatomy of Power*, Boston: Houghton Mifflin; Naim (2013).

15   Eisenstadt (2006), pp. 189-190.

16   The fact that the original Euromaidan protests began with a Facebook post has now become legendary. The use of technology — specifically smartphones — for communications during the actual protests has also been well documented (see for example: Gruzd, Anatoliy and Tsyganova, Ksenia (April 2015) "Information Wars and Online Activism During the 2013/2014 Crisis in Ukraine: Examining the Social Structures of Pro- and Anti-Maidan Groups" *Policy and Internet;* Onuch, Olga (April 2015) "'Facebook Helped Me Do It': Understanding the EuroMaidan Protester 'Tool-Kit'" *Studies in Ethnicity and Nationalism,* as has the use of social media for resource mobilization during the early months of the war in the Donbas (e.g. Kotsyuba, Oleh (22 Oct. 2015) "The Conflict/War and Social Media: Politics of Information and Communication during Euromaidan and War in Donbas" *Krytyka.* Ref: https://krytyka.com/en/community/blogs/conflictwar-and-social-media-politics-information-and-communication-during. However, the Internet is an instrument of communication, not an explanation of the phenomenon of collective agency. In order for social media to be effective, users must transmit messages that are not only read and commented on, but also mobilize network participants to action beyond cyberspace.

17   Gerbaudo, Paolo (2012) *Tweets and the Streets: Social Media and Contemporary Activism,* London: Pluto Press, and Onuch, Olga (2015) "Euromaidan Protests in Ukraine: Social Media versus Social Networks" *Problems of Post-Communism,* vol. 62, issue 4.

18   Rosen, Michael (2012) *Dignity: Its History and Meaning,* Cambridge: Harvard University Press, pp. 11-12.

19   Rosen (2012), p. 11.

20   Rosen (2012), pp. 40-41.

21   Preamble to the UN Universal Declaration: "Whereas recognition of the inherent dignity and of the equal and inalienable rights of all members of the human family is the foundation of freedom, justice and peace in the world…" Rule 90 of International Humanitarian Law reads: "Torture, cruel or inhuman treatment and outrages upon personal dignity, in particular humiliating and degrading treatment, are prohibited." Article 1 of Germany's Basic Law: "Human dignity shall be inviolable. To respect and protect it shall be the duty of all state authority."

22   Waldron, Jeremy (2012) *Dignity, Rank and Rights,* New York: Oxford University Press, p. 33.

23   *Словник української мови* «гідність». Ref: http://sum.in.ua/s/ghidnistj

24   This same dichotomy is present in Toftul, M.H. *Етика* (2005), Kyiv: Kyiv-Mohyla Academy Press.

25   In his reply to Rosen, who enjoins Aquinas' formulation of "dignity" as signifying an inherent virtue of the person-created-in-God's-image, Jeremy Waldron states "I know of no consistent or respectable (modern) use of "dignity" that treats it as a synonym for "goodness" — understood as a praiseworthy quality of conduct or the possession of virtues." (Waldron 2012:138). It is highly unfortunate that the author does not speak Ukrainian.

26   This translation reflects the fact that in the 1627 edition of "Leksikoni Slavenosskim" compiled by Pamvo Berynda, the term "hidnist" is cited as a synonym of "dostoynist". See Chaban, V. M. (2014) "Концептосфера гідність в українській лінгвокультурі", Ivan Franko National University of Lviv. Ref: https://naub.oa.edu.ua/2014/kontseptosfera-hidnist-v-ukrajinskij-linhvokulturi/

27   Chaban (2014).

28   Interestingly, the Russian word "negodiay" (equivalent to the Ukrainian "nehid-
      nyk") is derived from "ne-ugodnyi" – one who dissents or disapproves of the heg-
      emonic order.
29   In this sense, the adjective "dostoynyi'" translates almost exactly into the German
      "wuerdig" which means both "deserving" and "dignified" (see Rosen 2012:19). It
      was in this sense that Hobbes used the term "dignity".
30   For more on the discussion of Wuerde and its use by Kant in the context of debates
      on the status of "dignity", see Waldron (2012:23-27) and Rosen (2012:19-31).
31   Rosen, Michael (2012) "Dignity Past and Present" *Dignity, Rank and Rights*, New
      York: Oxford University Press, p. 95.
32   Given the prevalence of the phenomenon of "Birth of a Nation" during the Maidan
      protests and thereafter (discussed in Chapter 8), it is not surprising that in the
      Ukrainian case, a discourse of "dignity" should be tied to patriotism and national
      self-identification.
33   Williams, Thomas D. and Bengtsson, Jan Olof, Edward N. Zalta (ed.) (Summer
      2016 Edition) "Personalism" *The Stanford Encyclopedia of Philosophy*. Ref:
      https://plato.stanford.edu/archives/sum2016/entries/personalism/
34   Smith, Christian (2010) *What is a Person? Rethinking Humanity, Social Life, and the
      Moral Good from the Person Up*, Chicago: University of Chicago Press, p. 474.
35   See Aquas, Jove J. S. (June 2009) "The Notions of the Human Person and Human
      Dignity in Aquinas and Wojtyla" *Kritike*, vol. 3, no. 1, pp. 40-60.
36   Rourke, Thomas R. and Chazarretta Rourke, Rosita A. (2005) *A Theory of Personal-
      ism*, Lexington Books, p. 11.
37   This is the feeling that I tried to express in the Facebook post quoted at the start of
      the Preface.
38   Mounier, Emmanuel (1950) *Personalism*, London: Routledge, p. 23.
39   Rourke and Chazarreta Rourke (2005), p. 8.
40   Rourke and Chazarreta Rourke (2005), p. 75.
41   Rourke and Chazarreta Rourke (2005), p. 71.
42   Rourke and Chazarreta Rourke (2005), p. 67.
43   Since 2002, this author has presented two questions from the individualism/col-
      lectivism scale developed by G. Hofstede to multiple business school classes: the
      first measures respondents' attitudes to individual rights and freedoms, while the
      second measures their attitudes to individual/collective responsibility. Without
      fail, Ukrainians score exceptionally high in their value of individual freedom, and
      exceptionally high in their value of collective responsibility. This informal research
      is based on previous work conducted by Pavlo Sheremeta – see: Rozhen,
      Oleksandr (24 May 2002) "Чи заважає наша ментальність життєвому успіху?"
      Dzerkalo Tyzhnia. Ref: https://dt.ua/SCIENCE/chi_zavazhae_nasha_mentalnist_
      zhittevomu_uspihu.html
44   Oxford Dictionaries, s. v. "communication". Ref: https://en.oxforddictionaries.
      com/definition/communication and Merriam-Webster, s. v. "communication".
      Ref: www.merriam-webster.com/dictionary/communication
45   See *Civil Society Index*. Ref: www.odi.org/publications/5389-csi-civil-society-index
46   Surprisingly, Maidan and post-Maidan civil society were rarely connected to the
      pre-2013 NGO sector that had received funding from western donors. During the
      1990's, virtually all observers of Ukraine's post-Soviet democratic development
      noted a dearth of civil society organizations – a fact that resulted in the channeling
      by donors such as USAID and Open Society Foundation (Soros) of significant fi-
      nancial resources into the largely artificial creation of an NGO sector. During the

run-up to the Orange Revolution in 2004 many Ukrainian NGO's received significant funding, training and political support from the US (via proxy organizations such as FreedomHouse, NDI, etc.) leading some to conclude that they were nothing more than "foreign agents" of soft power imperialism (this view was especially propagated by the Kremlin). In the early 2010's, foreign grants to Ukraine's "third sector" was reduced significantly, and by 2013-14, US government funding of Ukrainian NGO's was negligible; George Soros was reportedly on the verge of closing his Renaissance Foundation office in Kyiv just before Maidan. As it turned out, the NGO's that had previously received funding from western sources, in fact played a relatively marginal role in the course of the protests.

47   "Благодійність і волонтерство-2016: результати соціологічного опитування" (21 Feb. 2017) *Democratic Initiatives Foundation*. Ref: https://dif.org.ua/article/blagodiynist-i-volonterstvo-2016-rezultati-sotsiologichnogo-doslidzhennya

48   "Постмайданна благодійність і волонтерство-2015: результати соцдослідження" (9 Dec. 2015) *Democratic Initiatives Foundation*. Ref: https://dif.org.ua/article/postmaydanna-blagodiynist-i-volonterstvo-2015-rezultati-sotsdoslidzhennya

49   Cited in Lozhkin (2016), p. 71. On the other hand, Holovakha claimed that Ukraine's volunteer movement cannot be considered a mass phenomenon: according to his data, throughout Ukraine's 2,5 decades of independence, 13% of survey respondents have claimed to be members of an NGO; the post-2014 volunteer phenomenon was merely an activation of this same 13% — see "Українці на шляху до щастя: 9 тез Євгена Головахи" (19 July 2015) *Tvoemisto*. Ref: http://tvoemisto.tv/news/ukraintsi_na_shlyahu_do_shchastya_9_tez_yevgena_golovahy_71728.html

50   As noted in Chapter 7, Hannah Arendt identified a "pathos of novelty" as a requisite characteristic of "great" revolutions — see Arendt (1963), p. 29.

51   "Modern theories of justice try to separate questions of fairness and rights from arguments about honor, virtue, and moral desert. They seek principles of justice that are neutral among ends, and enable people to choose and pursue their ends for themselves. Aristotle (384–322 B.C.) does not think justice can be neutral in this way. He believes that debates about justice are, unavoidably, debates about honor, virtue, and the nature of the good life." Sandel, Michael (2010) *Justice: What's the Right Thing to Do?*, New York: Farrar, Straus and Giroux, p. 99.

52   During the Parliamentary debates that led to the adoption of Ukraine's original Constitution in 1996, the formulation of the article declaring the country to be a "rule of law state" was hotly debated, and eventually the phrase "verkhovenstvo prava" was adopted. In the words of Deputy Hoshovska (see Constitutional debate transcripts — June 28, 1996): "pravo is the expression of the general will of the people, the nation, whereas zakony often express the particular will of a parliamentary majority." For more see Wynnyckyj, Mychailo (2009) "Ukraine 2006-2007: Building Elite Consensus through Conflict" in Luzhnycky, Andrej and Riabchuk, Mykola (eds.) *Ukraine on its Meandering Path Between East and West*, Peter Lang. The original research was presented in my MPhil dissertation ". The 1996 Constitution of Ukraine: A Reflection of the Values of the Political Elite" (1997), University of Cambridge.

53   "Spravedlyvist" was a concept central both to the Maidan protests, and to the social malaise that ensued in the years after Yanukovych's flight. Almost 5 years after the violence of the protests, not a single high-ranking member of the old regime, nor of the police and thugs who had maimed and killed, nor any of the snipers

responsible for mass killings in Kyiv's city-center had been found guilty and sentenced. Their trials were either ongoing, or they had escaped prosecution by fleeing to Russia.

54 Dymyd, Mychailo and Dymyd, Klementyia (2014) *Каміння Майдану*, Kyiv: Svichado.

55 The nominal organizer of the Donbas battalion, Semen Semenchenko (not his real name), refused to be seen without a balaklava mask throughout 2014. His anarchic worldview resulted in unpredictable behavior (some considered it erratic) once he was elected to Parliament, but Semenchenko's skepticism of government, and his ability to mobilize other disgruntled patriots proved highly effective in organizing the economic blockade of the occupied territories of the Donbas in 2016—a protest action that eventually became government policy in 2017 (see Chapter 6).

56 Quote from a volunteer battalion veteran who relayed his experiences informally to the author in March 2016.

57 The building's façade was renewed in time for Independence Day celebrations on 24 August 2018.

58 Plokhy, Serhii (2012) *The Cossack Myth: History and Nationhood in the Age of Empires*, Cambridge University Press.

59 The term "Otamanshchyna" refers to the period in Ukrainian history immediately following the 1917 coup d'état in St. Petersburg, when multiple independent leaders/warlords organized small bands of soldiers in the former southern regions of the Russian empire—each professing to represent the army of a new state, but often engaging in little more than looting.

60 "Як працює інклюзивна освіта в українських школах" (18 Dec. 2017) *24TV*. Ref: https://24tv.ua/yak_pratsyuye_inklyuzivna_osvita_v_ukrayinskih_shkolah_n903519

61 "В Україні дозволили пускати відвідувачів до пацієнтів в реанімації" (29 June 2016) *Ukrayinska Pravda (Zhyttia)*. Ref: https://life.pravda.com.ua/health/2016/06/29/214428/

62 "Енергозбереження: що робити і де взяти гроші?" (14 Aug. 2016) *Teplo.gov.ua*. Ref: http://teplo.gov.ua/energoefektivnist/poradi-shchodo-energozberezhennya/enerhozberezhennya.html

63 For more on Weber's concept of charisma and its institutionalization in modernity see: Friedland, William H. (Oct. 1964) "For a Sociological Concept of Charisma" *Social Forces*, vol. 43, no. 1, pp. 18-26; Shils, Edward (April 1965) "Charisma, Order, and Status" *American Sociological Review*, vol. 30, no. 2, pp. 199-213.

64 Weber, Max (1947) *The Theory of Social and Economic Organization*, New York: Free Press, p. 328.

65 Brooks, David (3 March 2014) "Putin Can't Stop" *The New York Times*. Ref: www.nytimes.com/2014/03/04/opinion/brooks-putin-cant-stop.html

66 Sorokin, Pitirim (2010) *Social & Cultural Dynamics, A Study of Change in Major Systems of Art, Truth, Ethics, Law, and Social Relationships*, New Brunswick: Transaction Publishers, pp. 699-704.

67 Sorokin (2010), pp. 24-29.

68 Richard, Michel P. (2010) "Introduction to the Transaction Edition" in Sorokin, Pitirim (2010) *Social & Cultural Dynamics, A Study of Change in Major Systems of Art, Truth, Ethics, Law, and Social Relationships*, New Brunswick: Transaction Publishers, pp. viii-ix.

69 Sorokin (2010), pp. 703-704.

70 Sorokin (2010), p. 346.

71 Arendt (1963), p. 125.

72 Later (in 2015 and thereafter) discourse switched to "freedom" in reaction to Russia's invasion—as a designation for the collective desire to remain free of foreign domination. Nevertheless, the label "Revolution of Dignity" as a marker for the Maidan protests stuck.

73 See for example: Acemoglu, Daron and Robinson, James (2012) *Why Nations Fail: The Origins of Power, Prosperity, and Poverty*, Crown Business; Fukuyama, Francis (2011) *The Origins of Political Order*, New York: Farrar, Straus and Giroux ; North, Douglass (1990) *Institutions, Institutional Change and Economic Performance*, University of Cambridge.

Chapter 11 — Moving Forward

1 Paragraph 2 of Article 4 of the UN Charter specifically forbids violations of the "territorial integrity and political independence of any state" by another, and Paragraph 7 of the same Article commends both the UN and its members to avoid intervening in "matters which are essentially within the domestic jurisdiction of any state."

2 Umland, Andreas (12 Aug. 2015) "Ukraine Crisis is Not Only About Ukraine" *Atlantic Council*. Ref: www.atlanticcouncil.org/blogs/ukrainealert/ukraine-crisis-is-not-only-about-ukraine

3 Van Voren, Robert (12 Oct. 2015) "Putin has not won – the world has lost" *Euromaidan Press*. Ref: http://euromaidanpress.com/2015/10/12/putin-has-not-won-the-world-has-lost/

4 Micaleff, Joseph (17 Jan. 2017) "Vladimir Putin: The Art of the Bluff" *Military.com*. Ref: www.military.com/daily-news/2017/01/17/vladimir-putin-the-art-of-the-bluff.html

5 This phrase was one of three of the campaign planks of Bill Clinton's successful Presidential election campaign in 1992. It remained a paradigmatic mainstay of US policy-makers throughout the subsequent two decades.

6 Galeotti, Mark (4 Aug. 2015) "Time for a New Strategy in Russia" *Foreign Affairs*. Ref: www.foreignaffairs.com/articles/russia-fsu/2015-08-04/time-new-strategy-russia

7 Dickinson, Peter (13 March 2018) "From Crimea to Salisbury: Time to Acknowledge Putin's Global Hybrid War" *Atlantic Council Blog*. Ref: www.atlanticcouncil.org/blogs/ukrainealert/from-crimea-to-salisbury-time-to-acknowledge-putin-s-global-hybrid-war

8 The term "hybrid war" has been criticized for its ambiguity: "In practice, any threat can be hybrid as long as it is not limited to a single form and dimension of warfare. When any threat or use of force is defined as hybrid, the term loses its value and causes confusion instead of clarifying the "reality" of modern warfare." Van Puyvelde, Damien (2015) "Hybrid war – does it even exist?" *NATO Review Magazine*. Ref: www.nato.int/docu/review/2015/also-in-2015/hybrid-modern-future-warfare-russia-ukraine/EN/index.htm

9 Archer, Christon I. (2002) *World History of Warfare*, University of Nebraska Press.

10 For a comprehensive study of the writings of Alexander Dugin see: Umland, Andreas *Post-Soviet* (23 Jan. 2007) *'Uncivil Society' and the Rise of Aleksandr Dugin: A*

Case Study of the Extraparliamentary Radical Right in Contemporary Russia, Dissertation submitted to the Faculty of Social and Political Sciences of the University of Cambridge for the degree of Doctor of Philosophy.

11   Brookes (2014).

12   Goble, Paul (31 Dec. 2015) "When crisis becomes permanent: Russia vs. Ukraine" *Euromaidan Press*. Ref: http://euromaidanpress.com/2015/12/31/russia-vs-ukraine-when-crises-become-permanent/

13   For analysis see: Micaleff, Joseph (13 Sept. 2018) "Has Putin Become Russia's Tsar?" *Military.com*. Ref: www.military.com/daily-news/2018/09/13/has-putin-become-russias-tsar.html. For an example of the "Putin-as-savior" image, see www.youtube.com/watch?v=-9-5NBaAEsI. During the 2018 Presidential election campaign in Russia, Duma deputy Anna Kuvychko produced a propagandist video for a tune entitled "Dyadya Vova my s toboy!" (Uncle Vova we are with you). The video illustrates the Putin personality cult fostered by the country's elites: www.youtube.com/watch?v=jO08pAXiNvs

14   One might ask: if the long-term solution to the Russia problem (i.e. the existential threat to Ukraine, and the permanent threat to the West posed by the Kremlin) is the removal of Putin from office, why has this option not been explored by policymakers? The problem seems to lie in the belief that without Putin, Russia would disintegrate, and this scenario poses three substantial risks to the global geopolitical system:

a) Loss of control by Moscow over the Russian far east would likely result in the power vacuum being filled by China. In this scenario, China would gain direct and formal control (possibly peacefully) over the vast natural resources of Siberia and would thereby accelerate its economic and political rise as a global power—a prospect that may not be in the interests of the current global hegemon, the United States.

b) The disintegration of Russia would likely lead to religious and factional conflict in the Caucasus—an area whose population is largely Muslim, and whose local leaders could conceivably become radicalized and allied with Islamist groups based in Syria and Iraq. A reconstitution of borders in the region could also lead to a loss of control over nuclear weapons based there.

c) Factional and religious wars in European Russia would likely result in significant migratory pressures on Ukraine in the first place (minimal linguistic differences and close historical ties would make the country attractive for settlers fleeing violence and instability in Russia), and on Europe more broadly. A renewed refugee crisis is not in the interests of the EU.

15   I first wrote about the scenarios leading to Russia's disintegration (with Valerii Pekar) in 2015—see: Wynnyckyj, Mychailo and Pekar, Valerii (13 Feb. 2015) "Towards a Proactive Russia Policy: What Constitutes Checkmate?" *CircussBazaar*. Ref: www.circusbazaar.com/towards-a-proactive-russia-policy-what-constitutes-checkmate/. This theme was reiterated in 2019 by Bugajski, Janusz (9 Jan. 2019) "Managing Russia's Dissolution" *The Hill*. Ref: https://thehill.com/opinion/national-security/424511-managing-russias-dissolution?fbclid=IwAR2GMjlxDX5_igFHe_l5xC31UYilr44wUpTyc-eGEeFd6DOMUvxgxV9_0sk

16   Ukrainians, with their worldwide diaspora, and calamitous 20th century history (see Timothy Snyder's award-winning *Bloodlands* (2010), New York: Basic Books), have often been compared to Jews. Israel has received long-term infrastructural support from Western governments, consolidated in their desire to counter the

permanent existential threat it faces. For their part Israelis have built a uniquely successful state while surrounded by mortal enemies.

17   Wieseltier, Leon (19 May 2014) "The Russian War on Ukraine is One of the Proving Grounds of Principle in our Time" *The New Republic*. Ref: https://newrepublic.com/article/117817/leon-wieseltier-remarks-ukraine-thinking-together-conference

18   Portraying the Russo-Ukrainian conflict as a "civil war" was particularly widespread in academic and journalistic writing throughout 2015-2016. The release of the "Glazyev tapes" (see www.rferl.mobi/a/27948433.html) could potentially change this narrative, and if this were to occur, it would represent a formidable victory for Ukraine in the information war against Russia.

19   Plokhy, Serhii (2017) *Lost Kingdom: The Quest for Empire and the Making of the Russian Nation*, New York: Basic Books.

20   Fulford, Robert (1 April 2016) "Putin says Ukraine isn't a country. Too many in the West agree with him" *National Post*. Ref: https://nationalpost.com/opinion/robert-fulford-putin-says-ukraine-isnt-a-country-too-many-in-the-west-agree-with-him

21   On 5 January 2019, the Tomos granting Autocephaly to the Orthodox Church of Ukraine was signed by the Ecumenical Patriarch Bartholemew. The OCU was created on 15 December 2018 when bishops from the Ukrainian Orthodox Church (Kyiv Patriarchate), Ukrainian Autocephalous Orthodox Church, and several bishops of the Ukrainian Orthodox Church (Moscow Patriarchate) came together in a Synod, and proclaimed their unity. This process was vehemently opposed by Russia's Patriarch Kirill and resulted in a schism between Moscow and Constantinople.

22   Keyes, Ralph (2004) *The Post-Truth Era: Dishonesty and Deception in Contemporary Life*, New York: St. Martin's Press.

23   Giles, Keir (21 March 2016) *Russia's 'New' Tools for Confronting the West: Continuity and Innovation in Moscow's Exercise of Power*, London: Chatham House.

24   MacFarquhar, Neil (28 Aug. 2016) "A Powerful Russian Weapon: The Spread of False Stories" *The New York Times*. Ref: www.nytimes.com/2016/08/29/world/europe/russia-sweden-disinformation.html?partner=rss&emc=rss&smid=tw-nytimes&smtyp=cur&_r=1

25   Gerol, Ilya and Molyneux, Geoffrey (1988) *The Manipulators: Inside the Soviet Media*, Toronto: Stoddard.

26   "2015 Review: World finally wakes up to Russian infowar and begins to counter Kremlin fakes" (29 Dec. 2015) *BusinessUkraine*. Ref: http://bunews.com.ua/society/item/2015-review-world-finally-wakes-up-to-russian-infowar-and-begins-to-counter-kremlin-fakes

27   Pomarantsev wrote: "Russia's bombing raids in Syria also have the positive side effects (for Moscow) of distracting from the conflict in Ukraine and helping maintain a steady torrent of refugees to Europe, which in turn strengthens right-wing parties in countries such as France and Hungary that peddle anti-refugee fears, are supported by the Kremlin, and advocate dropping Western sanctions against Russia. What matters in the information age is not so much "military escalation dominance" — the Cold War doctrine emphasizing the ability to introduce more arms than the enemy into a conflict. Rather, it's "narrative escalation dominance" — being able to introduce more startling storylines than your opponent." See: Pomarantsev, Peter (29 Dec. 2015) "Brave New War" *The Atlantic*. Ref: https://www.

theatlantic.com/international/archive/2015/12/war-2015-china-russia-isis/4220
85/

28   Bullough (2015).

29   According to StopFake.org, of the 1001 false media stories proliferated by pro-Russian news sites in 2018, 461 portrayed Ukraine as a "Nazi state". See: www.
stopfake.org/en/year-in-review-1001-messages-of-pro-kremlin-disinformation/

30   Wynnyckyj, Mychailo (15 Feb. 2014) "Response to Washington Post Article by
Keith Darden and Lucan Way" *Euromaidan Press*. Ref: http://euromaidanpress.
com/2014/02/15/response-to-washington-post-article-by-keith-darden-and-
lucan-way-2/

31   Andrukhovych, Yuriy (22 Nov. 2014) "The price of pricelessness – Europe,
Ukraine, Maidan." *Euromaidan Press*. Ref: http://euromaidanpress.com/
2014/11/22/the-price-of-pricelessness-europe-ukraine-and-maidan/#arvlbdata.
Similar descriptions of the "magical" nature of Maidan can be found in Dymyd
and Dymyd (2015).

32   The original term "Homo Sovieticus" was coined by Zinovyev, Alekdandr (1986)
Homo Sovieticus, New York: Atlantic Monthly. The evolution of this phenomenon
in post-Soviet Russia was described in "The Long Life of Homo sovieticus" (10
Dec. 2011) *The Economist*. Ref: www.economist.com/briefing/2011/12/10/the-
long-life-of-homo-sovieticus

33   Throughout the 1990's and 2000's the practice of "buying legitimacy" by business
owners was widespread among owners of both privatized former Soviet enter-
prises and 'de novo' start-ups—see: Wynnyckyj, Mychailo (2003) *Institutions and
Entrepreneurs: Cultural Evolution in the 'De Novo' Market Sphere in Post-Soviet
Ukraine*, University of Cambridge and Söderbaum, Hannah (2018) *From Oligarch to
Benefactor? Legitimation Strategies among the Wealthy Elite in Post-Soviet Ukraine*, PhD
Dissertation, Uppsalla University.

34   Grytsenko, Oksana (2 Dec. 2015) "Volunteers help push changes in defense that
help frontline soldiers" *Ukraine's Success Stories: A Look at the Nation's Top Innova-
tors*, Kyiv: Kyiv Post.

35   Moscovici, Serge (1991) *The Invention of Society: Psychological Explanations for Social
Phenomena*, Hoboken: Wiley, pp. 191-2.

36   Karatnycky, Adrian and Motyl, Alexander (18 July 2018) "A Narrow Focus on Corruption Overlooks Remarkable Progress" *Foreign Affairs*. Ref: www.foreignaffairs
.com/articles/ukraine/2018-07-16/ukraines-promising-path-reform

37   Habermas, Jürgen (1962) *The Structural Transformation of the Public Sphere: An Inquiry into a Category of Bourgeois Societ*, Cambridge: MIT Press.

38   Bielieskov, Mykola (27 Feb. 2018) "Ukraine's Military is Back" *The National Interest*.
Ref: https://nationalinterest.org/blog/the-buzz/ukraines-military-back-24674

39   Goncharuk, Tetiana (21 Jan. 2018) "Where is Ukraine's new police force?" *Open
Democracy*. Ref: https://www.opendemocracy.net/od-russia/tetiana-goncharuk/
where-is-ukraines-new-police-force

40   Manthorpe, Rowland (20 Aug. 2018) "From the fires of revolution, Ukraine is rein-
venting government" *Wired*. Ref: www.wired.co.uk/article/ukraine-revolution-
government-procurement

41   Balmaceda, Margarita (2013) *The Politics of Energy Dependency: Ukraine, Belarus and
Lithuania between Domestic Oligarchs and Russian Pressure*, University of Toronto
Press.

42   Smolii, Yakiv (25 June 2018) "Restoring a Banking Sector to Health – the Ukrainian Experience" *International Banker*. Ref: https://internationalbanker.com/banking/restoring-a-banking-sector-to-health-the-ukrainian-experience/
43   Rabinovych, Maryna, Levitas, Anthony and Umland, Andreas (26 July 2018) *Kennan Cable No. 34: Revisiting Decentralization after Maidan: Achievements and Challenges of Ukraine's Local Governance Reform*, Washington: Woodrow Wilson Center.
44   Shandra, Alya (7 Dec. 2017) "Ukraine's education reform is a big step forward (beyond the language scandal)" *Euromaidan Press*. Ref: http://euromaidanpress.com/2017/12/07/ukraines-education-reform-is-a-big-step-forward-beyond-the-language-scandal/
45   Chernenko, Zoriana (20 Oct. 2017) "What Ukraine's healthcare reform is about" *Euromaidan Press*. Ref: http://euromaidanpress.com/2017/10/20/what-ukraines-healthcare-reform-is-about/
46   Bukatyuk, Ulana (8 Aug. 2018) "Гроші є – доріг немає. Чому місцева влада не поспішає з ремонтом автошляхів" *Espreso.tv*. Ref: https://espreso.tv/article/2018/08/08/groshi_ye_dorig_nemaye_chomu_misceva_vlada_ne_pospishaye_z_remontom_avtoshlyakhiv
47   Lough, John and Dubrovsky, Vladimir (Nov. 2018) *Are Ukraine's Anti-Corruption Reforms Working?*, Chatham House Research Paper.
48   Brinton (1938), p. 254.
49   In a September 2018 interview on CNN, President Poroshenko sarcastically "thanked" Vladimir Putin for enabling Ukraine's socio-economic and political shift towards Europe. See: "Poroshenko thanks Putin for making Ukraine "much more European" (video) (30 Sept. 2018) *UNIAN Information Agency*. Ref: www.unian.info/politics/10280577-poroshenko-thanks-putin-for-making-ukraine-much-more-european-video.html
50   Arendt (1963), Chapters 2-3.
51   Averchuk, Rostyslav (21 Nov. 2018) "The Pros and Cons of Tymoshenko's Constitutional Reform Proposal" *VoxUkraine*. Ref: https://voxukraine.org/en/the-pros-and-cons-of-tymoshenko-s-constitutional-reform-proposal/
52   President of Ukraine. Official website *President to submit constitutional amendments to the Parliament in order to consolidate the strategic movement of Ukraine towards NATO and EU membership* (28 June 2018). Ref: www.president.gov.ua/en/news/prezident-vnese-do-parlamentu-zmini-do-konstituciyi-shodo-za-48398
53   The first exception among potential Presidential candidates became Svyatoslav Vakarchuk when he published his musings on "spravedlyvist" and "zakonnist'". See: Vakarchuk, Svyatoslav (28 Sept. 2018) "Кому тут тюрма, кому – Дольче Віта" *Ukrayinska Pravda*. Ref: www.pravda.com.ua/articles/2018/09/28/7193394/
54   For example: www.youtube.com/watch?v=OpOvdT49SCo
55   In his speech to the nation on Independence Day (24 Aug. 2018), President Poroshenko proclaimed "The issue of the Tomos on autocephaly for the Orthodox Church of Ukraine goes beyond the religious framework...It is akin to strengthening the army, protecting the language, and struggling for membership with the European Union and NATO. This is another strategic reference point on our historical path. This is a nut and bolt of our independence."
56   Arendt (1963), Chapter 1.
57   Even in Donetsk and Luhansk, the separatist movement adopted the regional Donbass identity (traditionally strong) rather than openly calling for annexation to Russia along the Crimean model.

58   A popular joke among Ukrainians during the post-Yanukovych years focused on
      Crimea: if you want to understand whether a Russian-speaker is Ukrainian or Rus-
      sian, just ask him/her whom Crimea belongs to—"Chyy Krym?"

Afterword

1   Quoted by Forostyna (2015), in Wilson (ed.), p. 32.
2   This image even survived the events of 2013-15, making its way into US President
     Obama's January 2016 State of the Union Address, causing controversy in the US
     media, and requiring an explanation from the White House later. See "Many Puz-
     zled by Obama's Reference to Ukraine as Russian 'Client State'" (13 Jan. 2016)
     RFE/RL.   Ref: www.rferl.org/content/ukraine-obama-state-of-union-reference-
     puzzles-many/27486026.html
3   The visits by John McCain (Rep.) and Christopher Murphy (Dem.) were well re-
     ceived by the protesters, and condemned as constituting an intervention by the US
     into Ukraine's internal affairs by Russia. In retrospect, the two senators' visit con-
     stituted not much more than a media photo opportunity: neither made an effort to
     understand the real substance of the protest movement, nor did they affect the out-
     come in any meaningful way.
4   Piotr Sztompka coined this term with respect to the 1989 collapse of the Soviet bloc,
     and the abrupt discontinuity between the developmental (civilizational) paths fol-
     lowed by the Central European states before and after.
5   Garton Ash, Timothy (2002) *The Polish Revolution: Solidarity* 3rd edition, Yale Uni-
     versity Press, p. 290.

EAST EUROPEAN STUDIES: JOURNALS AND BOOK SERIES

SOVIET AND POST-SOVIET POLITICS AND SOCIETY

Editor: Andreas Umland

Founded in 2004 and refereed since 2007, SPPS makes available, to the academic community and general public, affordable English-, German- and Russian-language scholarly studies of various empirical aspects of the recent history and current affairs of the former Soviet bloc from the late Tsarist period to today. It publishes approximately 15–20 volumes per year, and focuses on issues in transitions to and from democracy such as economic crisis, identity formation, civil society development, and constitutional reform in CEE and the NIS. SPPS also aims to highlight so far understudied themes in East European studies such as right-wing radicalism, religious life, higher education, or human rights protection.

JOURNAL OF SOVIET AND POST-SOVIET POLITICS AND SOCIETY

Editor: Julie Fedor

Review Editor: Gergana Dimova

The Journal of Soviet and Post-Soviet Politics and Society is a new bi-annual journal that was launched in April 2015 as a companion journal to the Soviet and Post-Soviet Politics and Society book series (founded 2004 and edited by Andreas Umland, Dr. phil., PhD). Like the book series, the journal will provide an interdisciplinary forum for new original research on the Soviet and post-Soviet world. The journal aims to become known for publishing creative, intelligent, and lively writing tackling and illuminating significant issues and capable of engaging wider educated audiences beyond the academy.

ibidem
Press

CHANGING EUROPE

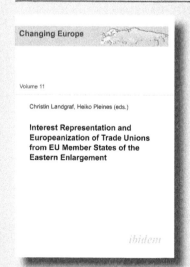

Changing Europe

Volume 11

Christin Landgraf, Heiko Pleines (eds.)

Interest Representation and Europeanization of Trade Unions from EU Member States of the Eastern Enlargement

ibidem

Editors: Sabine Fischer, Heiko Pleines, Hans-Henning Schröder

The book series Changing Europe contains edited volumes dealing with current political, economic and social affairs in Eastern Europe and the enlarged EU. The core of the series is formed by contributions to the Changing Europe Summer Schools, which are being organised by the Research Centre for East European Studies at the University of Bremen.

FORUM FÜR OSTEUROPÄISCHE IDEEN- UND ZEITGESCHICHTE

Editors: Leonid Luks, Gunter Dehnert, Nikolaus Lobkowicz, Alexei Rybakow, Andreas Umland

FORUM features interdisciplinary discussions by political scientists—literary, legal, and economic scholars—and philosophers on the history of ideas, and it reviews books on Central and Eastern European history. Through the translation and publication of documents and contributions from Russian, Polish, and Czech researchers, the journal offers Western readers critical insight into scientific discourses across Eastern Europe.

ibidem Press | Leuschnerstr. 40 | 30457 Hannover | Germany
Phone: +49 (0) 511 2 62 22 00 | Fax: +49 (0) 511 2 62 22 00 | sales@ibidem.eu

LITERATURE AND CULTURE IN CENTRAL AND EASTERN EUROPE

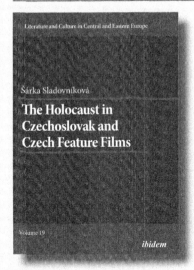

Editor: Reinhard Ibler

This series was founded to give a platform for the contemporary research into Literature and Culture of Middle and Eastern Europe. The profile of the series is geographical rather than philological, thriving on a variety of content and methods. Central subjects include the literary and cultural processing of the Holocaust, a focus born out of the successful Gießen project on comparative research of this important and productive issue, using Polish, Czech, Slovakian, and German material. Further, defining subjects are the discourse on modernity and avant-garde, questions of genre typology and history, as well as interdisciplinary aspects of aesthetics and literary and cultural theory, as far as it is grounded in Middle and Eastern European intellectual tradition.

JOURNAL OF ROMANIAN STUDIES

Editors: Lavinia Stan, Margarat Beissinger

Review Editor: Radu Cinpoes

The Journal of Romanian Studies, jointly developed by The Society for Romanian Studies and ibidem Press, is a biannual, peer-reviewed, and interdisciplinary journal. It examines critical issues in Romanian studies, linking work in that field to wider theoretical debates and issues of current relevance, and serving as a forum for junior and senior scholars. The journal also presents articles that connect Romania and Moldova comparatively with other states and their ethnic majorities and minorities, and with other groups by investigating the challenges of migration and globalization and the impact of the European Union.

ibidem.eu